第3巻

RG VEDA

聖伝

六星群嵐篇 II

STORY BY
大川七瀬
AGEHA OHKAWA

COMIC BY
もこなあぱぱ
MOKONA

新書館

PLANNING
CLAMP

Publication

Serial Publication

WINGS

WINGS COMICS

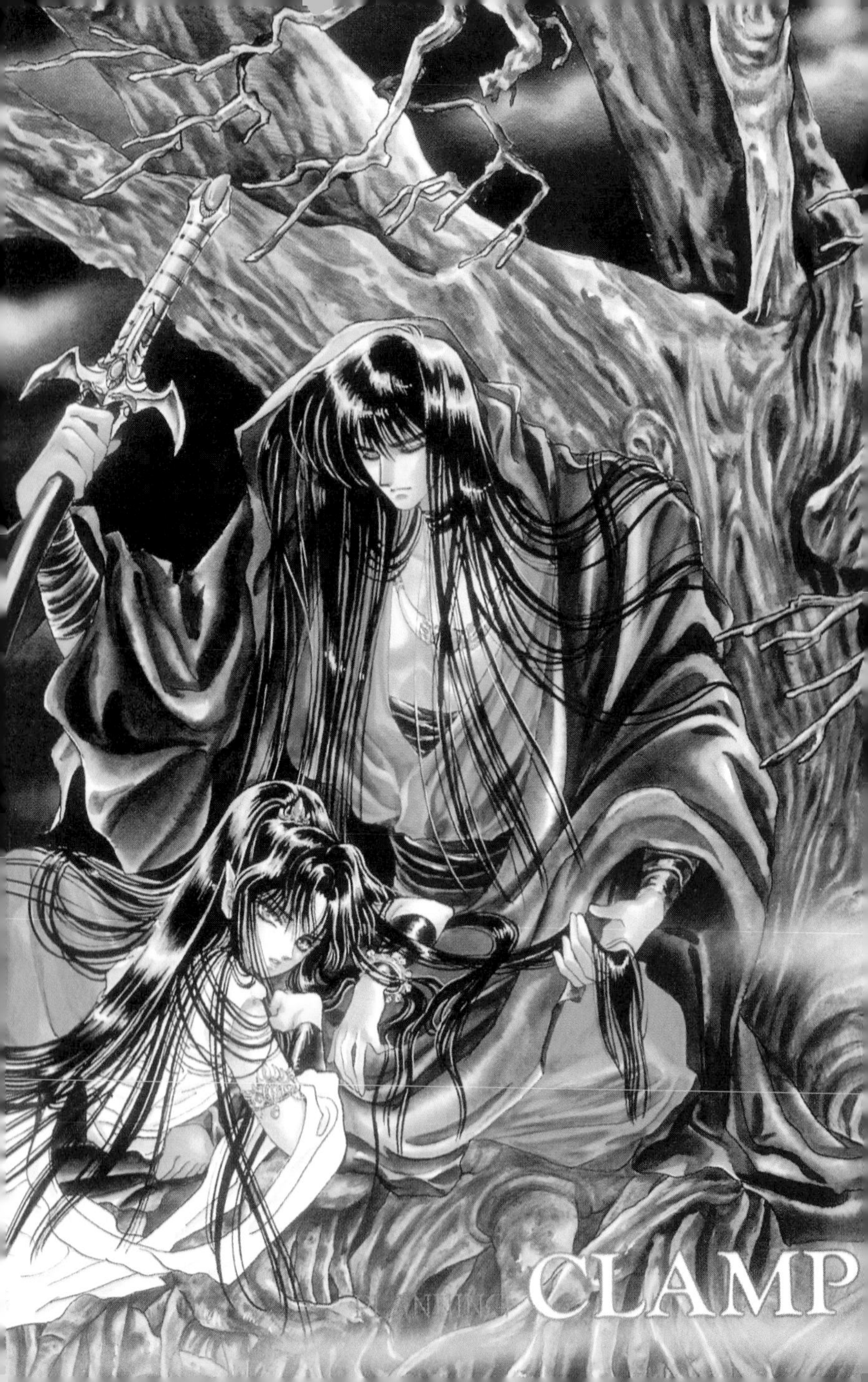
CLAMP

R G VEDA
聖伝

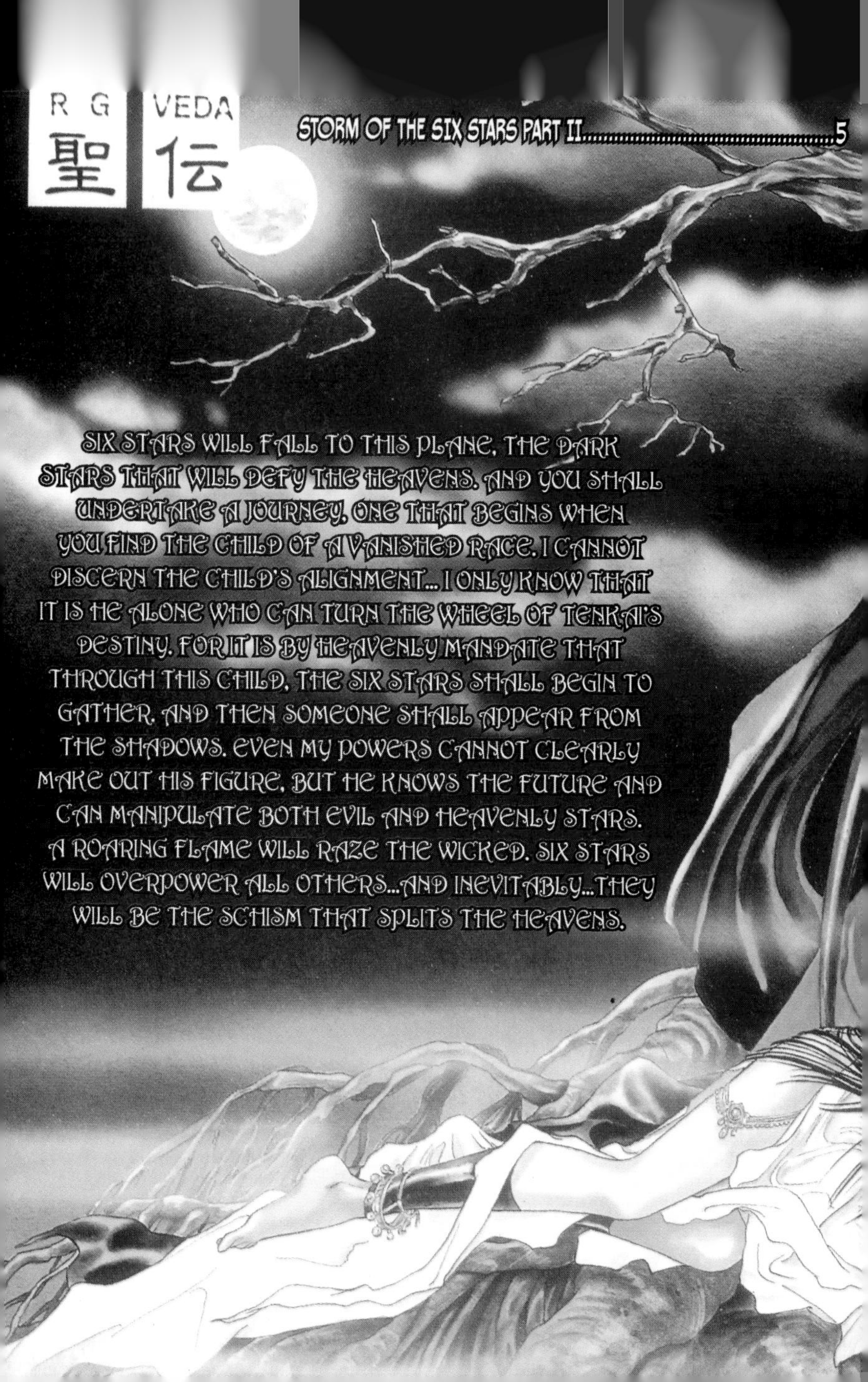

SIX STARS WILL FALL TO THIS PLANE, THE DARK STARS THAT WILL DEFY THE HEAVENS. AND YOU SHALL UNDERTAKE A JOURNEY, ONE THAT BEGINS WHEN YOU FIND THE CHILD OF A VANISHED RACE. I CANNOT DISCERN THE CHILD'S ALIGNMENT... I ONLY KNOW THAT IT IS HE ALONE WHO CAN TURN THE WHEEL OF TENKAI'S DESTINY. FOR IT IS BY HEAVENLY MANDATE THAT THROUGH THIS CHILD, THE SIX STARS SHALL BEGIN TO GATHER. AND THEN SOMEONE SHALL APPEAR FROM THE SHADOWS. EVEN MY POWERS CANNOT CLEARLY MAKE OUT HIS FIGURE, BUT HE KNOWS THE FUTURE AND CAN MANIPULATE BOTH EVIL AND HEAVENLY STARS. A ROARING FLAME WILL RAZE THE WICKED. SIX STARS WILL OVERPOWER ALL OTHERS...AND INEVITABLY...THEY WILL BE THE SCHISM THAT SPLITS THE HEAVENS.

HOSHIGA NAGARERU

Main

CLAMP MEMBERS

STORY
大川七瀬
AGEHA OHKAWA

COMIC
もこなあぱぱ
MOKONA

Book Designer
大川七瀬
AGEHA OHKAWA

Director
もこなあぱぱ
MOKONA

Short Comic
猫井みっく
TSUBAKI NEKOI

Art Assistants
猫井みっく
TSUBAKI NEKOI

五十嵐さつき
SATSUKI IGARASHI

CLAMP MEMBERS

YOU WILL BE THE SCHISM THAT SPLITS HEAVEN.

PLANNING & PRESENTED by

CLAMP

VOLUME 3

BY
CLAMP

HAMBURG // LONDON // LOS ANGELES // TOKYO

RG Veda Vol. 3
created by CLAMP

Translation - Haruko Furukawa
English Adaptation - Christine Schilling
Copy Editors - Jane Wohlgethan and Emily Wing
Retouch and Lettering - Irene Woori Choi
Production Artist - Rafael Najarian
Cover Design - Jorge Negrete

Editor - Carol Fox
Digital Imaging Manager - Chris Buford
Production Managers - Jennifer Miller and Mutsumi Miyazaki
Managing Editor - Lindsey Johnston
VP of Production - Ron Klamert
Publisher and E.I.C. - Mike Kiley
President and C.O.O. - John Parker
C.E.O. - Stuart Levy

A  Manga

TOKYOPOP Inc.
5900 Wilshire Blvd. Suite 2000
Los Angeles, CA 90036

E-mail: info@TOKYOPOP.com
Come visit us online at www.TOKYOPOP.com

ISBN: 1-59532-486-0

First TOKYOPOP printing: October 2005
10 9 8 7 6 5 4 3 2 1
Printed in Canada

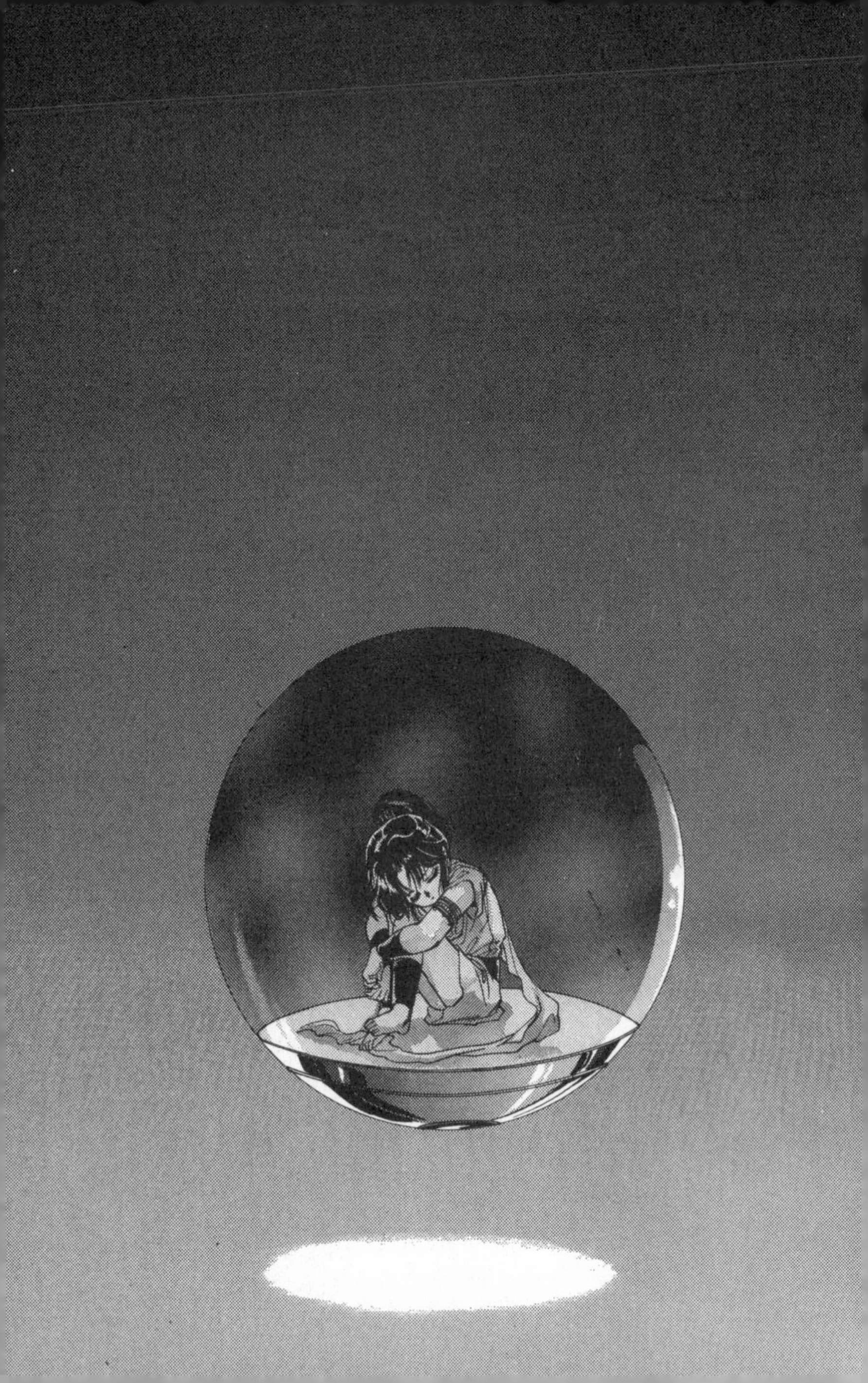

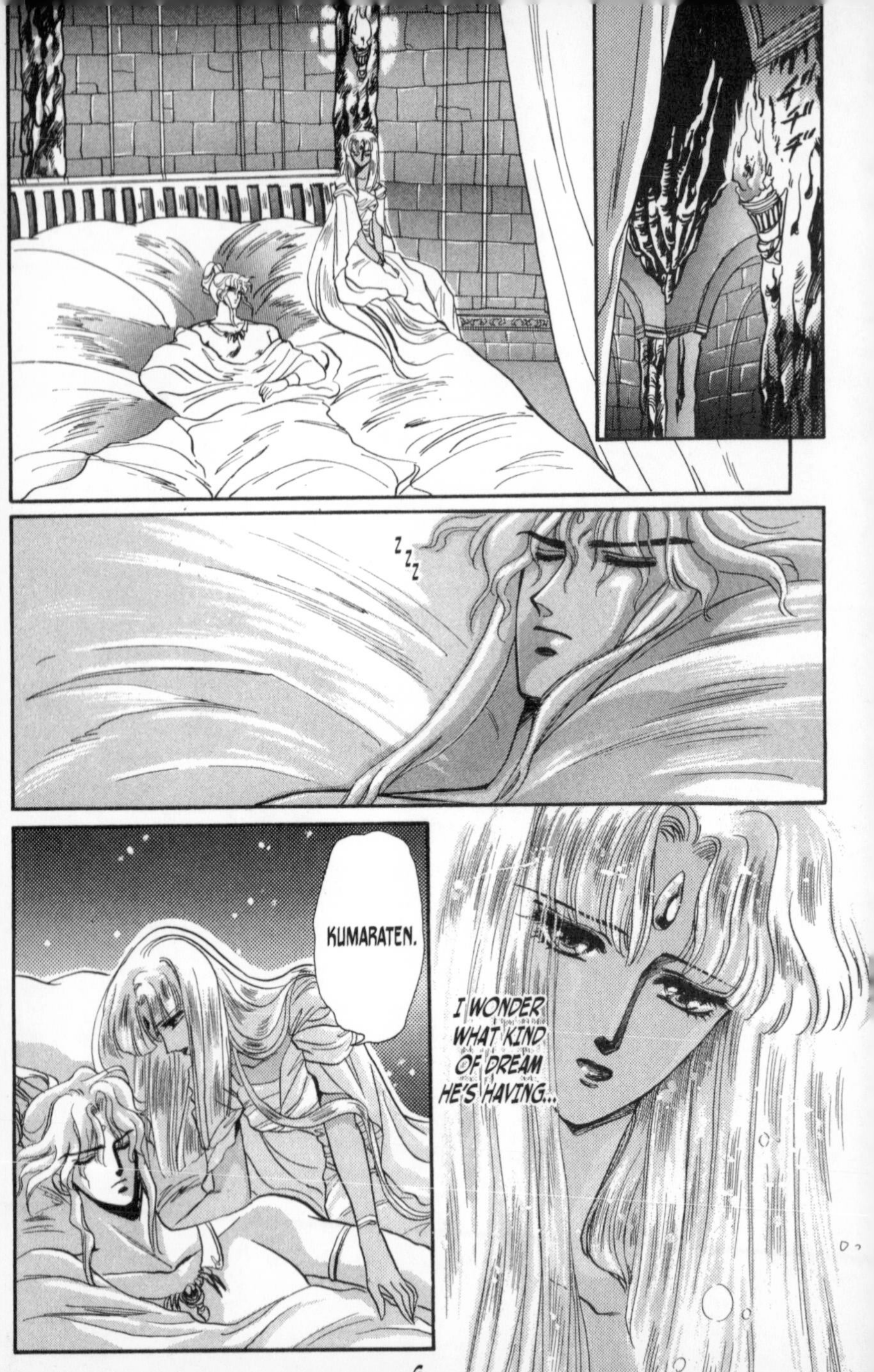
Z Z Z
KUMARATEN.
I WONDER WHAT KIND OF DREAM HE'S HAVING...

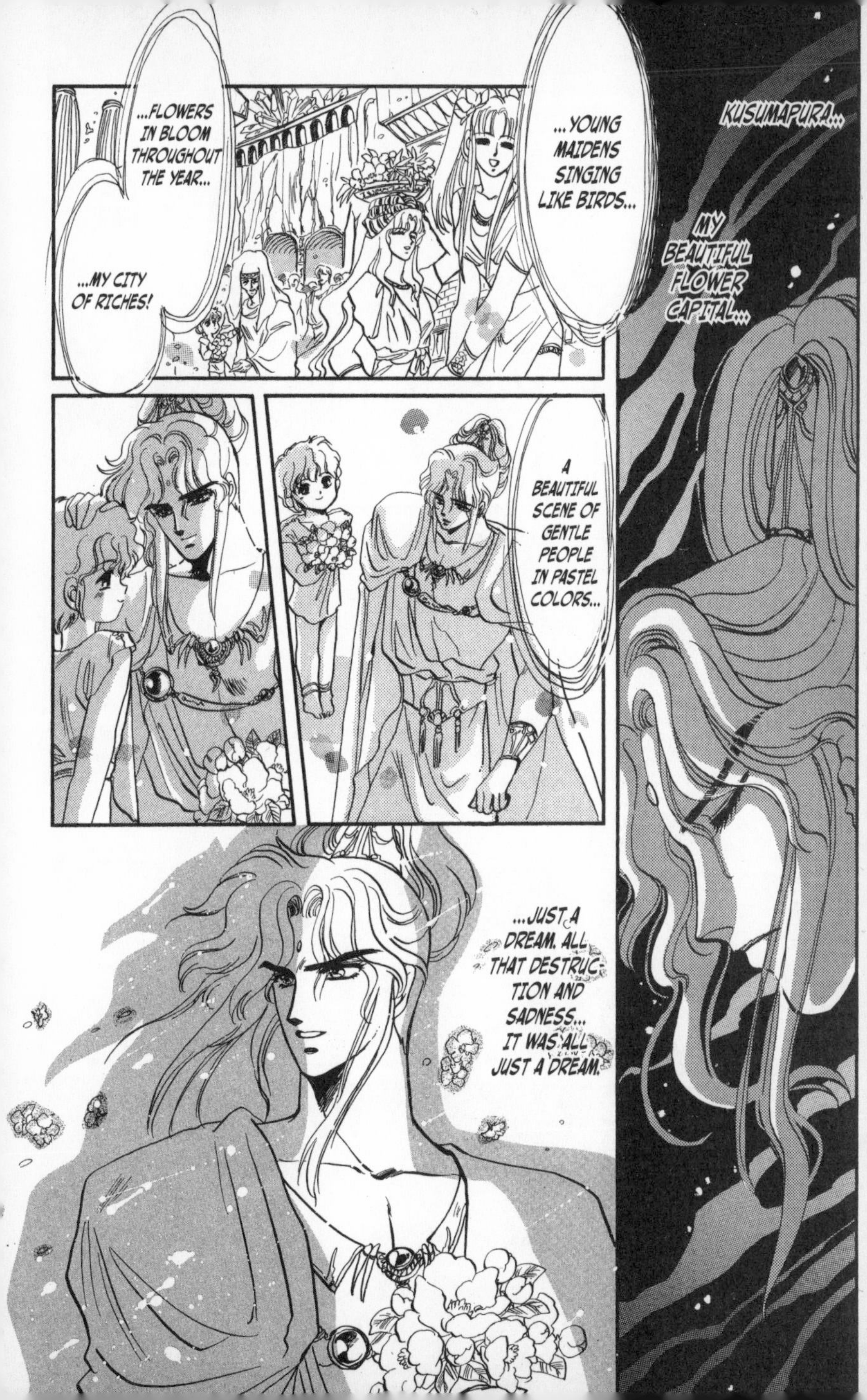
KUSUMAPURA...
MY BEAUTIFUL FLOWER CAPITAL...
...YOUNG MAIDENS SINGING LIKE BIRDS...
...FLOWERS IN BLOOM THROUGHOUT THE YEAR...
...MY CITY OF RICHES!
A BEAUTIFUL SCENE OF GENTLE PEOPLE IN PASTEL COLORS...
...JUST A DREAM. ALL THAT DESTRUCTION AND SADNESS... IT WAS ALL JUST A DREAM.

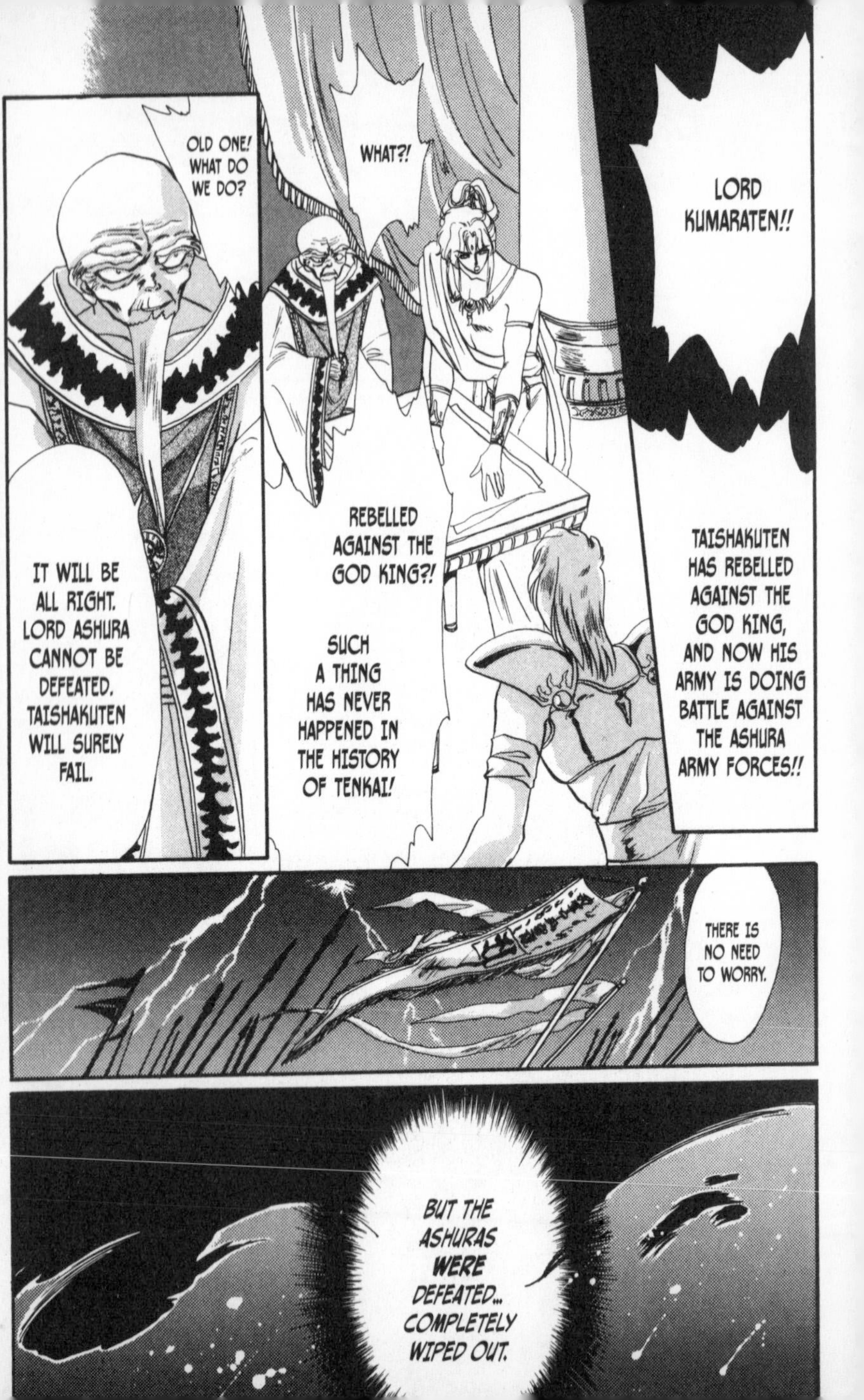
LORD KUMARATEN!!
TAISHAKUTEN HAS REBELLED AGAINST THE GOD KING, AND NOW HIS ARMY IS DOING BATTLE AGAINST THE ASHURA ARMY FORCES!!
WHAT?!
REBELLED AGAINST THE GOD KING?!
SUCH A THING HAS NEVER HAPPENED IN THE HISTORY OF TENKAI!
OLD ONE! WHAT DO WE DO?
IT WILL BE ALL RIGHT. LORD ASHURA CANNOT BE DEFEATED. TAISHAKUTEN WILL SURELY FAIL.
THERE IS NO NEED TO WORRY.
BUT THE ASHURAS WERE DEFEATED... COMPLETELY WIPED OUT.

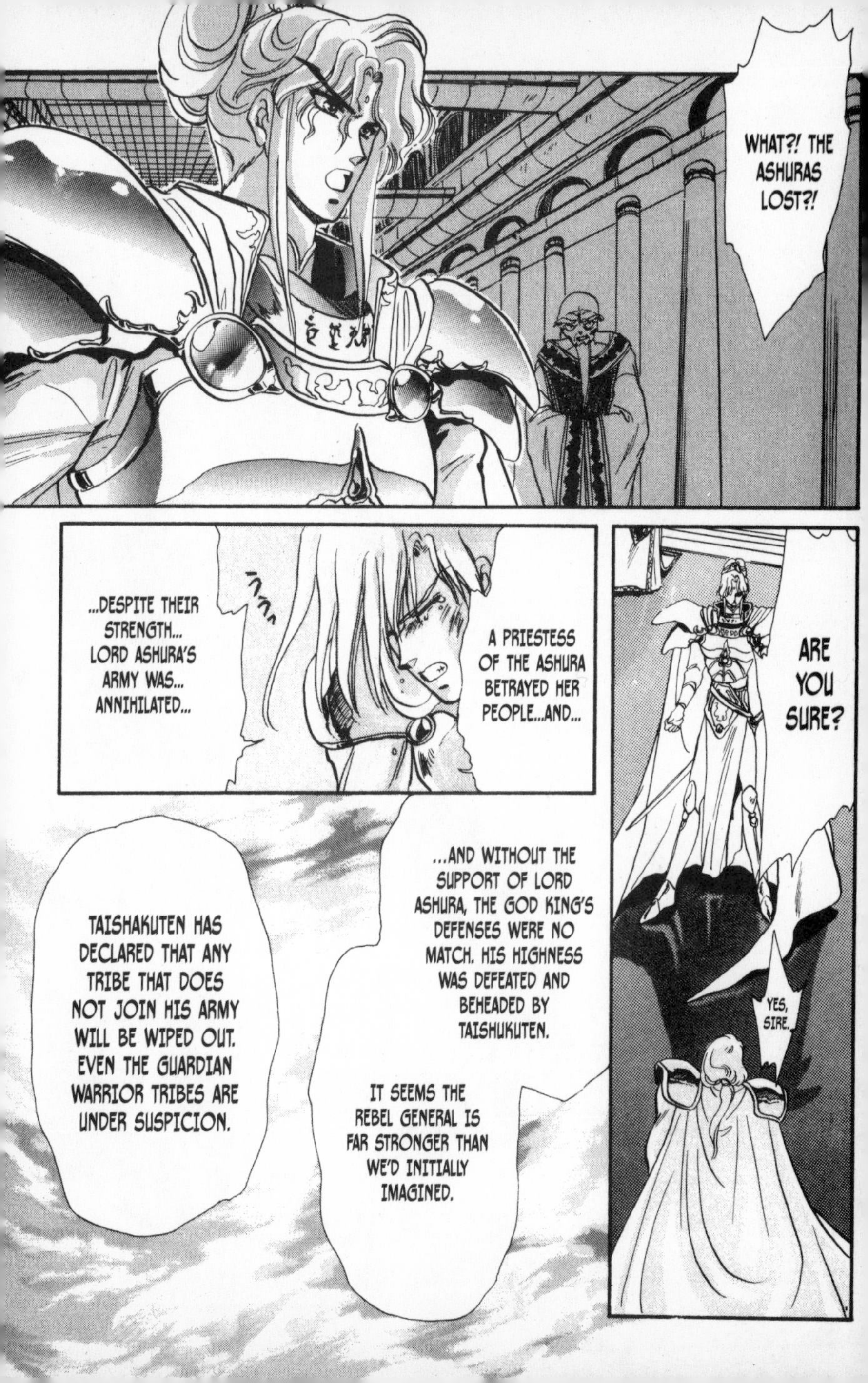
WHAT?! THE ASHURAS LOST?!
ARE YOU SURE?
YES, SIRE.
A PRIESTESS OF THE ASHURA BETRAYED HER PEOPLE...AND...
...DESPITE THEIR STRENGTH... LORD ASHURA'S ARMY WAS... ANNIHILATED...
...AND WITHOUT THE SUPPORT OF LORD ASHURA, THE GOD KING'S DEFENSES WERE NO MATCH. HIS HIGHNESS WAS DEFEATED AND BEHEADED BY TAISHUKUTEN.
IT SEEMS THE REBEL GENERAL IS FAR STRONGER THAN WE'D INITIALLY IMAGINED.
TAISHAKUTEN HAS DECLARED THAT ANY TRIBE THAT DOES NOT JOIN HIS ARMY WILL BE WIPED OUT. EVEN THE GUARDIAN WARRIOR TRIBES ARE UNDER SUSPICION.

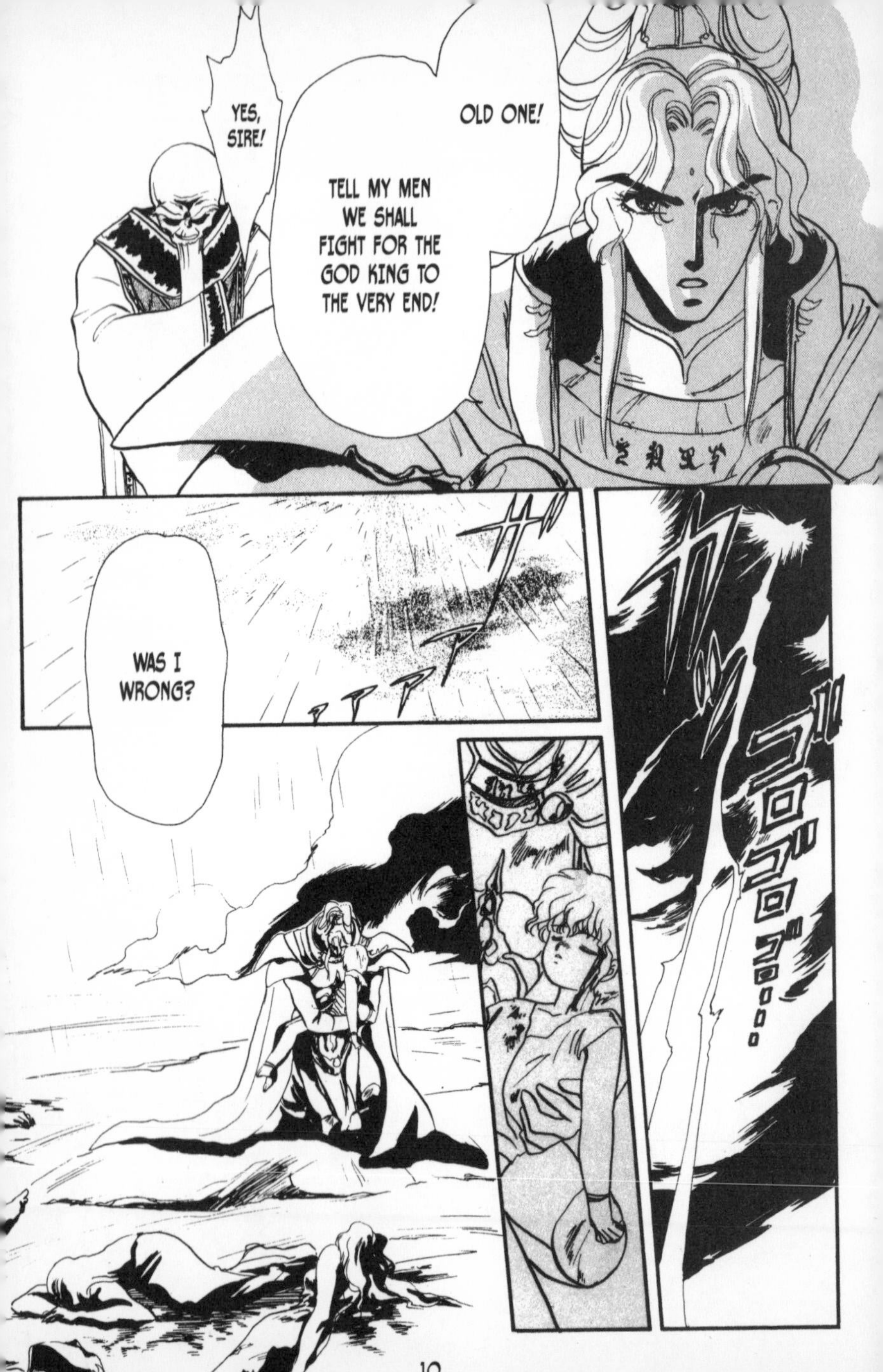
OLD ONE!
TELL MY MEN WE SHALL FIGHT FOR THE GOD KING TO THE VERY END!
YES, SIRE!
WAS I WRONG?

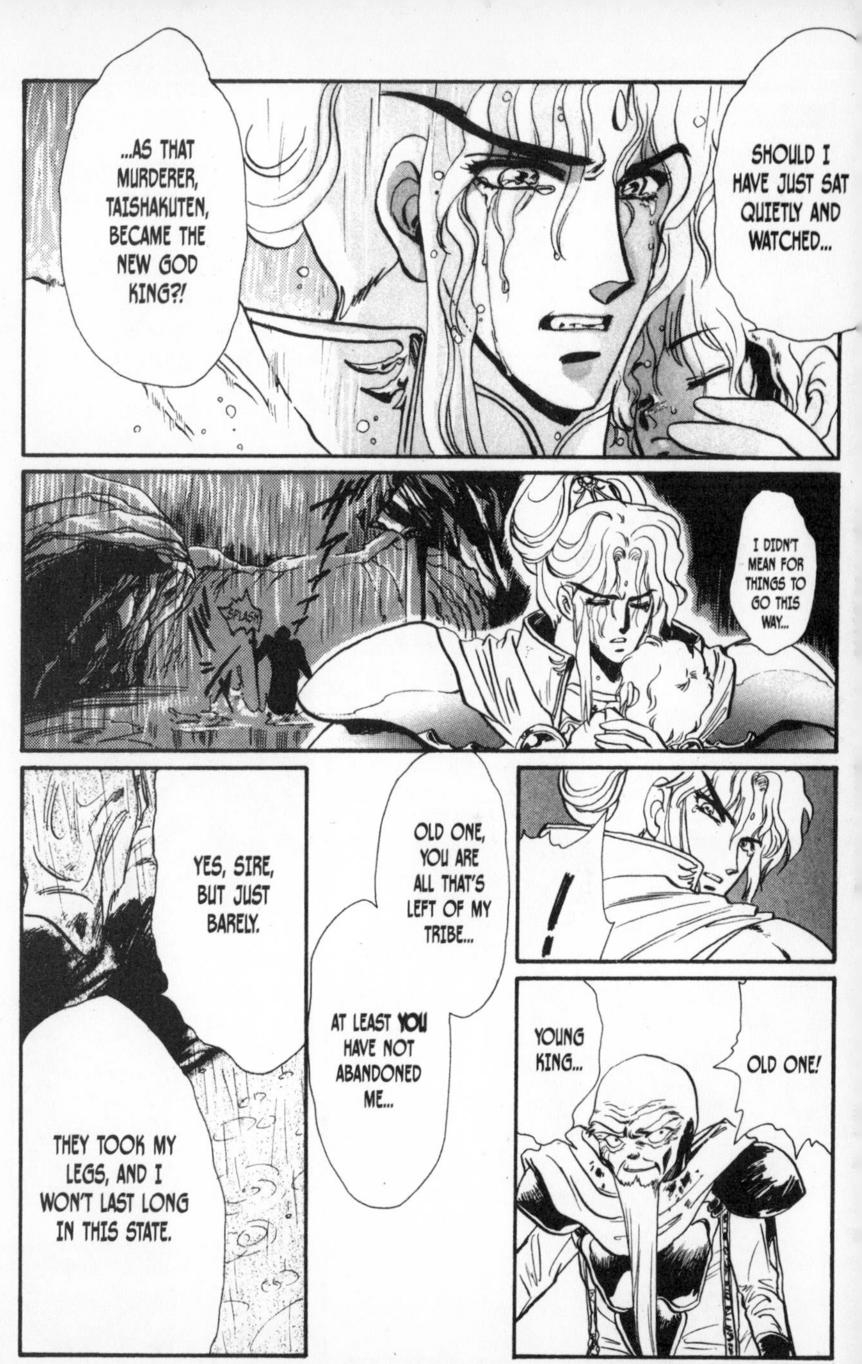
SHOULD I HAVE JUST SAT QUIETLY AND WATCHED...
...AS THAT MURDERER, TAISHAKUTEN, BECAME THE NEW GOD KING?!
I DIDN'T MEAN FOR THINGS TO GO THIS WAY...
SPLASH
!
OLD ONE!
YOUNG KING...
OLD ONE, YOU ARE ALL THAT'S LEFT OF MY TRIBE...
AT LEAST YOU HAVE NOT ABANDONED ME...
YES, SIRE, BUT JUST BARELY.
THEY TOOK MY LEGS, AND I WON'T LAST LONG IN THIS STATE.

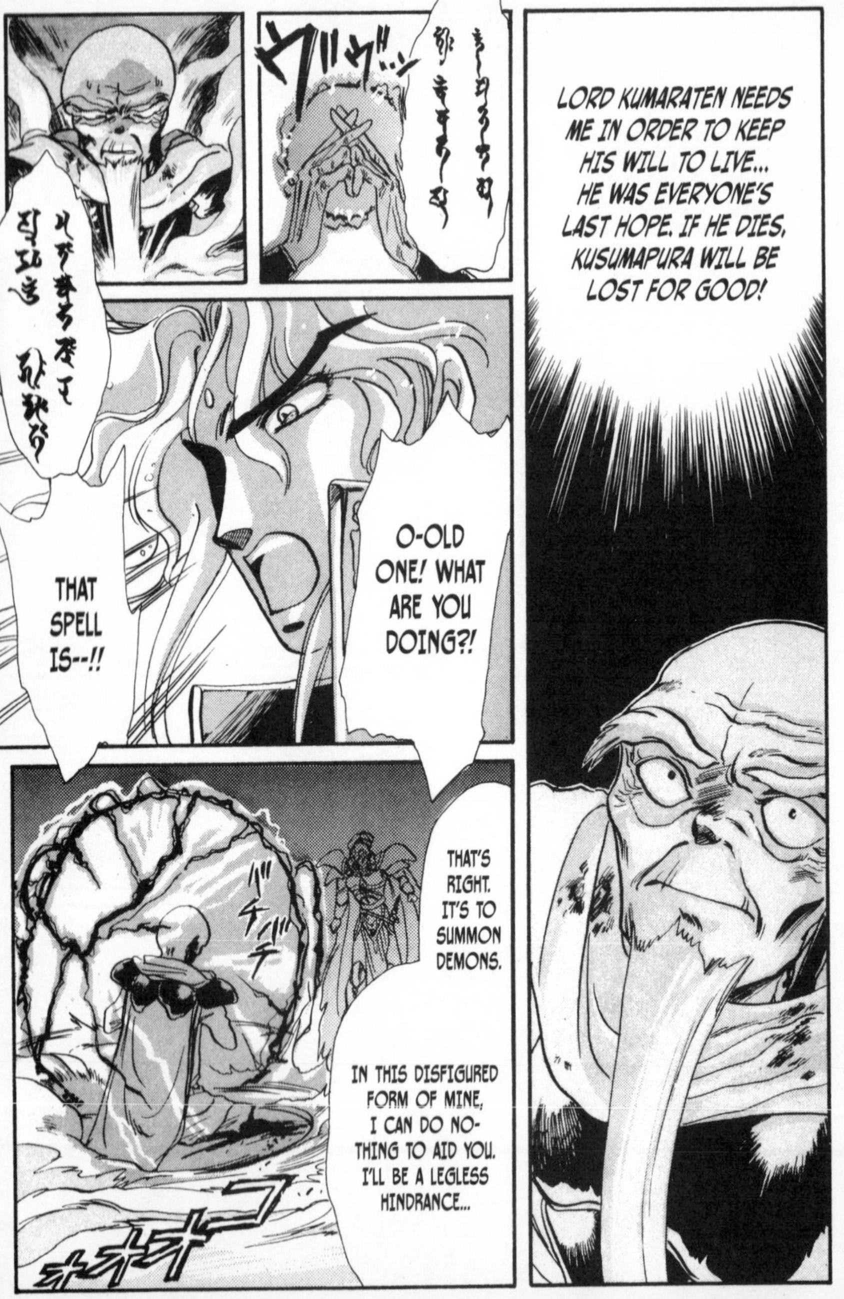
LORD KUMARATEN NEEDS ME IN ORDER TO KEEP HIS WILL TO LIVE... HE WAS EVERYONE'S LAST HOPE. IF HE DIES, KUSUMAPURA WILL BE LOST FOR GOOD!
O-OLD ONE! WHAT ARE YOU DOING?!
THAT SPELL IS--!!
THAT'S RIGHT. IT'S TO SUMMON DEMONS.
IN THIS DISFIGURED FORM OF MINE, I CAN DO NO-THING TO AID YOU. I'LL BE A LEGLESS HINDRANCE...

...IT WILL ALLOW ME TO STAY BY MY KING'S SIDE. AND I VOW TO JOIN YOU IN THE DEPTHS OF KUSUMAPURA TO HELP YOU REBUILD YOUR CITY IN ALL ITS GLORY.

THIS NEW FORM MAY BE HIDEOUS, BUT...

THEREFORE, I WILL MAKE A PACT WITH A DEMON AND TRANSFER MY SOUL INTO ITS BODY. IF SUCCESSFUL, MY NEW FORM WILL LAST FOR CENTURIES.

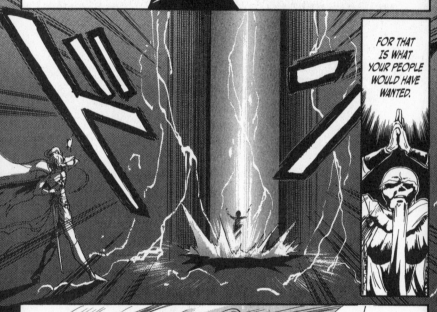

FOR THAT IS WHAT YOUR PEOPLE WOULD HAVE WANTED.

OLD ONE!!

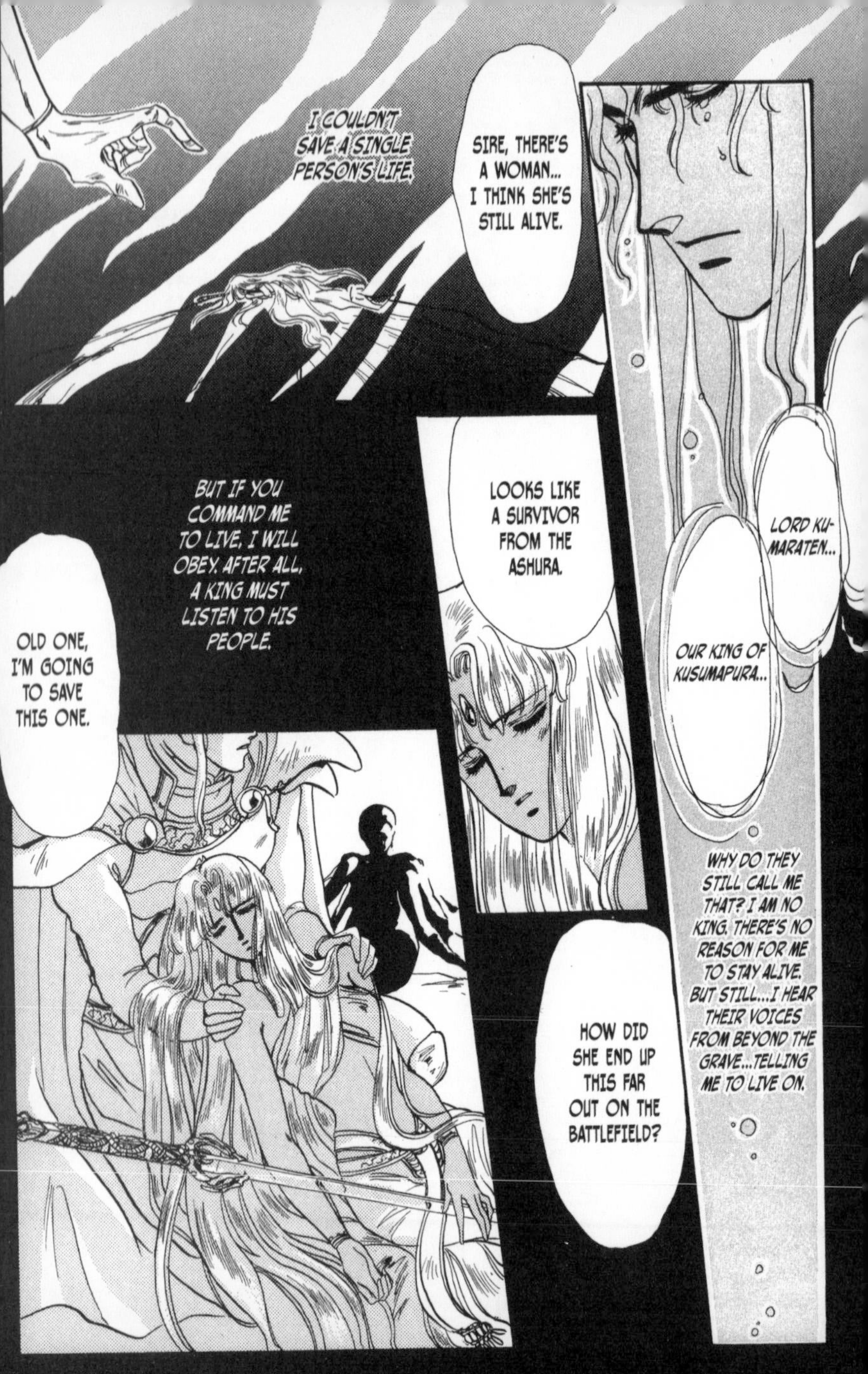
LORD KU-MARATEN...
OUR KING OF KUSUMAPURA...
WHY DO THEY STILL CALL ME THAT? I AM NO KING. THERE'S NO REASON FOR ME TO STAY ALIVE. BUT STILL...I HEAR THEIR VOICES FROM BEYOND THE GRAVE...TELLING ME TO LIVE ON.
I COULDN'T SAVE A SINGLE PERSON'S LIFE.
BUT IF YOU COMMAND ME TO LIVE, I WILL OBEY. AFTER ALL, A KING MUST LISTEN TO HIS PEOPLE.
SIRE, THERE'S A WOMAN... I THINK SHE'S STILL ALIVE.
LOOKS LIKE A SURVIVOR FROM THE ASHURA.
HOW DID SHE END UP THIS FAR OUT ON THE BATTLEFIELD?
OLD ONE, I'M GOING TO SAVE THIS ONE.

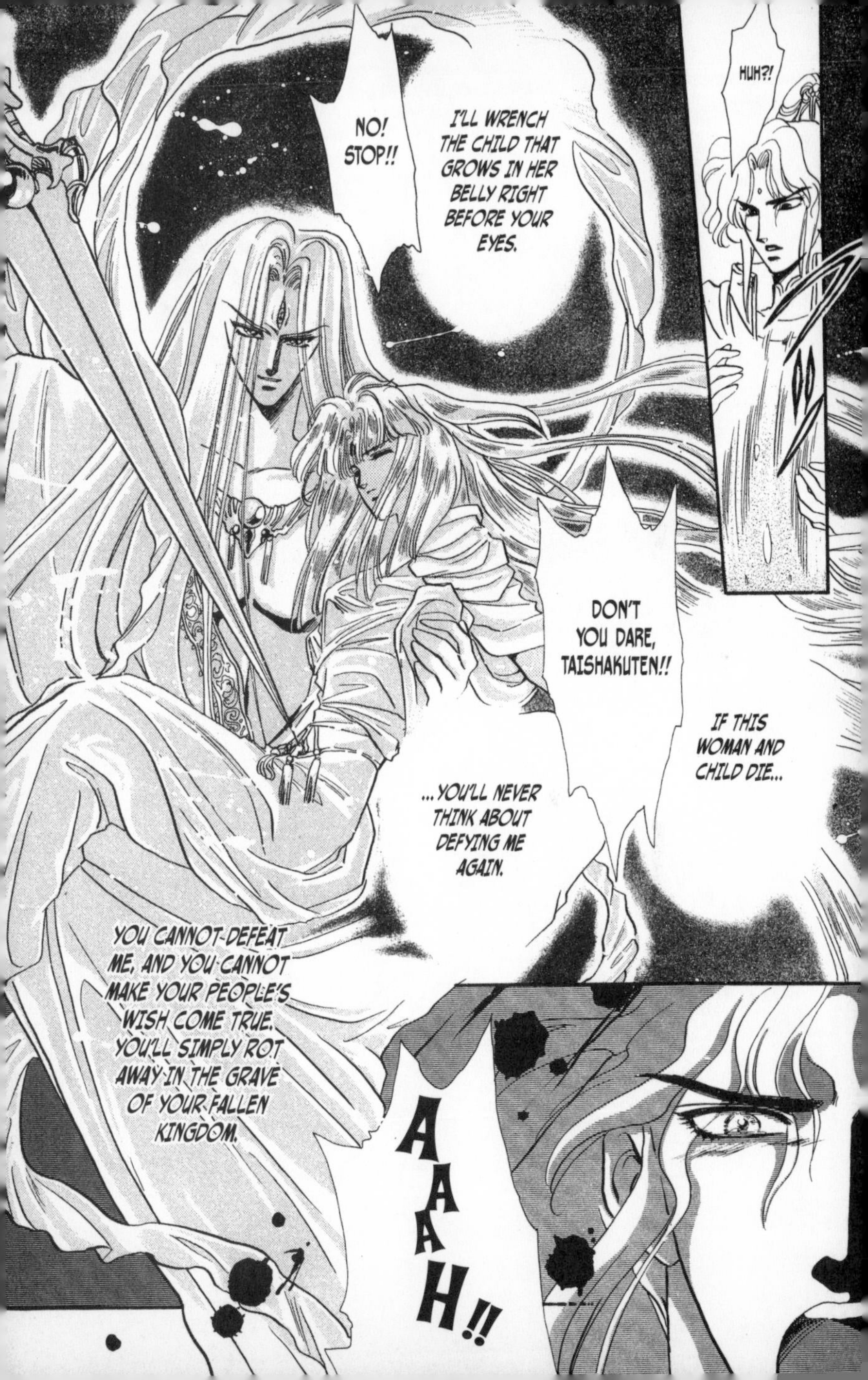
HUH?!
I'LL WRENCH THE CHILD THAT GROWS IN HER BELLY RIGHT BEFORE YOUR EYES.
NO! STOP!!
DON'T YOU DARE, TAISHAKUTEN!!
IF THIS WOMAN AND CHILD DIE...
...YOU'LL NEVER THINK ABOUT DEFYING ME AGAIN.
YOU CANNOT DEFEAT ME, AND YOU CANNOT MAKE YOUR PEOPLE'S WISH COME TRUE. YOU'LL SIMPLY ROT AWAY IN THE GRAVE OF YOUR FALLEN KINGDOM.
AAAAH!!

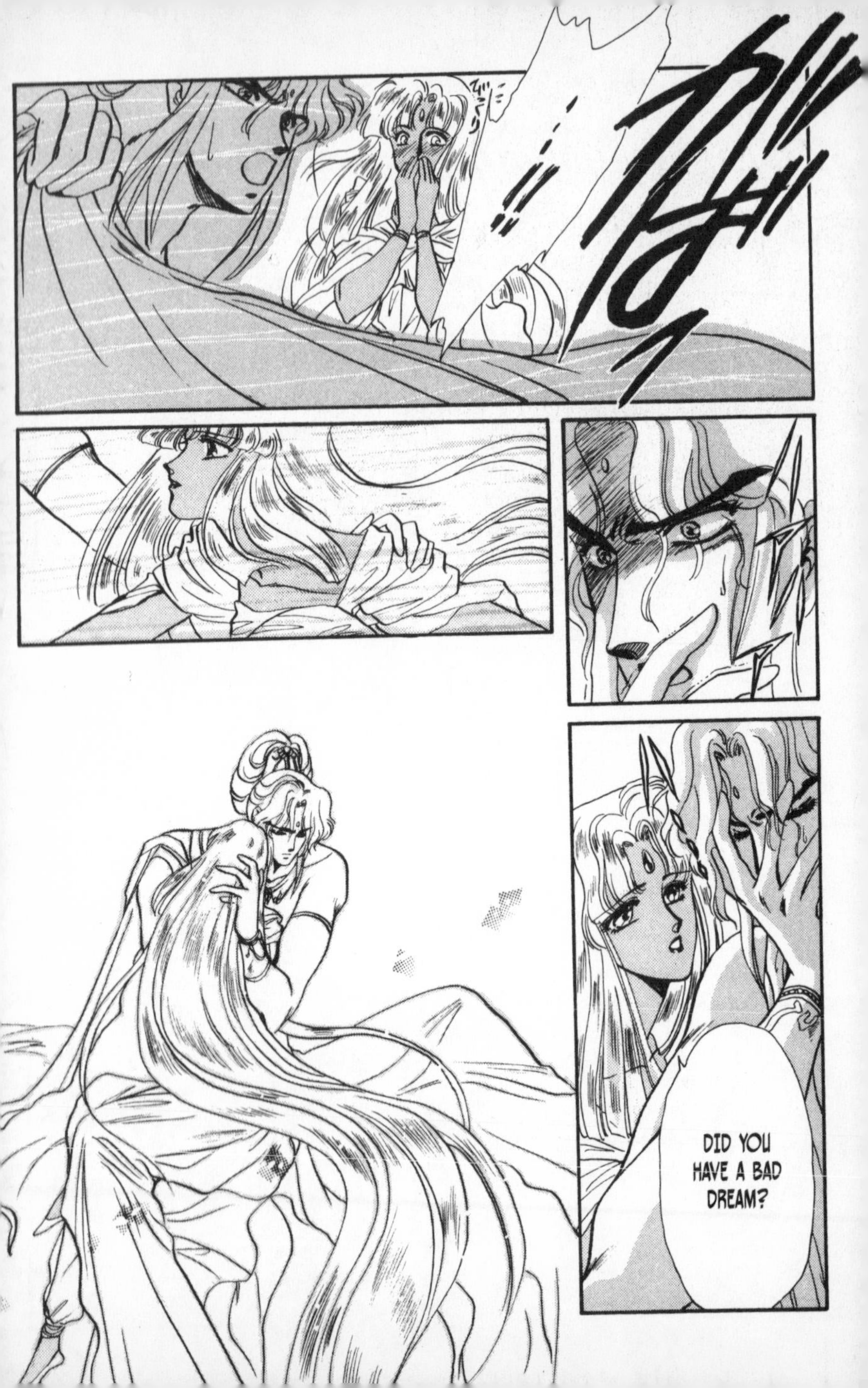
DID YOU HAVE A BAD DREAM?

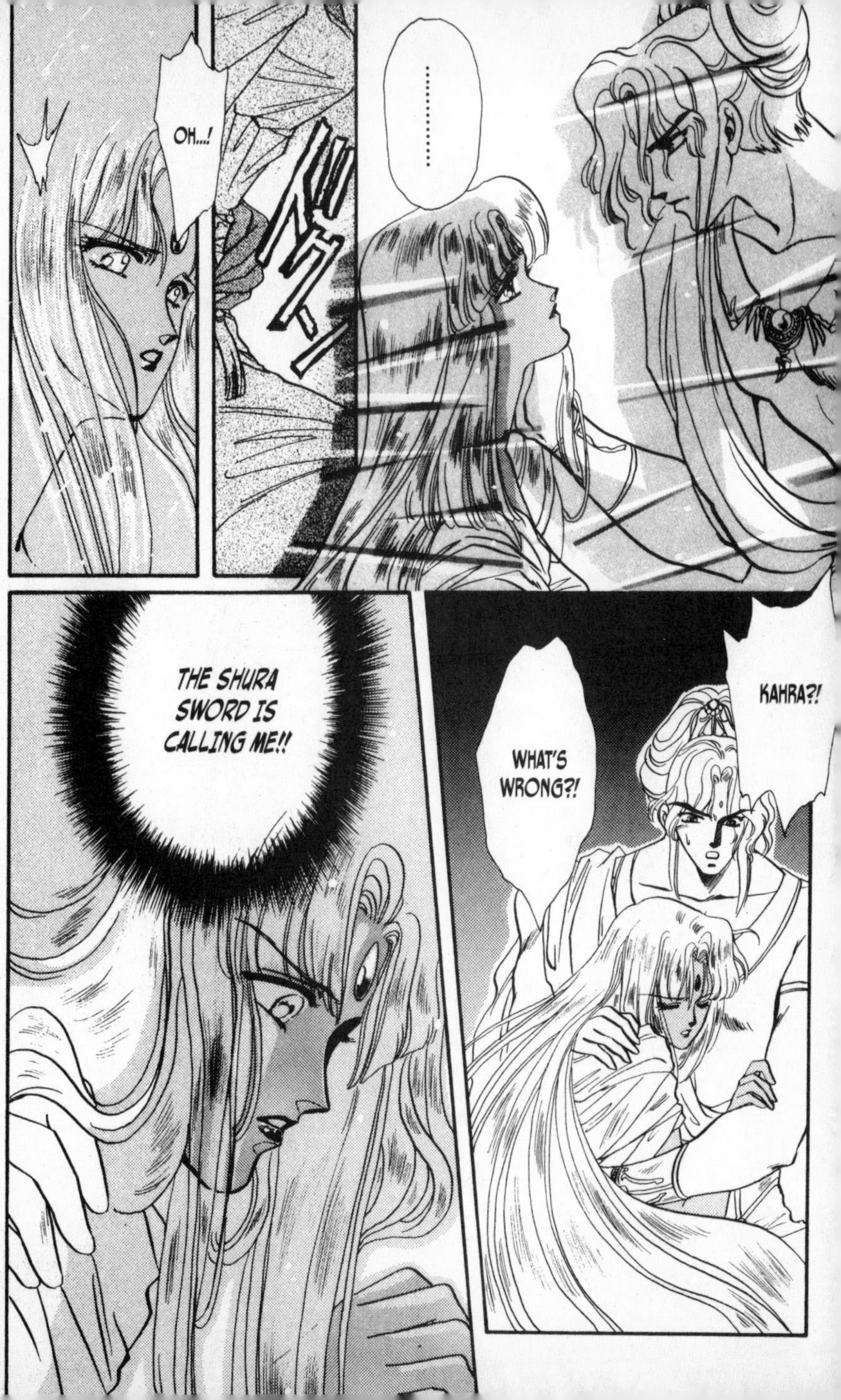

......
OH...!
KAHRA?!
WHAT'S WRONG?!
THE SHURA SWORD IS CALLING ME!!

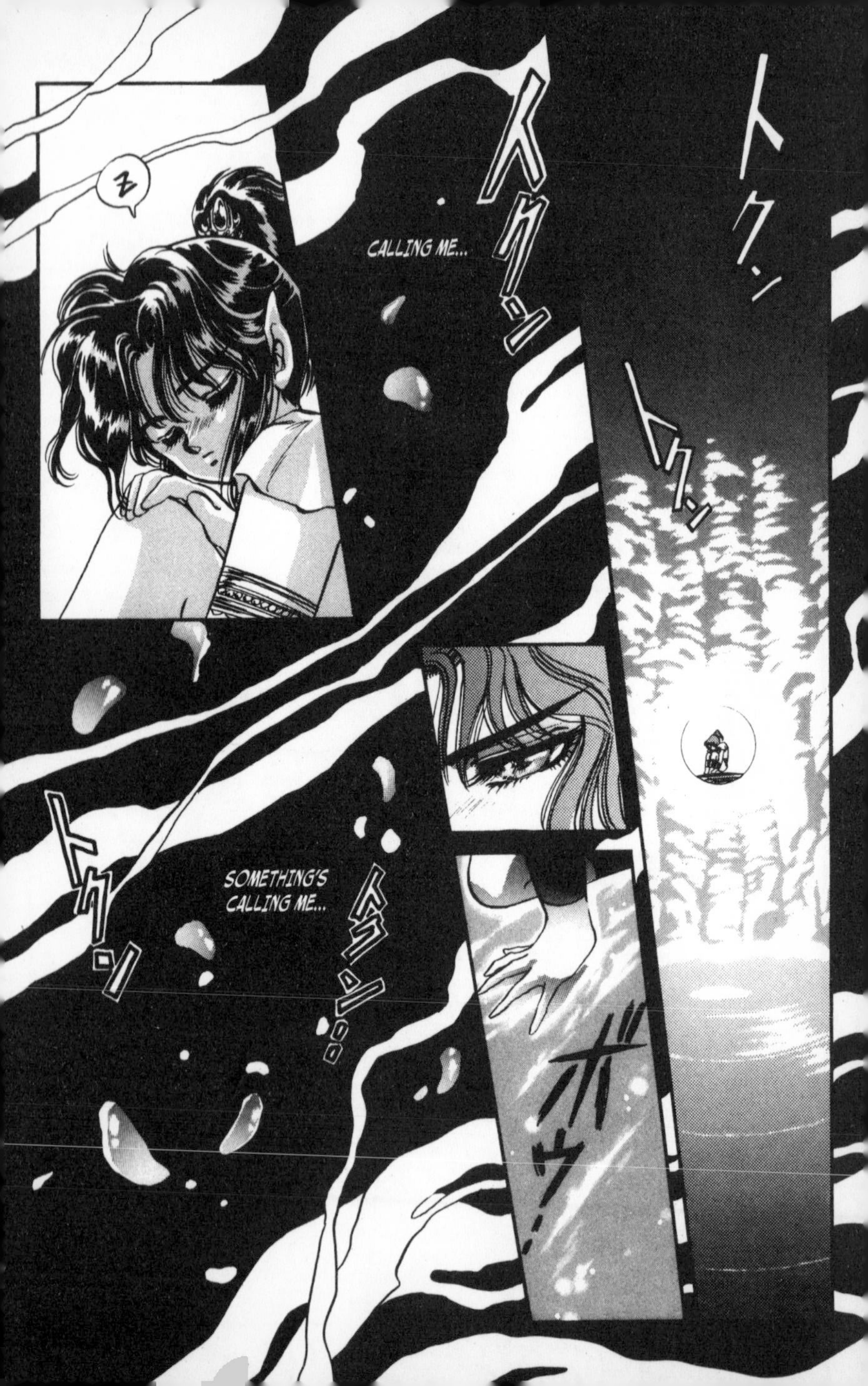
CALLING ME...
Z
SOMETHING'S CALLING ME...

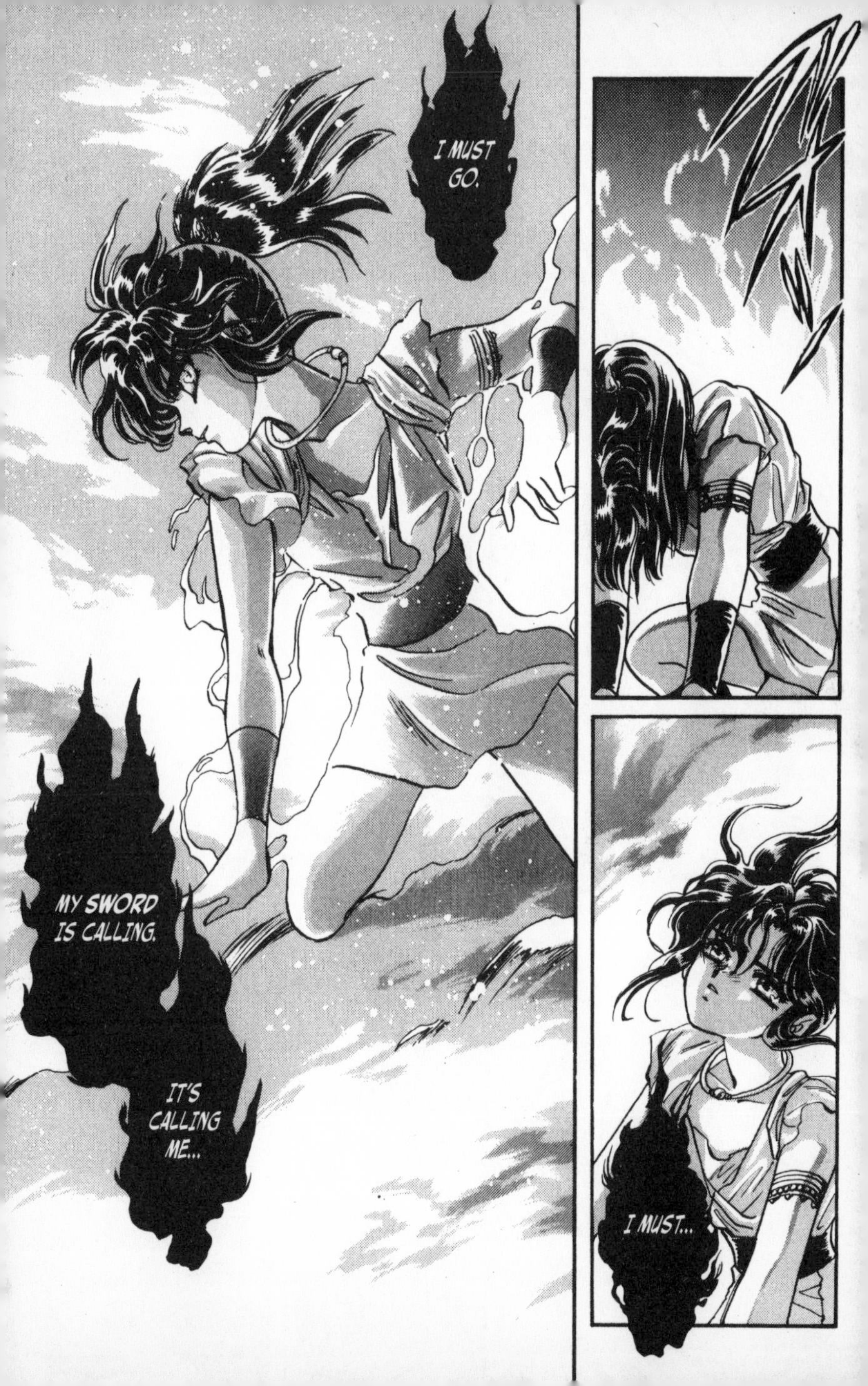
I MUST...
I MUST GO.
MY SWORD IS CALLING.
IT'S CALLING ME...

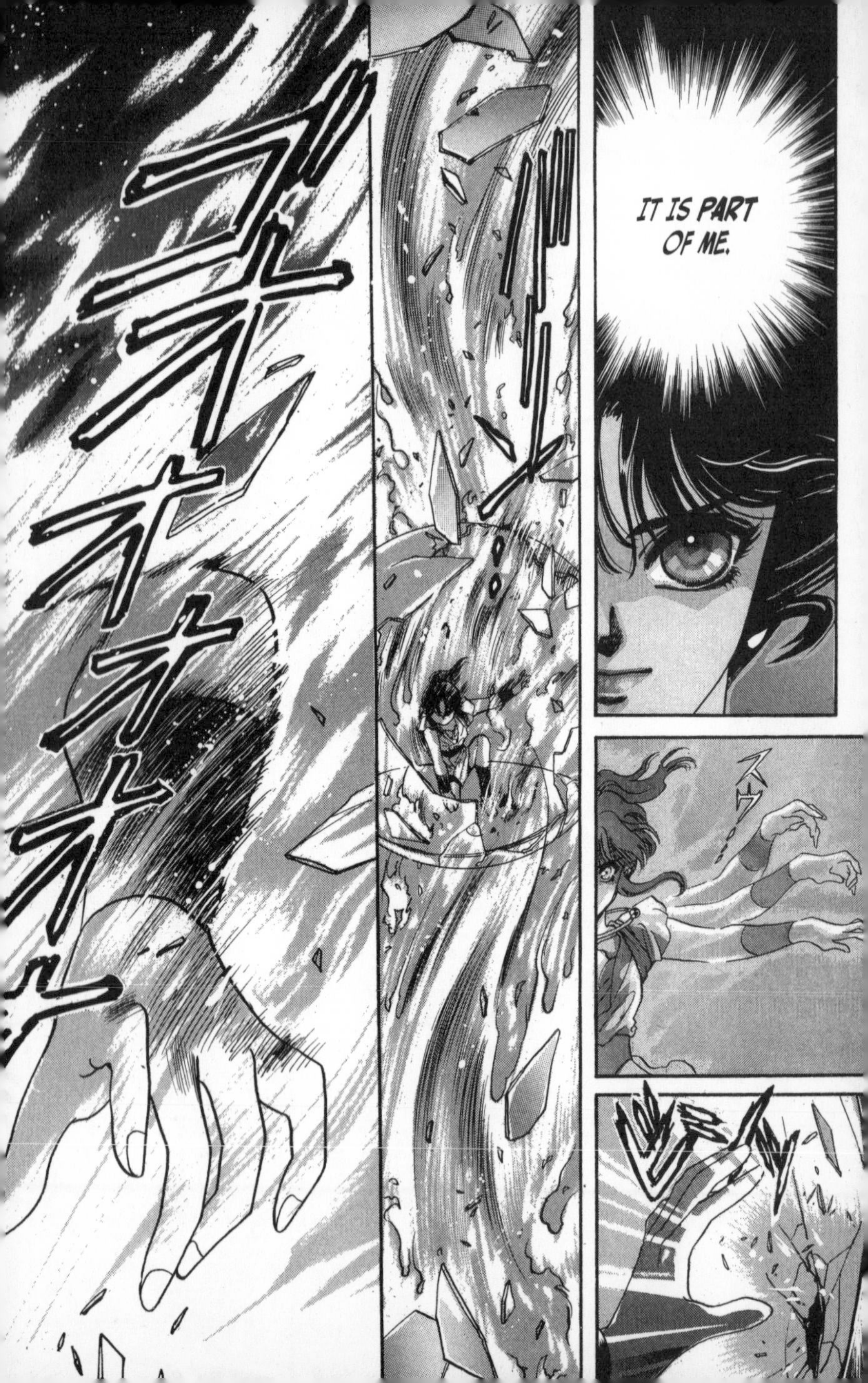
IT IS PART OF ME.

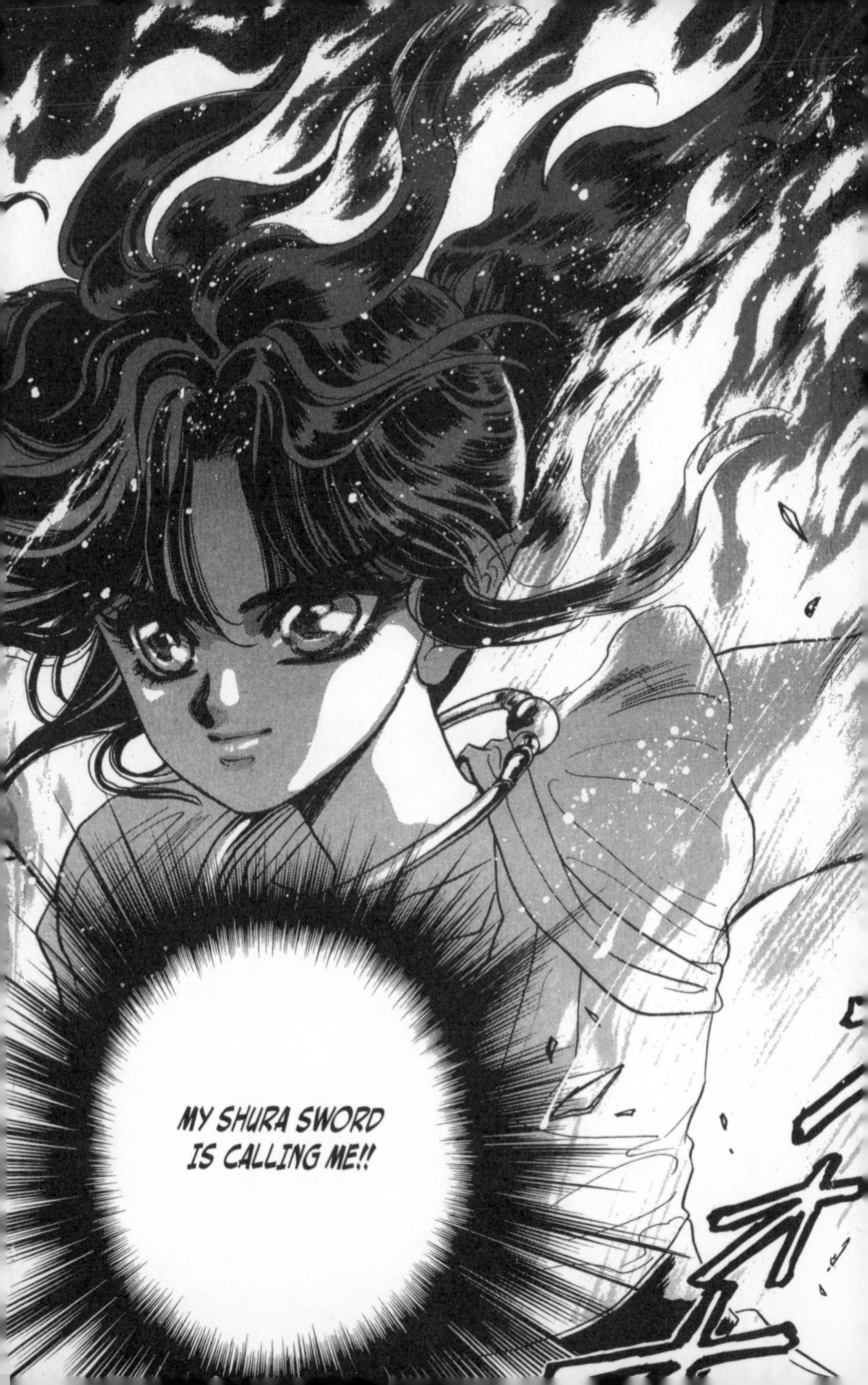
MY SHURA SWORD IS CALLING ME!!

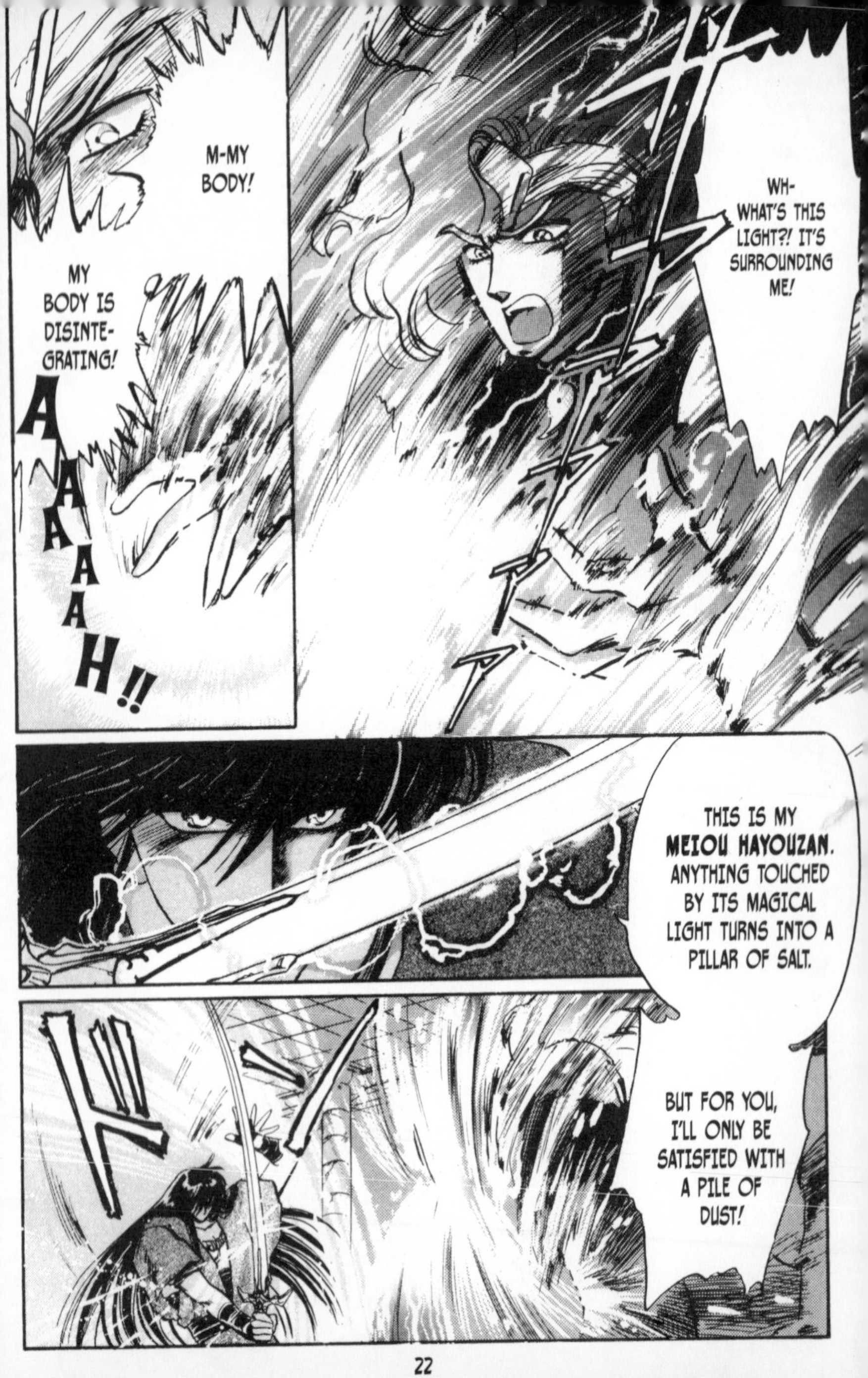
WH- WHAT'S THIS LIGHT?! IT'S SURROUNDING ME!
M-MY BODY!
MY BODY IS DISINTE-GRATING!
AAAAAAH!!
THIS IS MY **MEIOU HAYOUZAN.** ANYTHING TOUCHED BY ITS MAGICAL LIGHT TURNS INTO A PILLAR OF SALT.
BUT FOR YOU, I'LL ONLY BE SATISFIED WITH A PILE OF DUST!

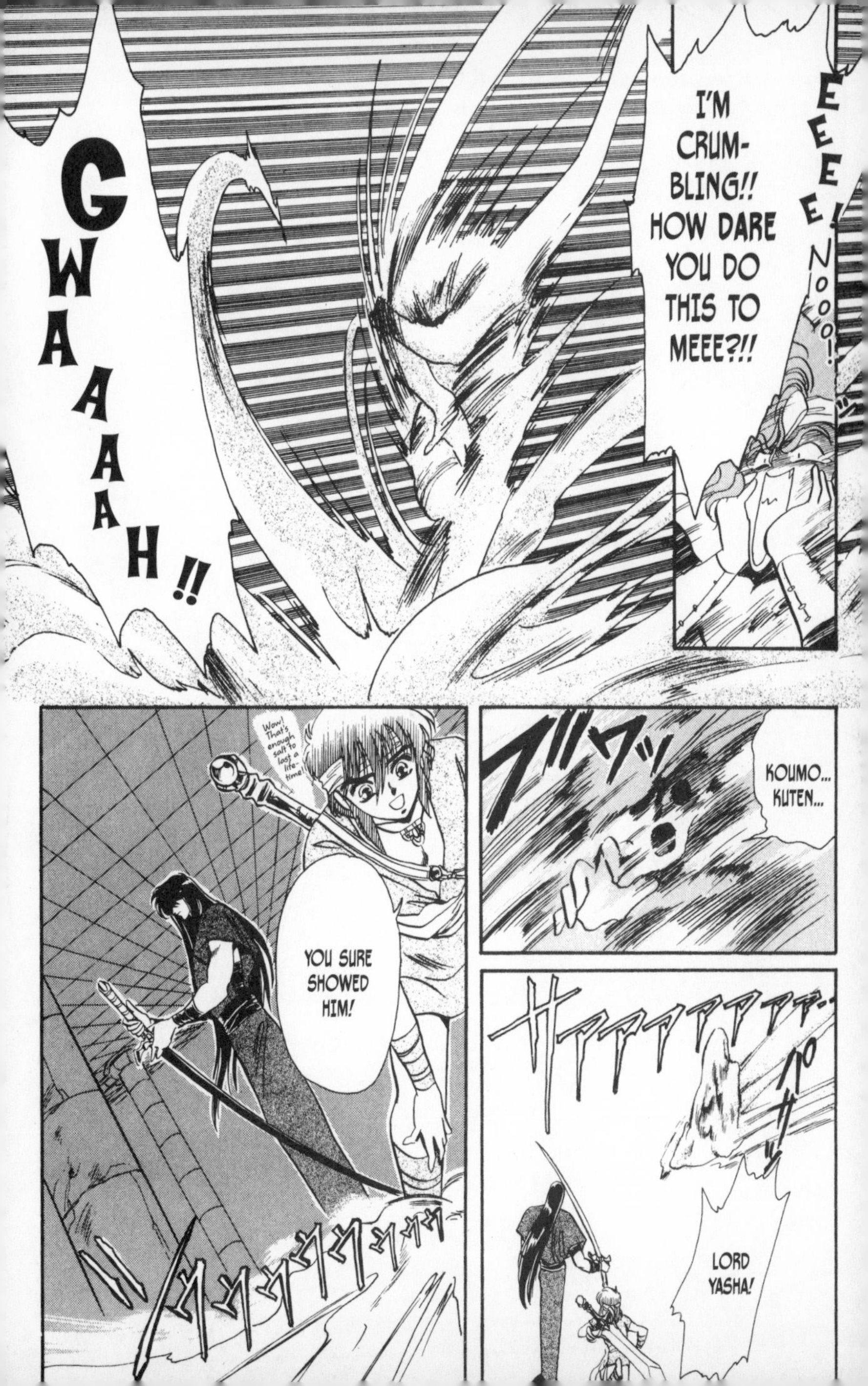
GWAAAAH!!
I'M CRUMBLING!! HOW DARE YOU DO THIS TO MEEE?!!
EEEE! NOOOO!
Wow! That's enough salt to last a lifetime!
YOU SURE SHOWED HIM!
KOUMO... KUTEN...
LORD YASHA!

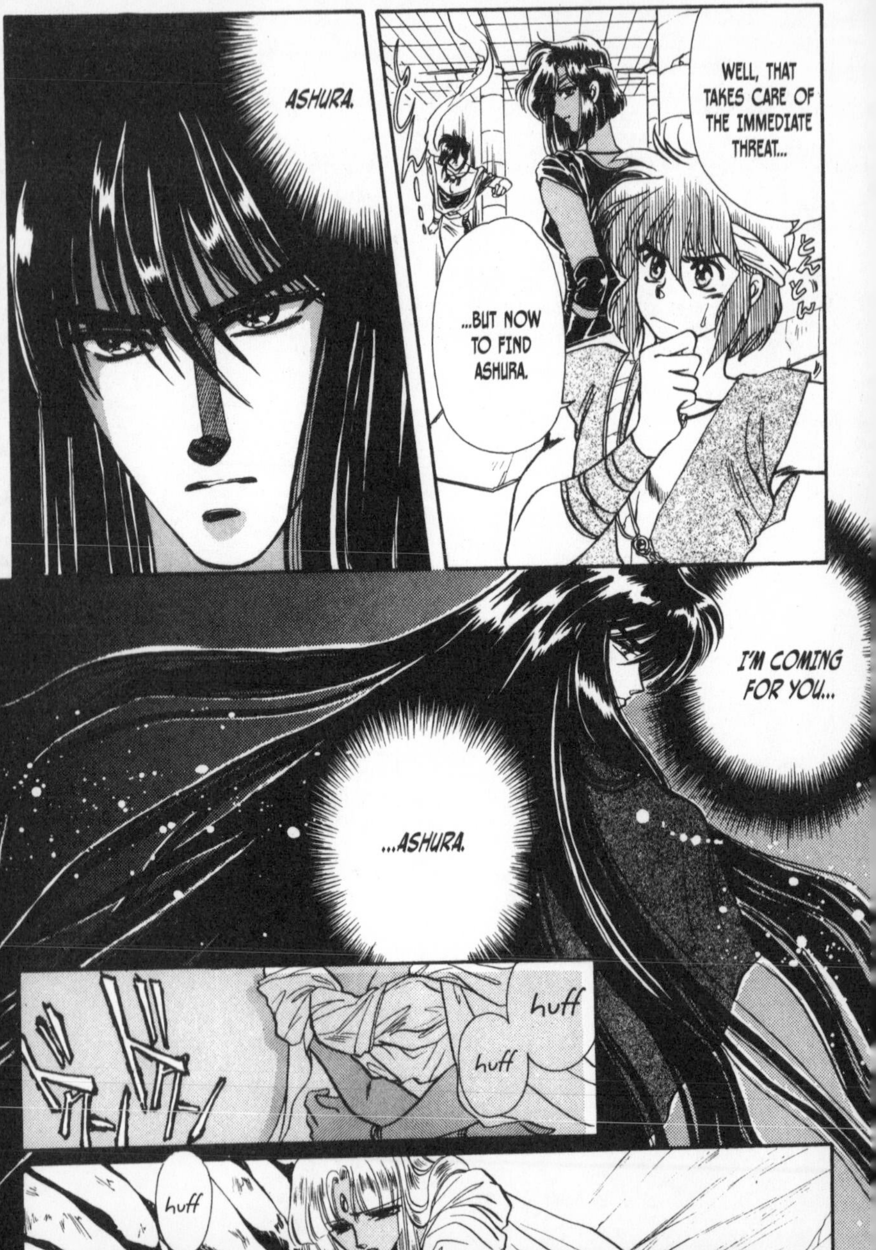
WELL, THAT TAKES CARE OF THE IMMEDIATE THREAT...
とんとん
...BUT NOW TO FIND ASHURA.
ASHURA.
I'M COMING FOR YOU...
...ASHURA.
huff
huff
huff

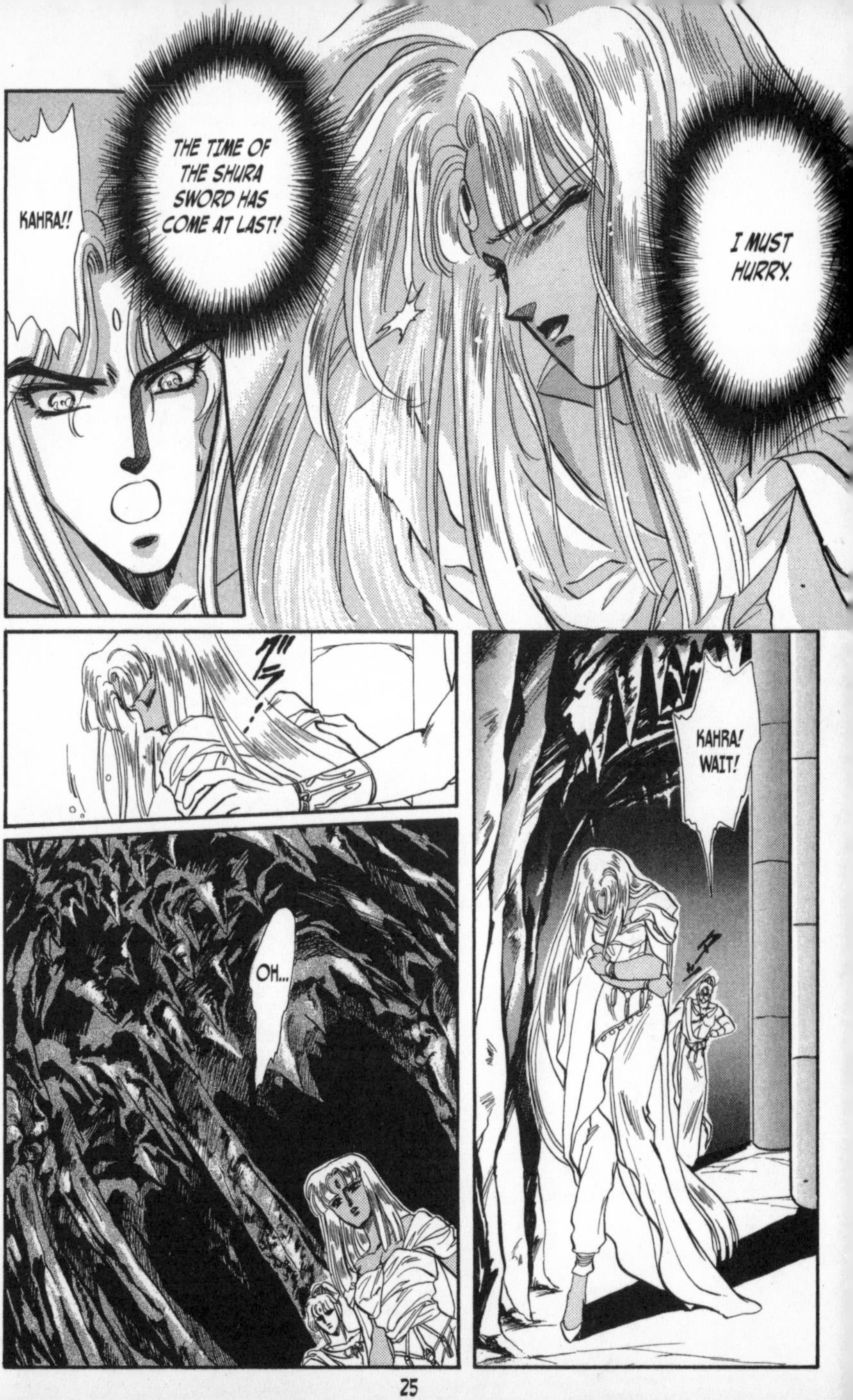
KAHRA!!
THE TIME OF THE SHURA SWORD HAS COME AT LAST!
I MUST HURRY.
KAHRA! WAIT!
OH...

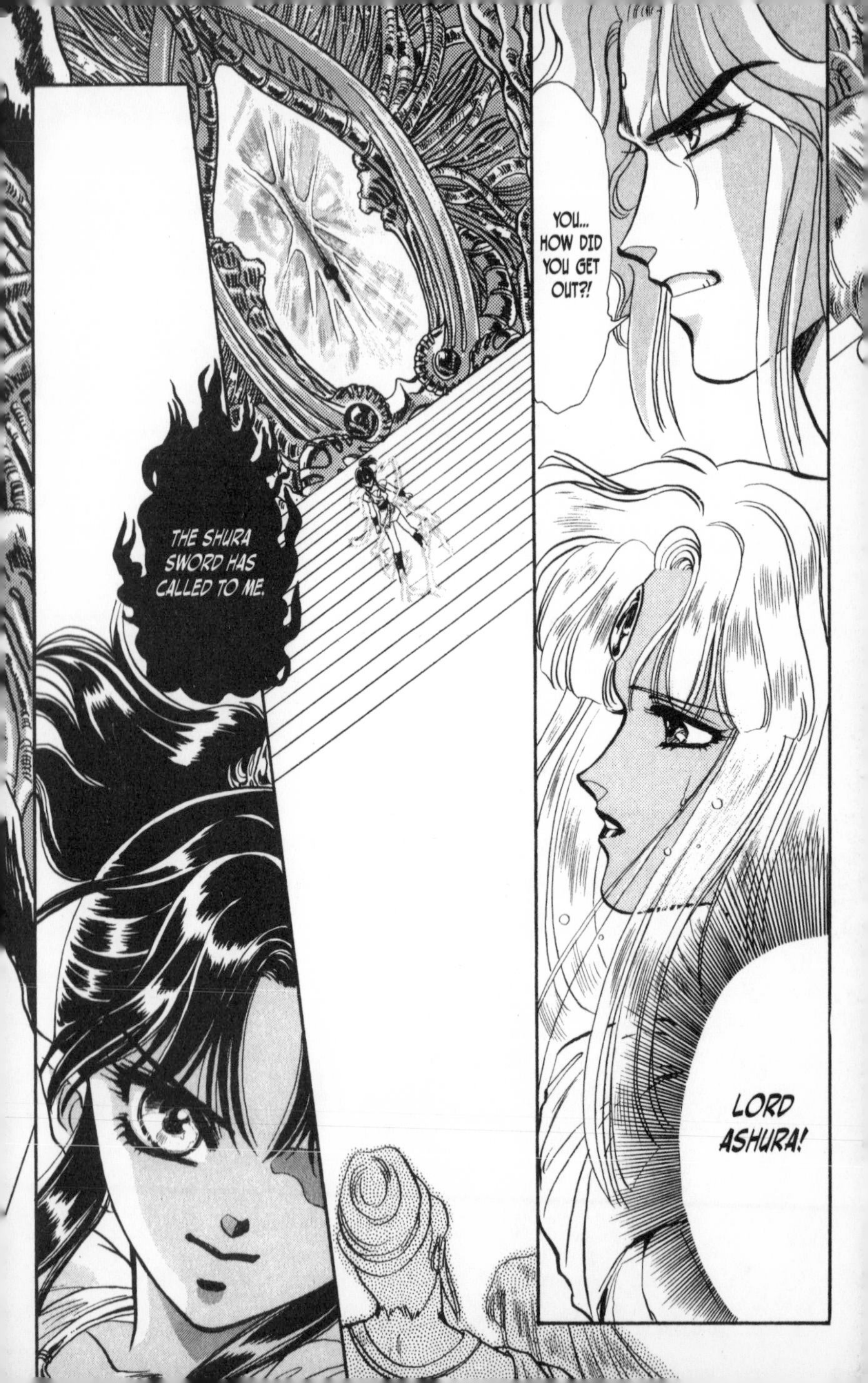
YOU... HOW DID YOU GET OUT?!
LORD ASHURA!
THE SHURA SWORD HAS CALLED TO ME.

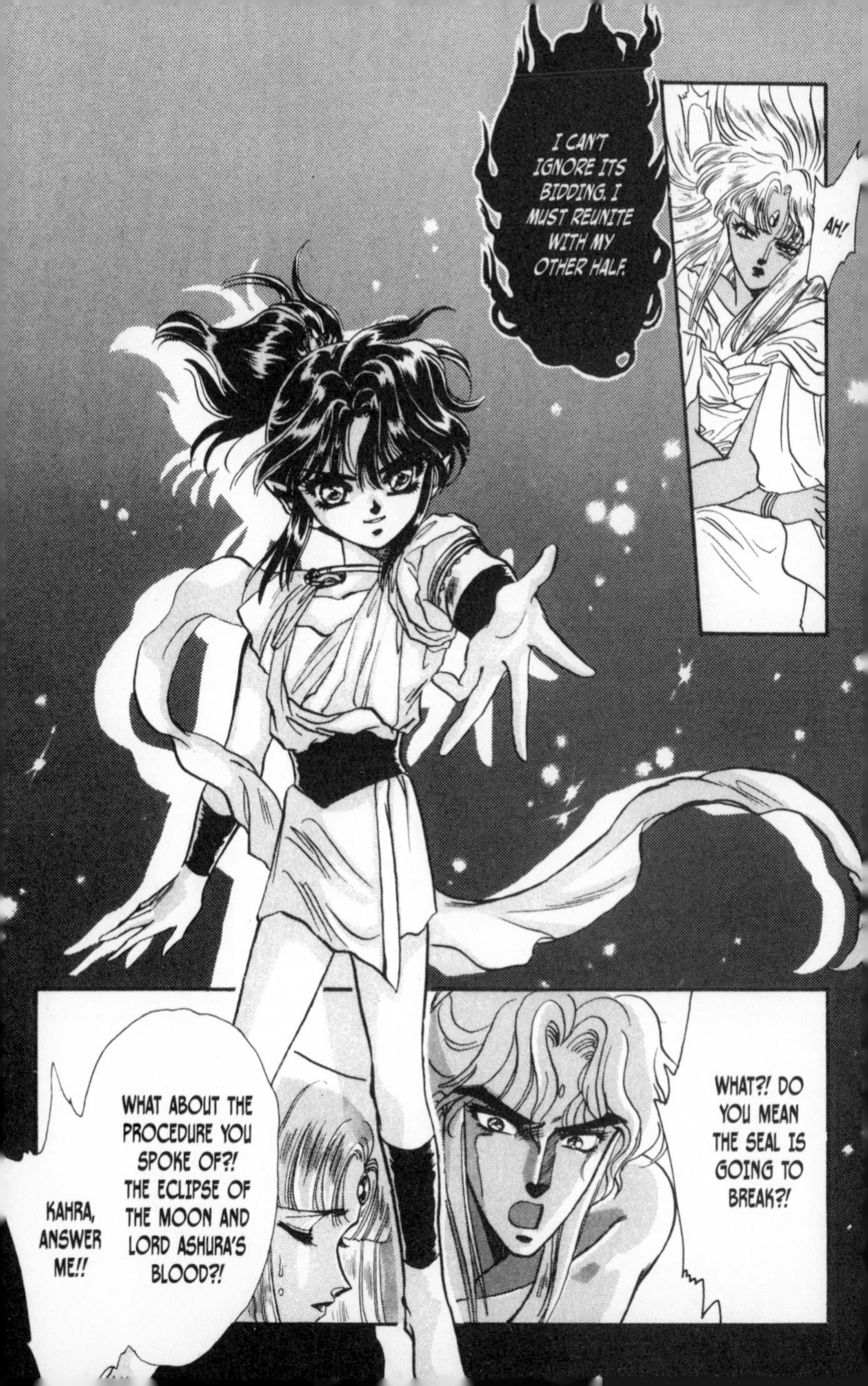
AH!
I CAN'T IGNORE ITS BIDDING. I MUST REUNITE WITH MY OTHER HALF.
WHAT?! DO YOU MEAN THE SEAL IS GOING TO BREAK?!
WHAT ABOUT THE PROCEDURE YOU SPOKE OF?! THE ECLIPSE OF THE MOON AND LORD ASHURA'S BLOOD?!
KAHRA, ANSWER ME!!

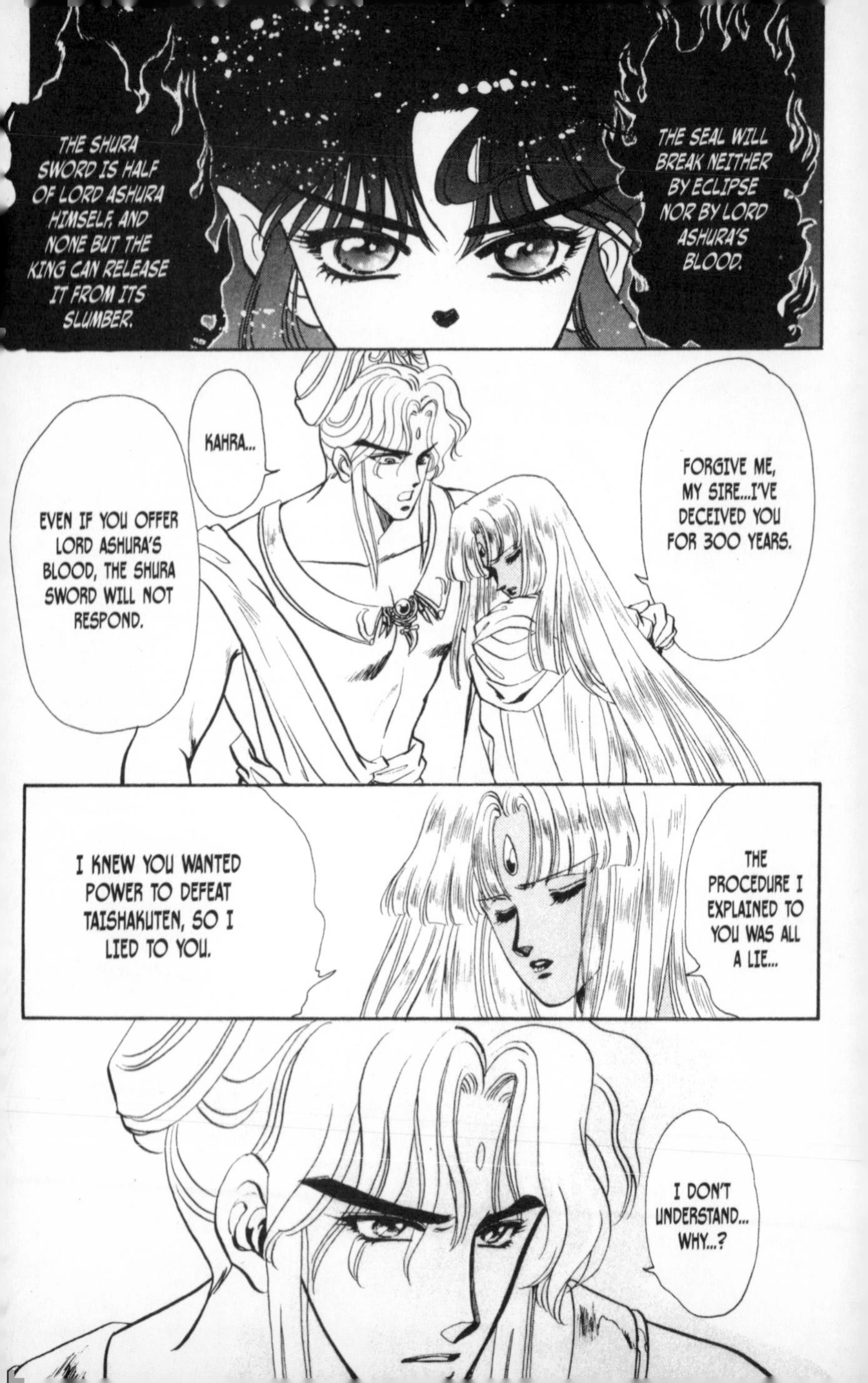

THE SEAL WILL BREAK NEITHER BY ECLIPSE NOR BY LORD ASHURA'S BLOOD.
THE SHURA SWORD IS HALF OF LORD ASHURA HIMSELF, AND NONE BUT THE KING CAN RELEASE IT FROM ITS SLUMBER.
FORGIVE ME, MY SIRE...I'VE DECEIVED YOU FOR 300 YEARS.
KAHRA...
EVEN IF YOU OFFER LORD ASHURA'S BLOOD, THE SHURA SWORD WILL NOT RESPOND.
THE PROCEDURE I EXPLAINED TO YOU WAS ALL A LIE...
I KNEW YOU WANTED POWER TO DEFEAT TAISHAKUTEN, SO I LIED TO YOU.
I DON'T UNDERSTAND... WHY...?

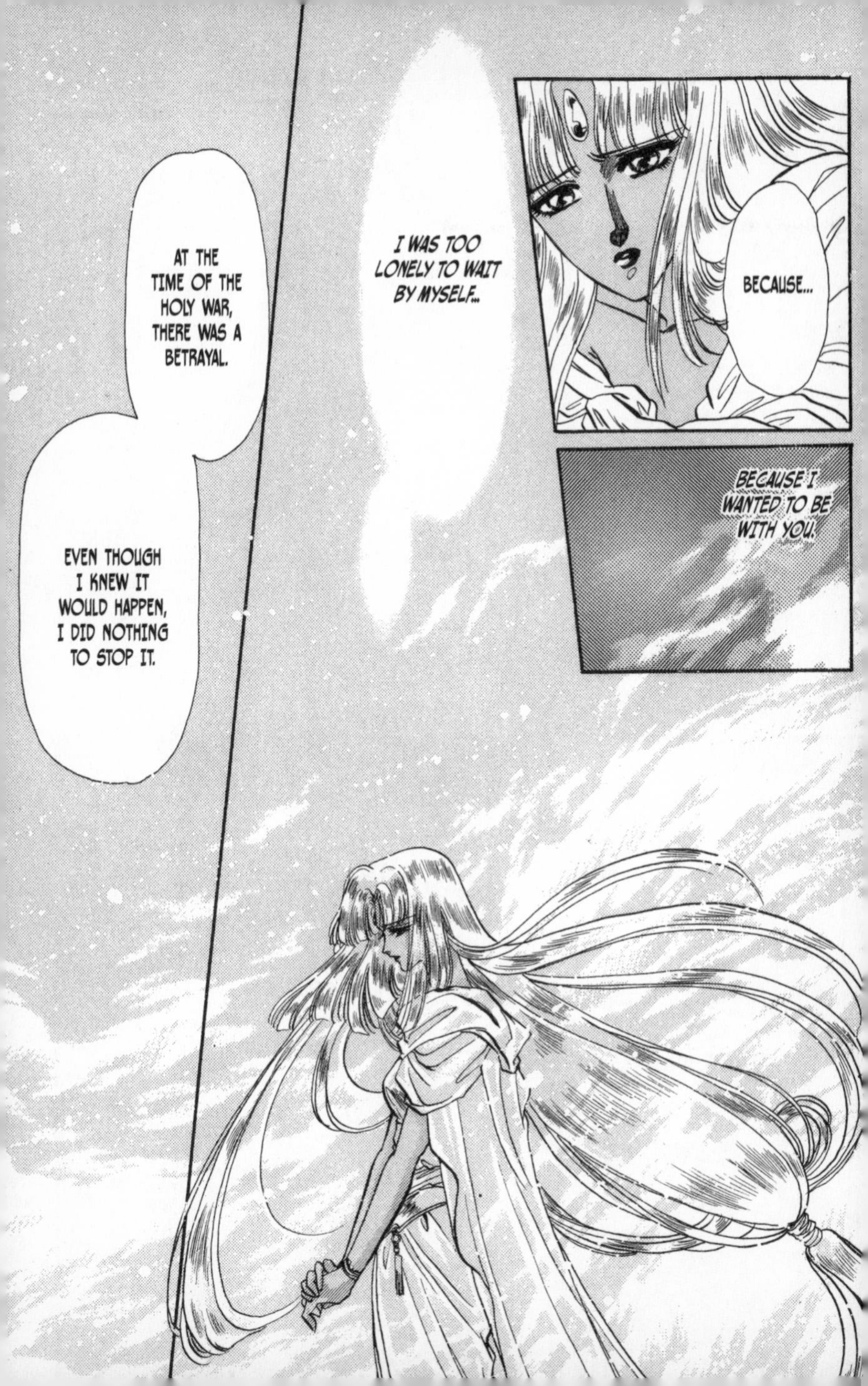
BECAUSE...
BECAUSE I WANTED TO BE WITH YOU.
I WAS TOO LONELY TO WAIT BY MYSELF...
AT THE TIME OF THE HOLY WAR, THERE WAS A BETRAYAL.
EVEN THOUGH I KNEW IT WOULD HAPPEN, I DID NOTHING TO STOP IT.

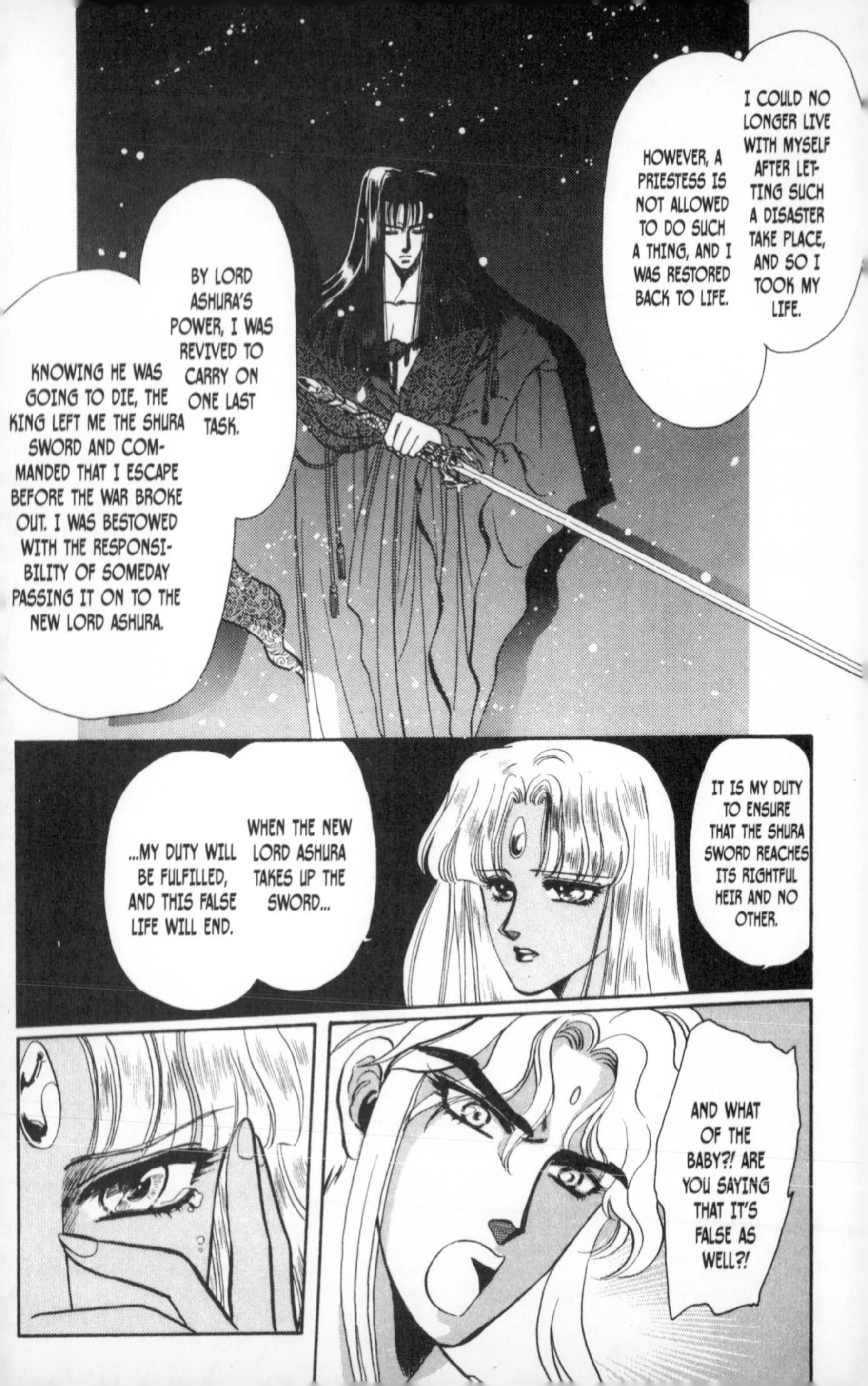
I COULD NO LONGER LIVE WITH MYSELF AFTER LETTING SUCH A DISASTER TAKE PLACE, AND SO I TOOK MY LIFE.
HOWEVER, A PRIESTESS IS NOT ALLOWED TO DO SUCH A THING, AND I WAS RESTORED BACK TO LIFE.
BY LORD ASHURA'S POWER, I WAS REVIVED TO CARRY ON ONE LAST TASK.
KNOWING HE WAS GOING TO DIE, THE KING LEFT ME THE SHURA SWORD AND COMMANDED THAT I ESCAPE BEFORE THE WAR BROKE OUT. I WAS BESTOWED WITH THE RESPONSIBILITY OF SOMEDAY PASSING IT ON TO THE NEW LORD ASHURA.
IT IS MY DUTY TO ENSURE THAT THE SHURA SWORD REACHES ITS RIGHTFUL HEIR AND NO OTHER.
WHEN THE NEW LORD ASHURA TAKES UP THE SWORD...
...MY DUTY WILL BE FULFILLED, AND THIS FALSE LIFE WILL END.
AND WHAT OF THE BABY?! ARE YOU SAYING THAT IT'S FALSE AS WELL?!

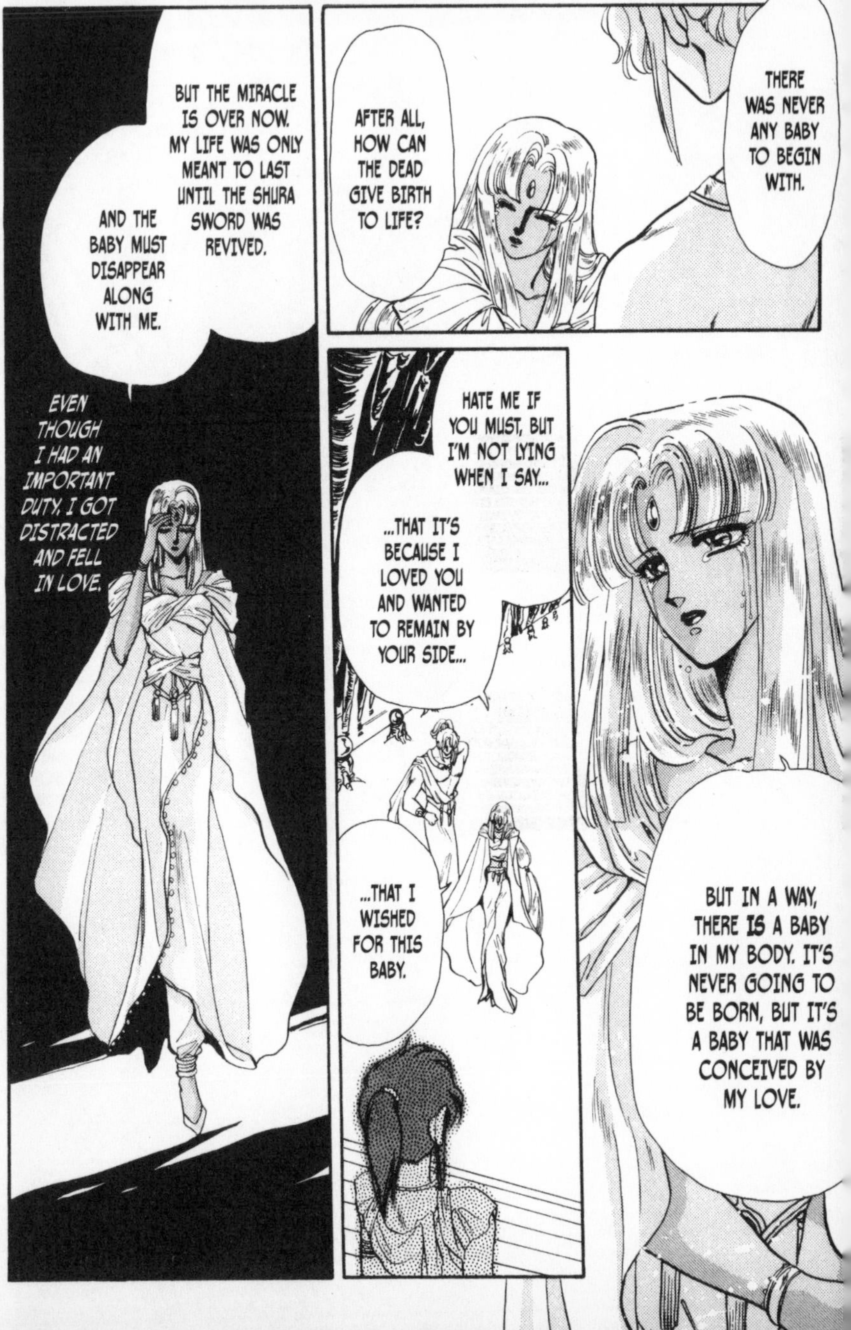
THERE WAS NEVER ANY BABY TO BEGIN WITH.
AFTER ALL, HOW CAN THE DEAD GIVE BIRTH TO LIFE?
HATE ME IF YOU MUST, BUT I'M NOT LYING WHEN I SAY...
...THAT IT'S BECAUSE I LOVED YOU AND WANTED TO REMAIN BY YOUR SIDE...
...THAT I WISHED FOR THIS BABY.
BUT IN A WAY, THERE IS A BABY IN MY BODY. IT'S NEVER GOING TO BE BORN, BUT IT'S A BABY THAT WAS CONCEIVED BY MY LOVE.
BUT THE MIRACLE IS OVER NOW. MY LIFE WAS ONLY MEANT TO LAST UNTIL THE SHURA SWORD WAS REVIVED.
AND THE BABY MUST DISAPPEAR ALONG WITH ME.
EVEN THOUGH I HAD AN IMPORTANT DUTY, I GOT DISTRACTED AND FELL IN LOVE.

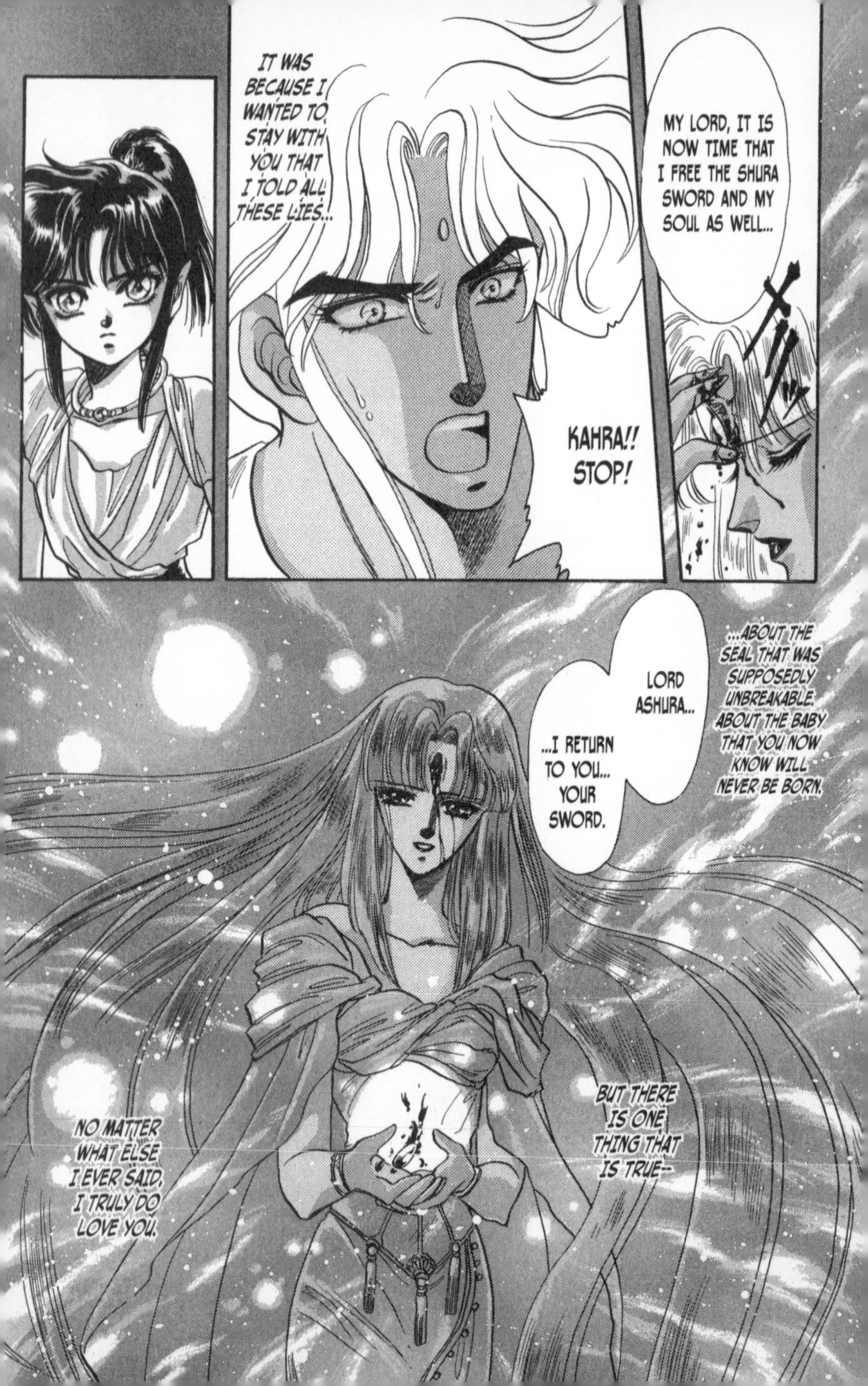

MY LORD, IT IS NOW TIME THAT I FREE THE SHURA SWORD AND MY SOUL AS WELL...
KAHRA!! STOP!
IT WAS BECAUSE I WANTED TO STAY WITH YOU THAT I TOLD ALL THESE LIES...
...ABOUT THE SEAL THAT WAS SUPPOSEDLY UNBREAKABLE. ABOUT THE BABY THAT YOU NOW KNOW WILL NEVER BE BORN.
LORD ASHURA...
...I RETURN TO YOU... YOUR SWORD.
BUT THERE IS ONE THING THAT IS TRUE-
NO MATTER WHAT ELSE I EVER SAID, I TRULY DO LOVE YOU.

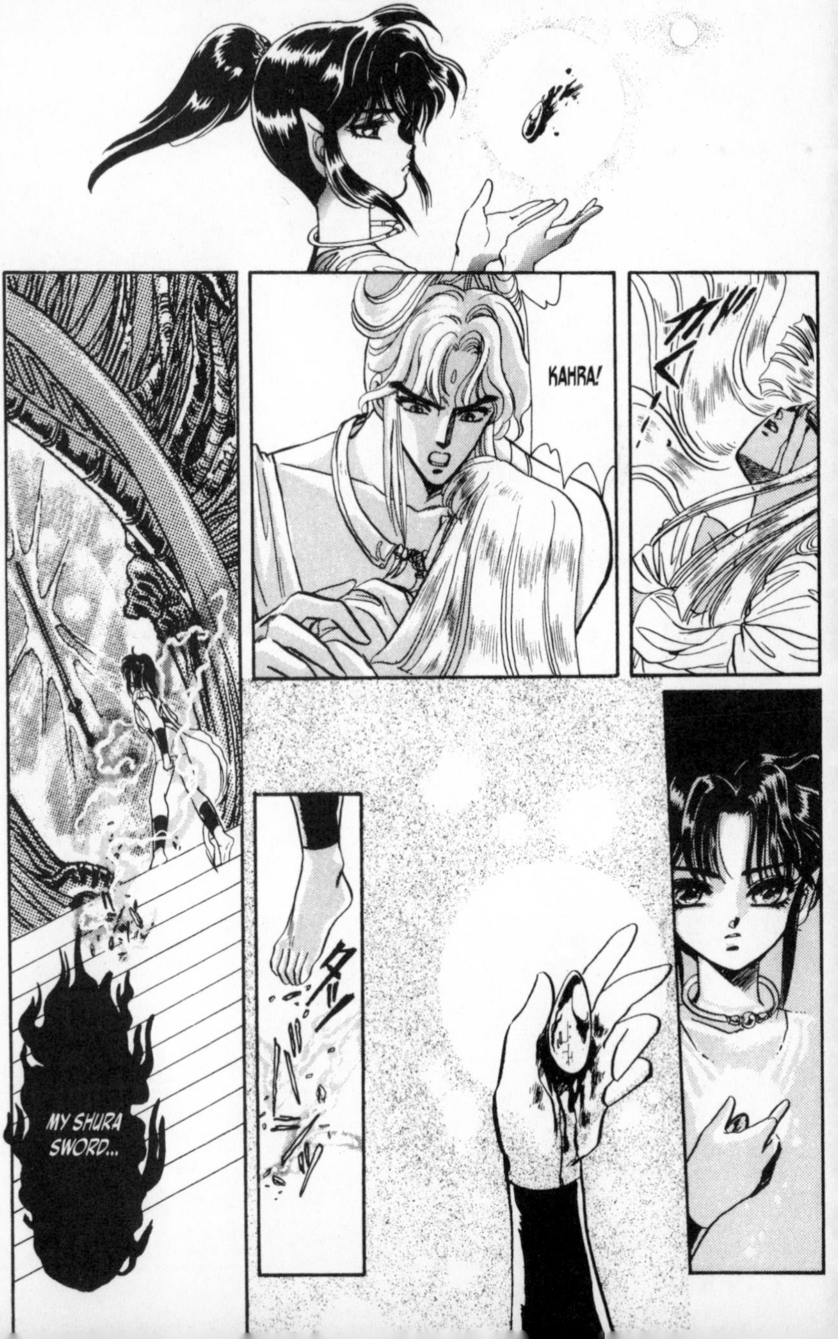
KAHRA!
MY SHURA SWORD...

I'VE KEPT YOU WAITING LONG ENOUGH.

IT'S TIME TO WAKE UP...

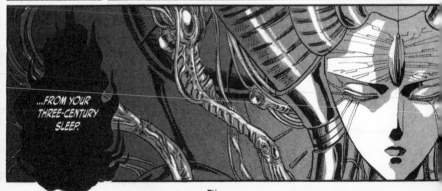

...FROM YOUR THREE-CENTURY SLEEP.

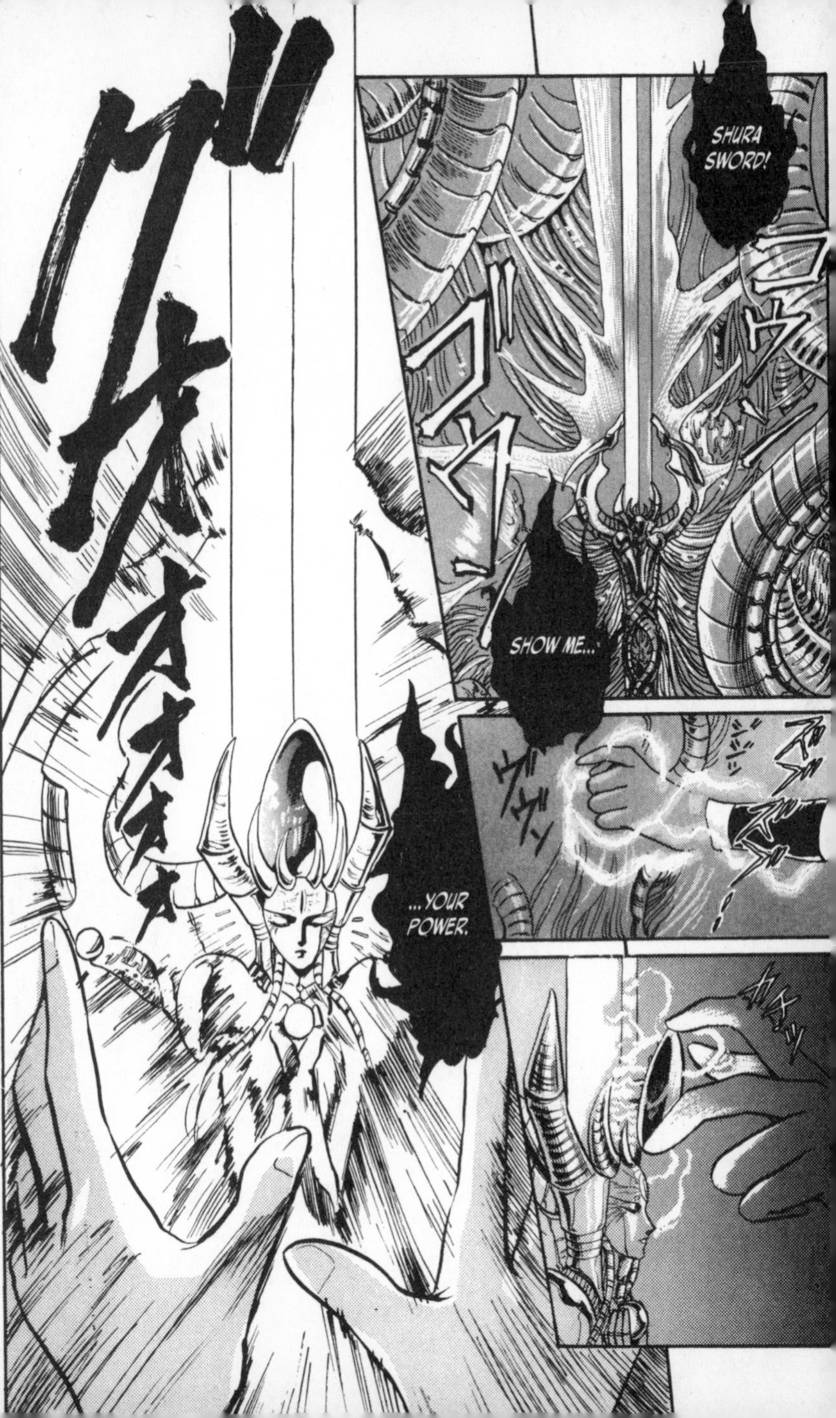
SHURA SWORD!
SHOW ME...
...YOUR POWER.

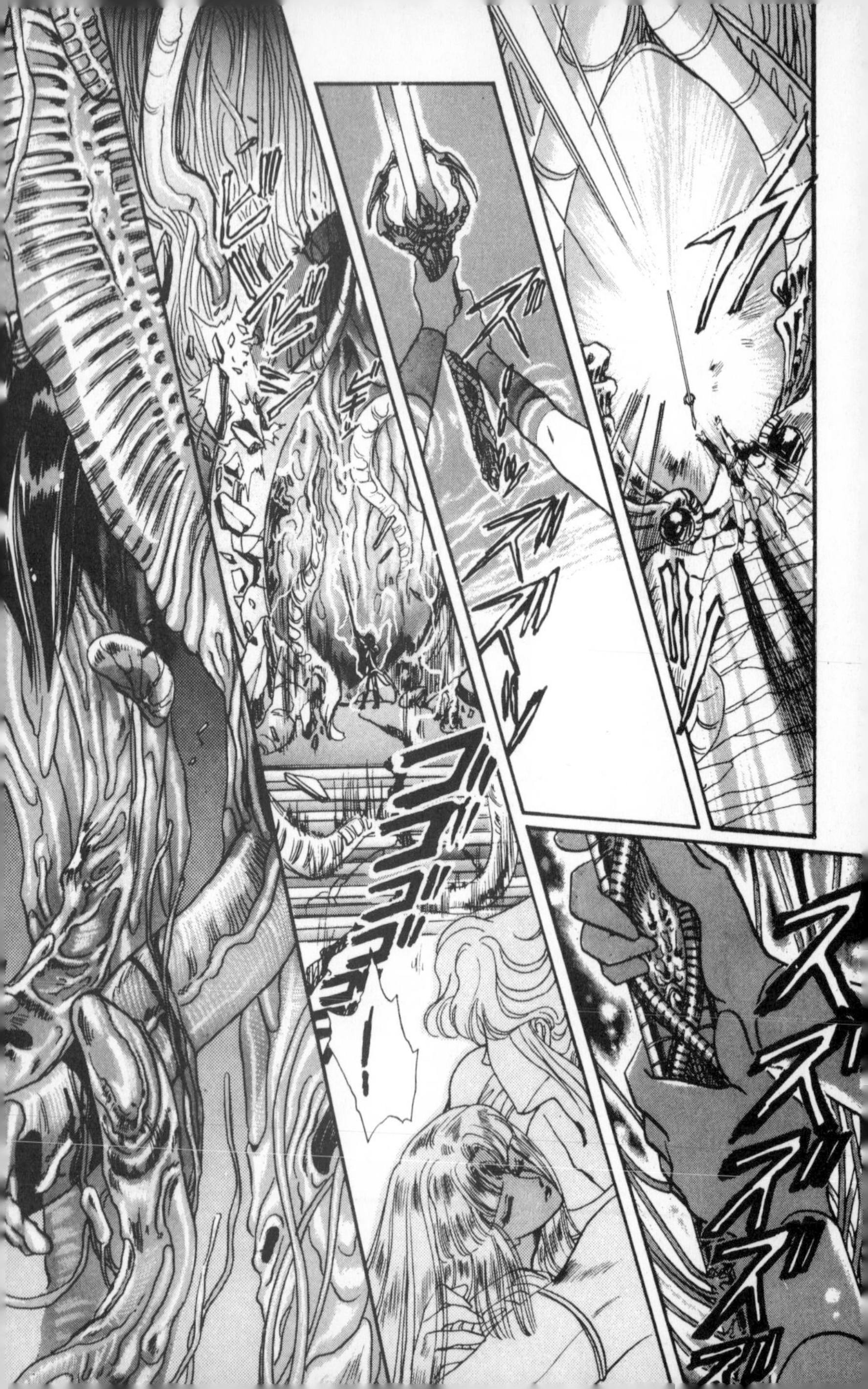
ゴゴゴゴ

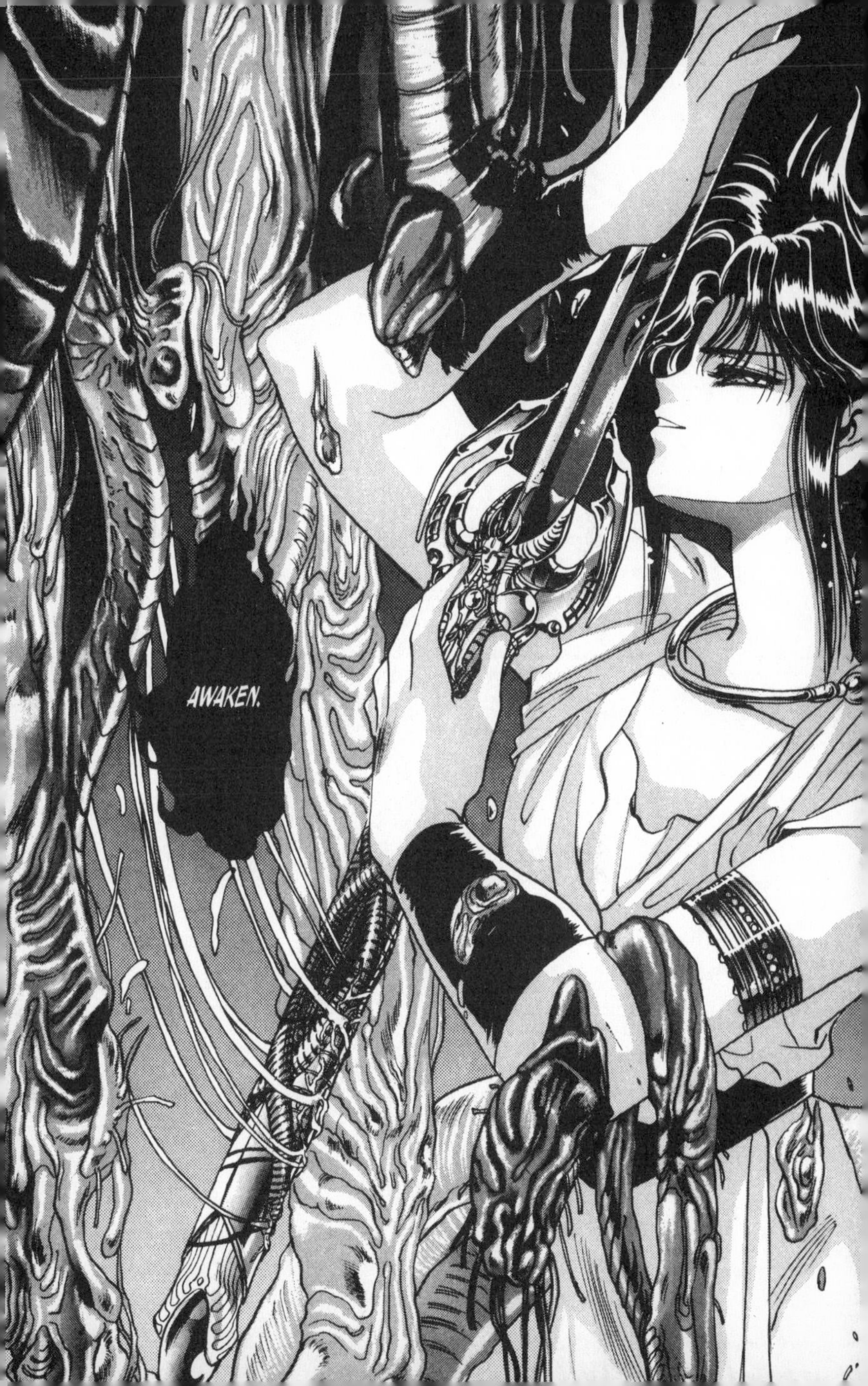
AWAKEN.

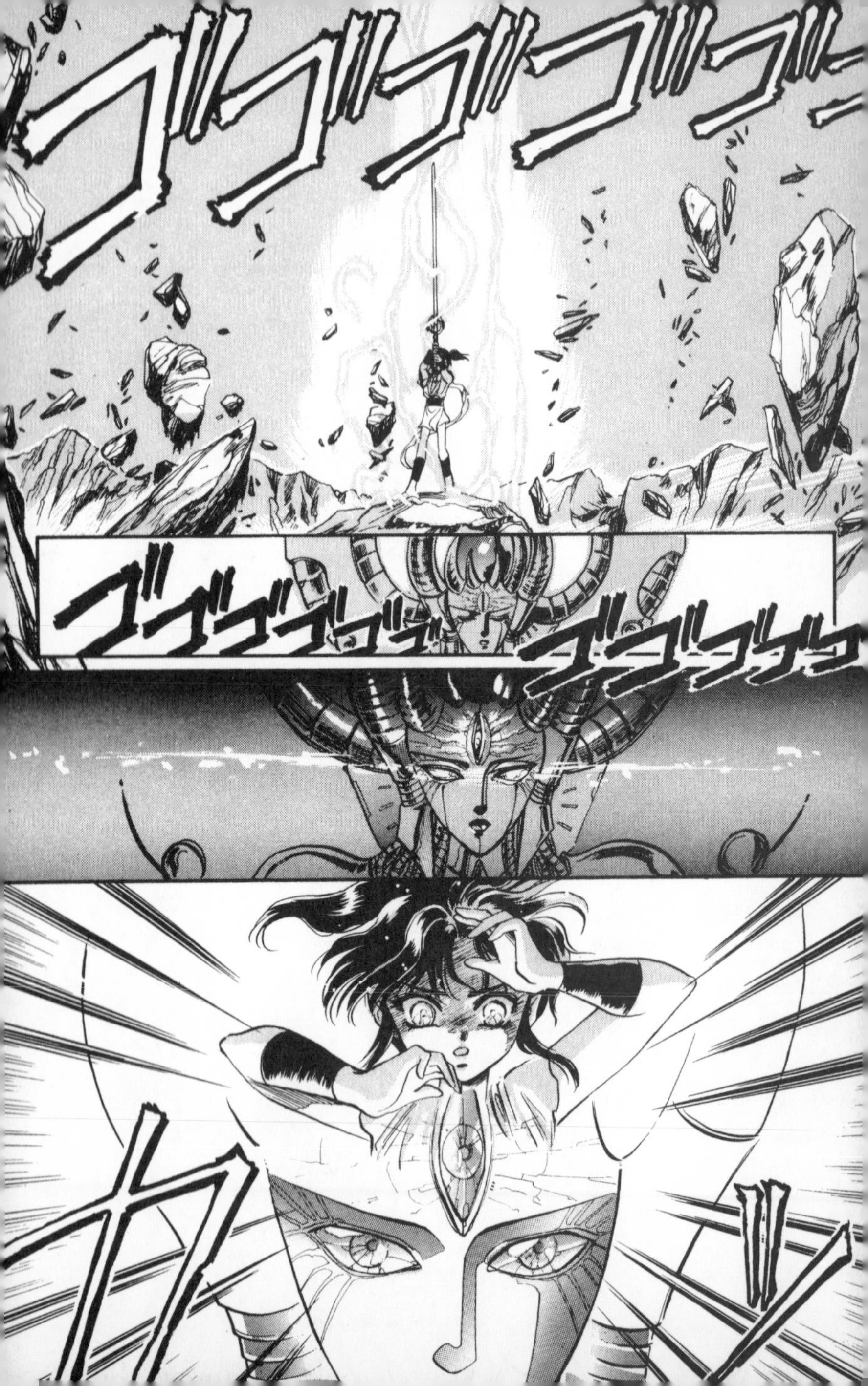

ゴゴゴゴー
ゴゴゴゴゴゴ
ゴゴゴゴ
カッ

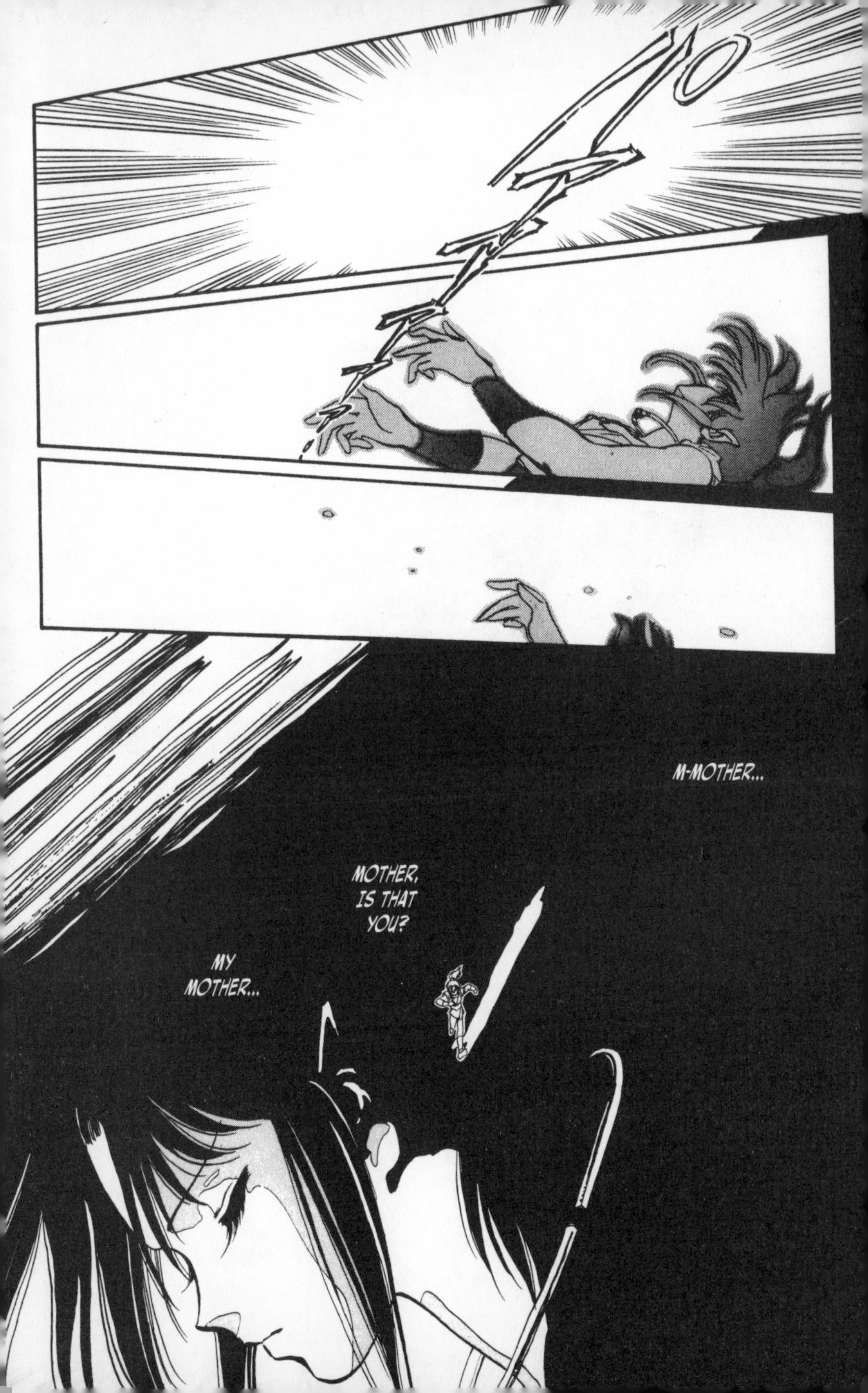
M-MOTHER...
MOTHER, IS THAT YOU?
MY MOTHER...

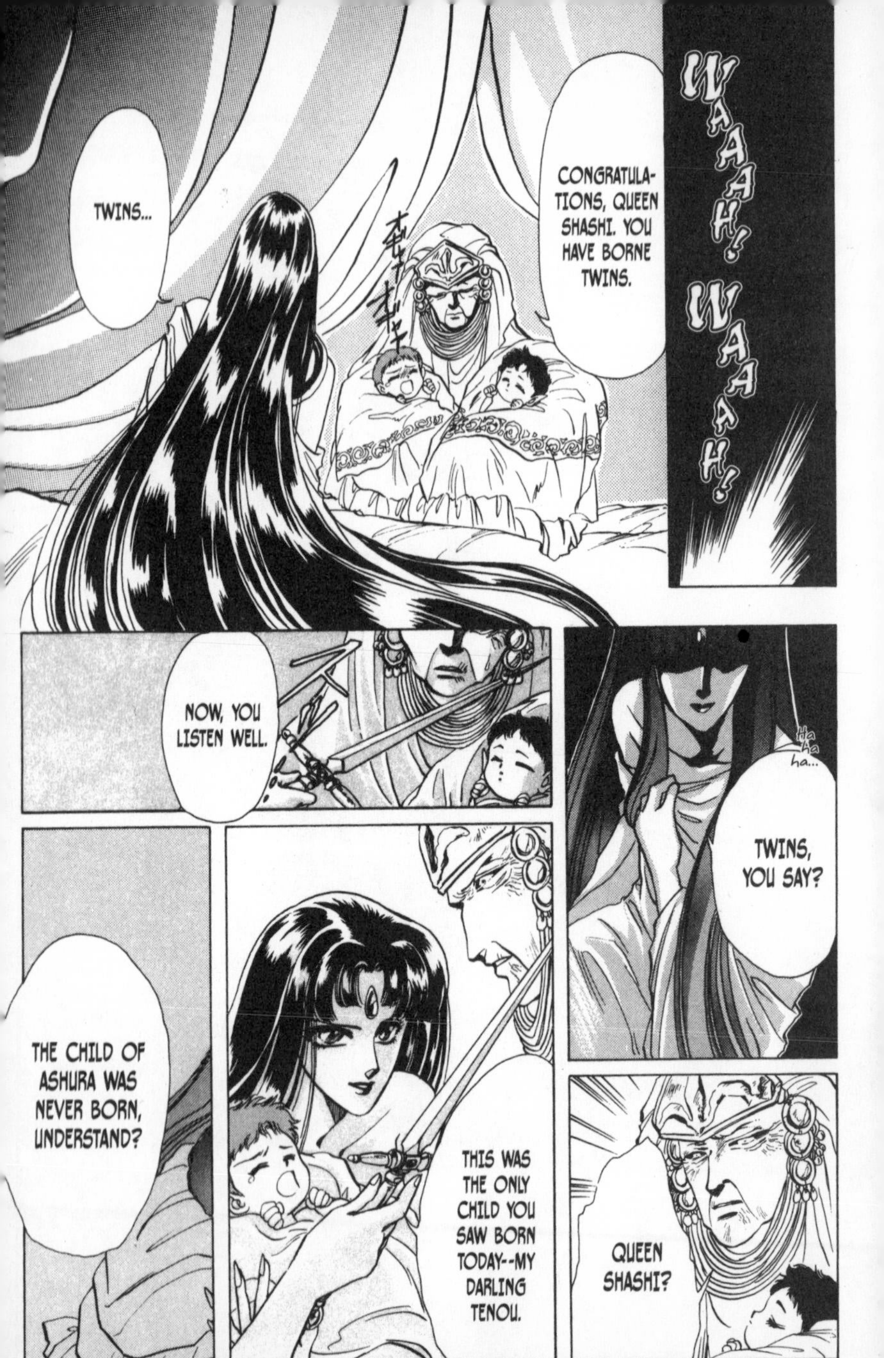
WAAAH! WAAAH!
CONGRATULATIONS, QUEEN SHASHI. YOU HAVE BORNE TWINS.
TWINS...
Ha ha ha...
TWINS, YOU SAY?
NOW, YOU LISTEN WELL.
QUEEN SHASHI?
THIS WAS THE ONLY CHILD YOU SAW BORN TODAY--MY DARLING TENOU.
THE CHILD OF ASHURA WAS NEVER BORN, UNDERSTAND?

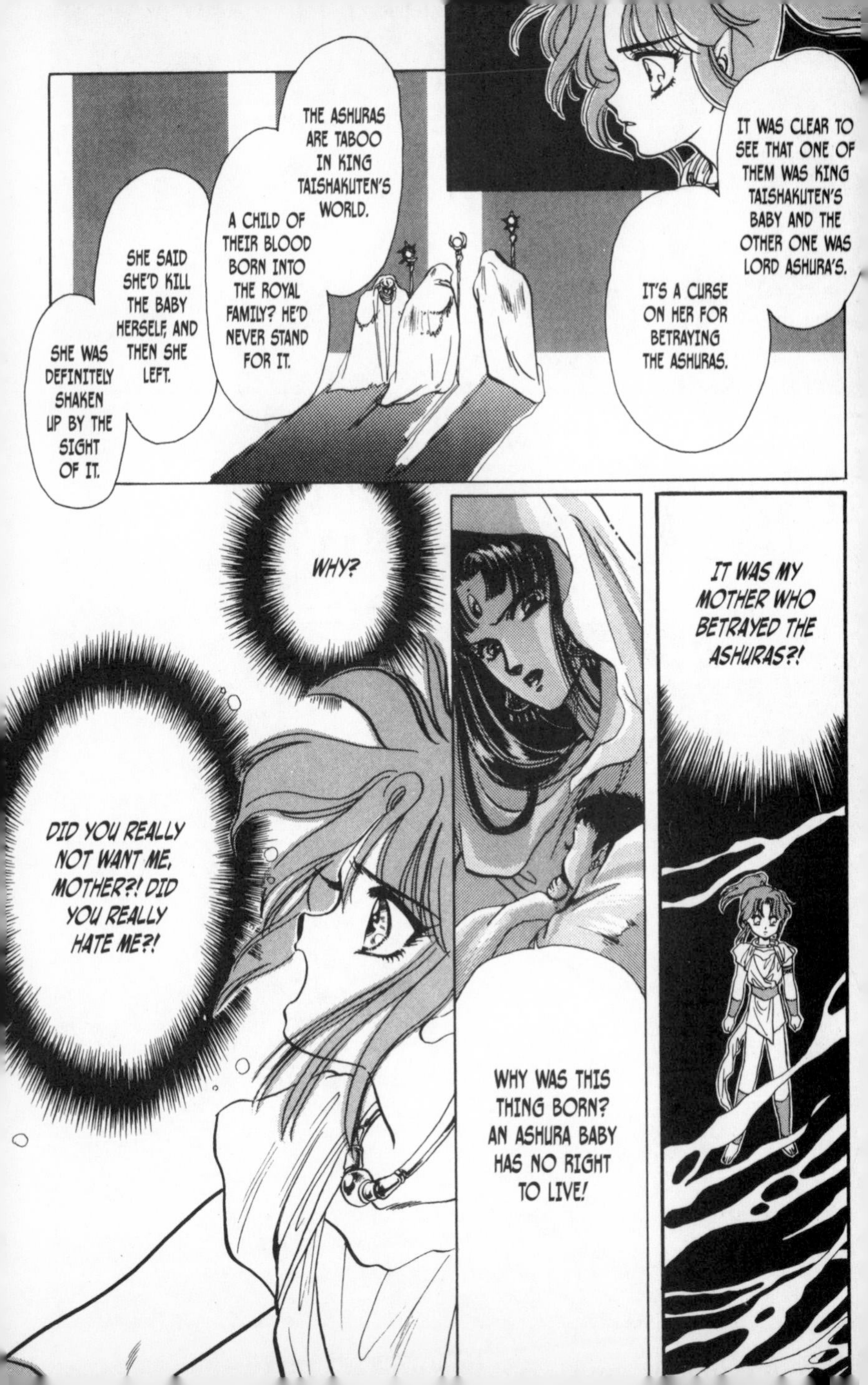
IT WAS CLEAR TO SEE THAT ONE OF THEM WAS KING TAISHAKUTEN'S BABY AND THE OTHER ONE WAS LORD ASHURA'S.
IT'S A CURSE ON HER FOR BETRAYING THE ASHURAS.
THE ASHURAS ARE TABOO IN KING TAISHAKUTEN'S WORLD.
A CHILD OF THEIR BLOOD BORN INTO THE ROYAL FAMILY? HE'D NEVER STAND FOR IT.
SHE SAID SHE'D KILL THE BABY HERSELF, AND THEN SHE LEFT.
SHE WAS DEFINITELY SHAKEN UP BY THE SIGHT OF IT.
IT WAS MY MOTHER WHO BETRAYED THE ASHURAS?!
WHY WAS THIS THING BORN? AN ASHURA BABY HAS NO RIGHT TO LIVE!
WHY?
DID YOU REALLY NOT WANT ME, MOTHER?! DID YOU REALLY HATE ME?!

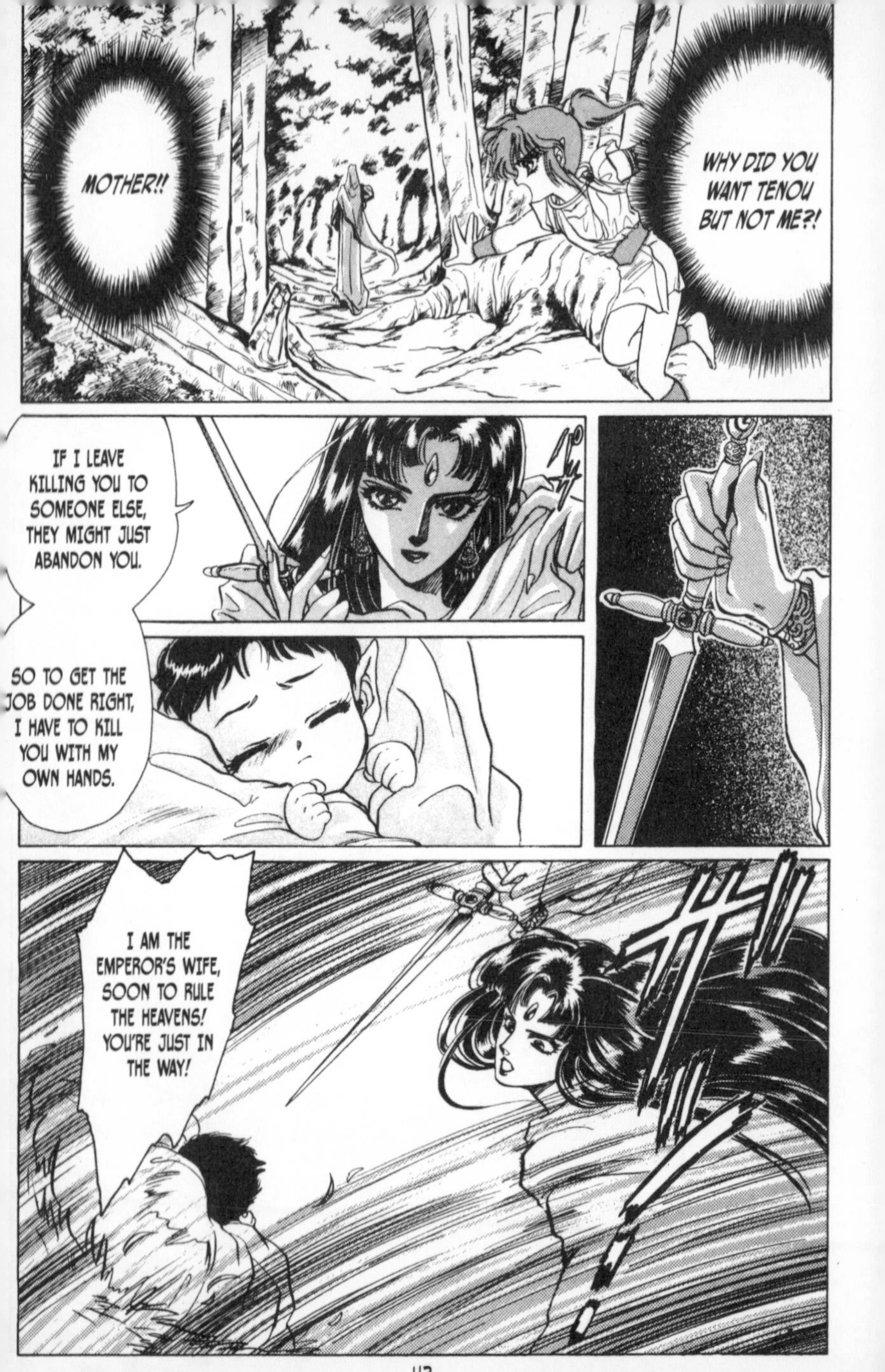
WHY DID YOU WANT TENOU BUT NOT ME?!
MOTHER!!
IF I LEAVE KILLING YOU TO SOMEONE ELSE, THEY MIGHT JUST ABANDON YOU.
SO TO GET THE JOB DONE RIGHT, I HAVE TO KILL YOU WITH MY OWN HANDS.
I AM THE EMPEROR'S WIFE, SOON TO RULE THE HEAVENS! YOU'RE JUST IN THE WAY!

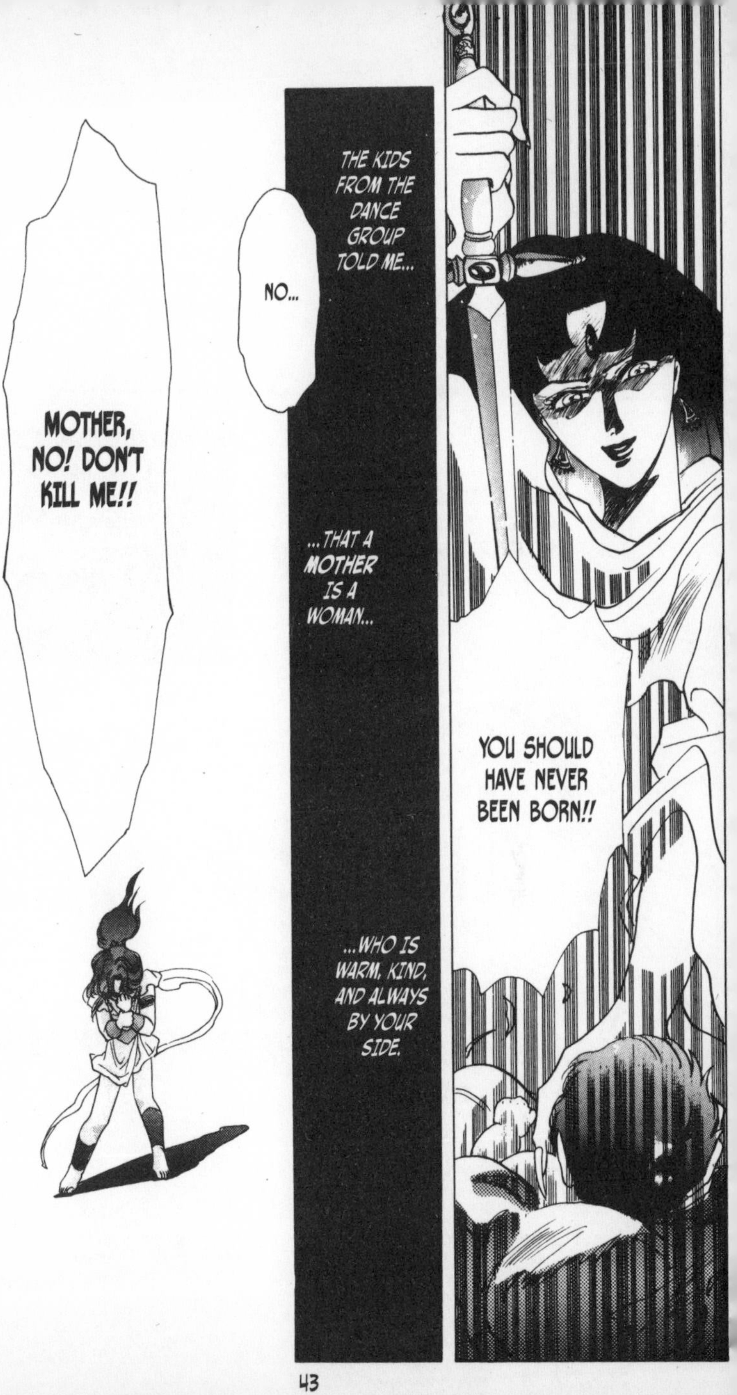
YOU SHOULD HAVE NEVER BEEN BORN!!
THE KIDS FROM THE DANCE GROUP TOLD ME...
...THAT A MOTHER IS A WOMAN...
...WHO IS WARM, KIND, AND ALWAYS BY YOUR SIDE.
NO...
MOTHER, NO! DON'T KILL ME!!

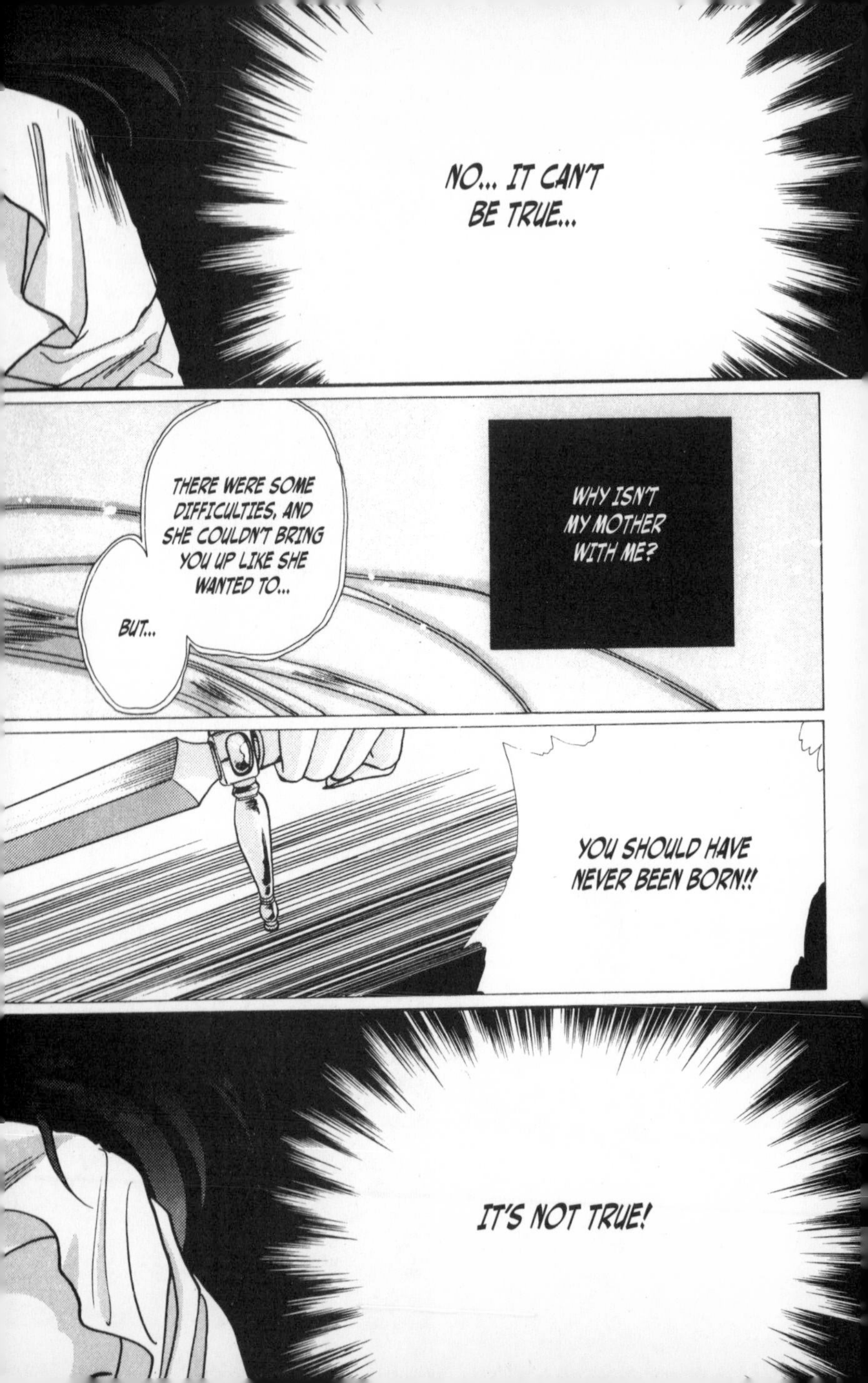
NO... IT CAN'T BE TRUE...
WHY ISN'T MY MOTHER WITH ME?
THERE WERE SOME DIFFICULTIES, AND SHE COULDN'T BRING YOU UP LIKE SHE WANTED TO...
BUT...
YOU SHOULD HAVE NEVER BEEN BORN!!
IT'S NOT TRUE!

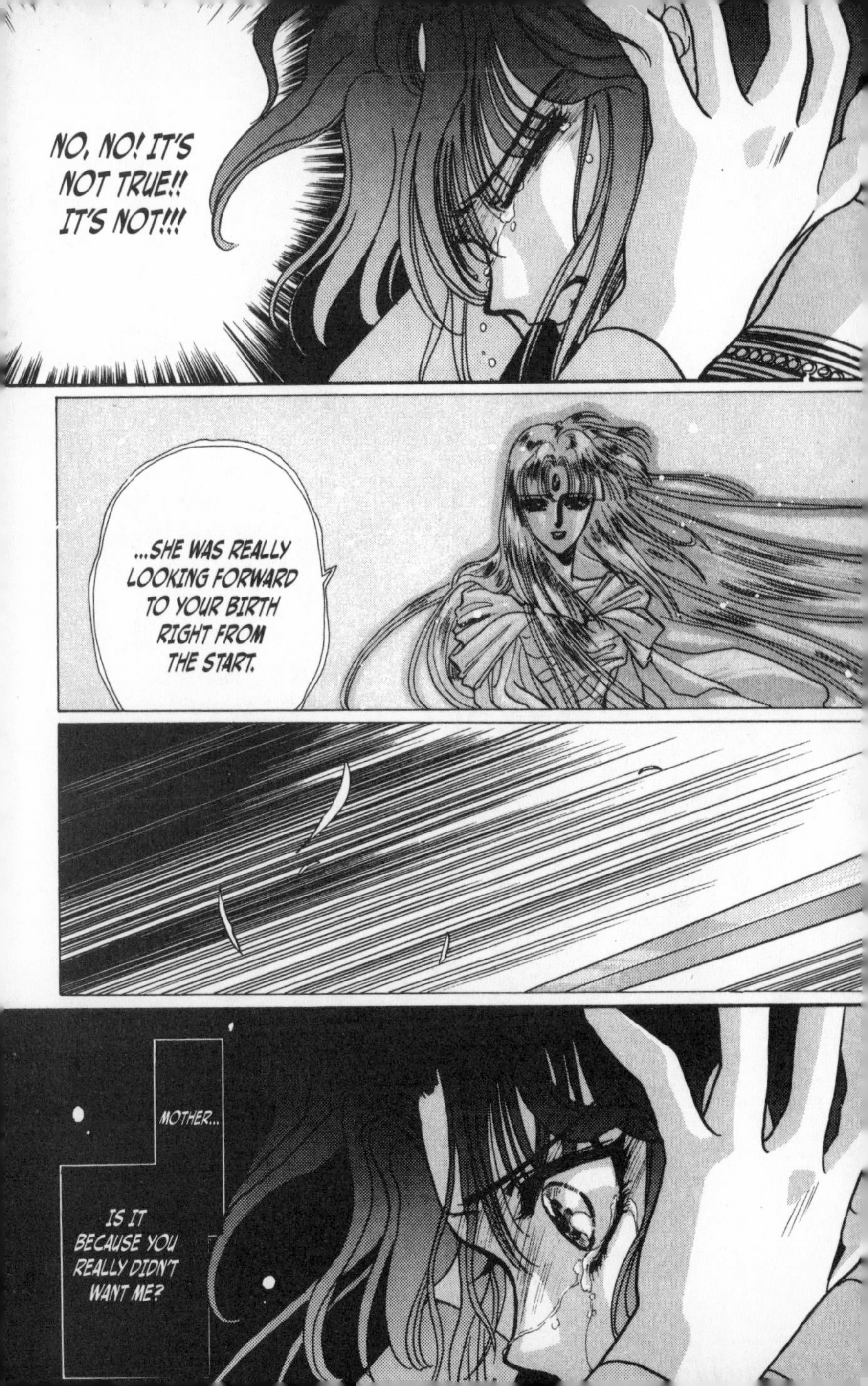
NO, NO! IT'S NOT TRUE!! IT'S NOT!!!
...SHE WAS REALLY LOOKING FORWARD TO YOUR BIRTH RIGHT FROM THE START.
MOTHER...
IS IT BECAUSE YOU REALLY DIDN'T WANT ME?

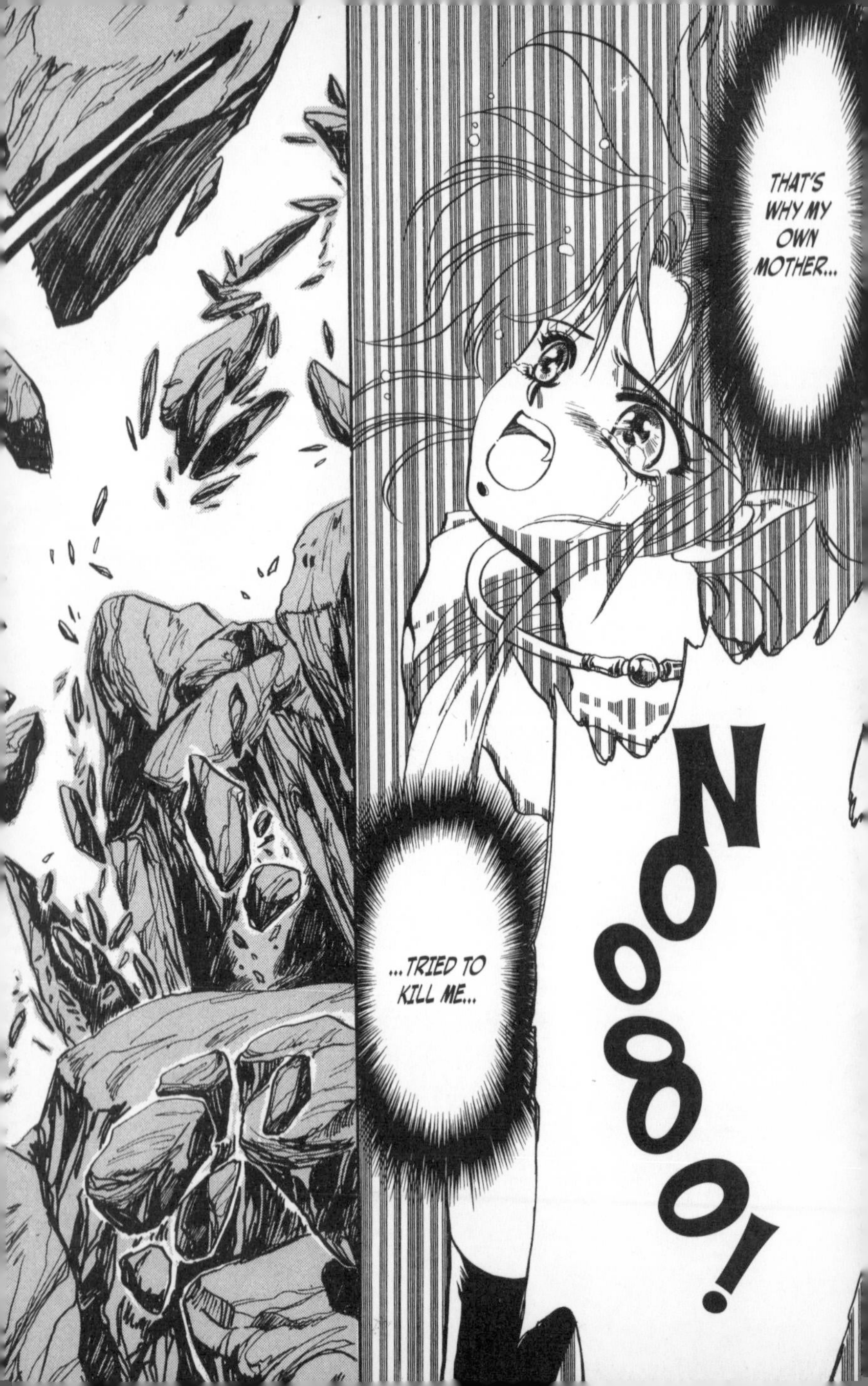
THAT'S WHY MY OWN MOTHER...
...TRIED TO KILL ME...
NOOOOO!

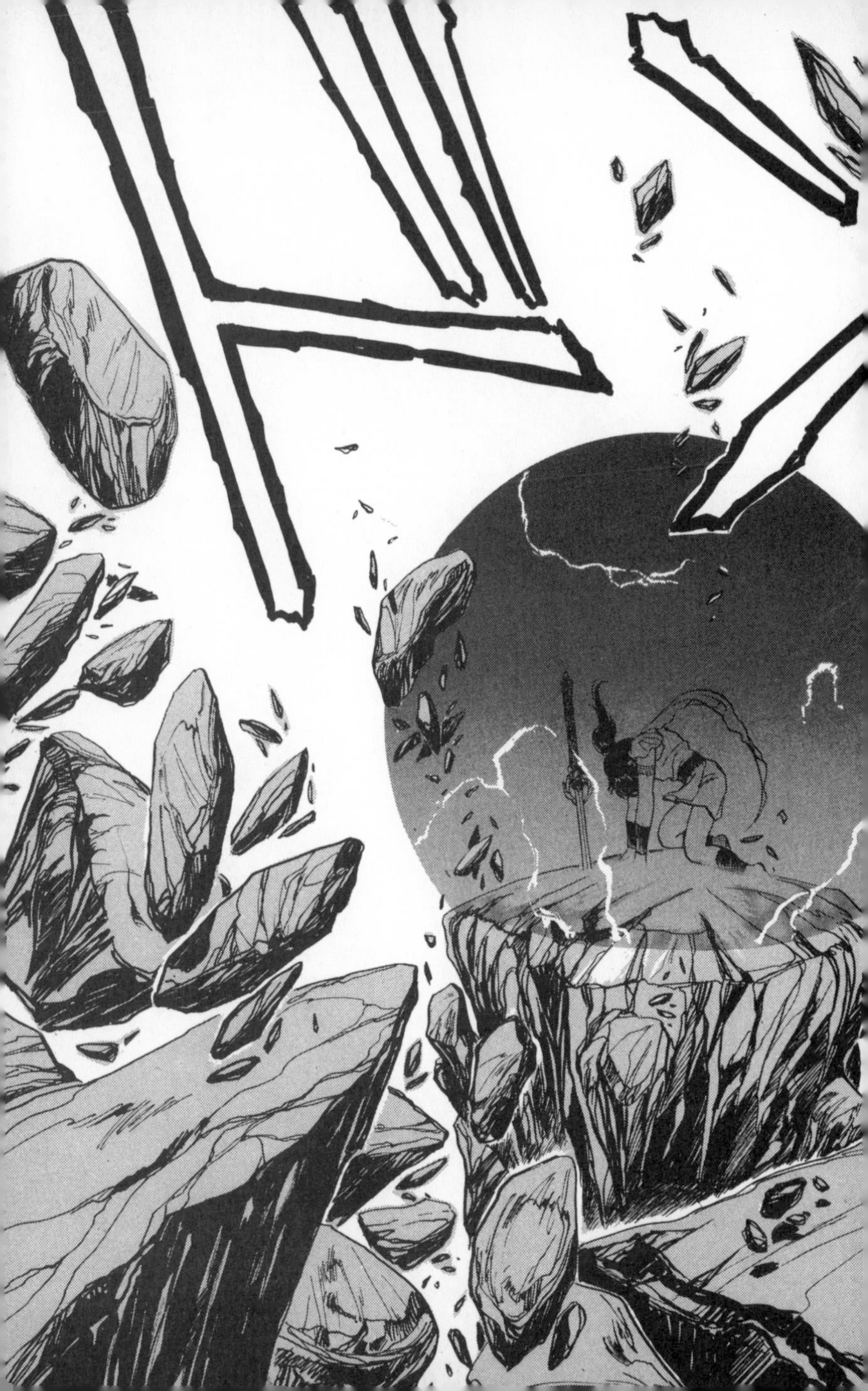

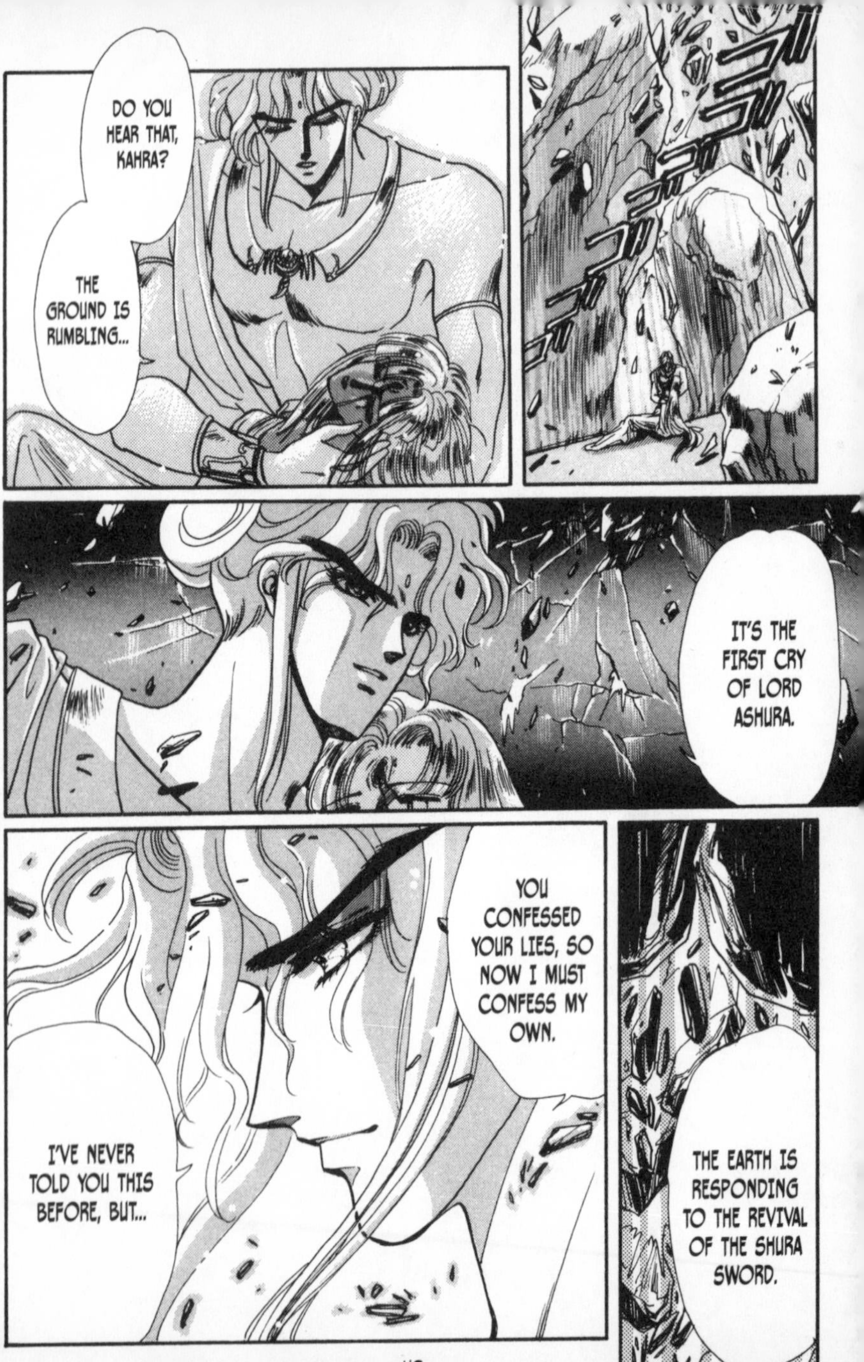
DO YOU HEAR THAT, KAHRA?
THE GROUND IS RUMBLING...
IT'S THE FIRST CRY OF LORD ASHURA.
THE EARTH IS RESPONDING TO THE REVIVAL OF THE SHURA SWORD.
YOU CONFESSED YOUR LIES, SO NOW I MUST CONFESS MY OWN.
I'VE NEVER TOLD YOU THIS BEFORE, BUT...

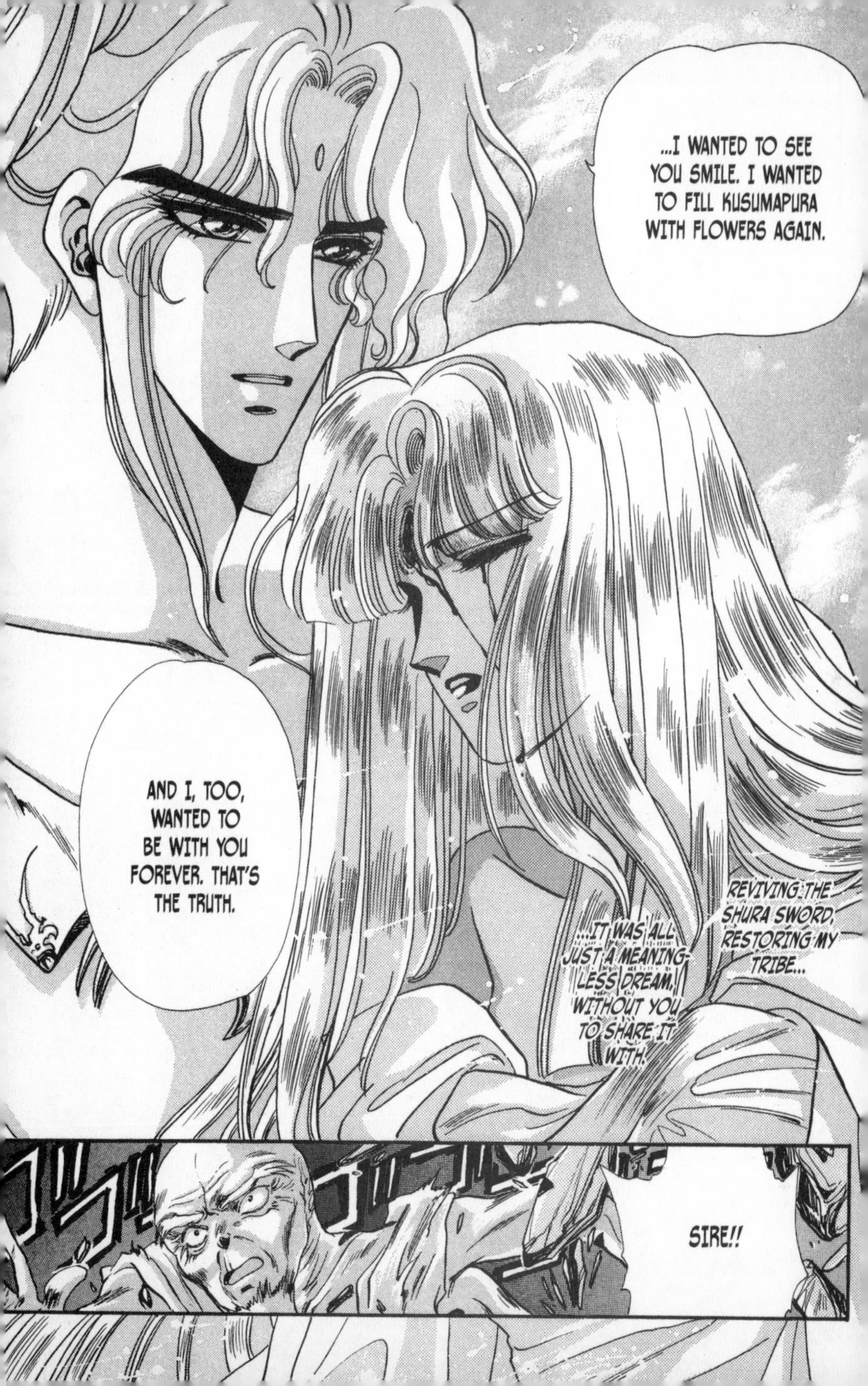

...I WANTED TO SEE YOU SMILE. I WANTED TO FILL KUSUMAPURA WITH FLOWERS AGAIN.
AND I, TOO, WANTED TO BE WITH YOU FOREVER. THAT'S THE TRUTH.
REVIVING THE SHURA SWORD, RESTORING MY TRIBE...
...IT WAS ALL JUST A MEANINGLESS DREAM, WITHOUT YOU TO SHARE IT WITH.
SIRE!!

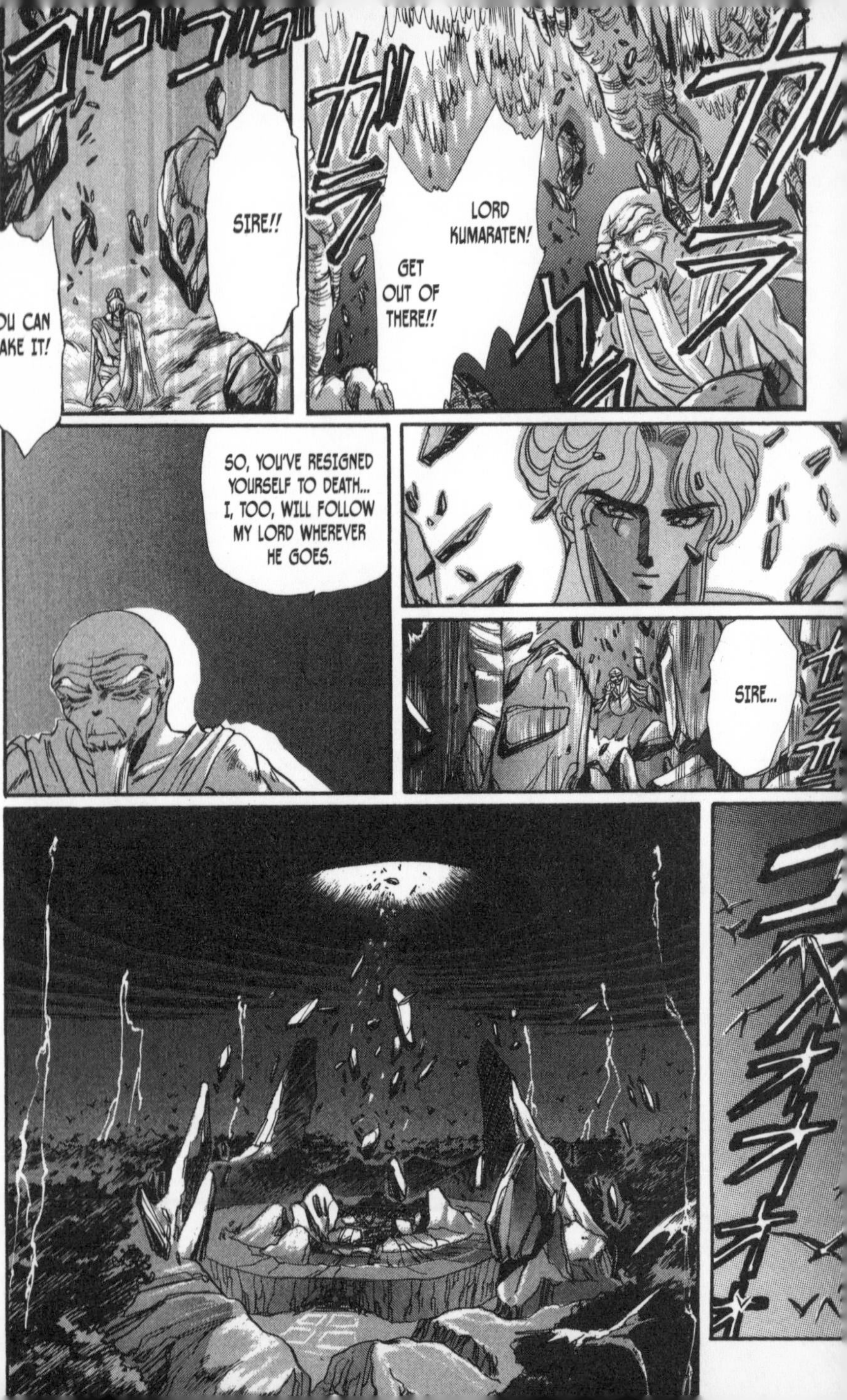
LORD KUMARATEN!
GET OUT OF THERE!!
SIRE!!
YOU CAN MAKE IT!
SIRE...
SO, YOU'VE RESIGNED YOURSELF TO DEATH... I, TOO, WILL FOLLOW MY LORD WHEREVER HE GOES.

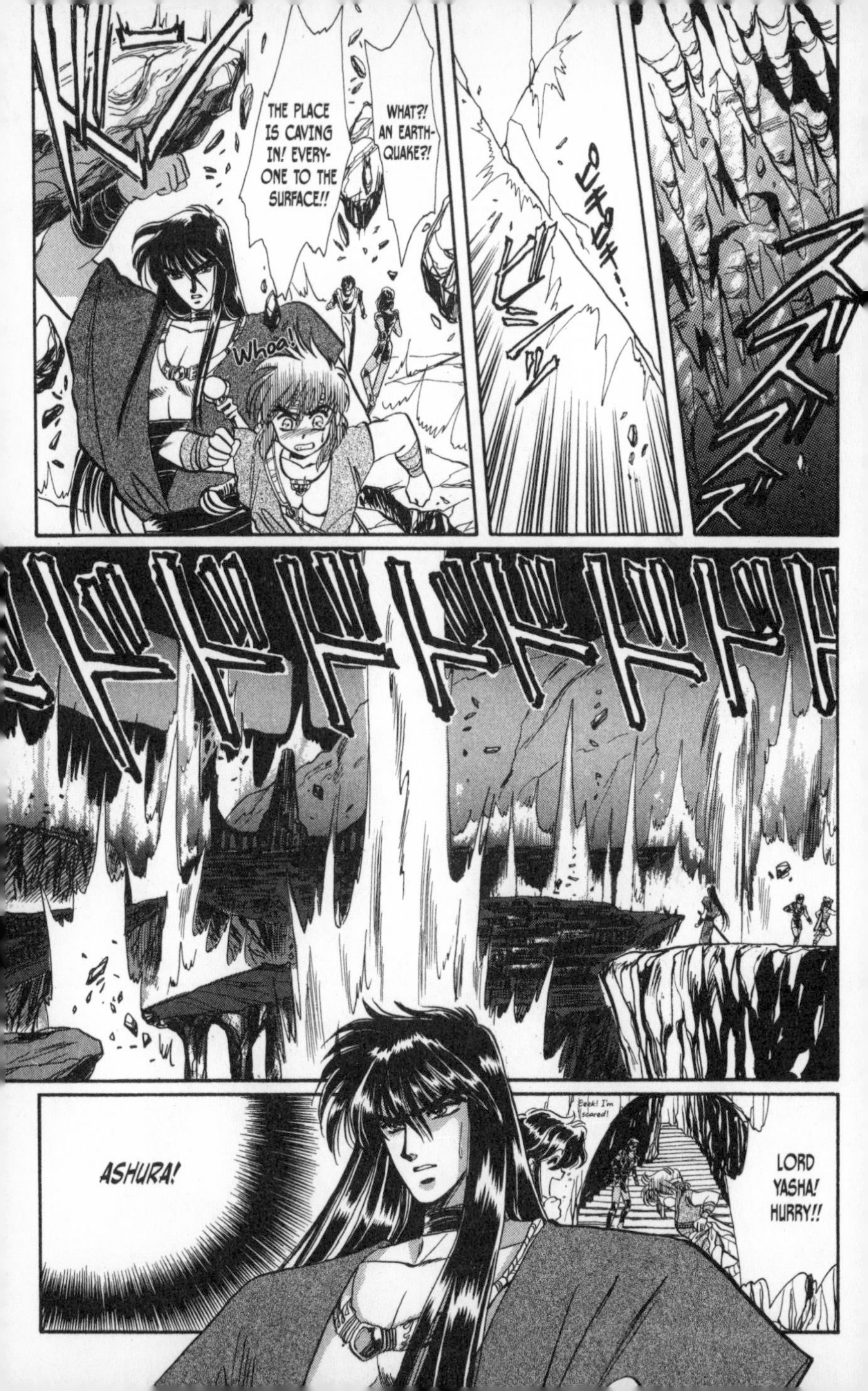
WHAT?! AN EARTH-QUAKE?!
THE PLACE IS CAVING IN! EVERY-ONE TO THE SURFACE!!
Whoa!
LORD YASHA! HURRY!!
Eeek! I'm scared!
ASHURA!

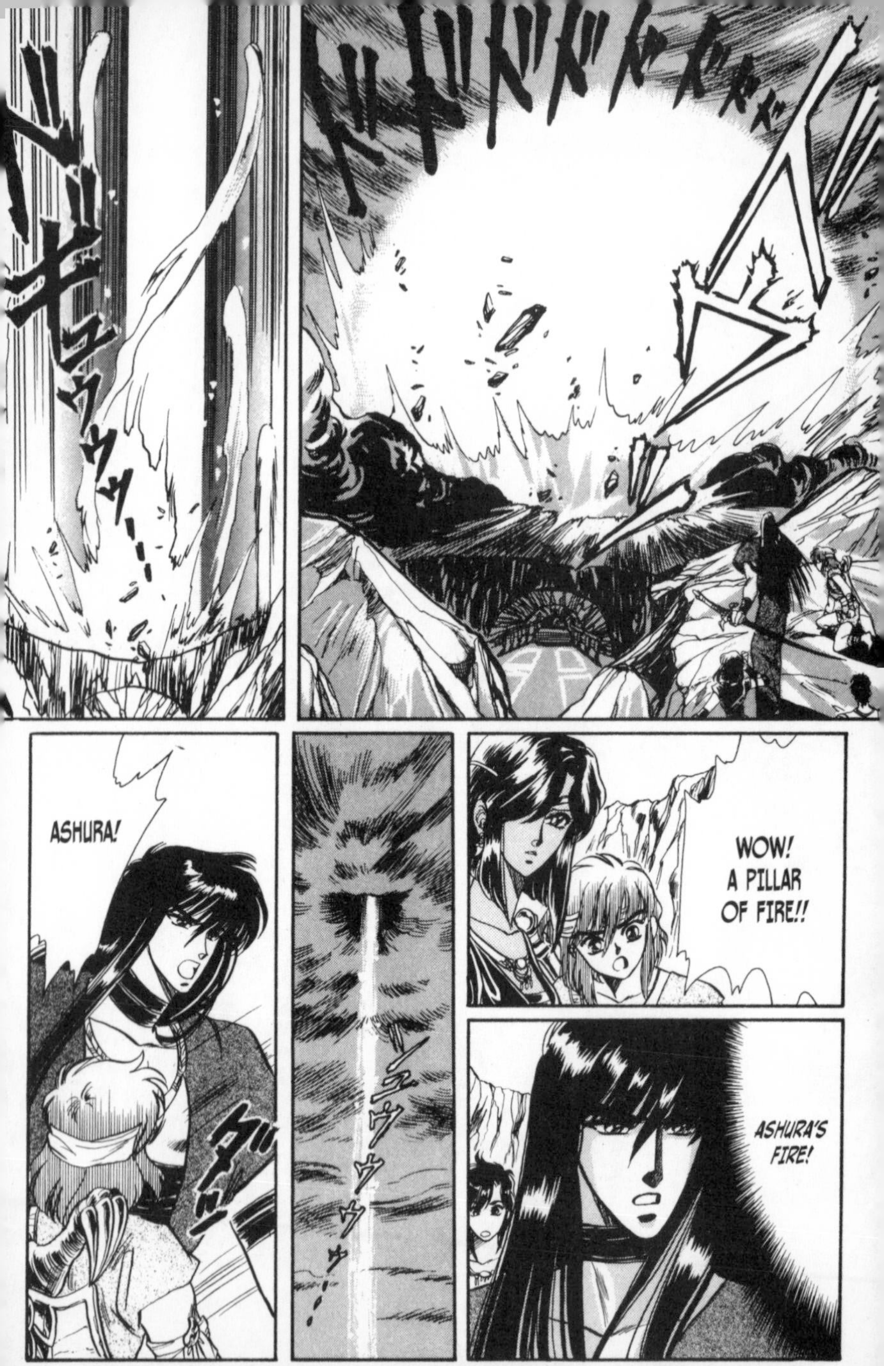
WOW! A PILLAR OF FIRE!!
ASHURA'S FIRE!
ASHURA!

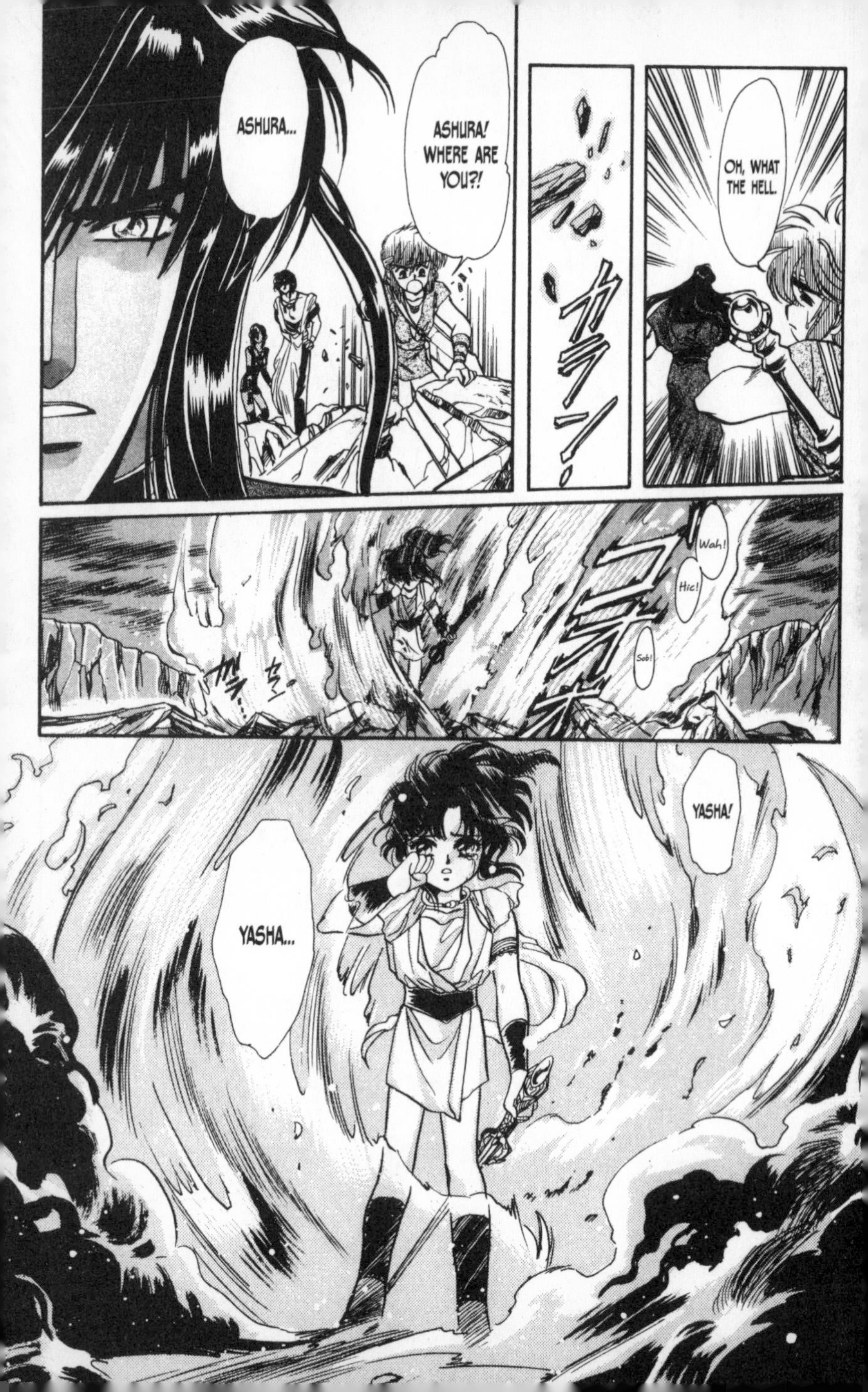
OH, WHAT THE HELL.
ASHURA! WHERE ARE YOU?!
ASHURA...
Wah!
Hic!
Sob!
YASHA!
YASHA...

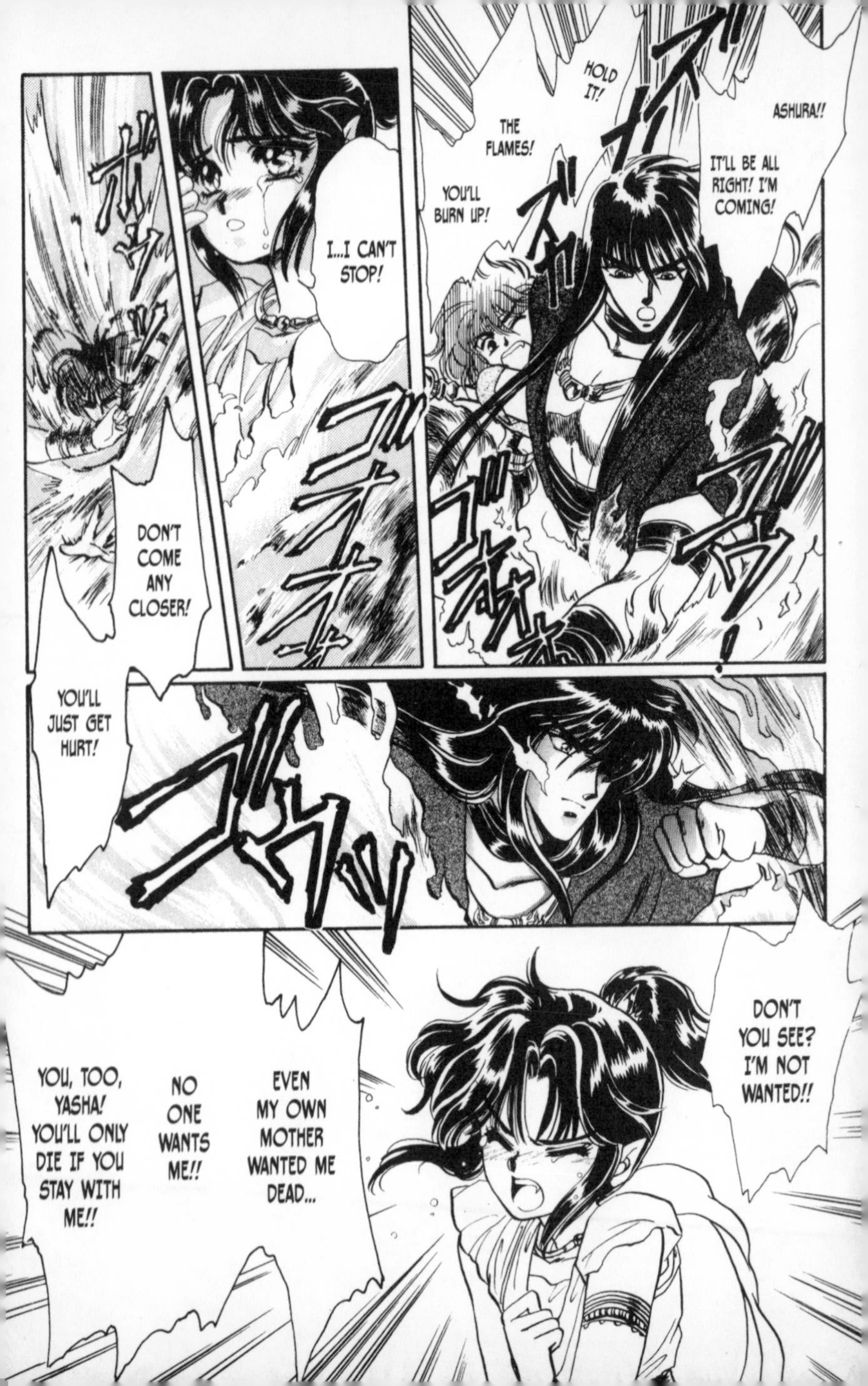
ASHURA!!
IT'LL BE ALL RIGHT! I'M COMING!
HOLD IT!
THE FLAMES!
YOU'LL BURN UP!
I...I CAN'T STOP!
DON'T COME ANY CLOSER!
YOU'LL JUST GET HURT!
DON'T YOU SEE? I'M NOT WANTED!!
EVEN MY OWN MOTHER WANTED ME DEAD...
NO ONE WANTS ME!!
YOU, TOO, YASHA! YOU'LL ONLY DIE IF YOU STAY WITH ME!!

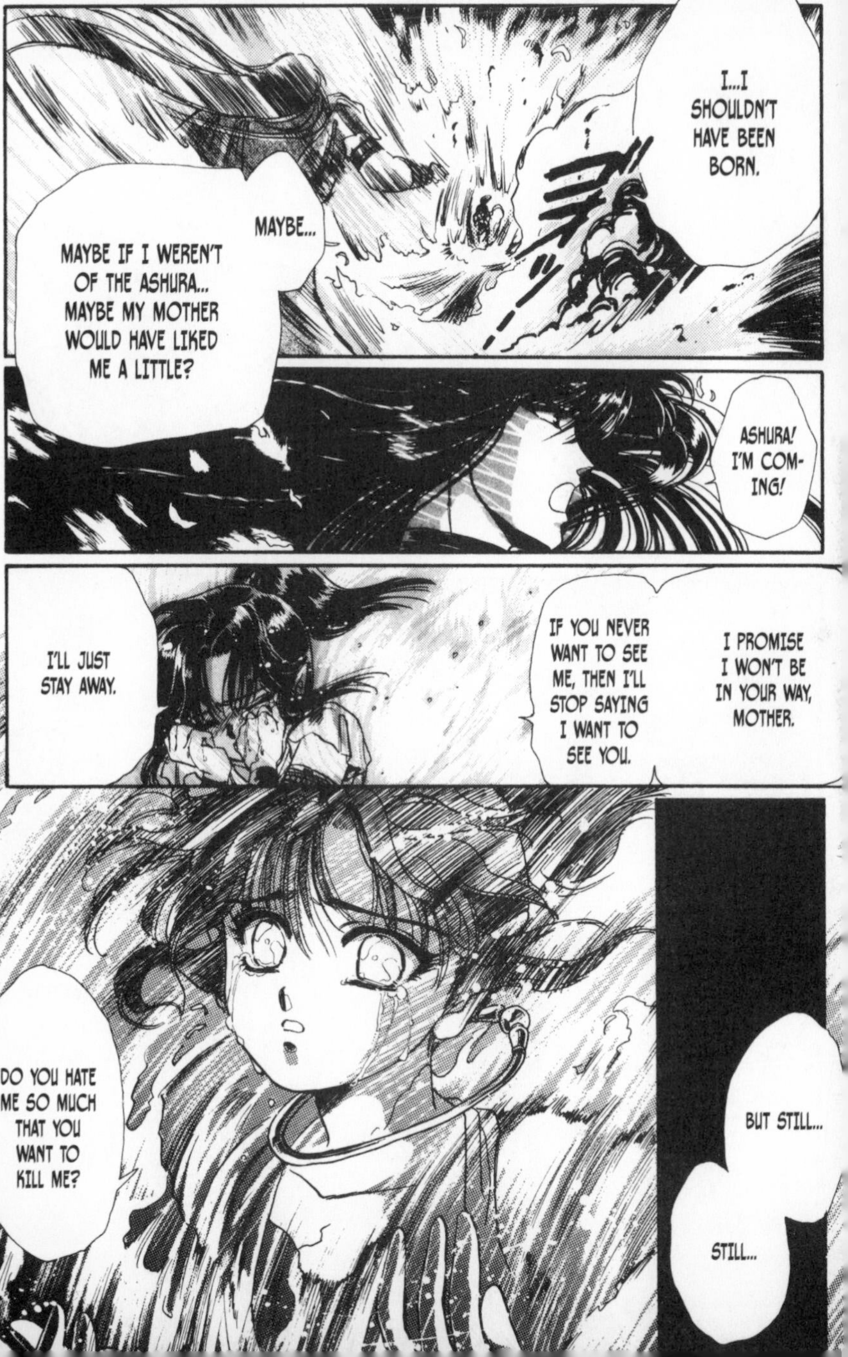
I...I SHOULDN'T HAVE BEEN BORN.
MAYBE...
MAYBE IF I WEREN'T OF THE ASHURA... MAYBE MY MOTHER WOULD HAVE LIKED ME A LITTLE?
ASHURA! I'M COMING!
I PROMISE I WON'T BE IN YOUR WAY, MOTHER.
IF YOU NEVER WANT TO SEE ME, THEN I'LL STOP SAYING I WANT TO SEE YOU.
I'LL JUST STAY AWAY.
BUT STILL...
STILL...
DO YOU HATE ME SO MUCH THAT YOU WANT TO KILL ME?

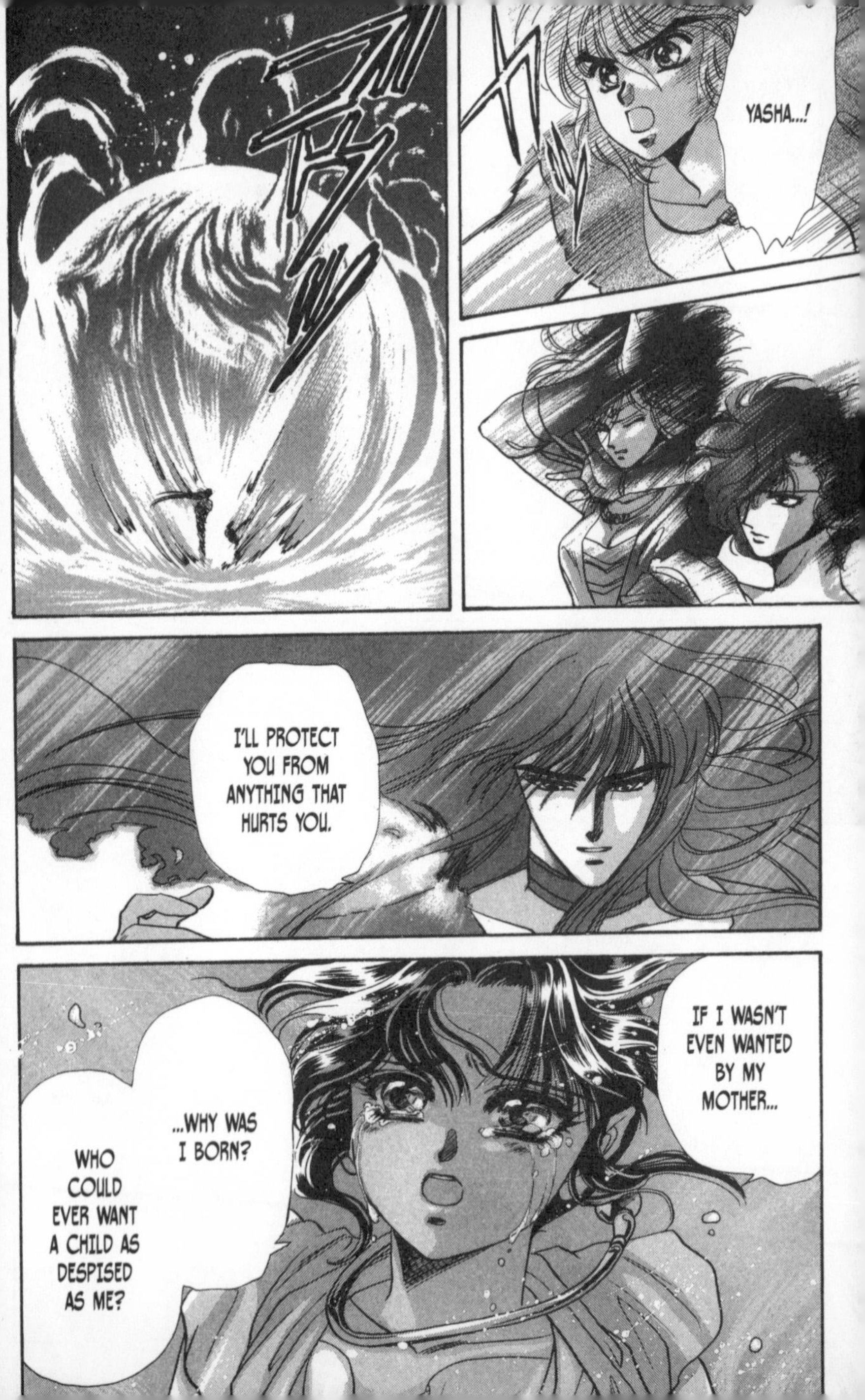
YASHA...!
I'LL PROTECT YOU FROM ANYTHING THAT HURTS YOU.
IF I WASN'T EVEN WANTED BY MY MOTHER...
...WHY WAS I BORN?
WHO COULD EVER WANT A CHILD AS DESPISED AS ME?

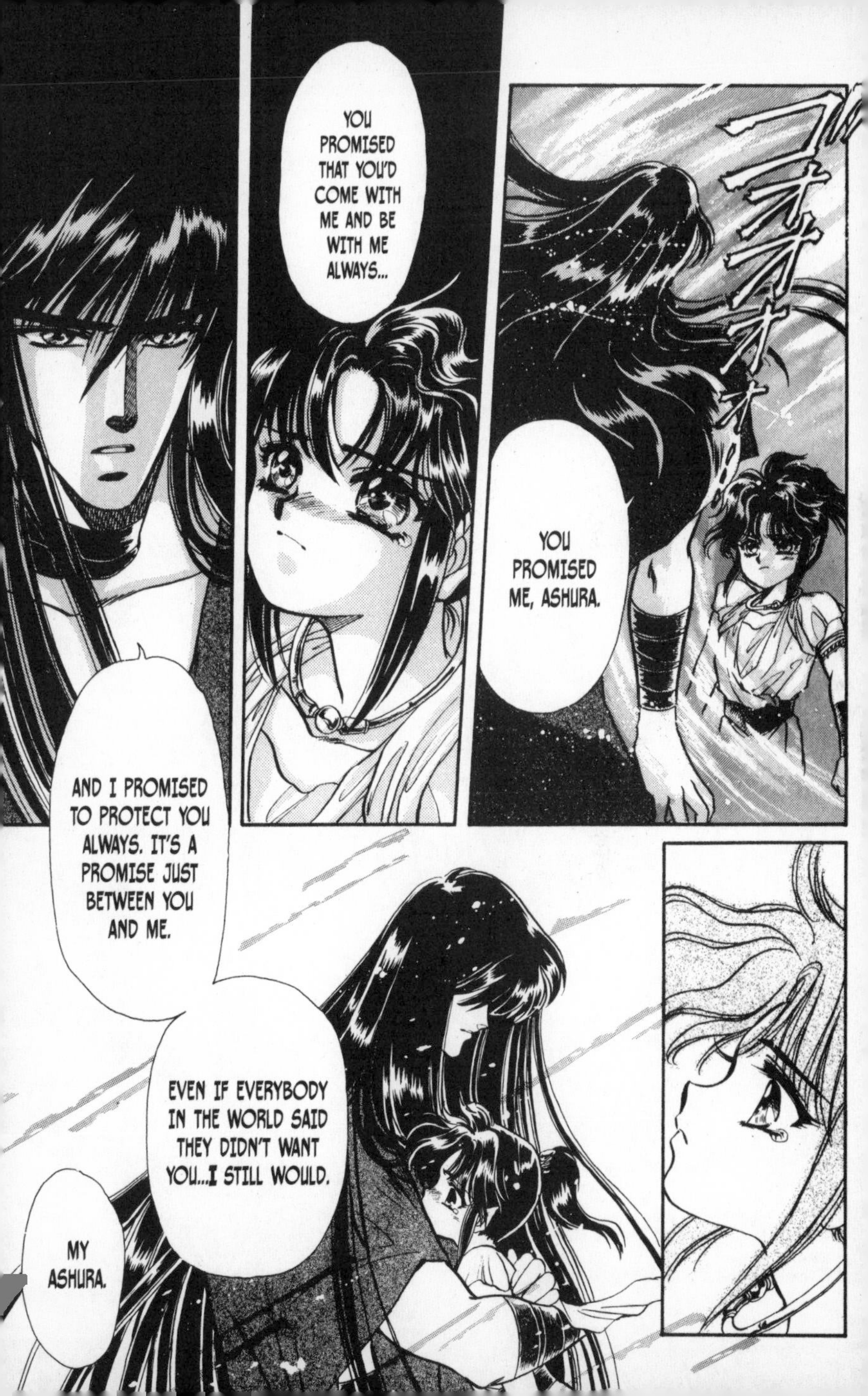
YOU PROMISED ME, ASHURA.
YOU PROMISED THAT YOU'D COME WITH ME AND BE WITH ME ALWAYS...
AND I PROMISED TO PROTECT YOU ALWAYS. IT'S A PROMISE JUST BETWEEN YOU AND ME.
EVEN IF EVERYBODY IN THE WORLD SAID THEY DIDN'T WANT YOU...I STILL WOULD.
MY ASHURA.

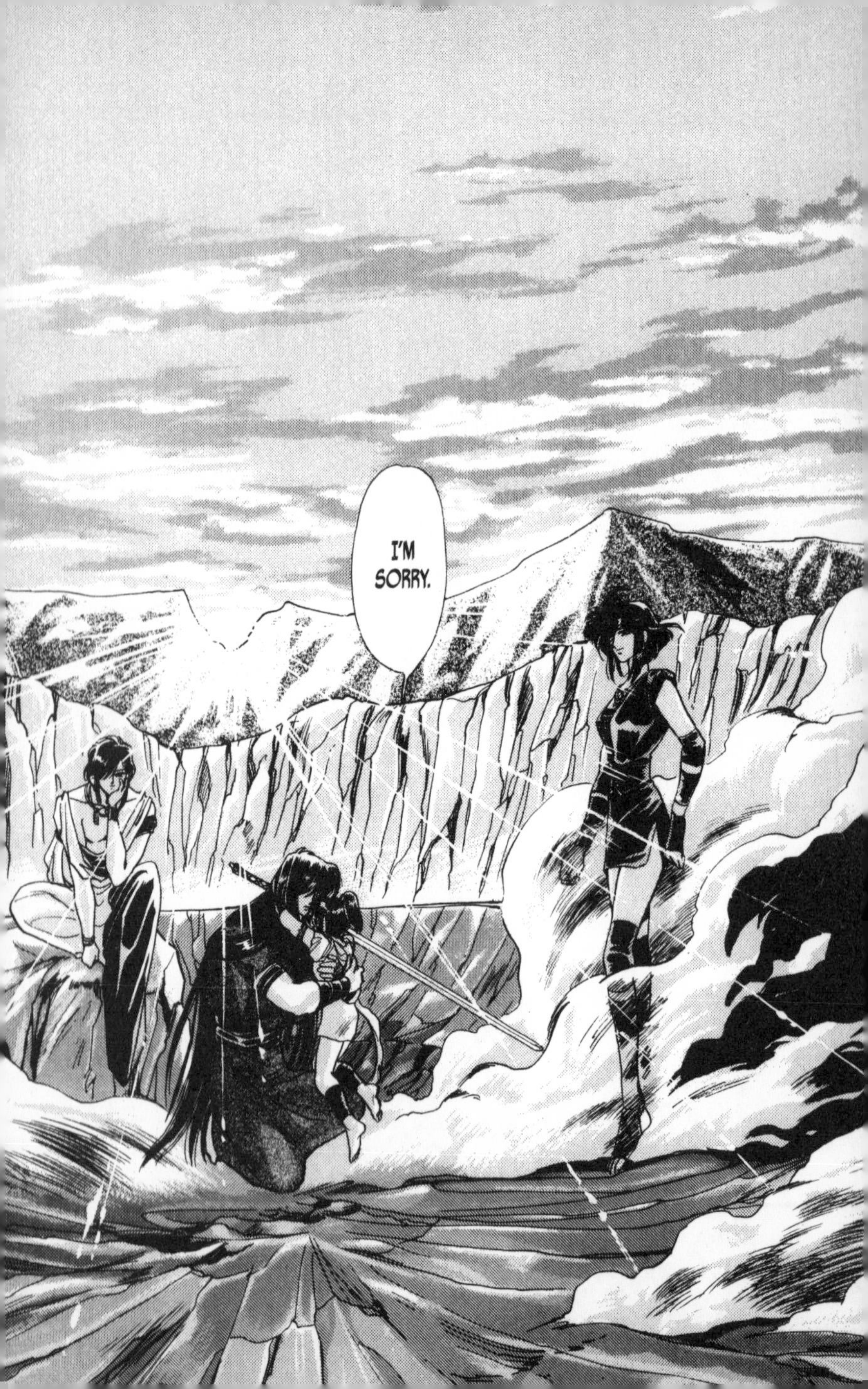
I'M SORRY.

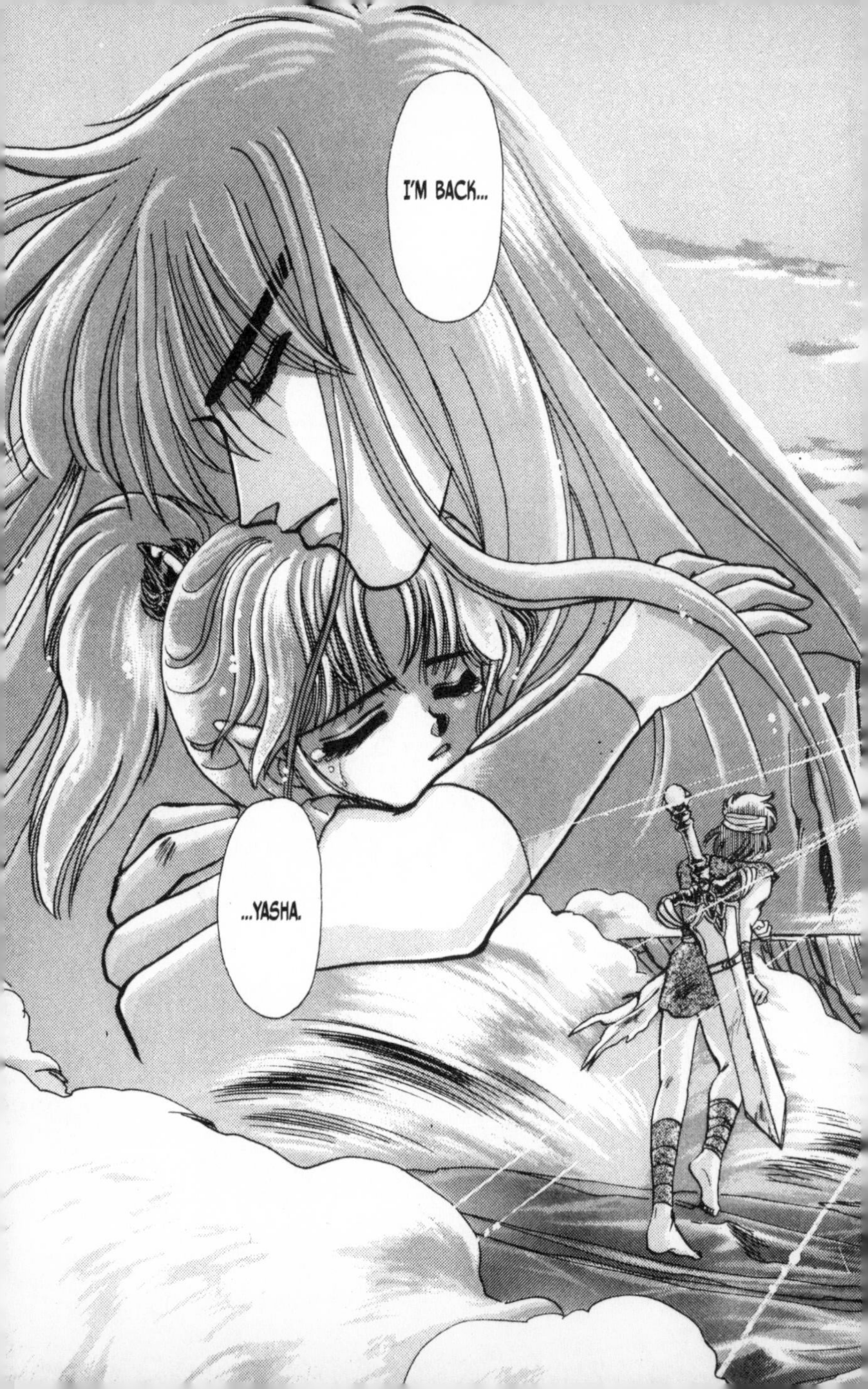
I'M BACK...
...YASHA.

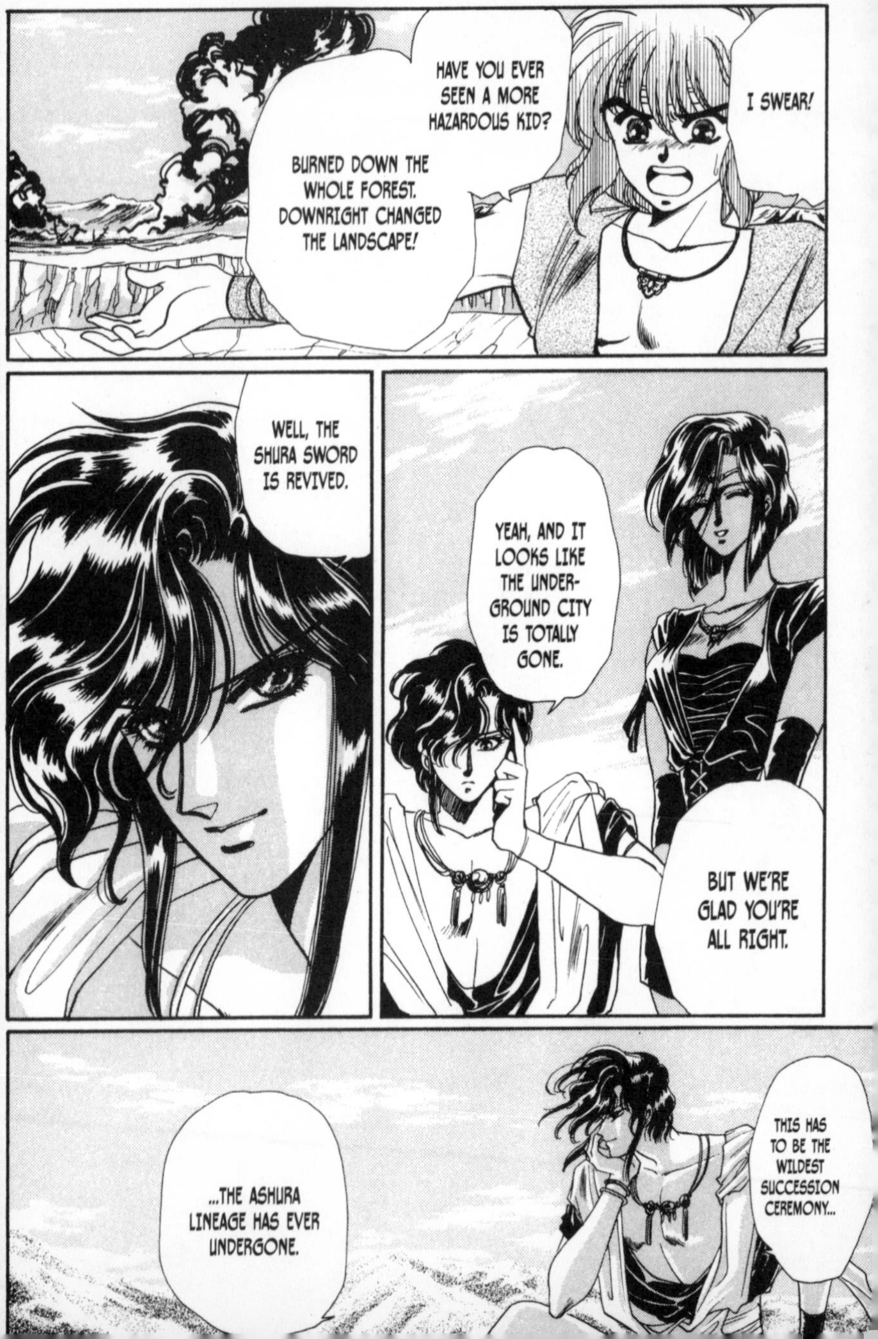
I SWEAR!
HAVE YOU EVER SEEN A MORE HAZARDOUS KID?
BURNED DOWN THE WHOLE FOREST. DOWNRIGHT CHANGED THE LANDSCAPE!
YEAH, AND IT LOOKS LIKE THE UNDER-GROUND CITY IS TOTALLY GONE.
BUT WE'RE GLAD YOU'RE ALL RIGHT.
WELL, THE SHURA SWORD IS REVIVED.
THIS HAS TO BE THE WILDEST SUCCESSION CEREMONY...
...THE ASHURA LINEAGE HAS EVER UNDERGONE.

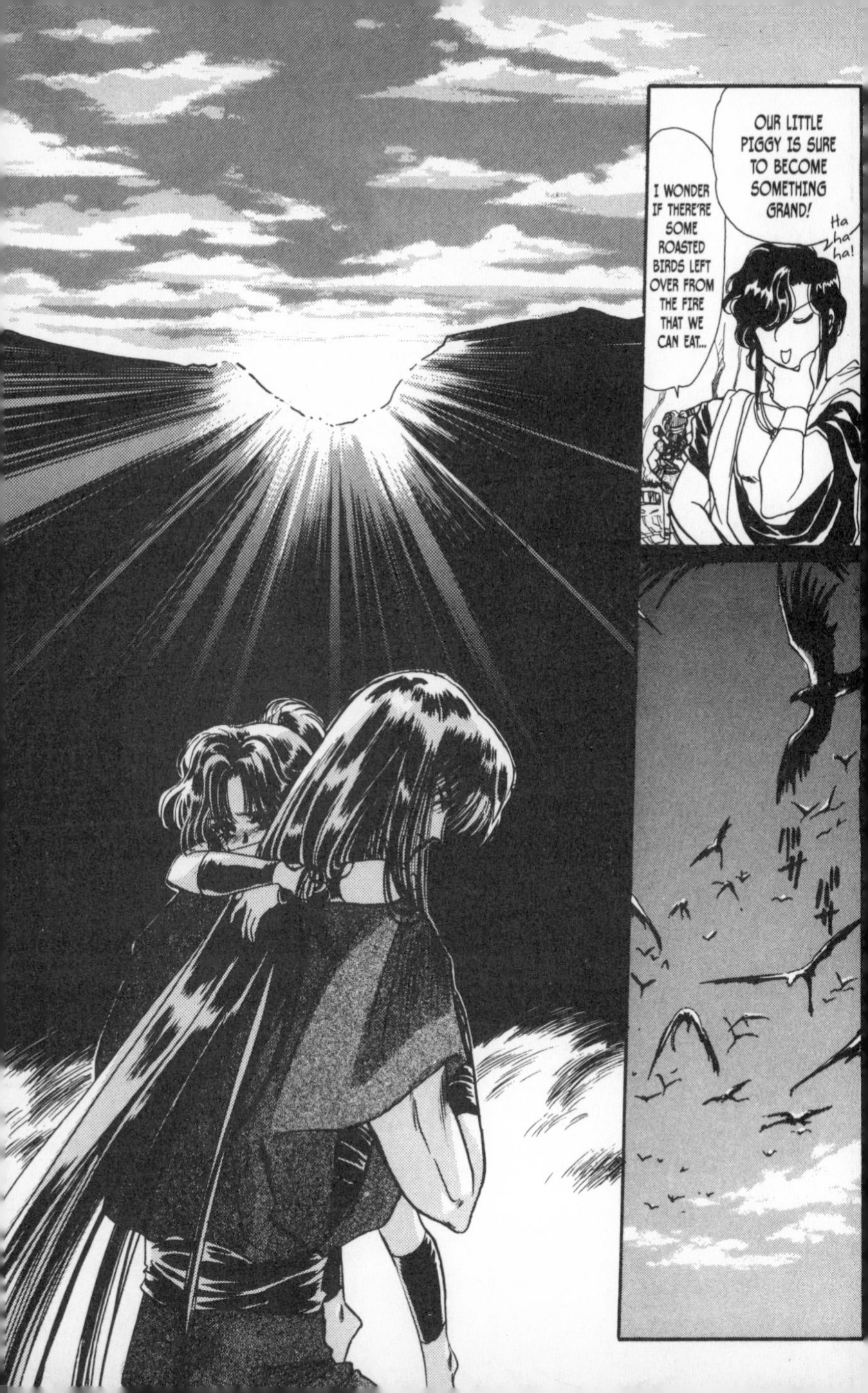
OUR LITTLE PIGGY IS SURE TO BECOME SOMETHING GRAND!
Ha ha ha!
I WONDER IF THERE'RE SOME ROASTED BIRDS LEFT OVER FROM THE FIRE THAT WE CAN EAT...

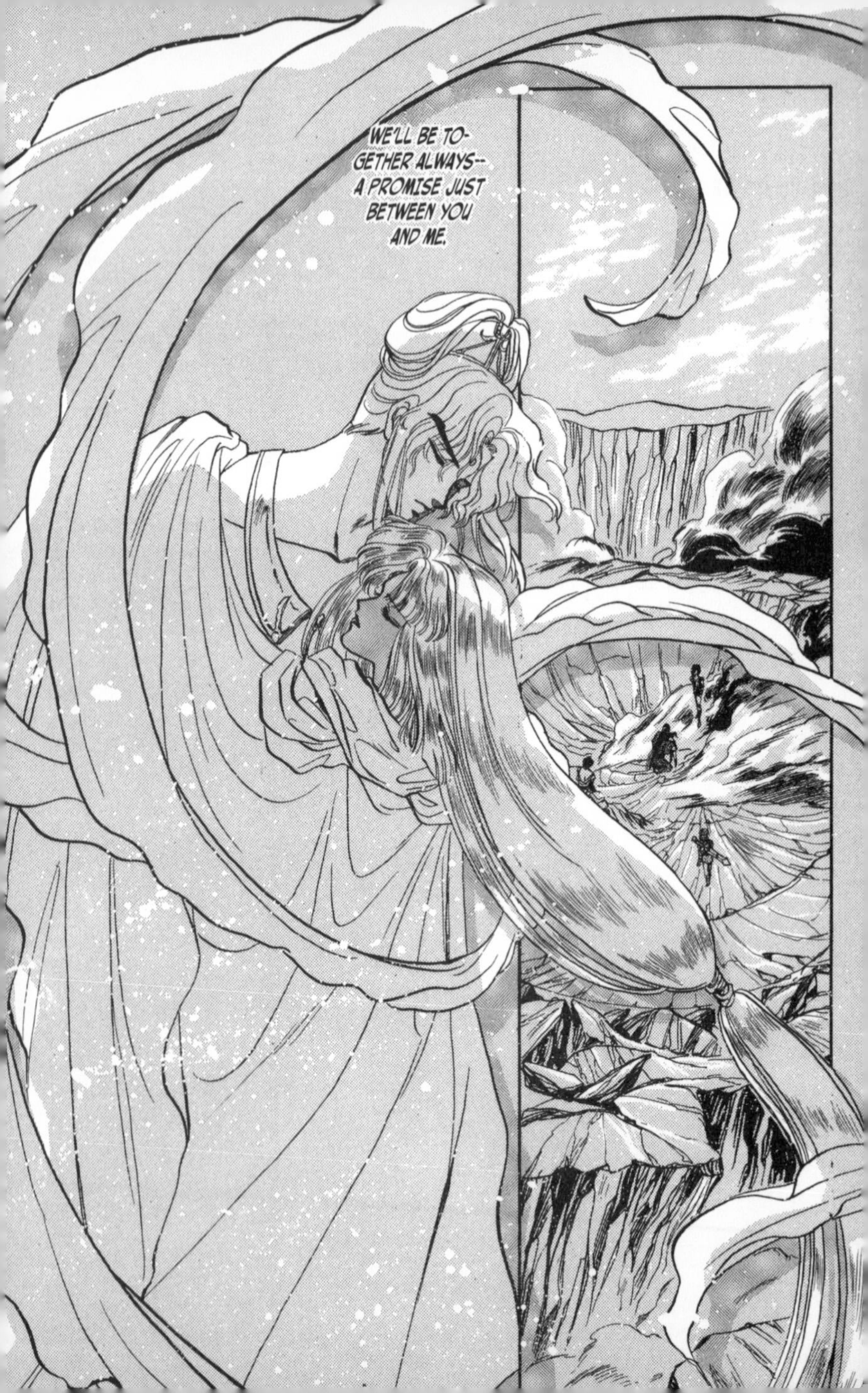
WE'LL BE TO-GETHER ALWAYS-- A PROMISE JUST BETWEEN YOU AND ME.

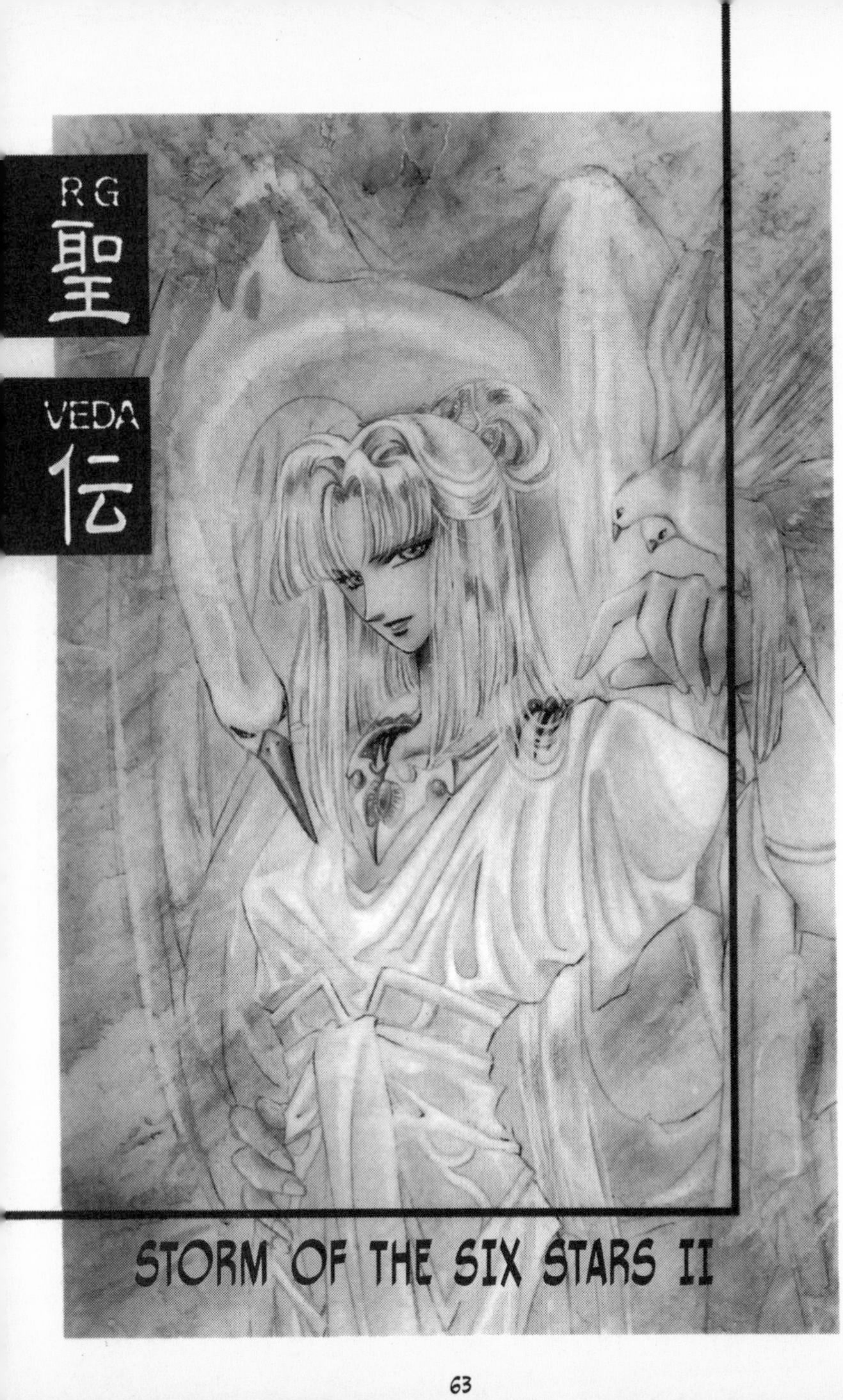
RG
聖
VEDA
伝
STORM OF THE SIX STARS II

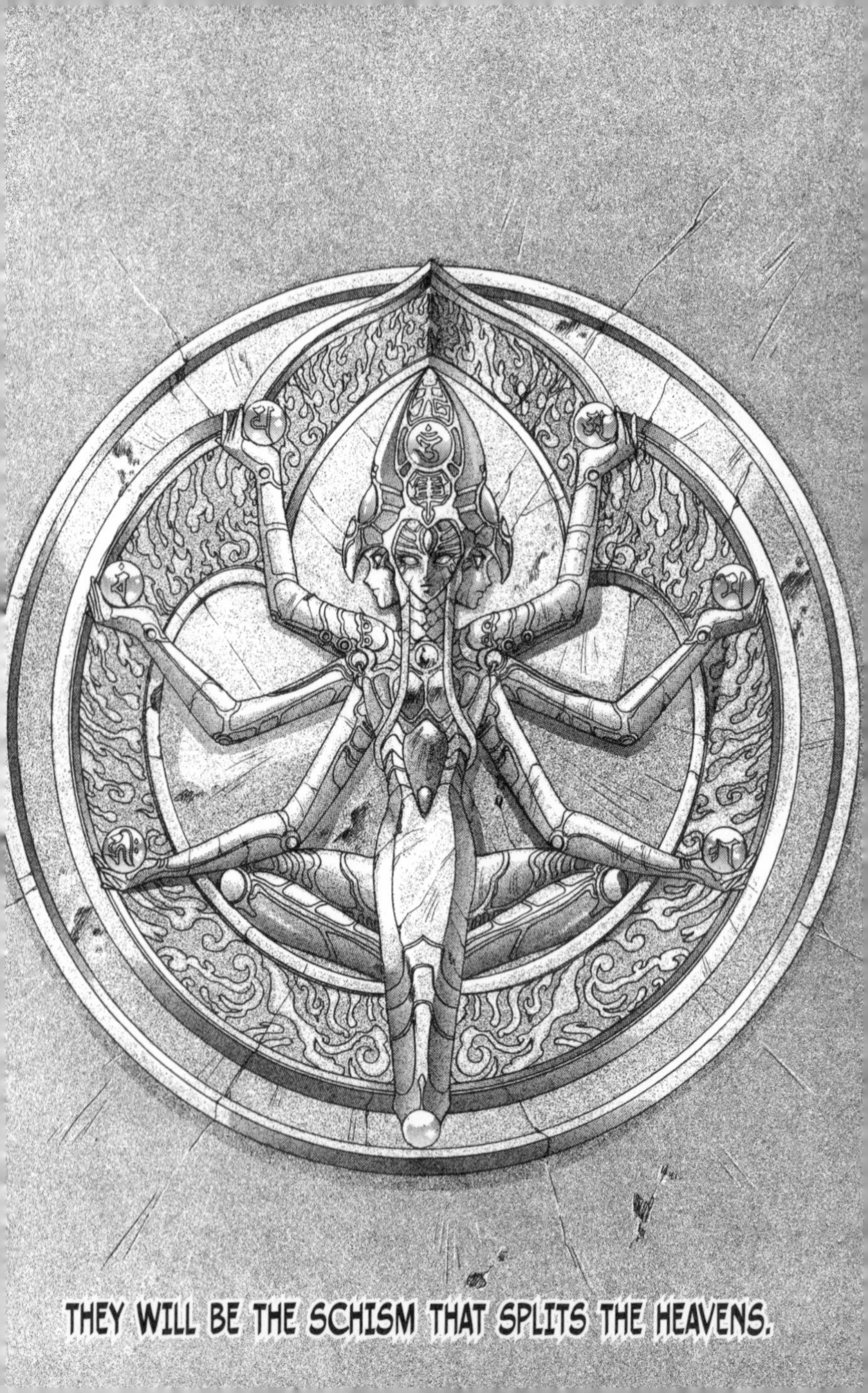
THEY WILL BE THE SCHISM THAT SPLITS THE HEAVENS.

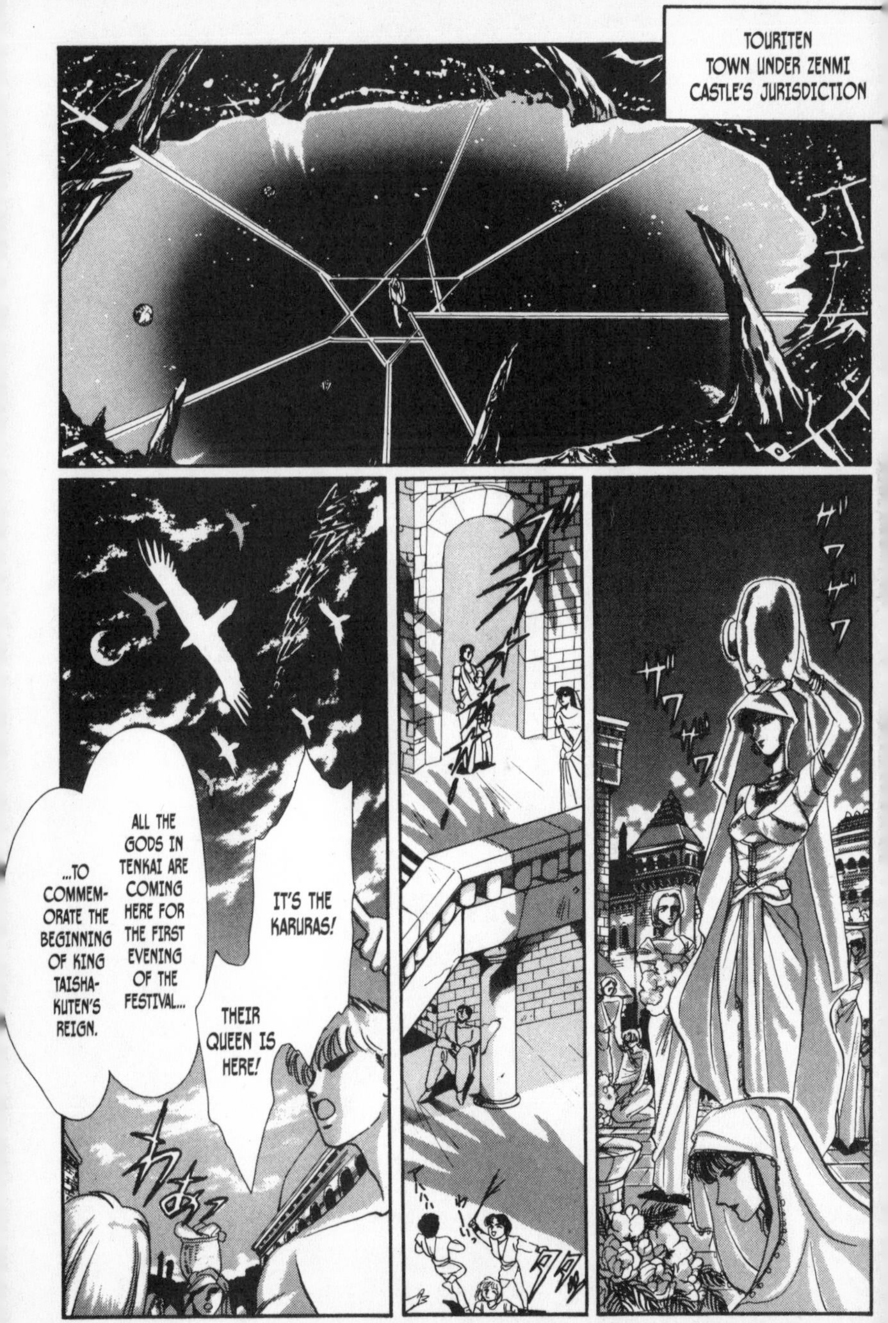
TOURITEN
TOWN UNDER ZENMI CASTLE'S JURISDICTION
IT'S THE KARURAS!
THEIR QUEEN IS HERE!
ALL THE GODS IN TENKAI ARE COMING HERE FOR THE FIRST EVENING OF THE FESTIVAL...
...TO COMMEMORATE THE BEGINNING OF KING TAISHAKUTEN'S REIGN.

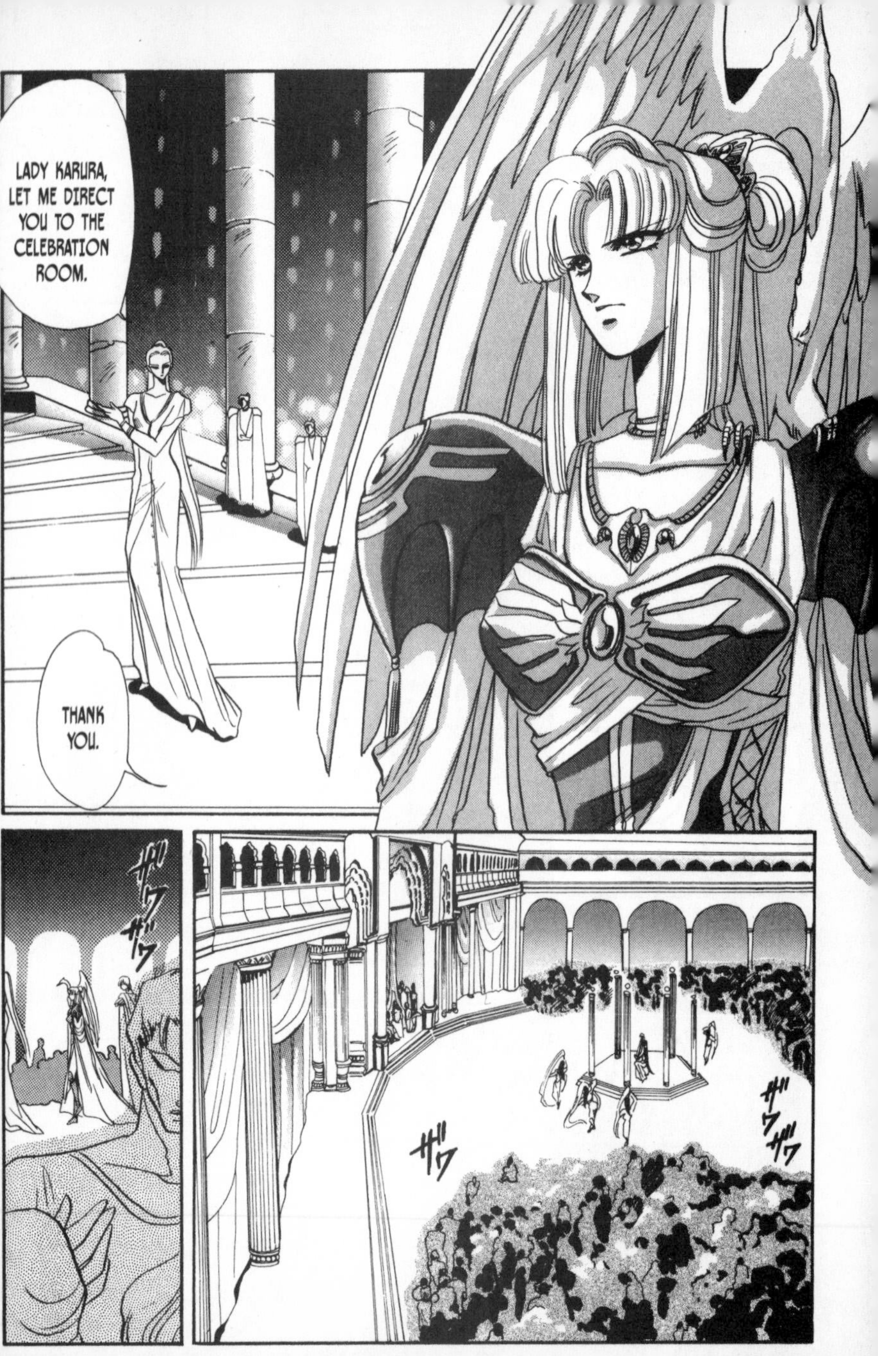
LADY KARURA, LET ME DIRECT YOU TO THE CELEBRATION ROOM.
THANK YOU.
ザワ ザワ ザワ
ザワ
ザワ ザワ

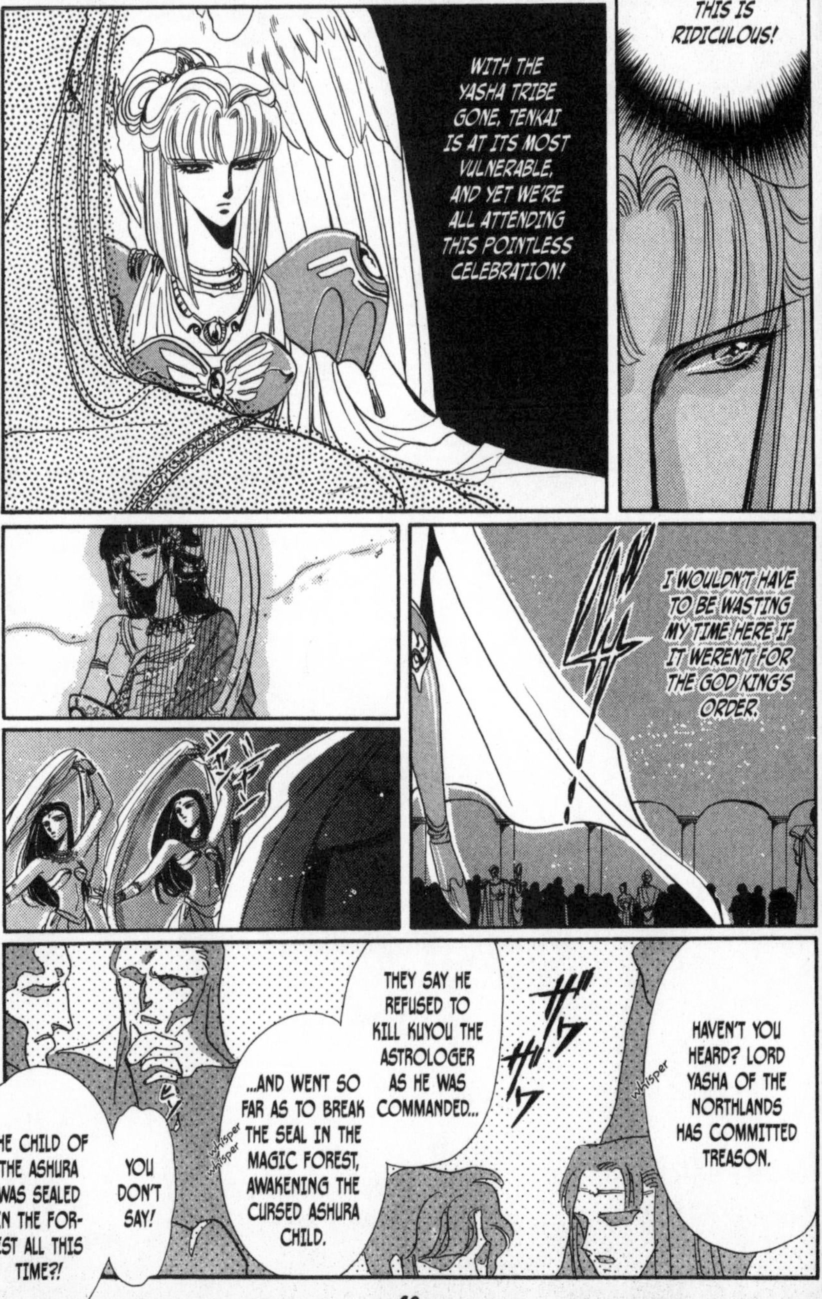
THIS IS RIDICULOUS!
WITH THE YASHA TRIBE GONE, TENKAI IS AT ITS MOST VULNERABLE, AND YET WE'RE ALL ATTENDING THIS POINTLESS CELEBRATION!
I WOULDN'T HAVE TO BE WASTING MY TIME HERE IF IT WEREN'T FOR THE GOD KING'S ORDER.
HAVEN'T YOU HEARD? LORD YASHA OF THE NORTHLANDS HAS COMMITTED TREASON.
whisper
THEY SAY HE REFUSED TO KILL KUYOU THE ASTROLOGER AS HE WAS COMMANDED...
...AND WENT SO FAR AS TO BREAK THE SEAL IN THE MAGIC FOREST, AWAKENING THE CURSED ASHURA CHILD.
whisper
whisper
YOU DON'T SAY!
THE CHILD OF THE ASHURA WAS SEALED IN THE FOREST ALL THIS TIME?!

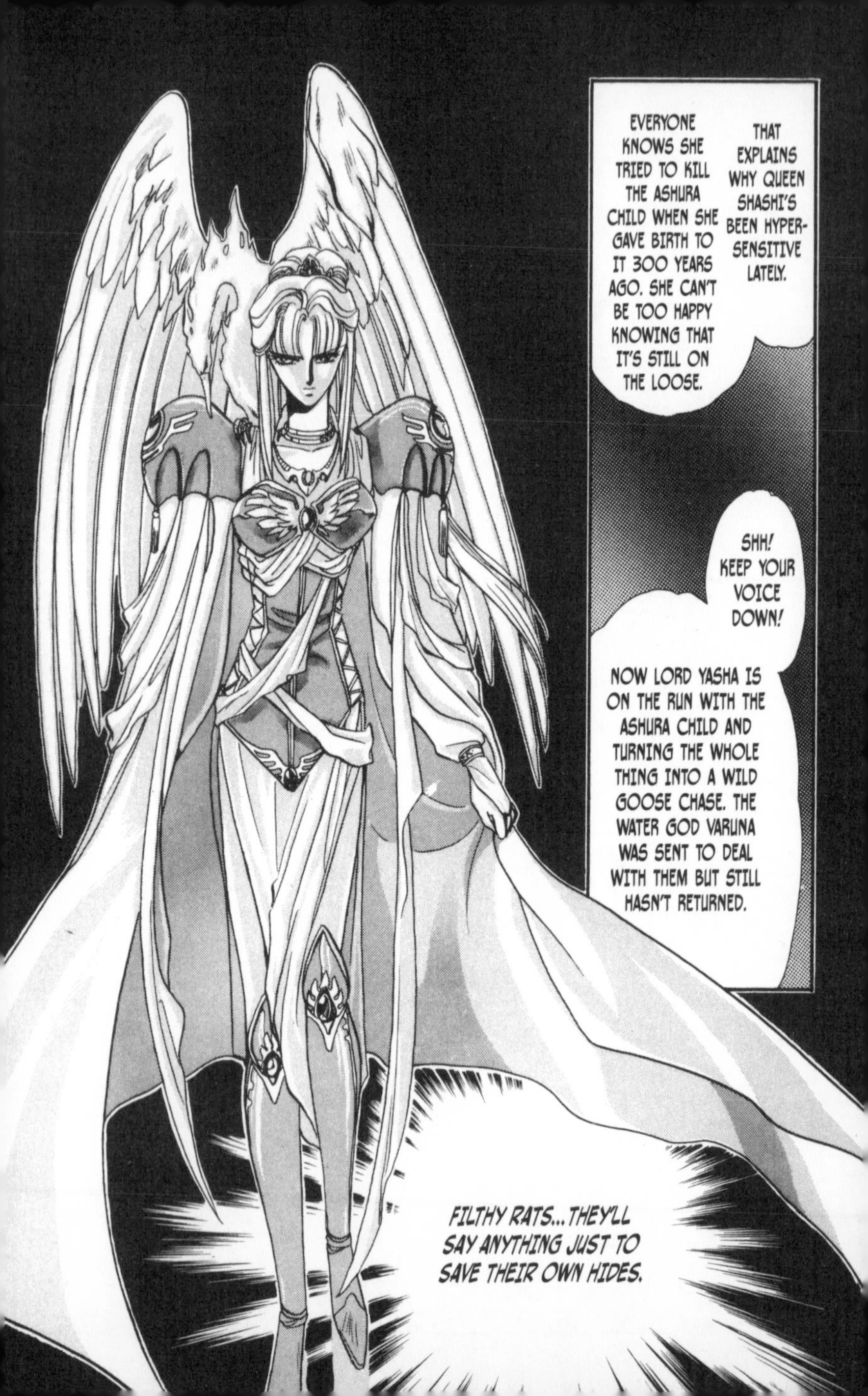
THAT EXPLAINS WHY QUEEN SHASHI'S BEEN HYPER-SENSITIVE LATELY.
EVERYONE KNOWS SHE TRIED TO KILL THE ASHURA CHILD WHEN SHE GAVE BIRTH TO IT 300 YEARS AGO. SHE CAN'T BE TOO HAPPY KNOWING THAT IT'S STILL ON THE LOOSE.
SHH! KEEP YOUR VOICE DOWN!
NOW LORD YASHA IS ON THE RUN WITH THE ASHURA CHILD AND TURNING THE WHOLE THING INTO A WILD GOOSE CHASE. THE WATER GOD VARUNA WAS SENT TO DEAL WITH THEM BUT STILL HASN'T RETURNED.
FILTHY RATS...THEY'LL SAY ANYTHING JUST TO SAVE THEIR OWN HIDES.

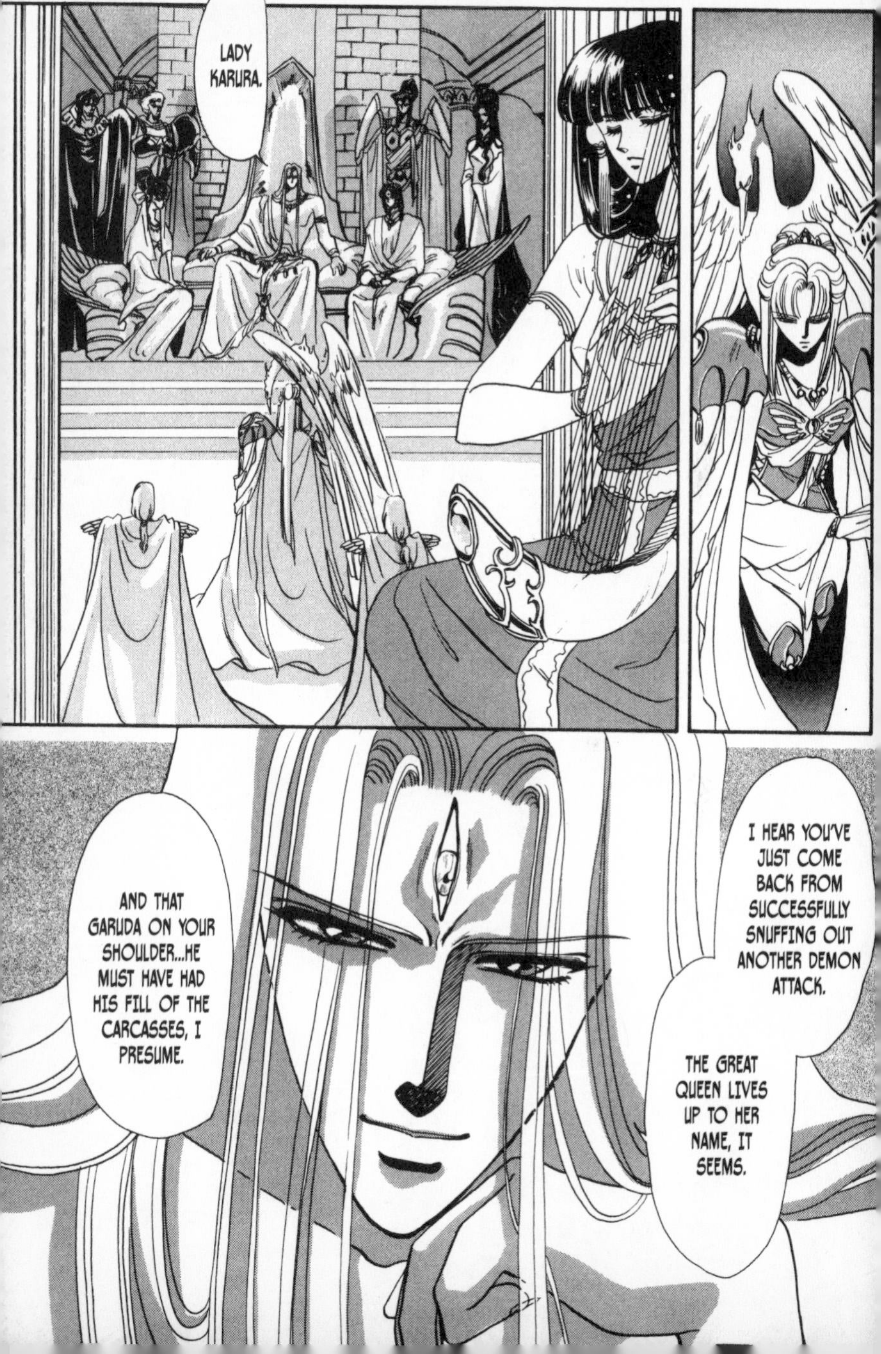
LADY KARURA.
I HEAR YOU'VE JUST COME BACK FROM SUCCESSFULLY SNUFFING OUT ANOTHER DEMON ATTACK.
THE GREAT QUEEN LIVES UP TO HER NAME, IT SEEMS.
AND THAT GARUDA ON YOUR SHOULDER...HE MUST HAVE HAD HIS FILL OF THE CARCASSES, I PRESUME.

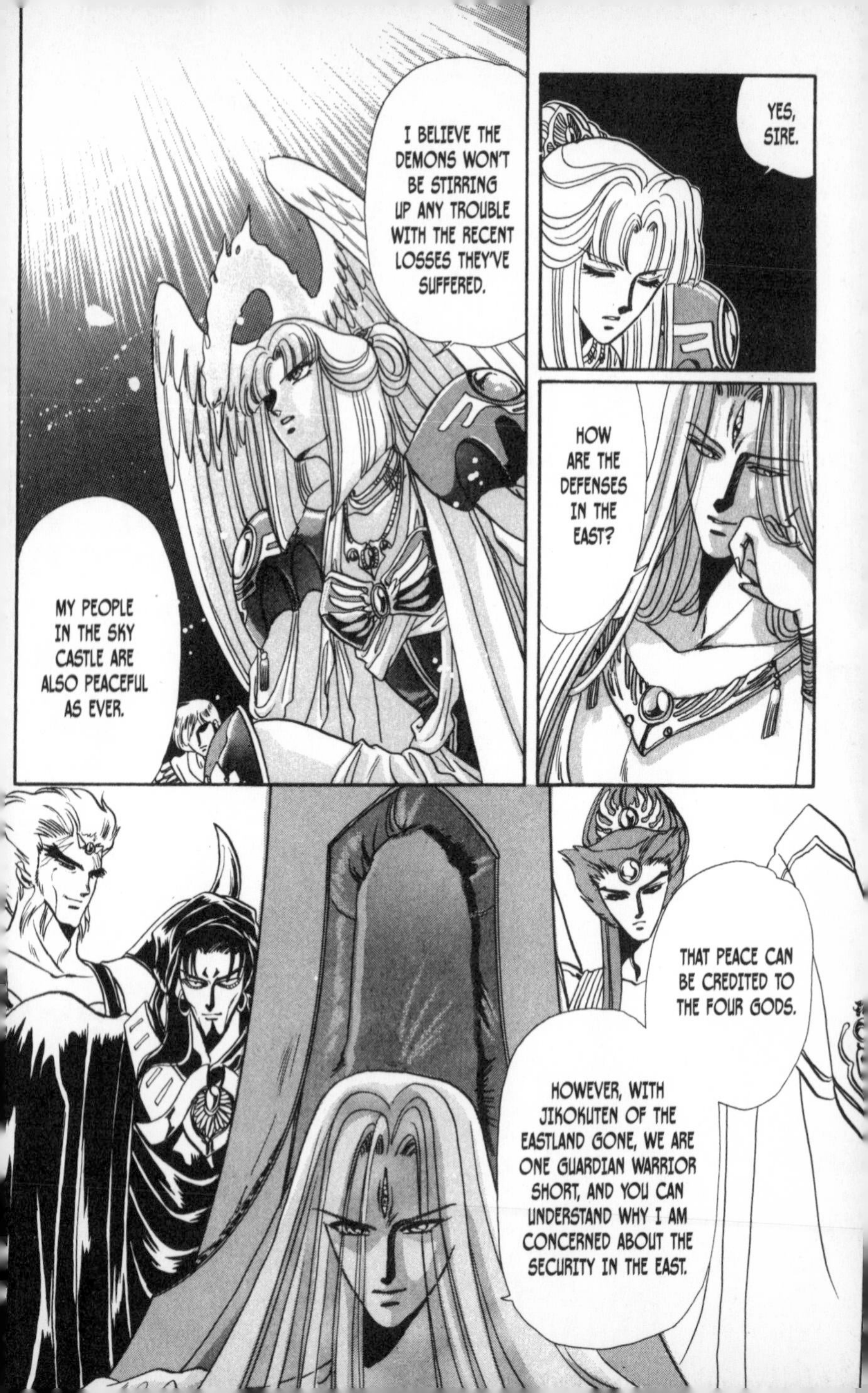
YES, SIRE.
I BELIEVE THE DEMONS WON'T BE STIRRING UP ANY TROUBLE WITH THE RECENT LOSSES THEY'VE SUFFERED.
MY PEOPLE IN THE SKY CASTLE ARE ALSO PEACEFUL AS EVER.
HOW ARE THE DEFENSES IN THE EAST?
THAT PEACE CAN BE CREDITED TO THE FOUR GODS.
HOWEVER, WITH JIKOKUTEN OF THE EASTLAND GONE, WE ARE ONE GUARDIAN WARRIOR SHORT, AND YOU CAN UNDERSTAND WHY I AM CONCERNED ABOUT THE SECURITY IN THE EAST.

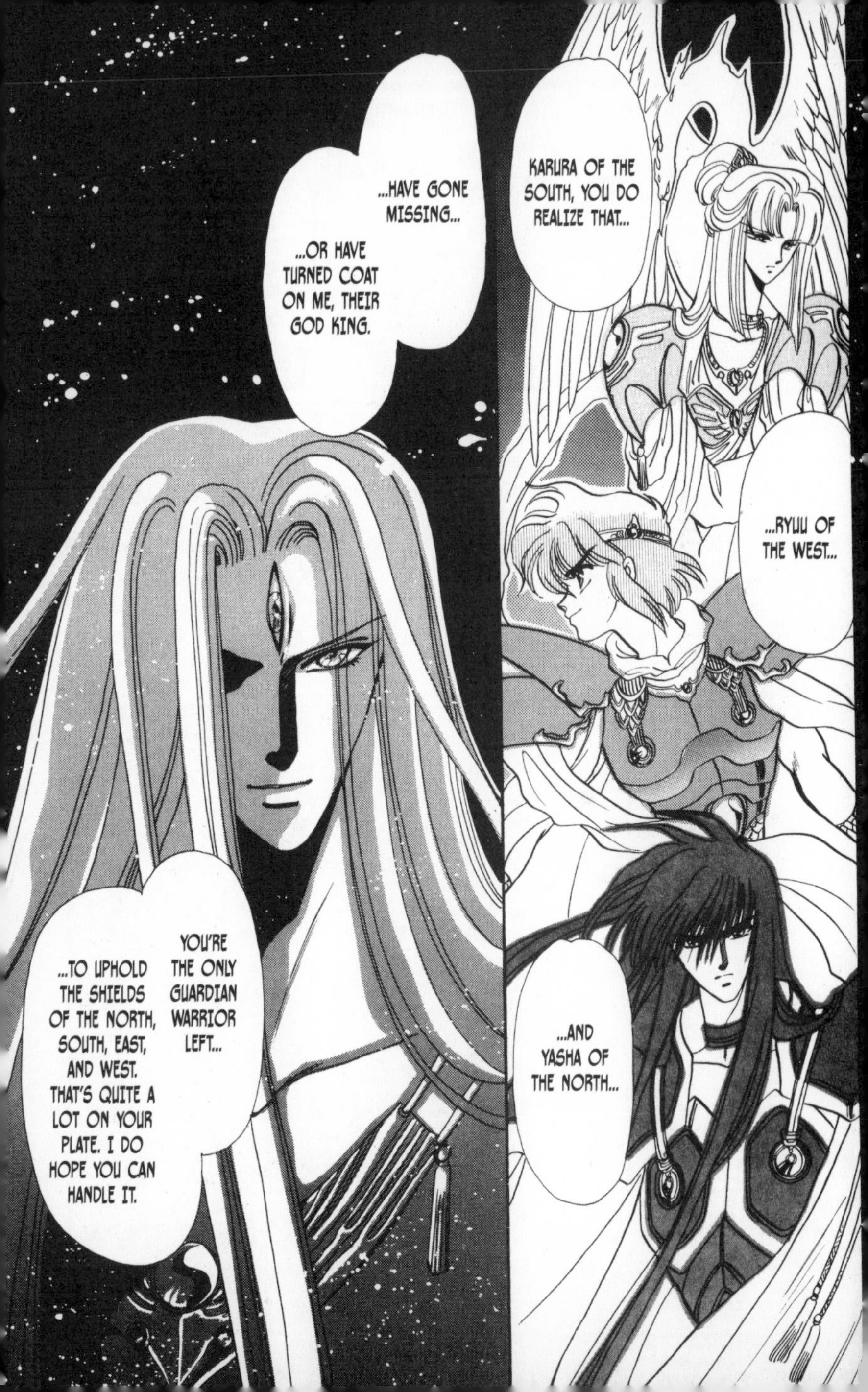
KARURA OF THE SOUTH, YOU DO REALIZE THAT...
...RYUU OF THE WEST...
...AND YASHA OF THE NORTH...
...HAVE GONE MISSING...
...OR HAVE TURNED COAT ON ME, THEIR GOD KING.
YOU'RE THE ONLY GUARDIAN WARRIOR LEFT...
...TO UPHOLD THE SHIELDS OF THE NORTH, SOUTH, EAST, AND WEST. THAT'S QUITE A LOT ON YOUR PLATE. I DO HOPE YOU CAN HANDLE IT.

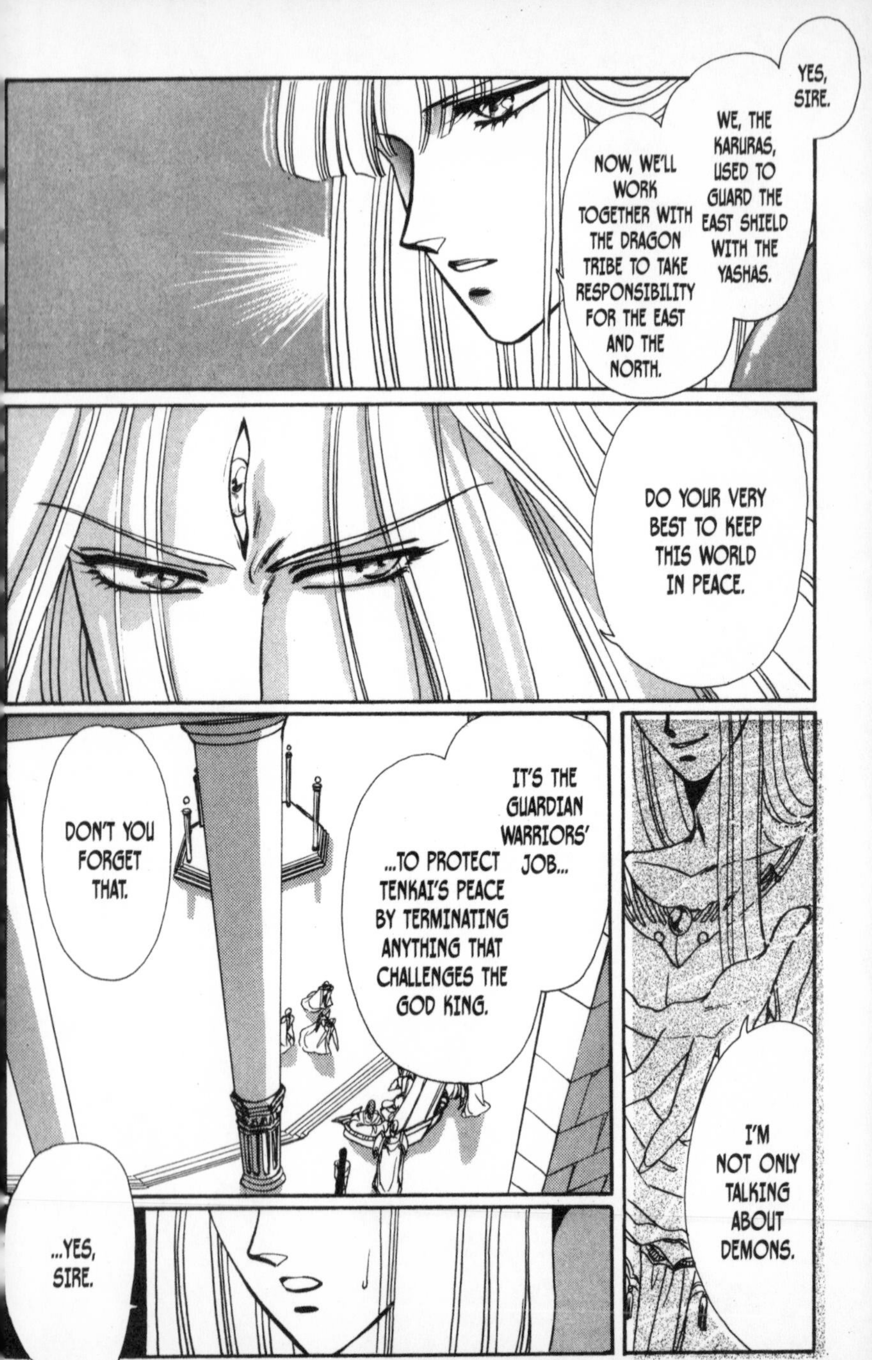
YES, SIRE.
WE, THE KARURAS, USED TO GUARD THE EAST SHIELD WITH THE YASHAS.
NOW, WE'LL WORK TOGETHER WITH THE DRAGON TRIBE TO TAKE RESPONSIBILITY FOR THE EAST AND THE NORTH.
DO YOUR VERY BEST TO KEEP THIS WORLD IN PEACE.
IT'S THE GUARDIAN WARRIORS' JOB...
...TO PROTECT TENKAI'S PEACE BY TERMINATING ANYTHING THAT CHALLENGES THE GOD KING.
DON'T YOU FORGET THAT.
I'M NOT ONLY TALKING ABOUT DEMONS.
...YES, SIRE.

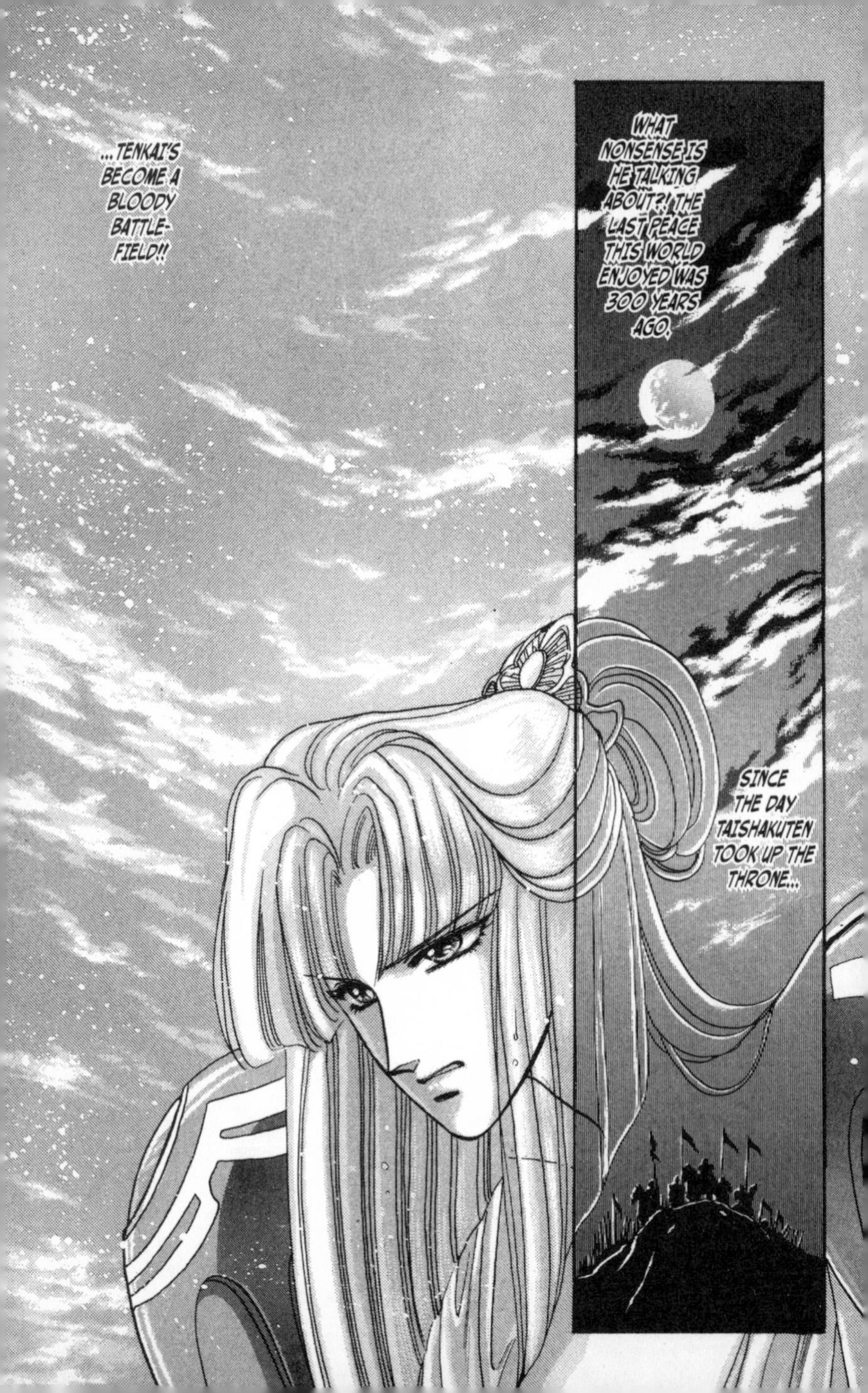
WHAT NONSENSE IS HE TALKING ABOUT?! THE LAST PEACE THIS WORLD ENJOYED WAS 300 YEARS AGO.
SINCE THE DAY TAISHAKUTEN TOOK UP THE THRONE...
...TENKAI'S BECOME A BLOODY BATTLE-FIELD!!

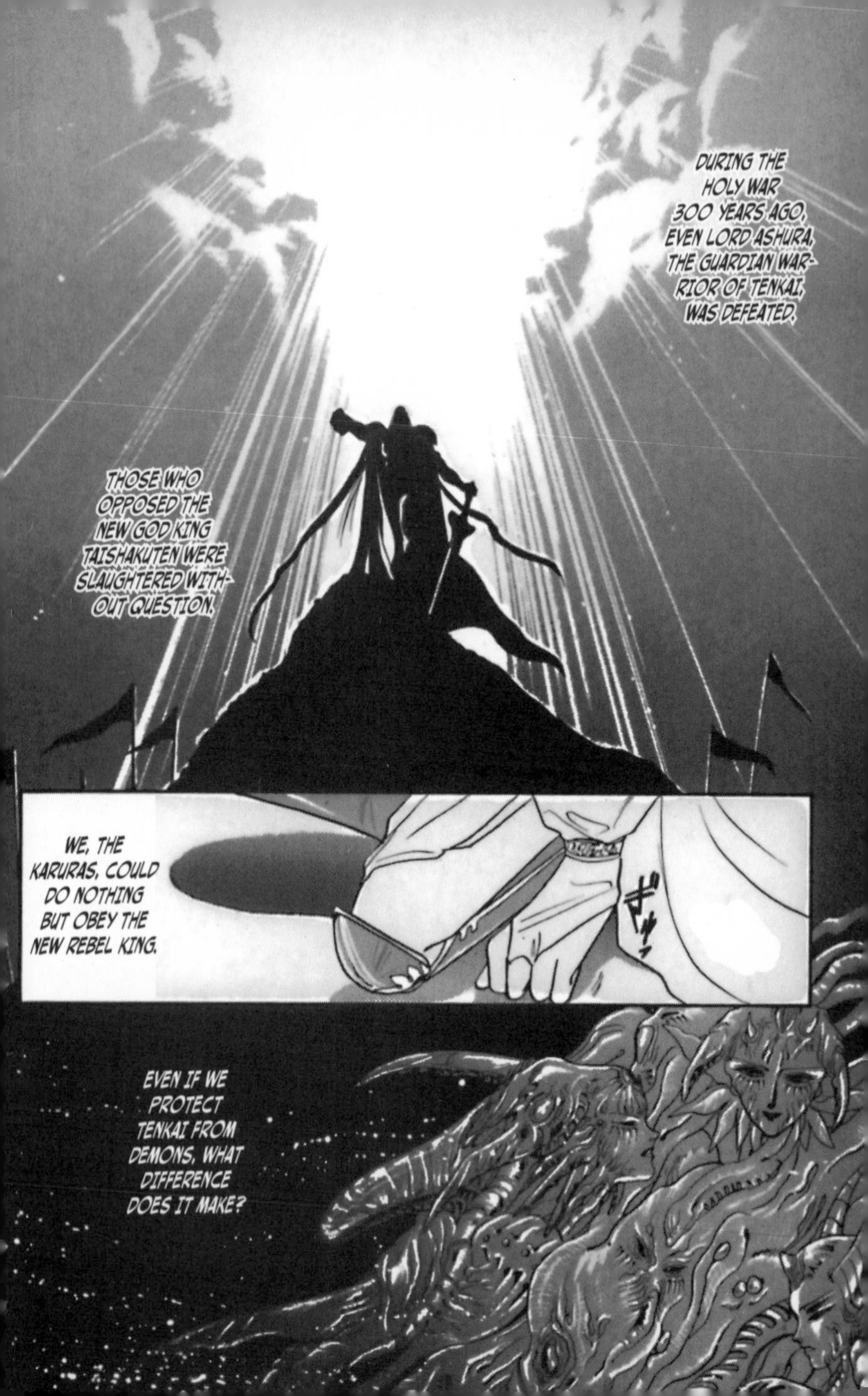

DURING THE HOLY WAR 300 YEARS AGO, EVEN LORD ASHURA, THE GUARDIAN WAR-RIOR OF TENKAI, WAS DEFEATED.
THOSE WHO OPPOSED THE NEW GOD KING TAISHAKUTEN WERE SLAUGHTERED WITH-OUT QUESTION.
WE, THE KARURAS, COULD DO NOTHING BUT OBEY THE NEW REBEL KING.
EVEN IF WE PROTECT TENKAI FROM DEMONS, WHAT DIFFERENCE DOES IT MAKE?

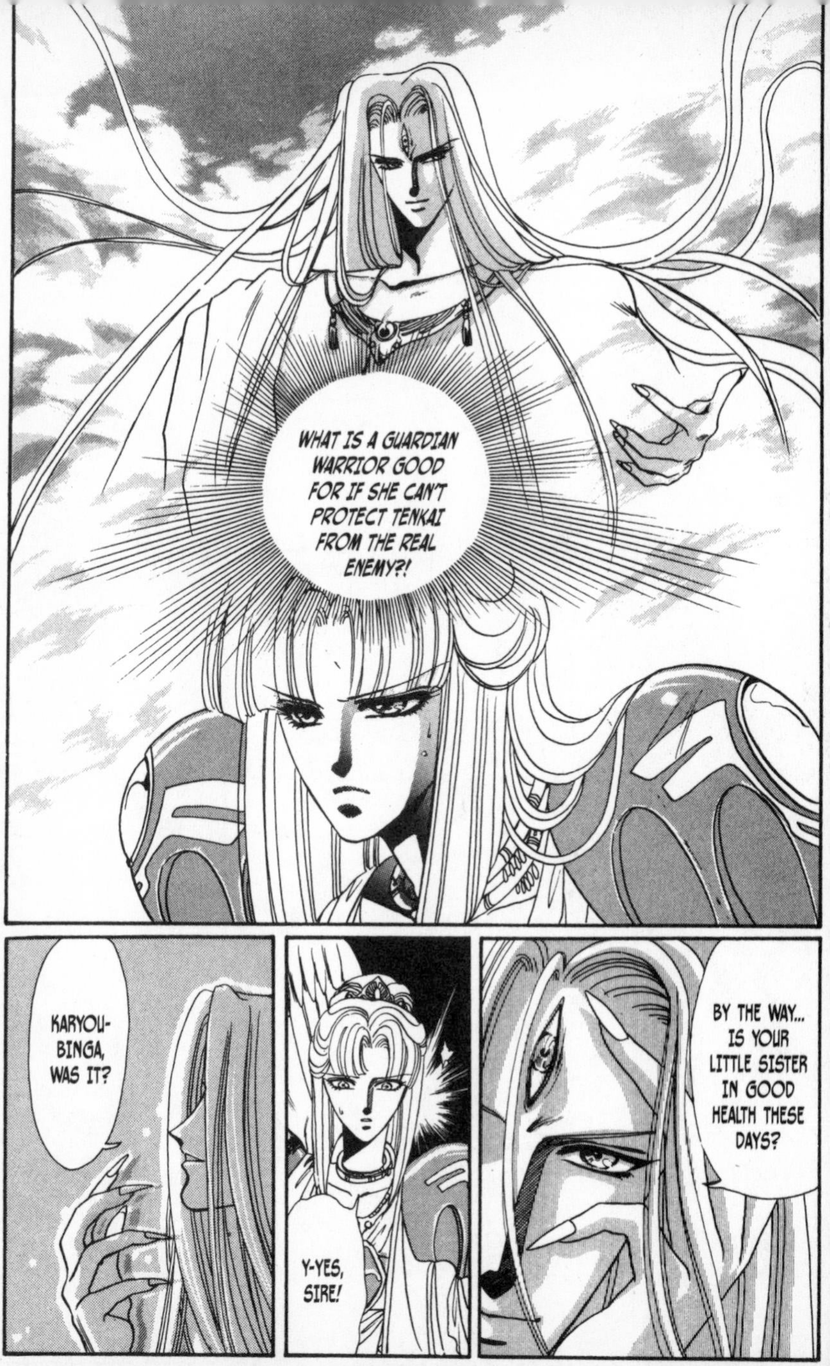
WHAT IS A GUARDIAN WARRIOR GOOD FOR IF SHE CAN'T PROTECT TENKAI FROM THE REAL ENEMY?!
BY THE WAY... IS YOUR LITTLE SISTER IN GOOD HEALTH THESE DAYS?
Y-YES, SIRE!
KARYOU-BINGA, WAS IT?

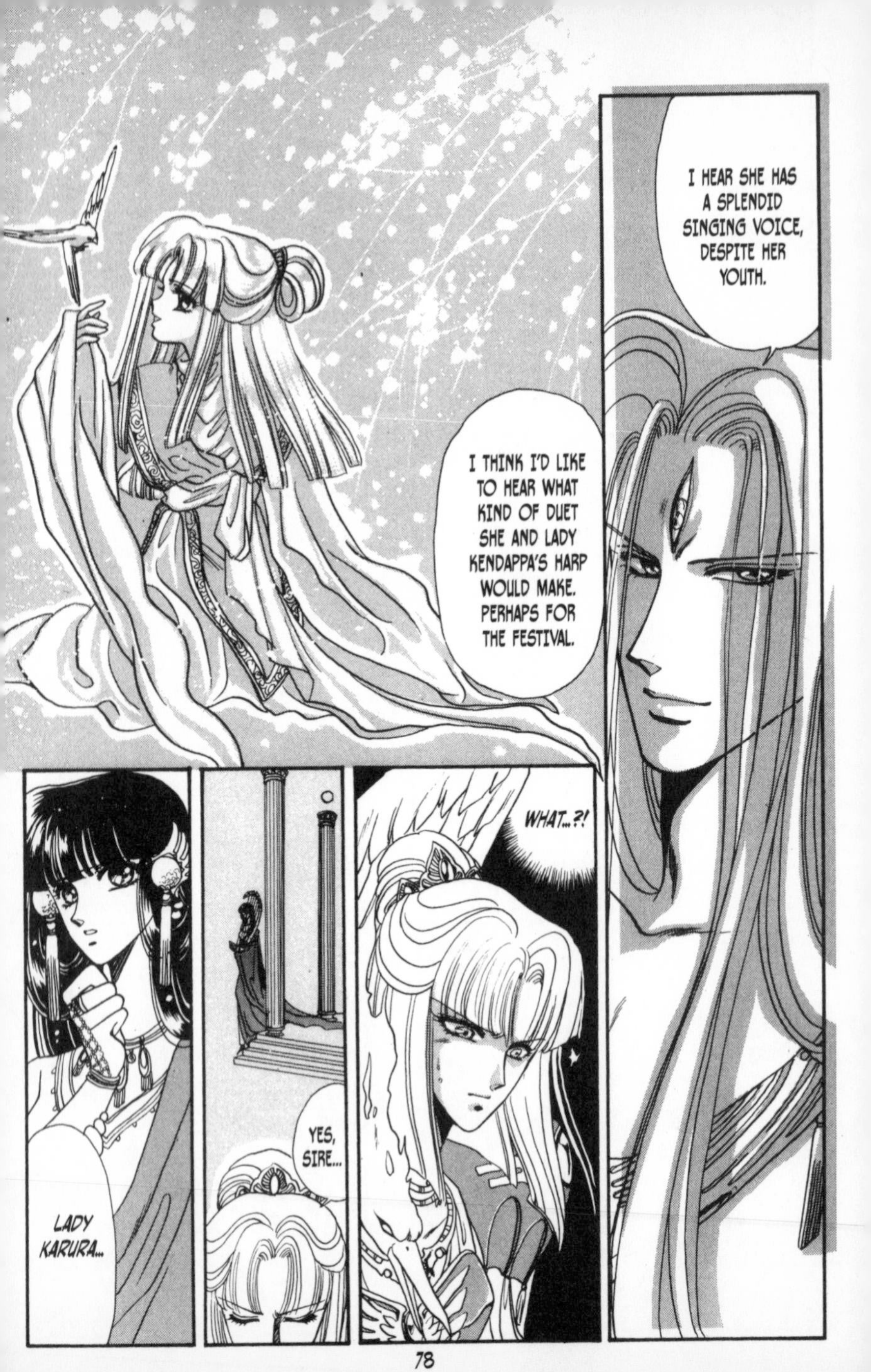
I HEAR SHE HAS A SPLENDID SINGING VOICE, DESPITE HER YOUTH.
I THINK I'D LIKE TO HEAR WHAT KIND OF DUET SHE AND LADY KENDAPPA'S HARP WOULD MAKE. PERHAPS FOR THE FESTIVAL.
WHAT...?!
YES, SIRE...
LADY KARURA...

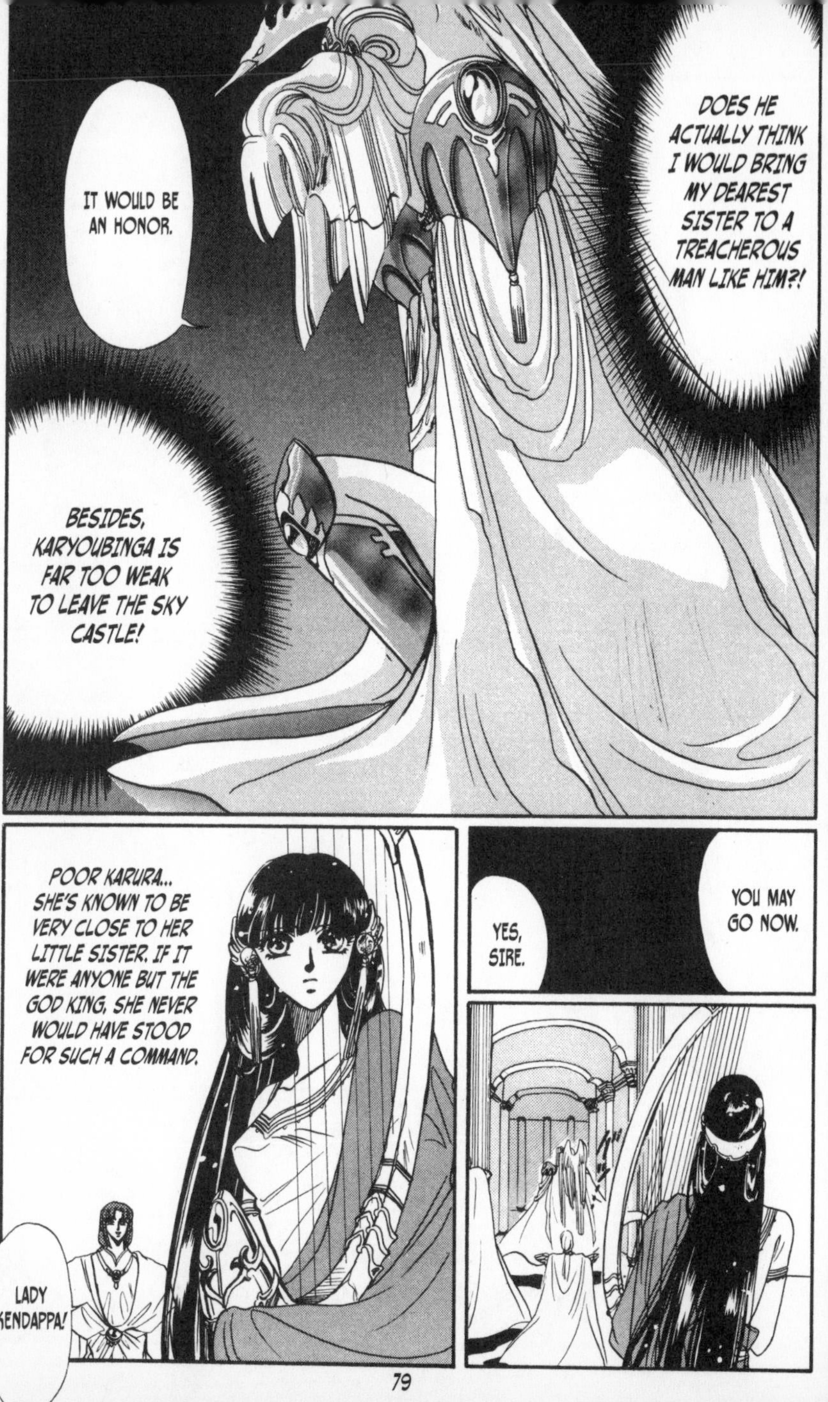
IT WOULD BE AN HONOR.
DOES HE ACTUALLY THINK I WOULD BRING MY DEAREST SISTER TO A TREACHEROUS MAN LIKE HIM?!
BESIDES, KARYOUBINGA IS FAR TOO WEAK TO LEAVE THE SKY CASTLE!
YOU MAY GO NOW.
YES, SIRE.
POOR KARURA... SHE'S KNOWN TO BE VERY CLOSE TO HER LITTLE SISTER. IF IT WERE ANYONE BUT THE GOD KING, SHE NEVER WOULD HAVE STOOD FOR SUCH A COMMAND.
LADY KENDAPPA!

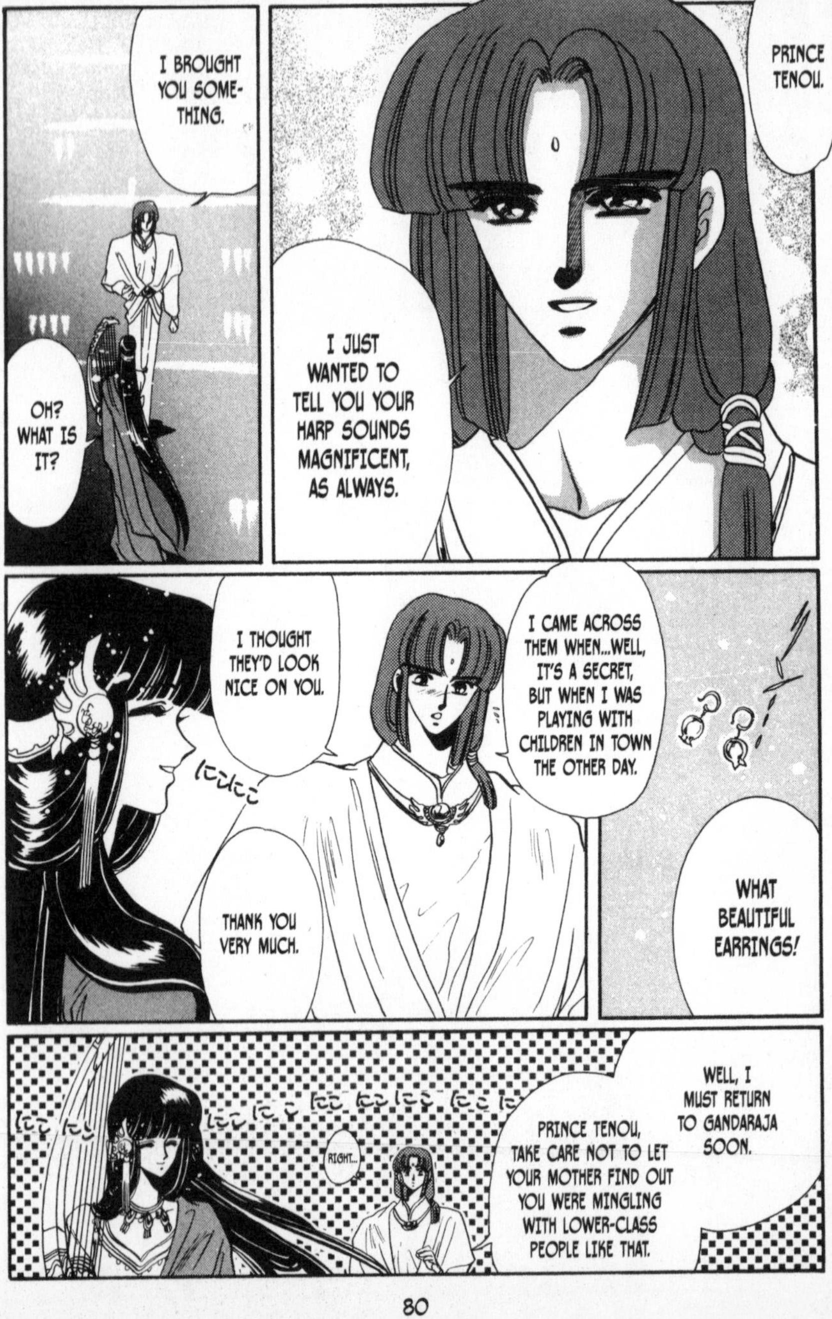
PRINCE TENOU.
I JUST WANTED TO TELL YOU YOUR HARP SOUNDS MAGNIFICENT, AS ALWAYS.
I BROUGHT YOU SOMETHING.
OH? WHAT IS IT?
WHAT BEAUTIFUL EARRINGS!
I CAME ACROSS THEM WHEN...WELL, IT'S A SECRET, BUT WHEN I WAS PLAYING WITH CHILDREN IN TOWN THE OTHER DAY.
I THOUGHT THEY'D LOOK NICE ON YOU.
にこにこ
THANK YOU VERY MUCH.
WELL, I MUST RETURN TO GANDARAJA SOON.
PRINCE TENOU, TAKE CARE NOT TO LET YOUR MOTHER FIND OUT YOU WERE MINGLING WITH LOWER-CLASS PEOPLE LIKE THAT.
RIGHT...

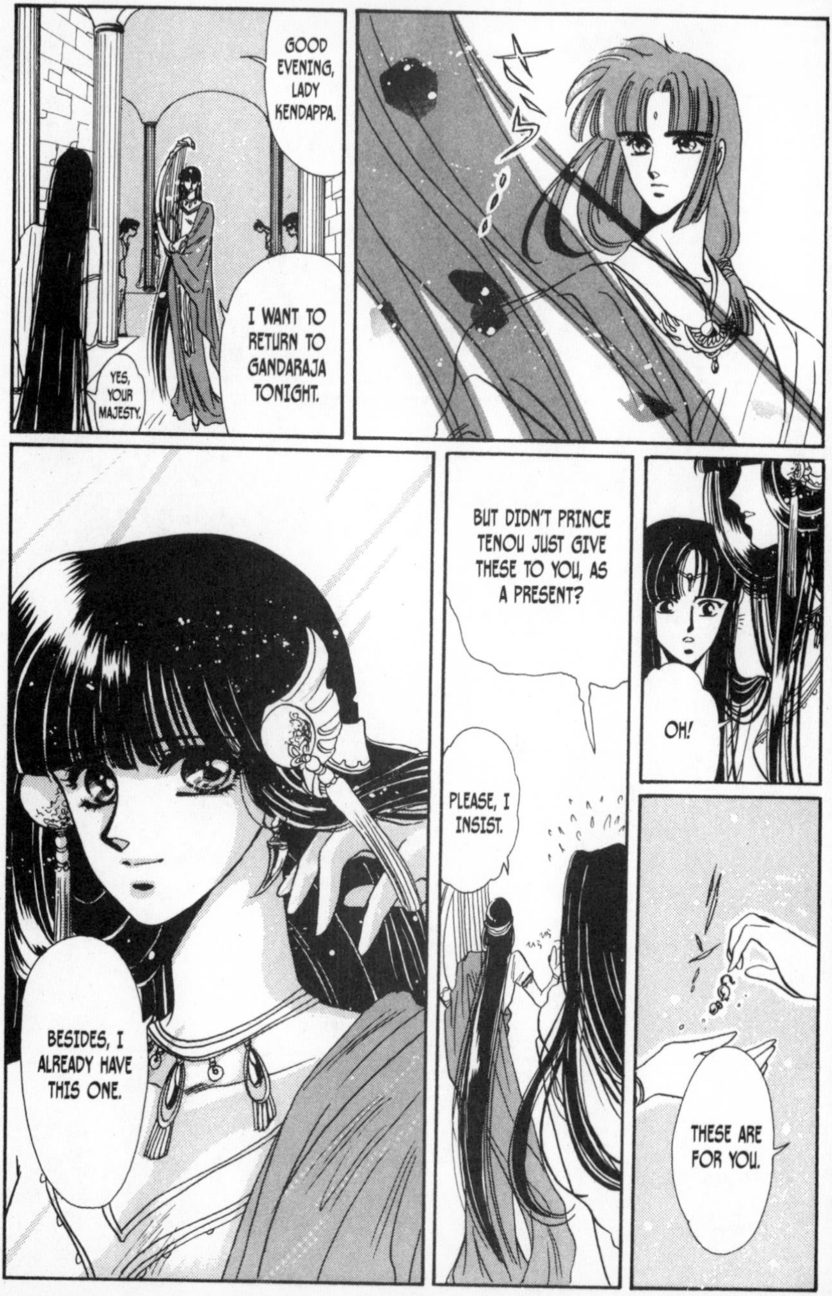
GOOD EVENING, LADY KENDAPPA.
I WANT TO RETURN TO GANDARAJA TONIGHT.
YES, YOUR MAJESTY.
OH!
THESE ARE FOR YOU.
BUT DIDN'T PRINCE TENOU JUST GIVE THESE TO YOU, AS A PRESENT?
PLEASE, I INSIST.
BESIDES, I ALREADY HAVE THIS ONE.

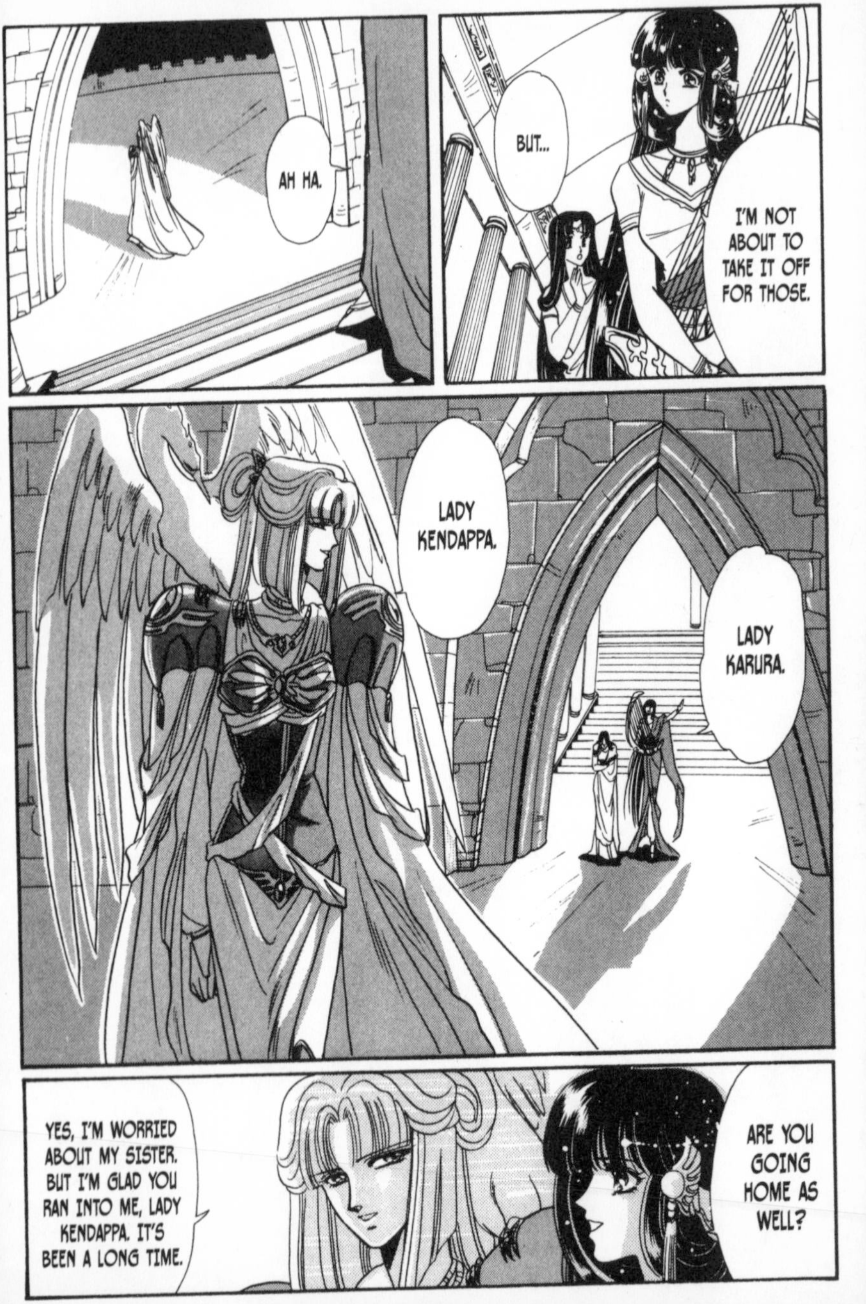
I'M NOT ABOUT TO TAKE IT OFF FOR THOSE.
BUT...
AH HA.
LADY KARURA.
LADY KENDAPPA.
ARE YOU GOING HOME AS WELL?
YES, I'M WORRIED ABOUT MY SISTER. BUT I'M GLAD YOU RAN INTO ME, LADY KENDAPPA. IT'S BEEN A LONG TIME.

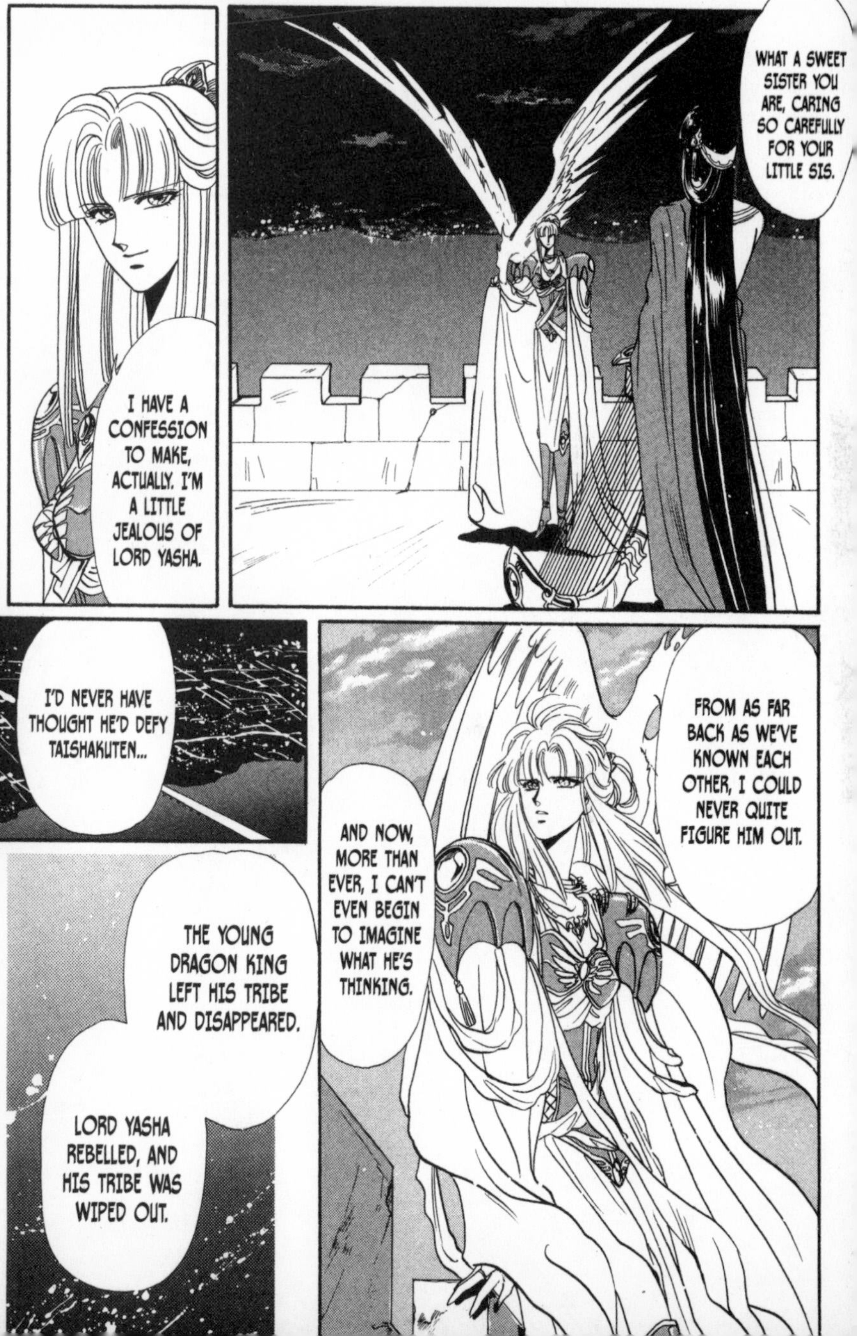
WHAT A SWEET SISTER YOU ARE, CARING SO CAREFULLY FOR YOUR LITTLE SIS.
I HAVE A CONFESSION TO MAKE, ACTUALLY. I'M A LITTLE JEALOUS OF LORD YASHA.
FROM AS FAR BACK AS WE'VE KNOWN EACH OTHER, I COULD NEVER QUITE FIGURE HIM OUT.
AND NOW, MORE THAN EVER, I CAN'T EVEN BEGIN TO IMAGINE WHAT HE'S THINKING.
I'D NEVER HAVE THOUGHT HE'D DEFY TAISHAKUTEN...
THE YOUNG DRAGON KING LEFT HIS TRIBE AND DISAPPEARED.
LORD YASHA REBELLED, AND HIS TRIBE WAS WIPED OUT.

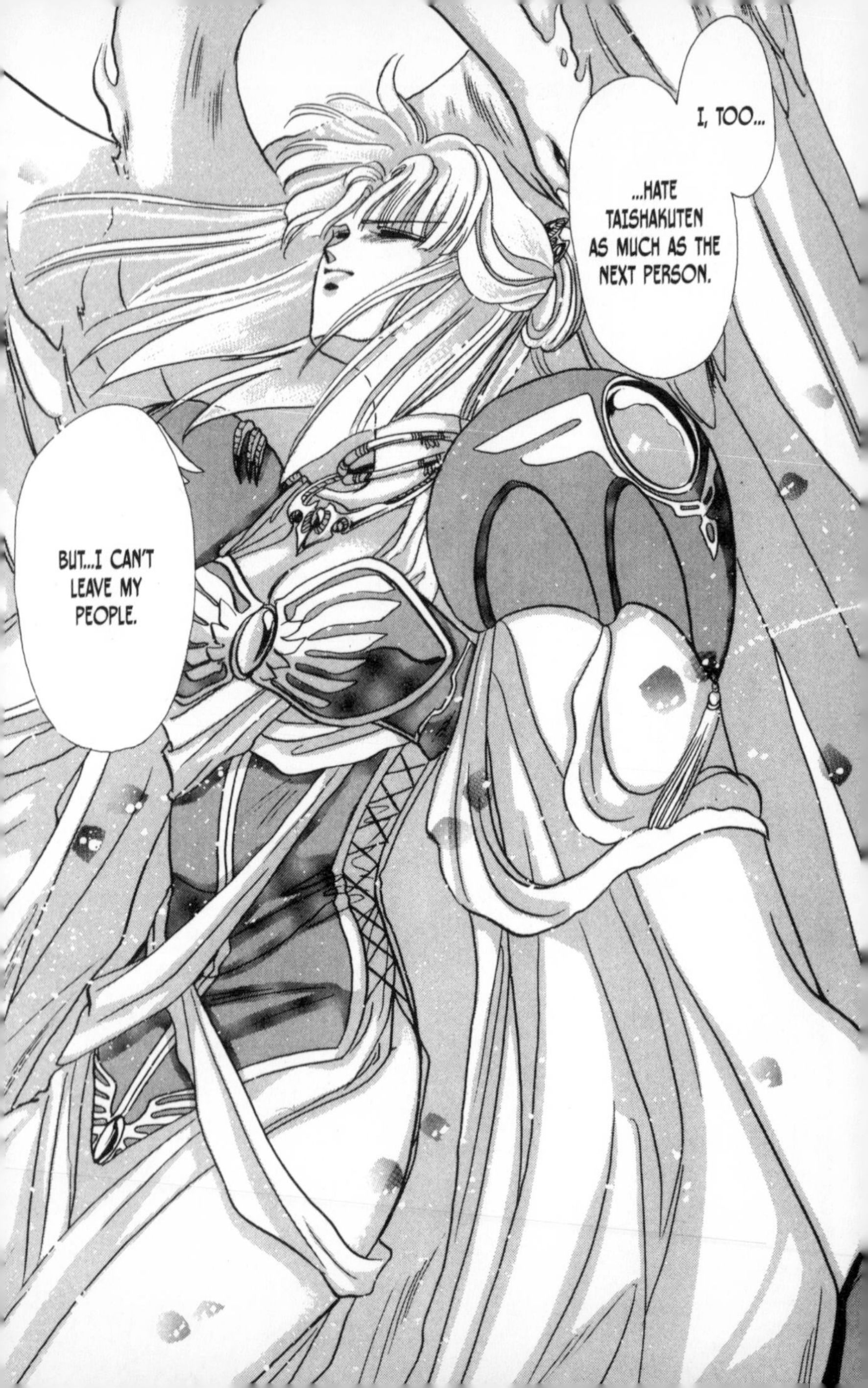

I, TOO...
...HATE TAISHAKUTEN AS MUCH AS THE NEXT PERSON.
BUT...I CAN'T LEAVE MY PEOPLE.

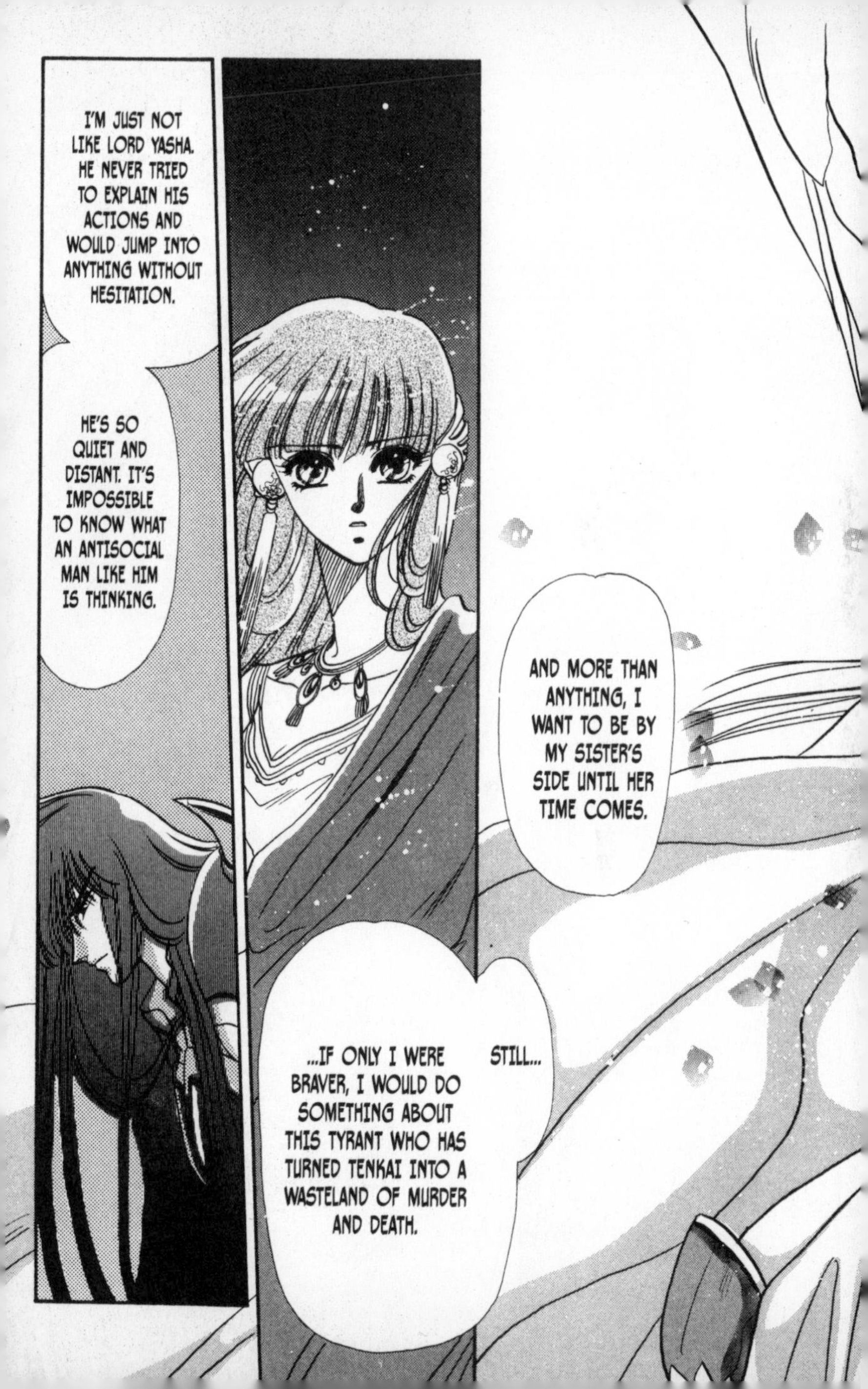
STILL...
...IF ONLY I WERE BRAVER, I WOULD DO SOMETHING ABOUT THIS TYRANT WHO HAS TURNED TENKAI INTO A WASTELAND OF MURDER AND DEATH.
I'M JUST NOT LIKE LORD YASHA. HE NEVER TRIED TO EXPLAIN HIS ACTIONS AND WOULD JUMP INTO ANYTHING WITHOUT HESITATION.
HE'S SO QUIET AND DISTANT. IT'S IMPOSSIBLE TO KNOW WHAT AN ANTISOCIAL MAN LIKE HIM IS THINKING.
AND MORE THAN ANYTHING, I WANT TO BE BY MY SISTER'S SIDE UNTIL HER TIME COMES.

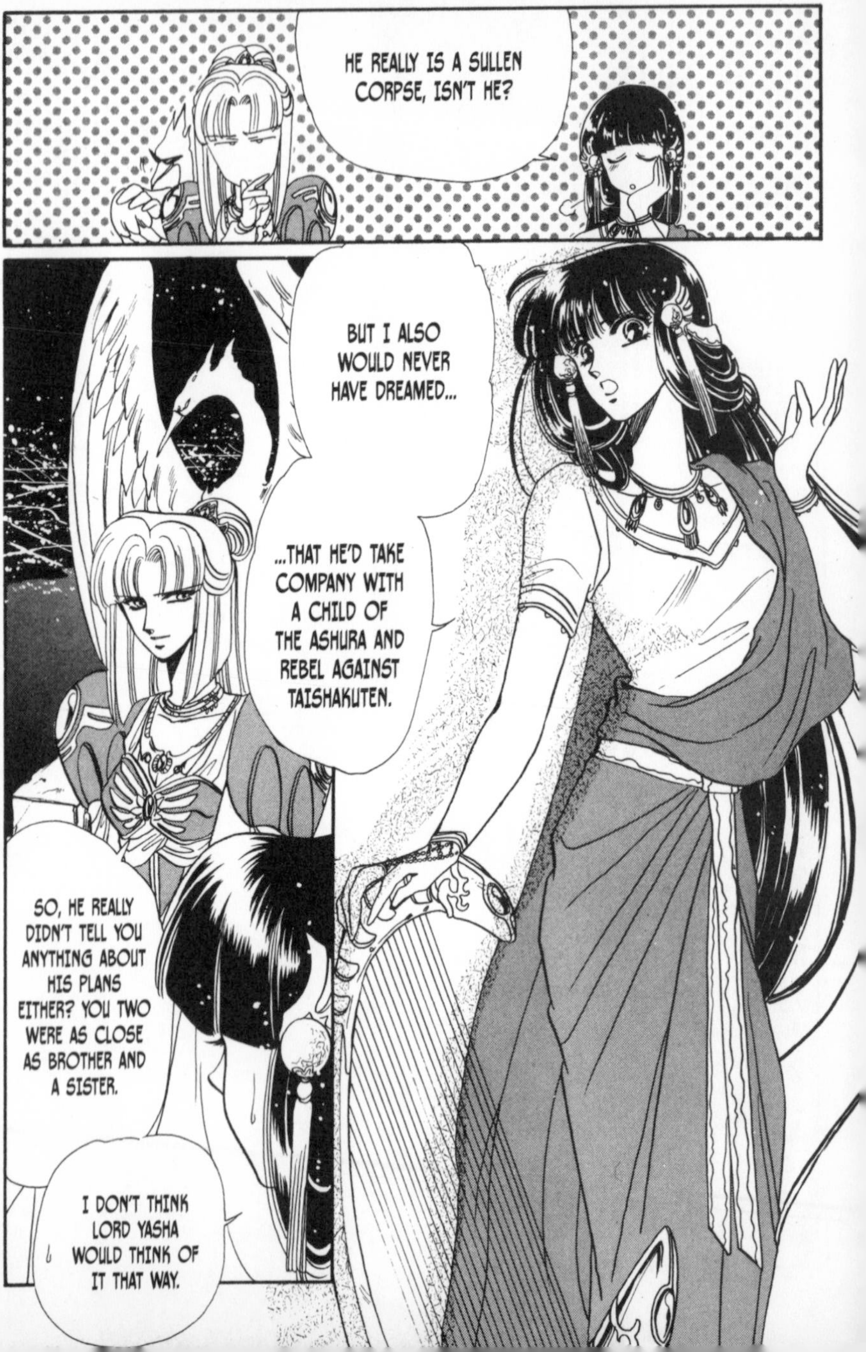
HE REALLY IS A SULLEN CORPSE, ISN'T HE?
BUT I ALSO WOULD NEVER HAVE DREAMED...
...THAT HE'D TAKE COMPANY WITH A CHILD OF THE ASHURA AND REBEL AGAINST TAISHAKUTEN.
SO, HE REALLY DIDN'T TELL YOU ANYTHING ABOUT HIS PLANS EITHER? YOU TWO WERE AS CLOSE AS BROTHER AND A SISTER.
I DON'T THINK LORD YASHA WOULD THINK OF IT THAT WAY.

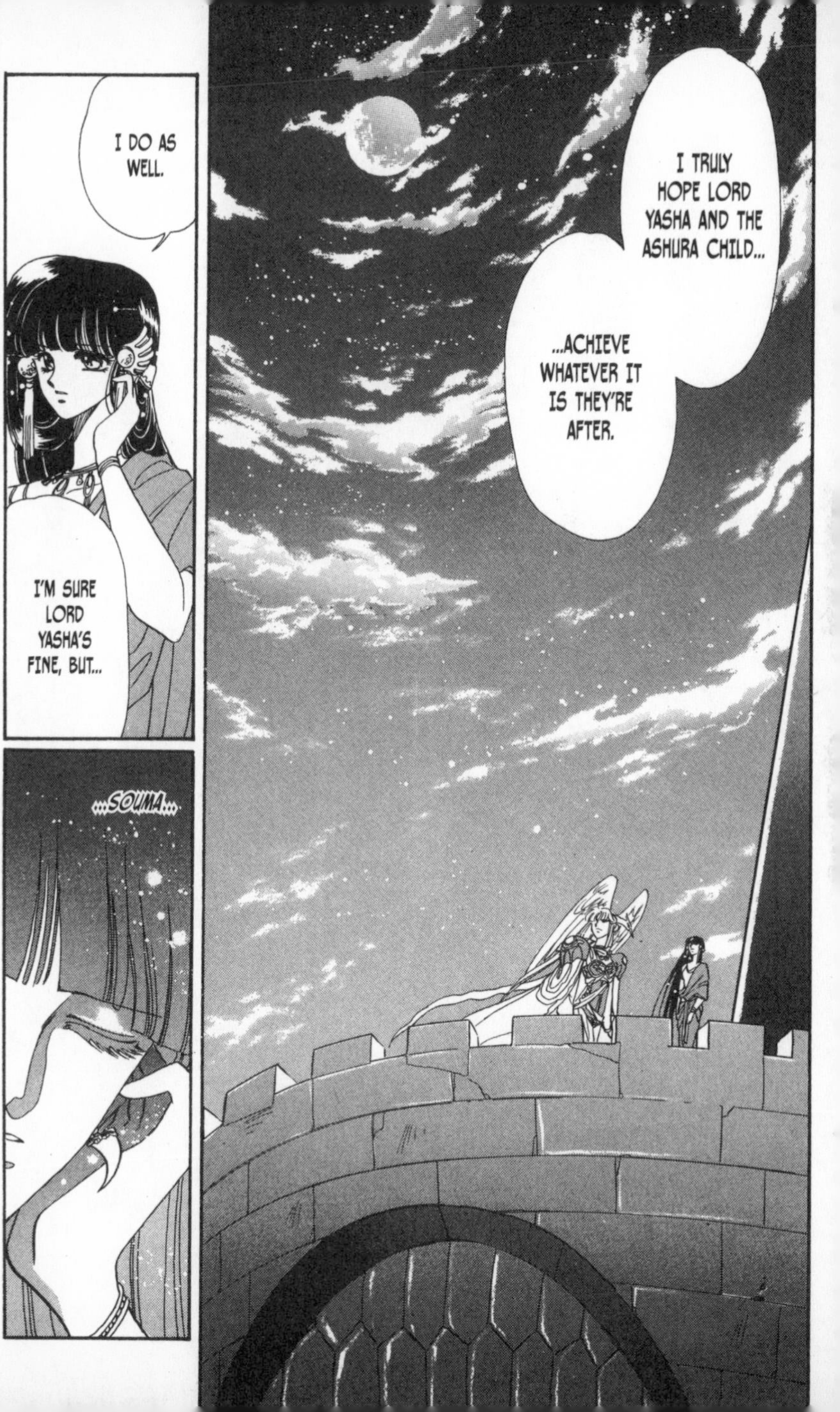
I TRULY HOPE LORD YASHA AND THE ASHURA CHILD...
...ACHIEVE WHATEVER IT IS THEY'RE AFTER.
I DO AS WELL.
I'M SURE LORD YASHA'S FINE, BUT...
...SOUMA...

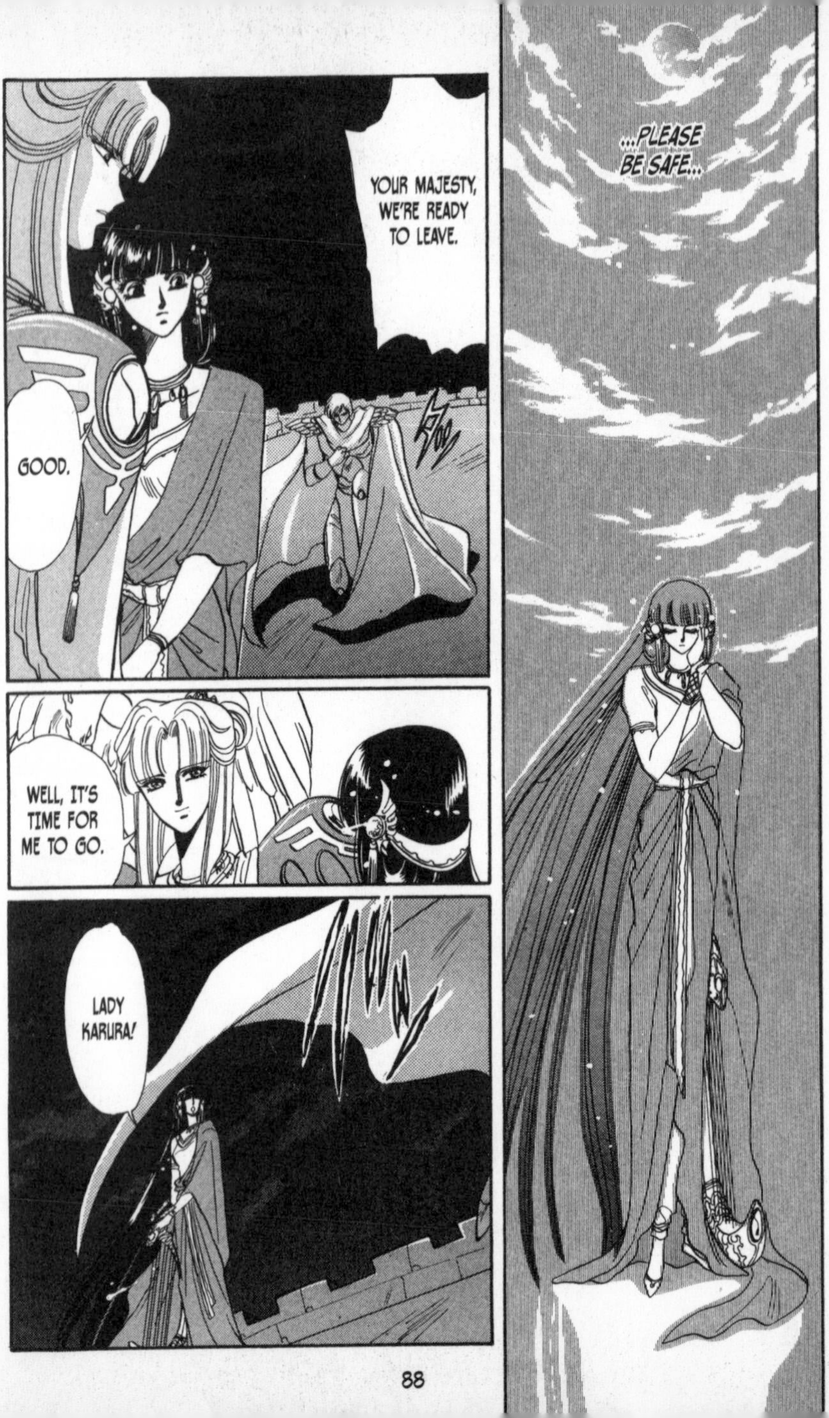

YOUR MAJESTY, WE'RE READY TO LEAVE.
GOOD.
...PLEASE BE SAFE...
WELL, IT'S TIME FOR ME TO GO.
LADY KARURA!

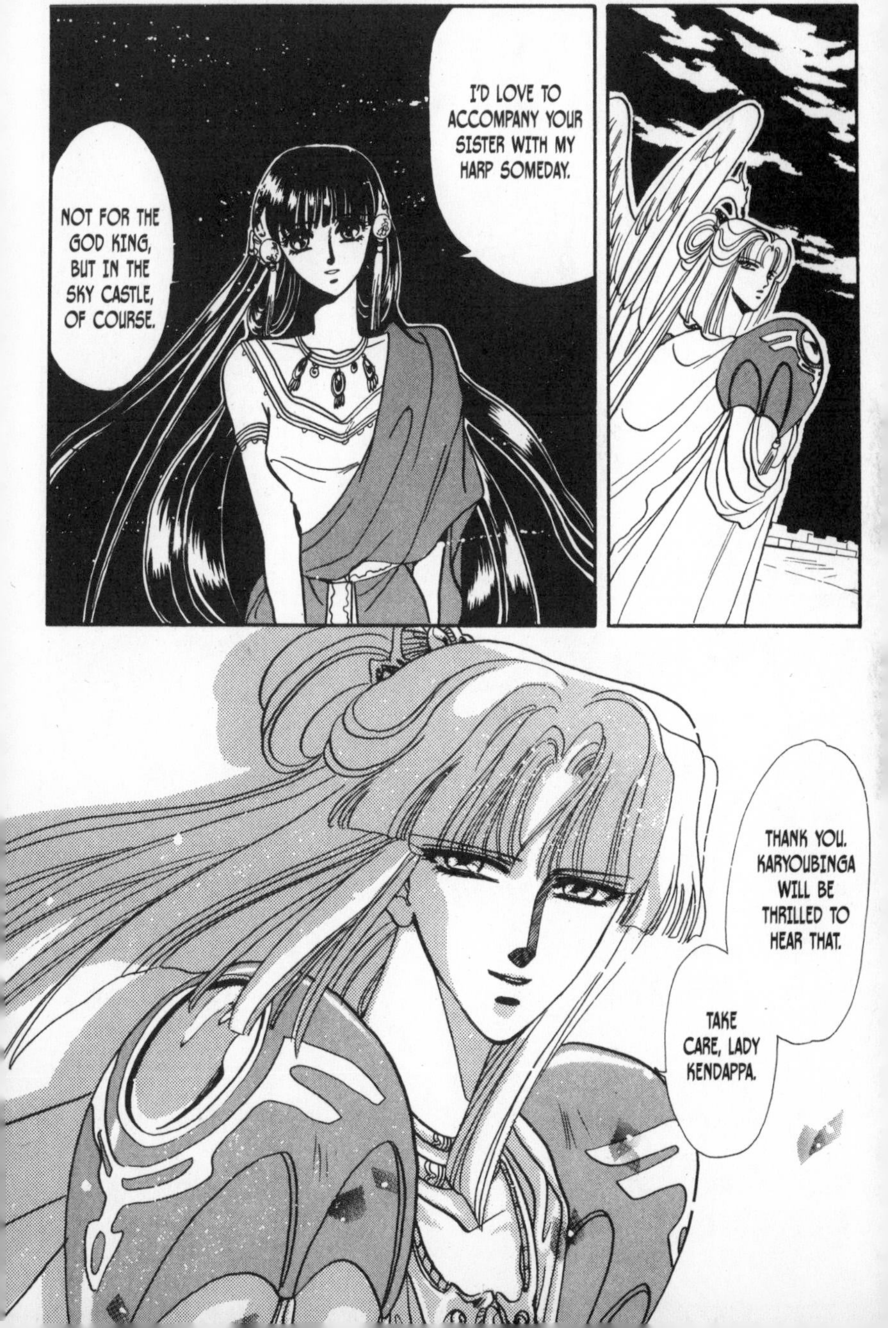
I'D LOVE TO ACCOMPANY YOUR SISTER WITH MY HARP SOMEDAY.
NOT FOR THE GOD KING, BUT IN THE SKY CASTLE, OF COURSE.
THANK YOU. KARYOUBINGA WILL BE THRILLED TO HEAR THAT.
TAKE CARE, LADY KENDAPPA.

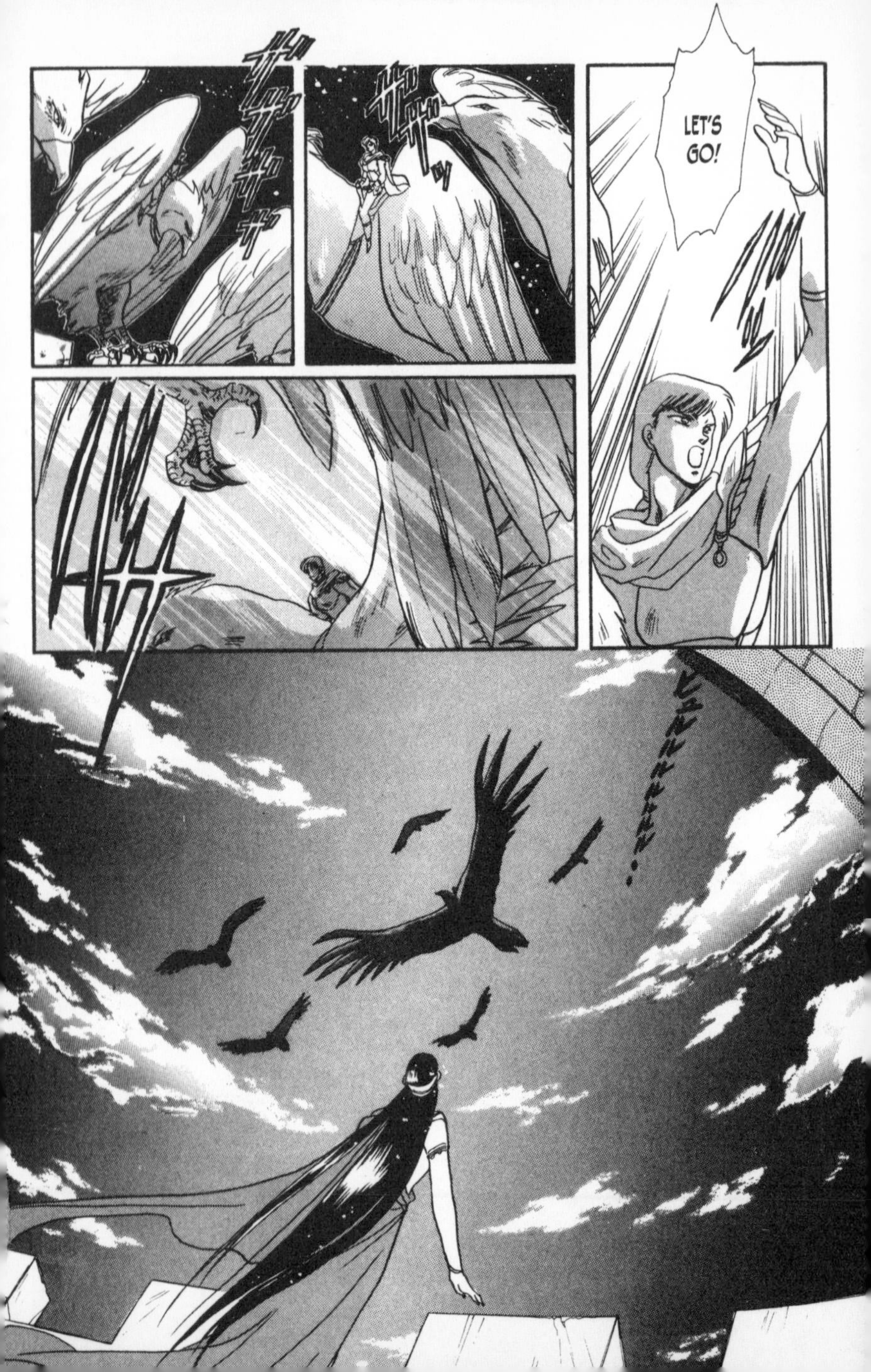
LET'S GO!

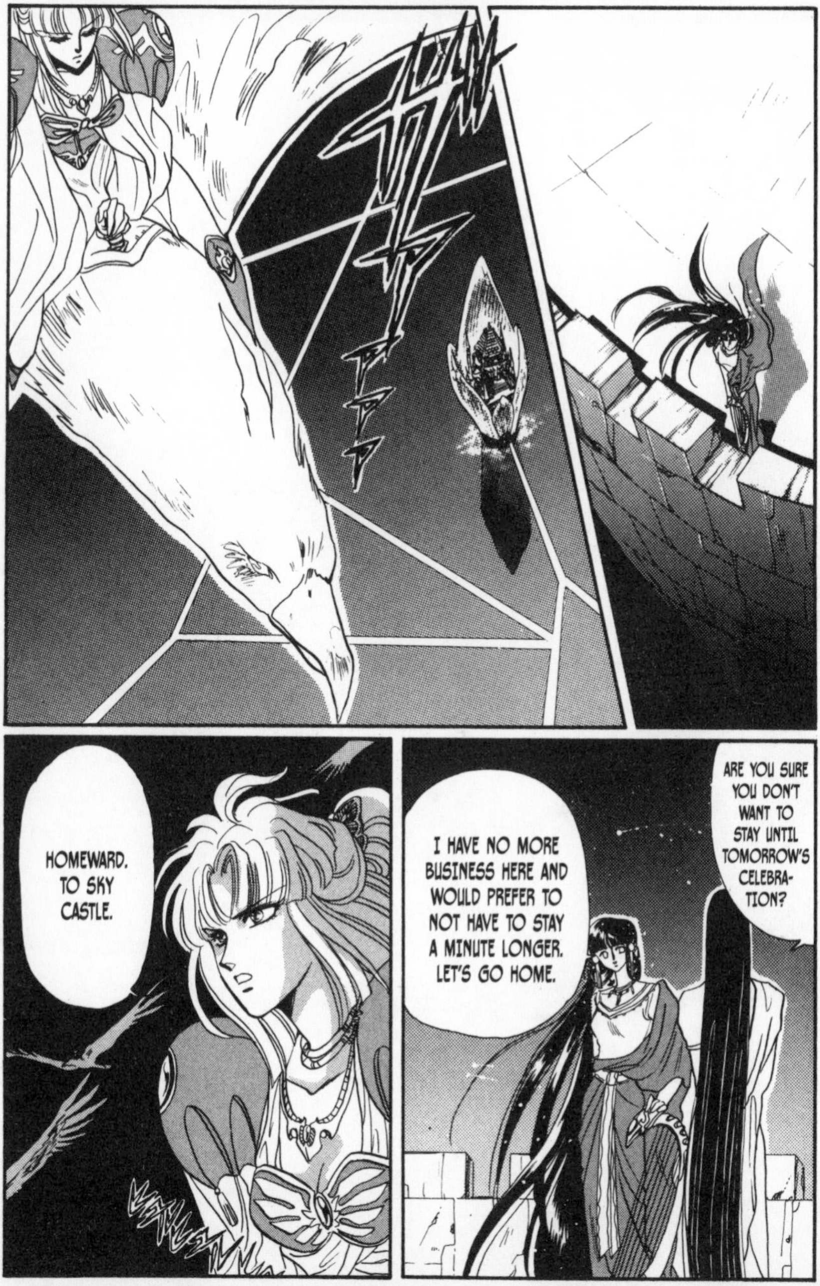

ARE YOU SURE YOU DON'T WANT TO STAY UNTIL TOMORROW'S CELEBRATION?
I HAVE NO MORE BUSINESS HERE AND WOULD PREFER TO NOT HAVE TO STAY A MINUTE LONGER. LET'S GO HOME.
HOMEWARD. TO SKY CASTLE.

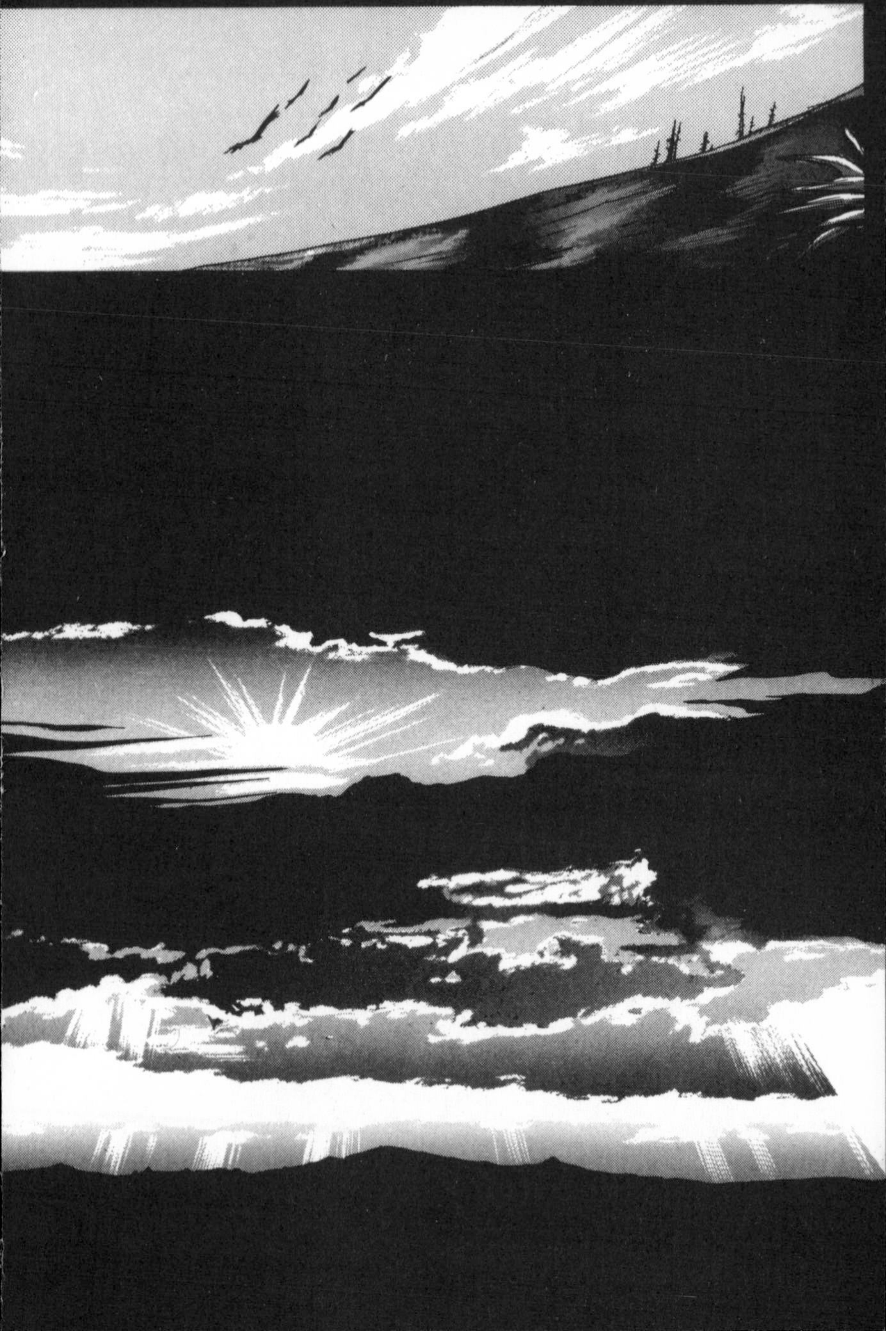

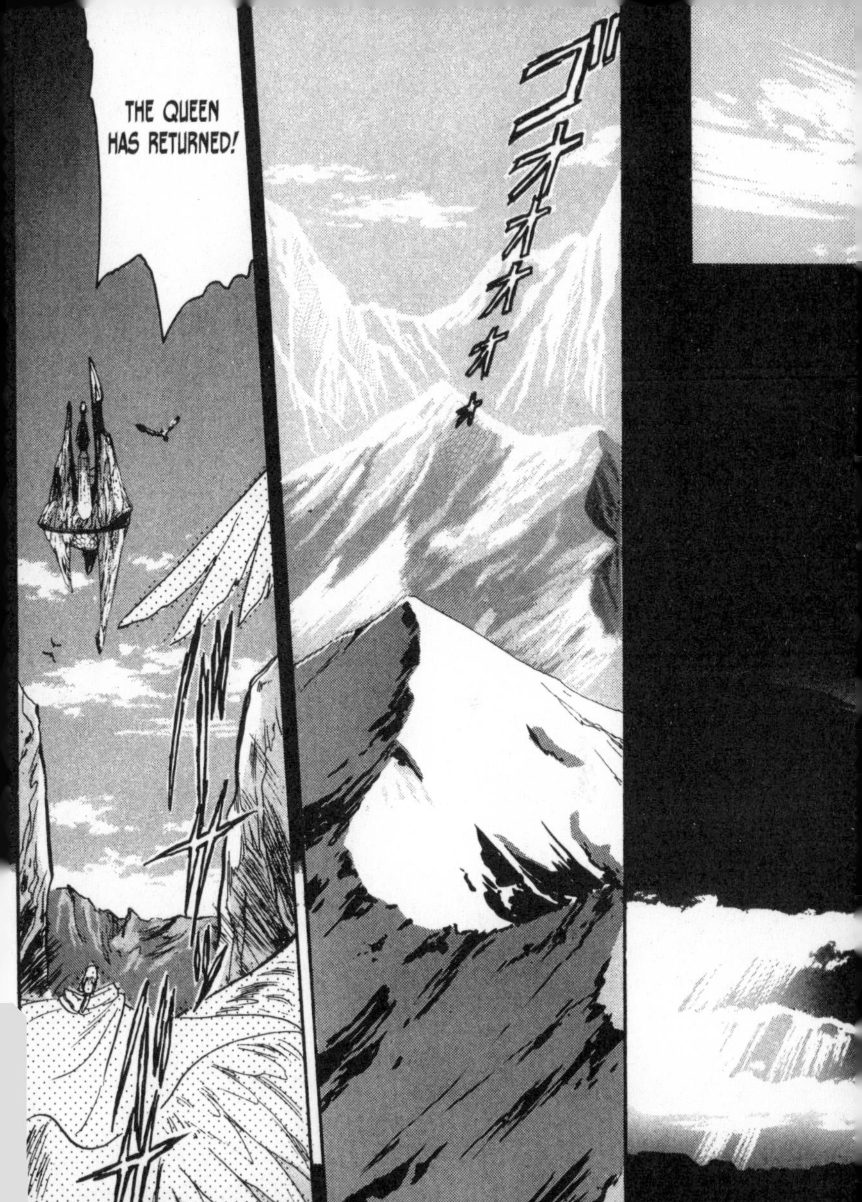
THE QUEEN HAS RETURNED!

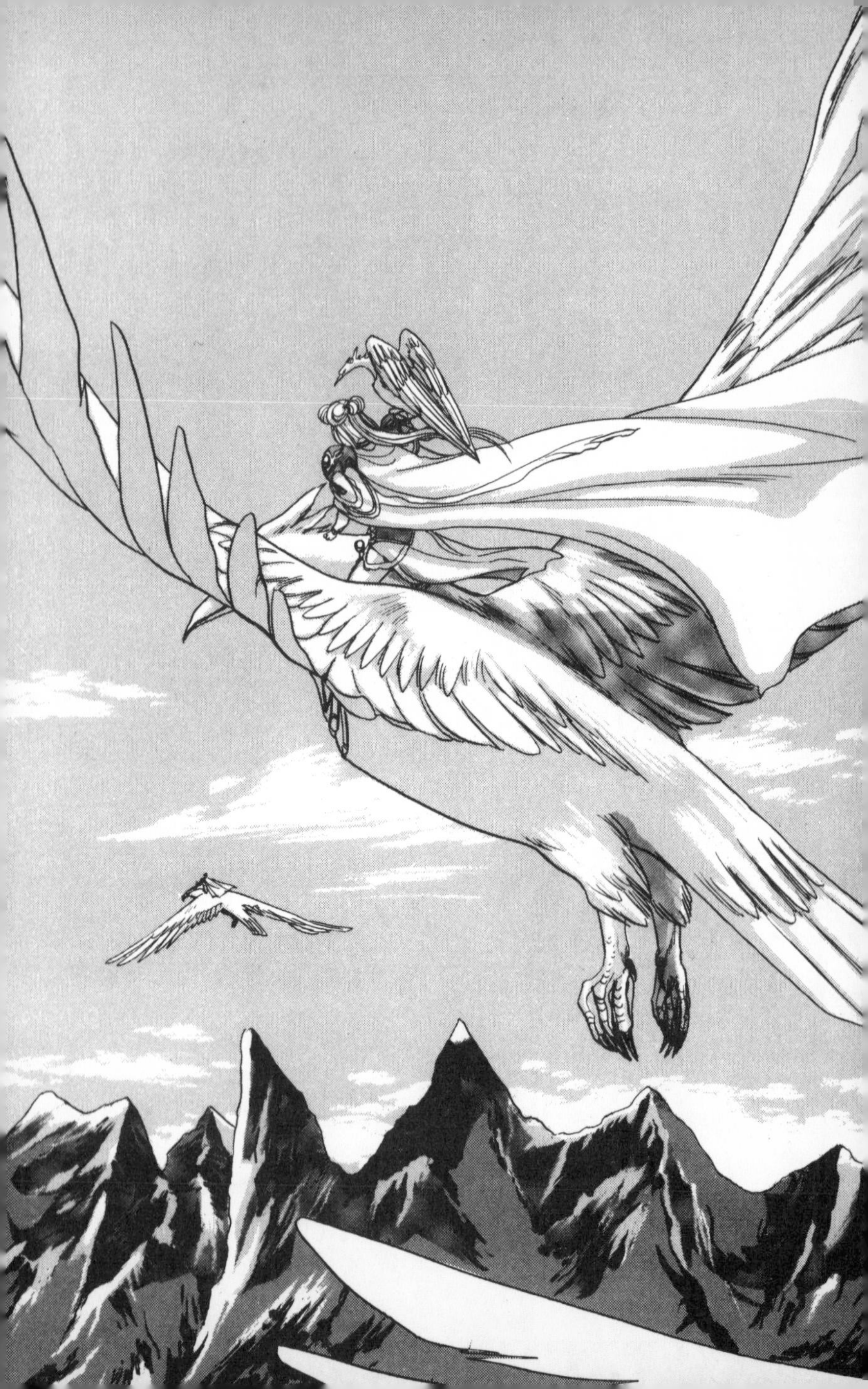

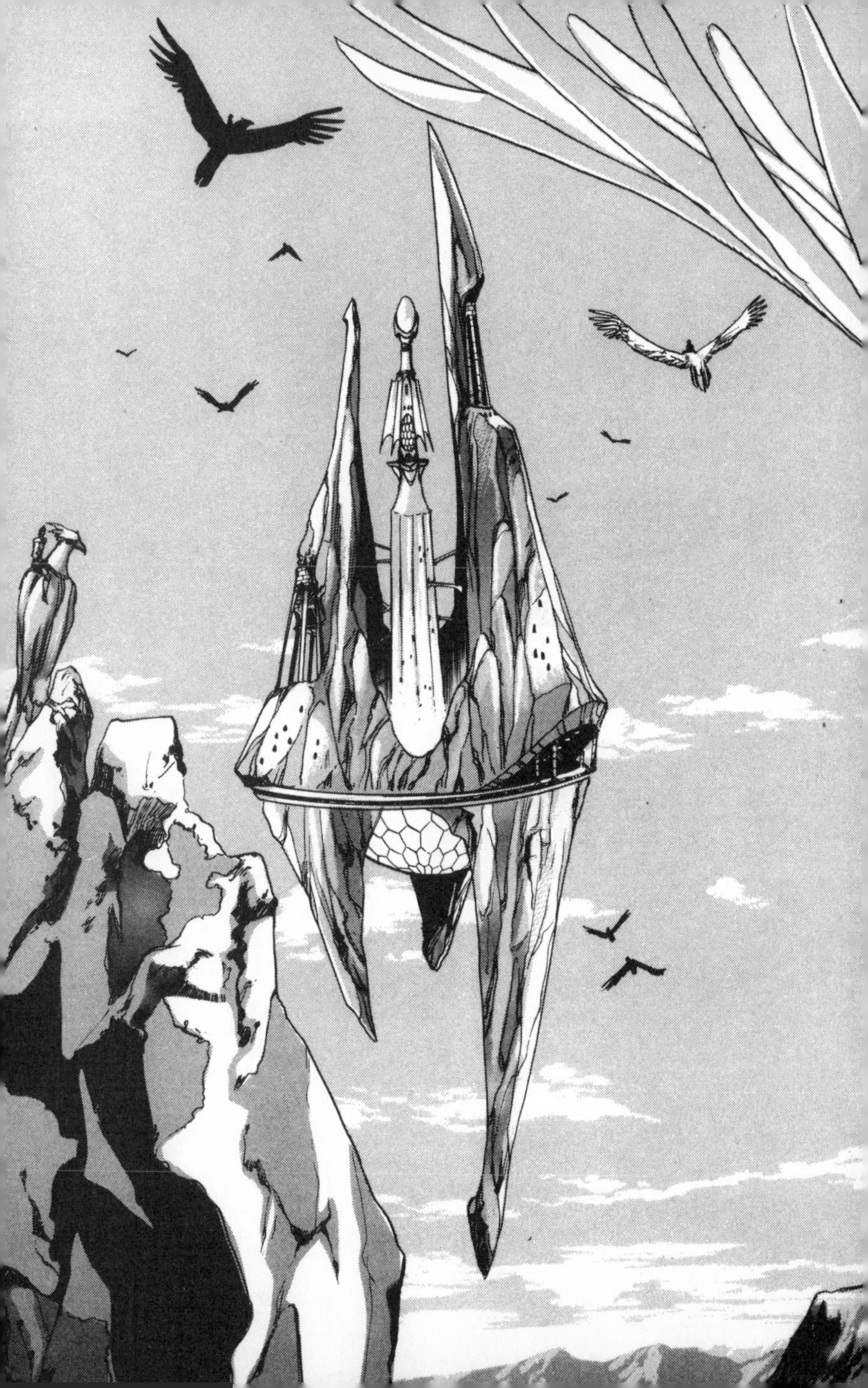

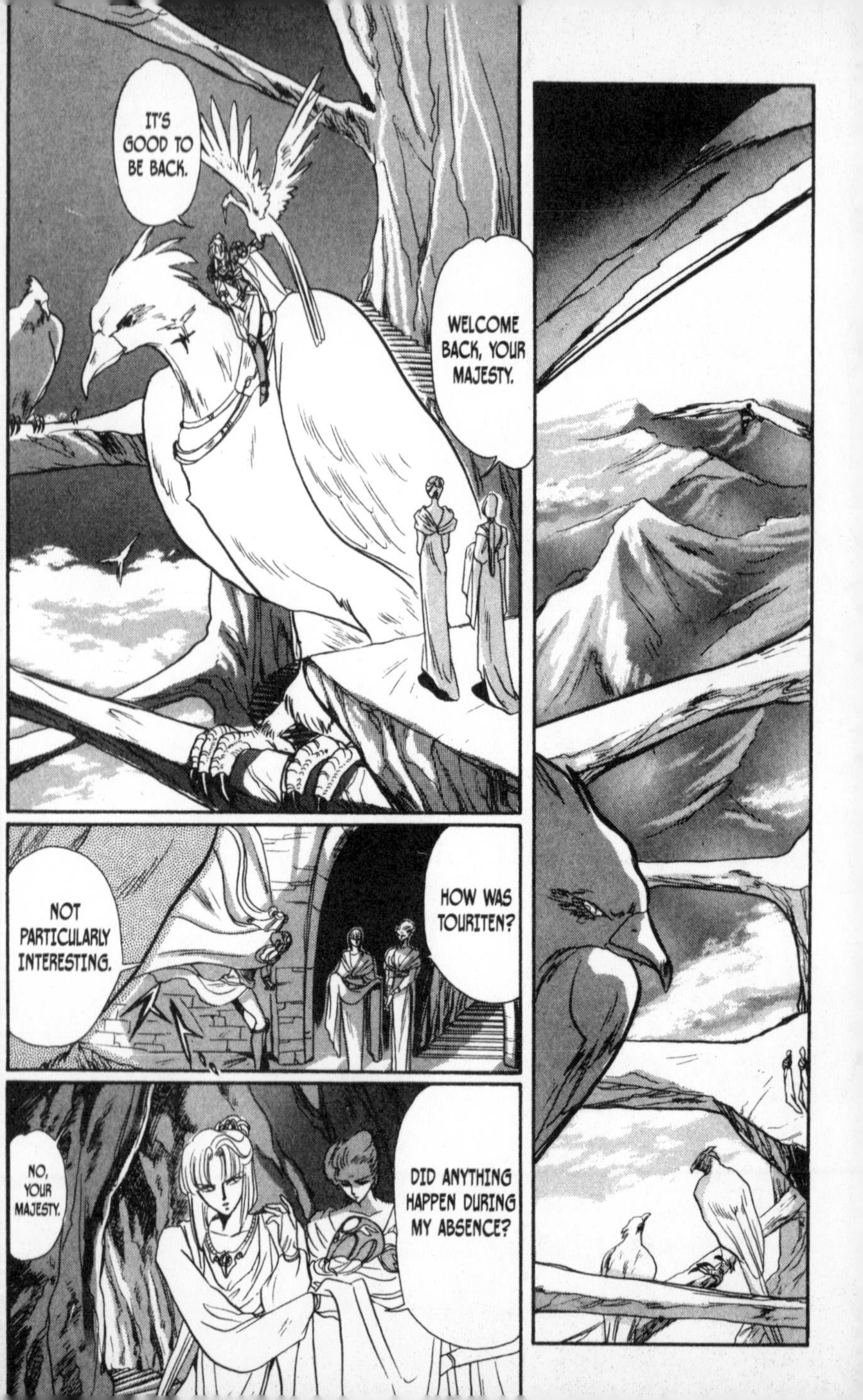
WELCOME BACK, YOUR MAJESTY.
IT'S GOOD TO BE BACK.
HOW WAS TOURITEN?
NOT PARTICULARLY INTERESTING.
DID ANYTHING HAPPEN DURING MY ABSENCE?
NO, YOUR MAJESTY.

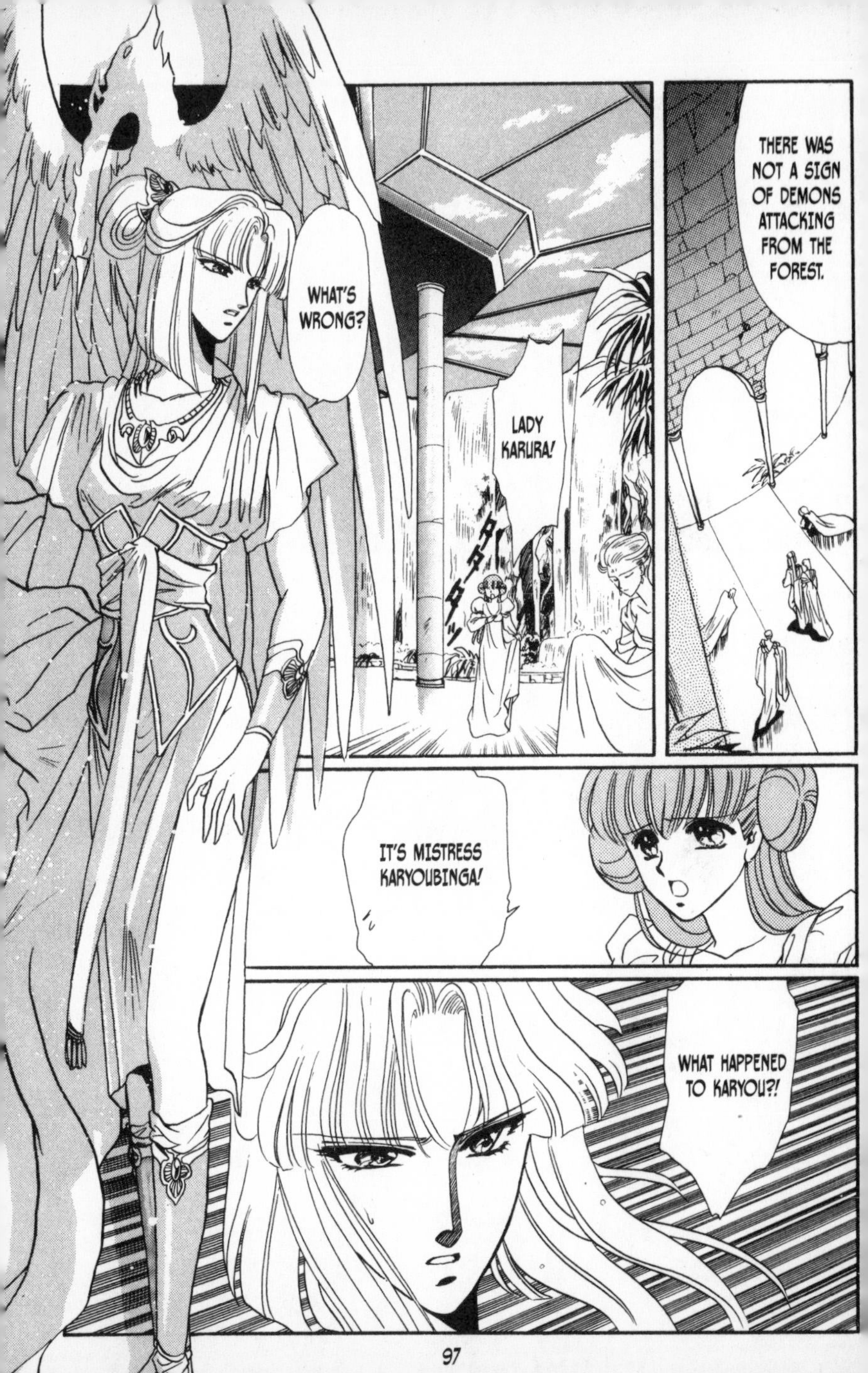
THERE WAS NOT A SIGN OF DEMONS ATTACKING FROM THE FOREST.
LADY KARURA!
WHAT'S WRONG?
IT'S MISTRESS KARYOUBINGA!
WHAT HAPPENED TO KARYOU?!

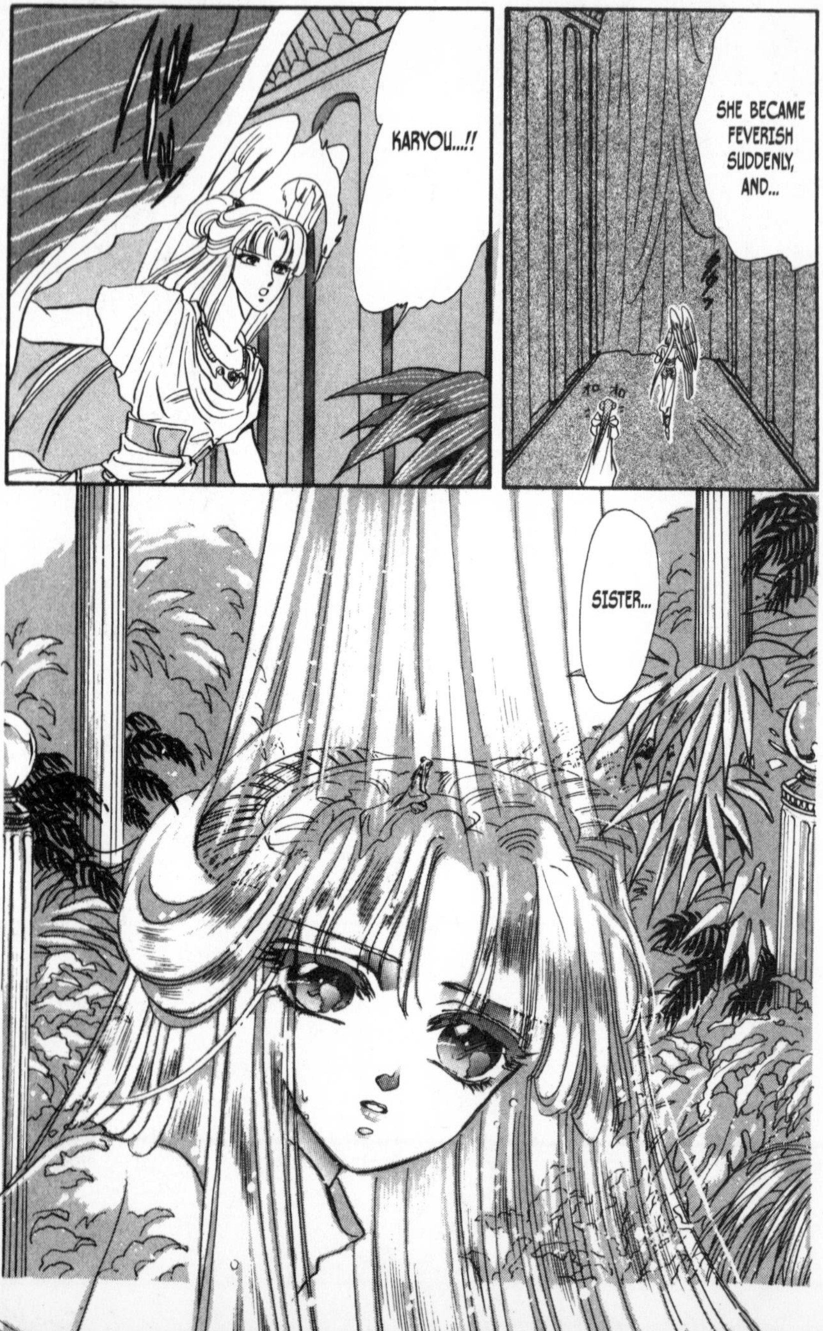
SHE BECAME FEVERISH SUDDENLY, AND...
KARYOU...!!
SISTER...

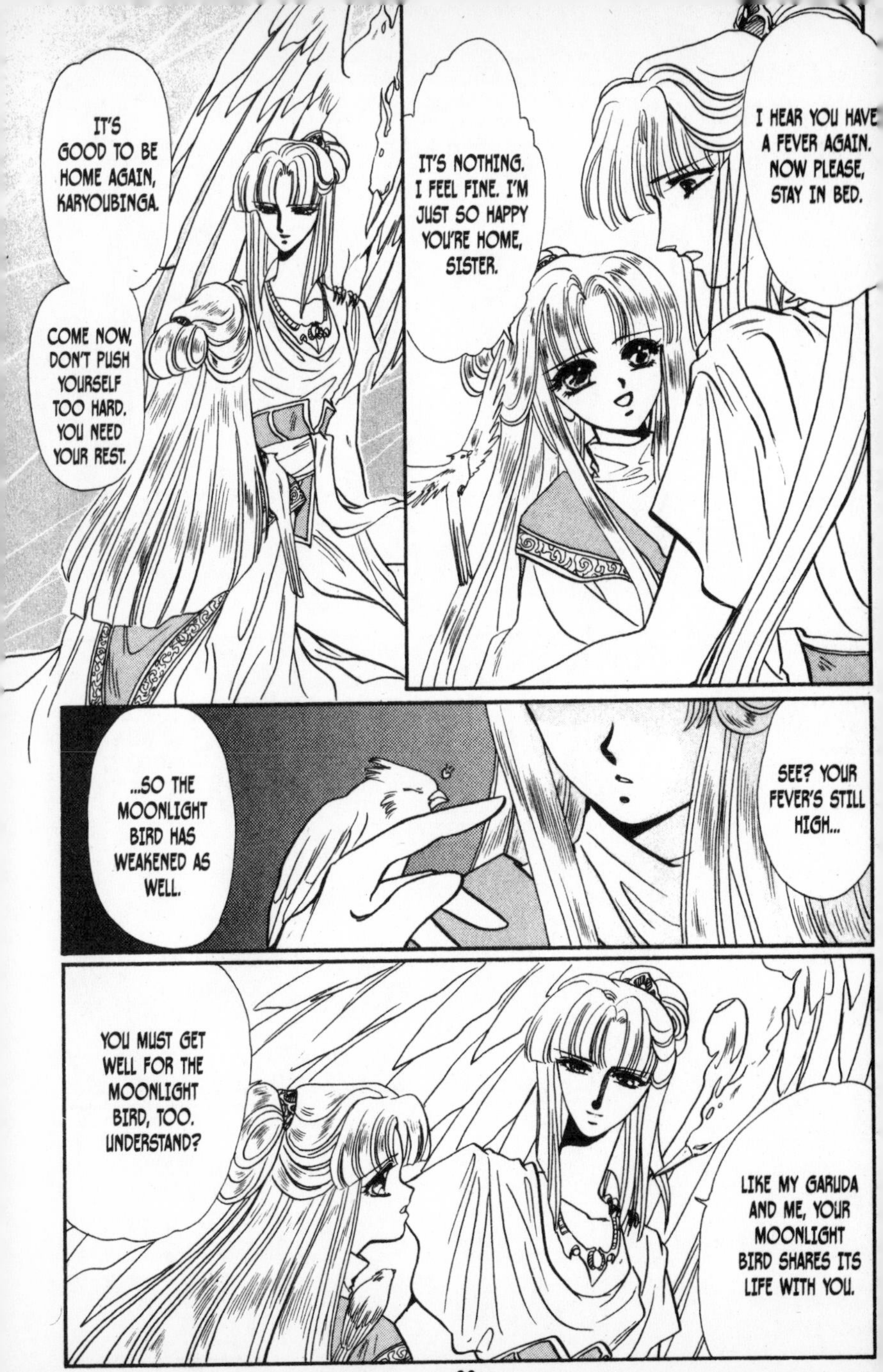
I HEAR YOU HAVE A FEVER AGAIN. NOW PLEASE, STAY IN BED.
IT'S NOTHING. I FEEL FINE. I'M JUST SO HAPPY YOU'RE HOME, SISTER.
IT'S GOOD TO BE HOME AGAIN, KARYOUBINGA.
COME NOW, DON'T PUSH YOURSELF TOO HARD. YOU NEED YOUR REST.
SEE? YOUR FEVER'S STILL HIGH...
...SO THE MOONLIGHT BIRD HAS WEAKENED AS WELL.
LIKE MY GARUDA AND ME, YOUR MOONLIGHT BIRD SHARES ITS LIFE WITH YOU.
YOU MUST GET WELL FOR THE MOONLIGHT BIRD, TOO. UNDERSTAND?

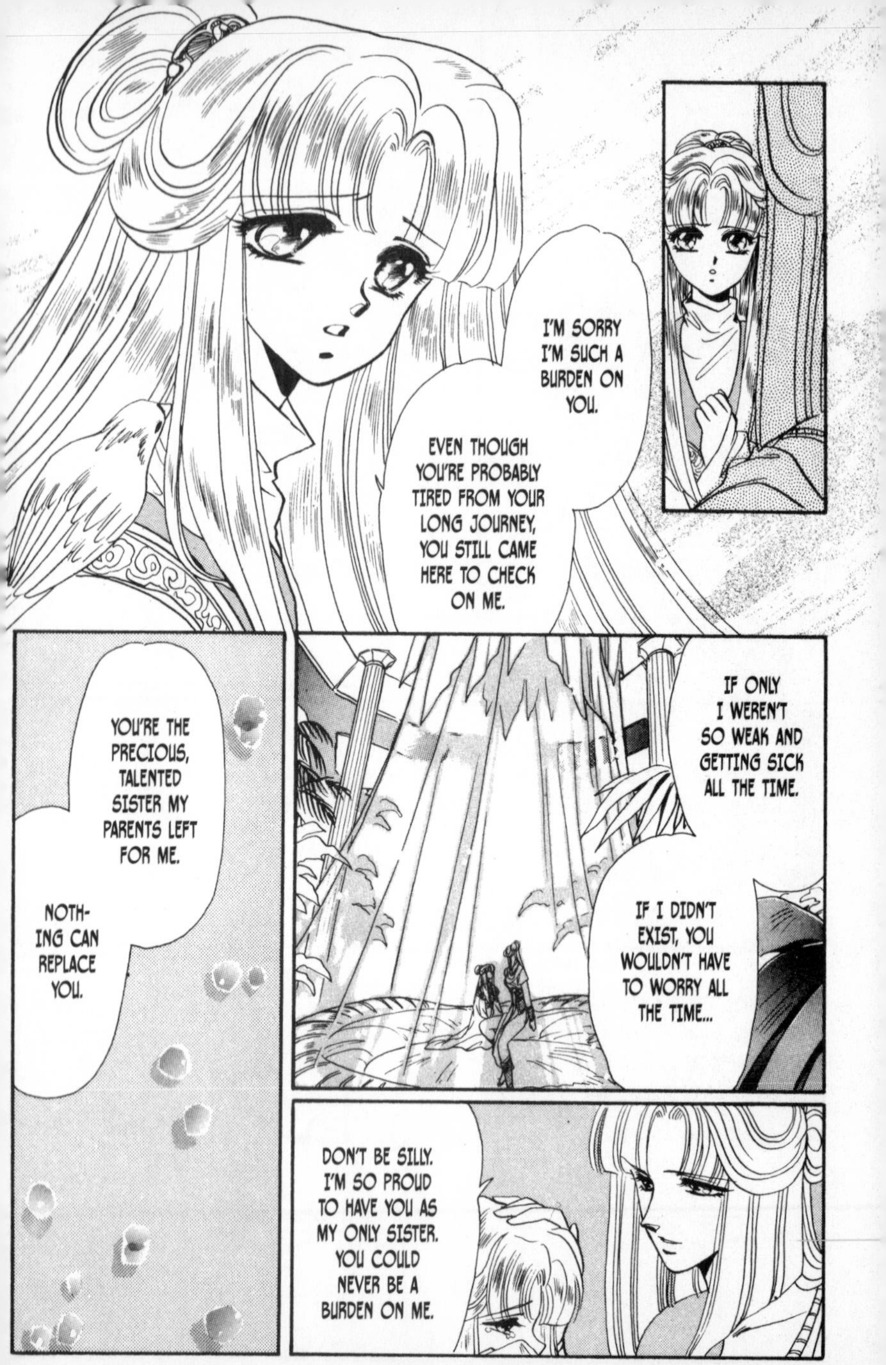
I'M SORRY I'M SUCH A BURDEN ON YOU.
EVEN THOUGH YOU'RE PROBABLY TIRED FROM YOUR LONG JOURNEY, YOU STILL CAME HERE TO CHECK ON ME.
IF ONLY I WEREN'T SO WEAK AND GETTING SICK ALL THE TIME.
IF I DIDN'T EXIST, YOU WOULDN'T HAVE TO WORRY ALL THE TIME...
DON'T BE SILLY. I'M SO PROUD TO HAVE YOU AS MY ONLY SISTER. YOU COULD NEVER BE A BURDEN ON ME.
YOU'RE THE PRECIOUS, TALENTED SISTER MY PARENTS LEFT FOR ME.
NOTH-ING CAN REPLACE YOU.

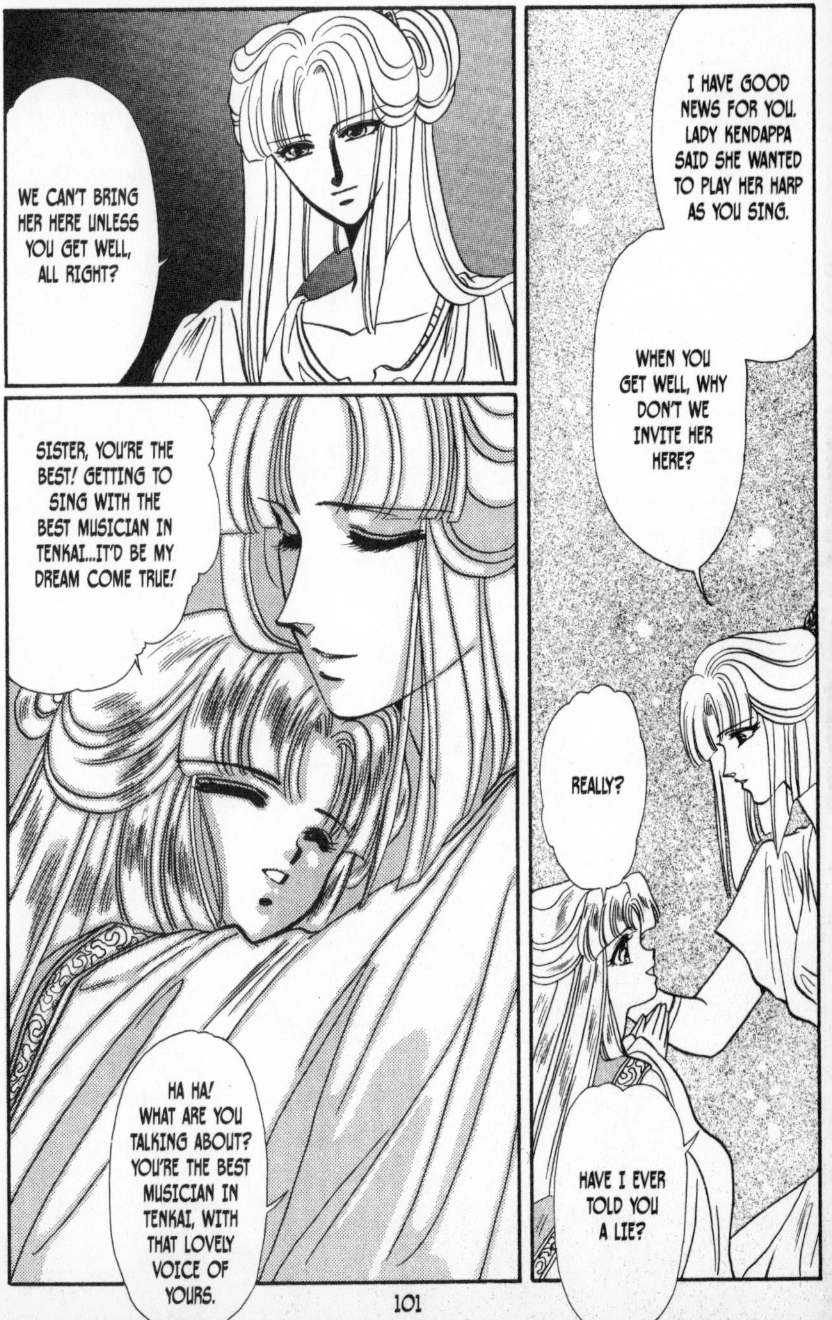
I HAVE GOOD NEWS FOR YOU. LADY KENDAPPA SAID SHE WANTED TO PLAY HER HARP AS YOU SING.
WHEN YOU GET WELL, WHY DON'T WE INVITE HER HERE?
REALLY?
HAVE I EVER TOLD YOU A LIE?
WE CAN'T BRING HER HERE UNLESS YOU GET WELL, ALL RIGHT?
SISTER, YOU'RE THE BEST! GETTING TO SING WITH THE BEST MUSICIAN IN TENKAI...IT'D BE MY DREAM COME TRUE!
HA HA! WHAT ARE YOU TALKING ABOUT? YOU'RE THE BEST MUSICIAN IN TENKAI, WITH THAT LOVELY VOICE OF YOURS.

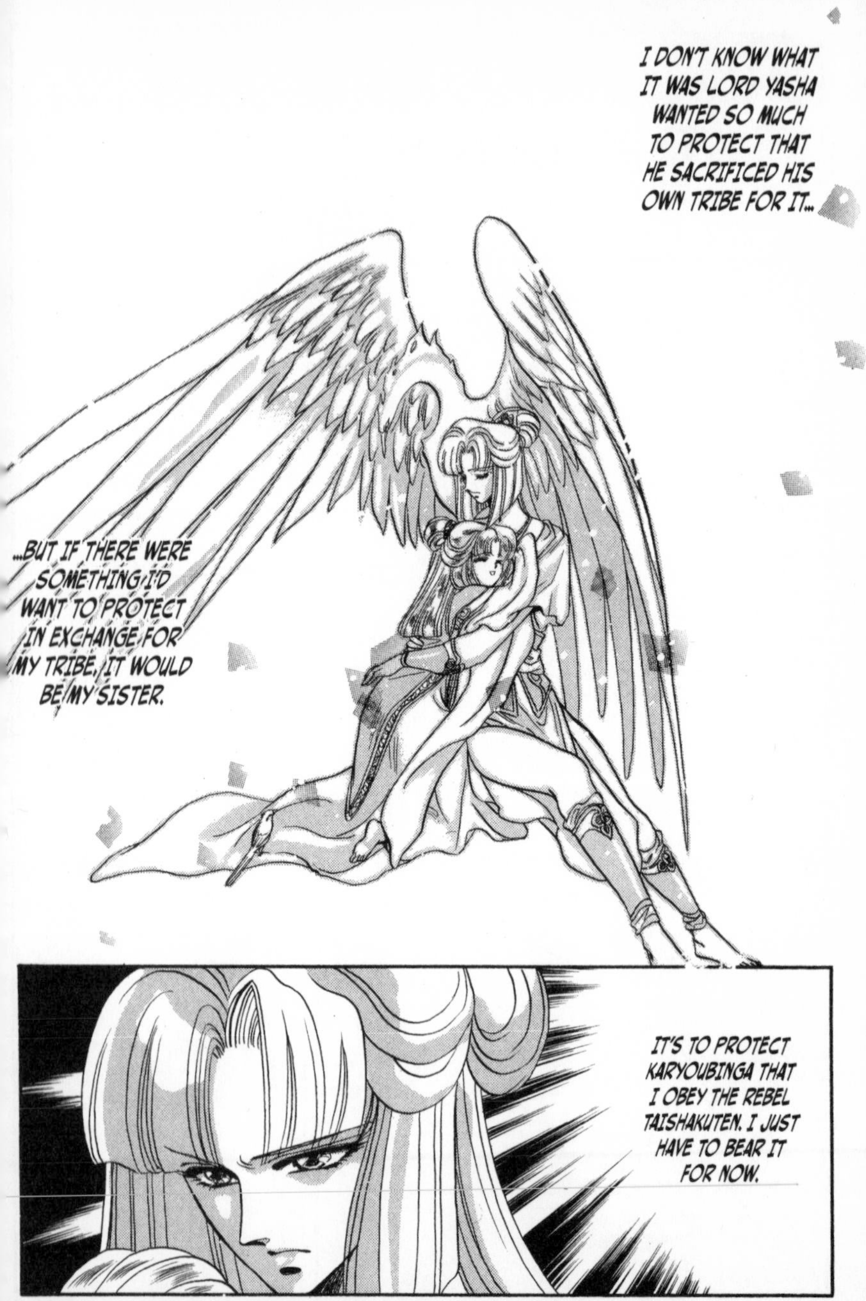
I DON'T KNOW WHAT IT WAS LORD YASHA WANTED SO MUCH TO PROTECT THAT HE SACRIFICED HIS OWN TRIBE FOR IT...
...BUT IF THERE WERE SOMETHING I'D WANT TO PROTECT IN EXCHANGE FOR MY TRIBE, IT WOULD BE MY SISTER.
IT'S TO PROTECT KARYOUBINGA THAT I OBEY THE REBEL TAISHAKUTEN. I JUST HAVE TO BEAR IT FOR NOW.

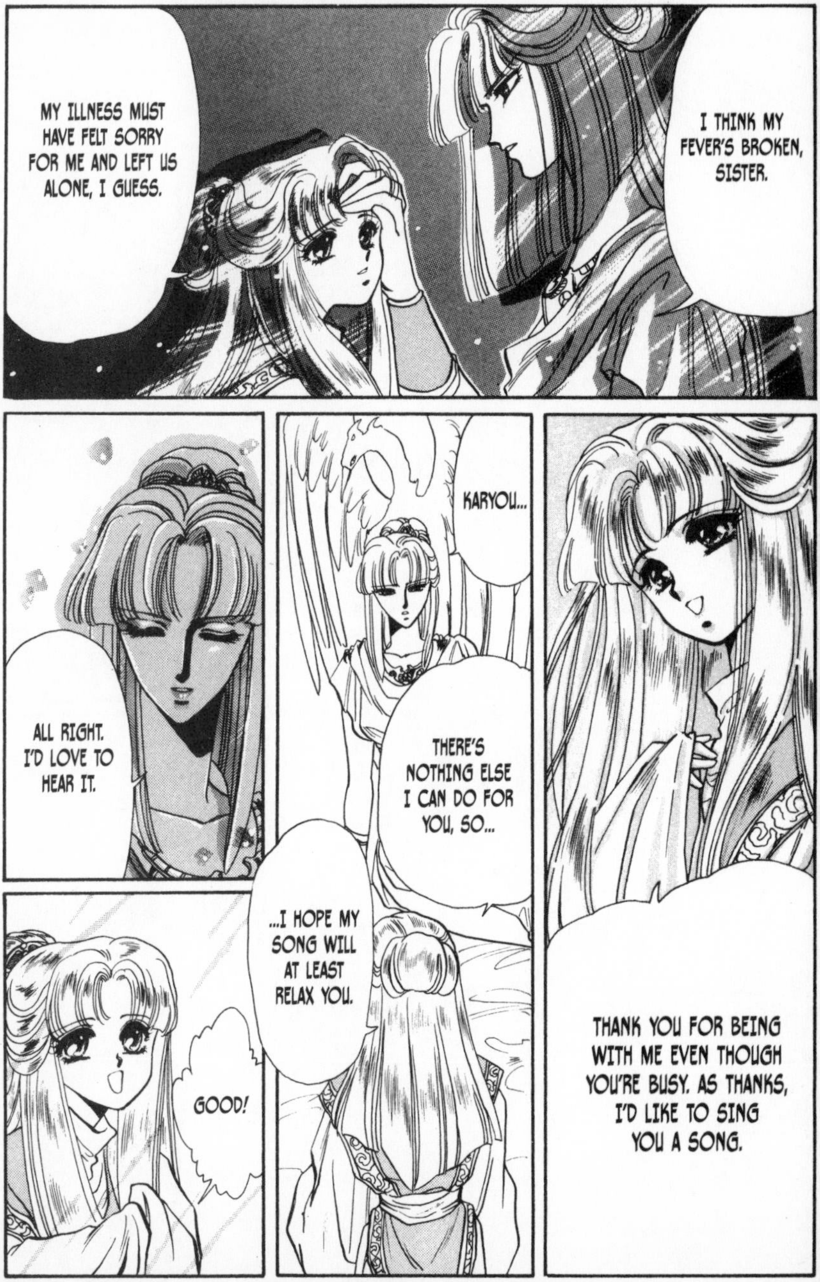
I THINK MY FEVER'S BROKEN, SISTER.
MY ILLNESS MUST HAVE FELT SORRY FOR ME AND LEFT US ALONE, I GUESS.
THANK YOU FOR BEING WITH ME EVEN THOUGH YOU'RE BUSY. AS THANKS, I'D LIKE TO SING YOU A SONG.
KARYOU...
ALL RIGHT. I'D LOVE TO HEAR IT.
THERE'S NOTHING ELSE I CAN DO FOR YOU, SO...
...I HOPE MY SONG WILL AT LEAST RELAX YOU.
GOOD!

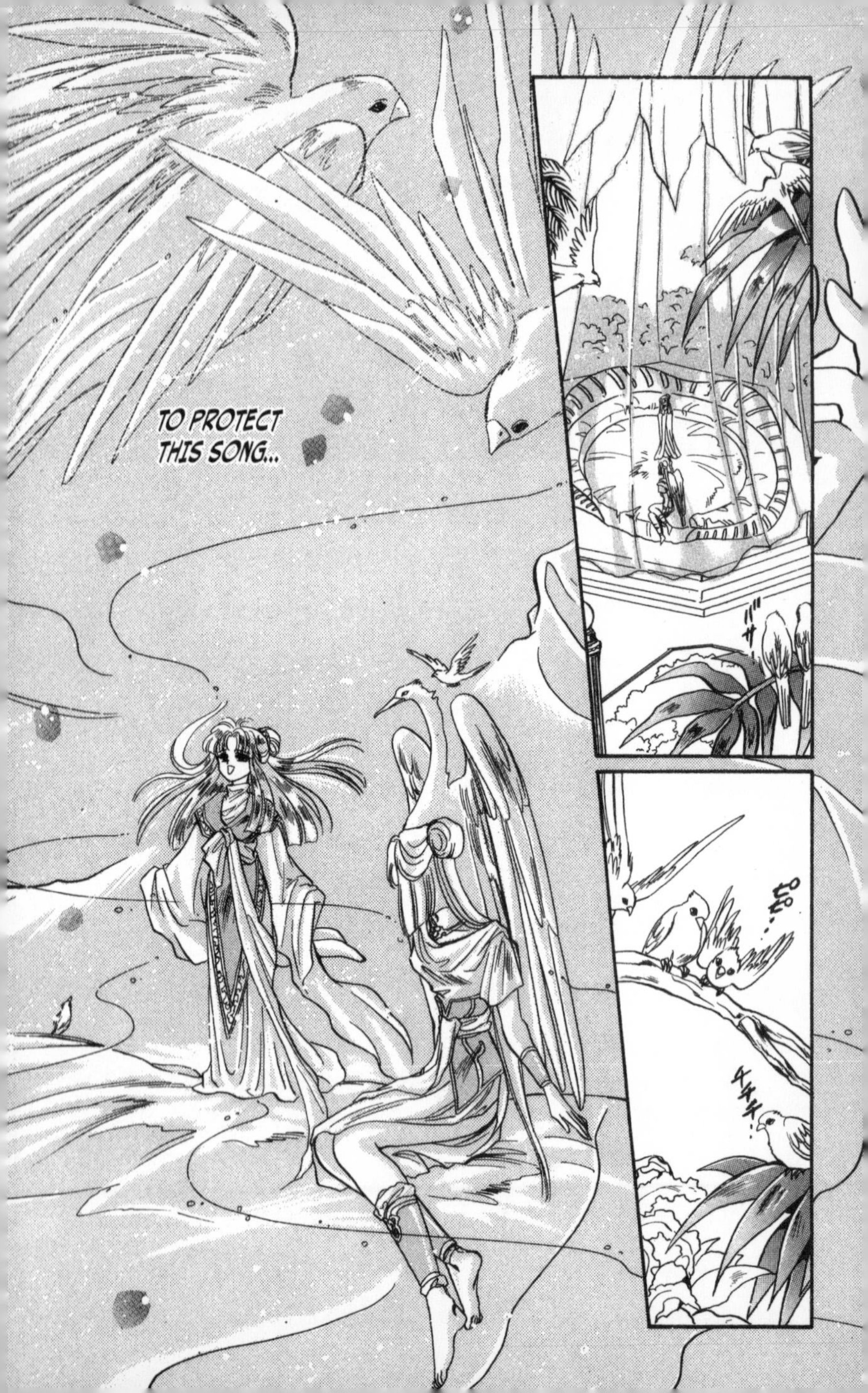
TO PROTECT THIS SONG...

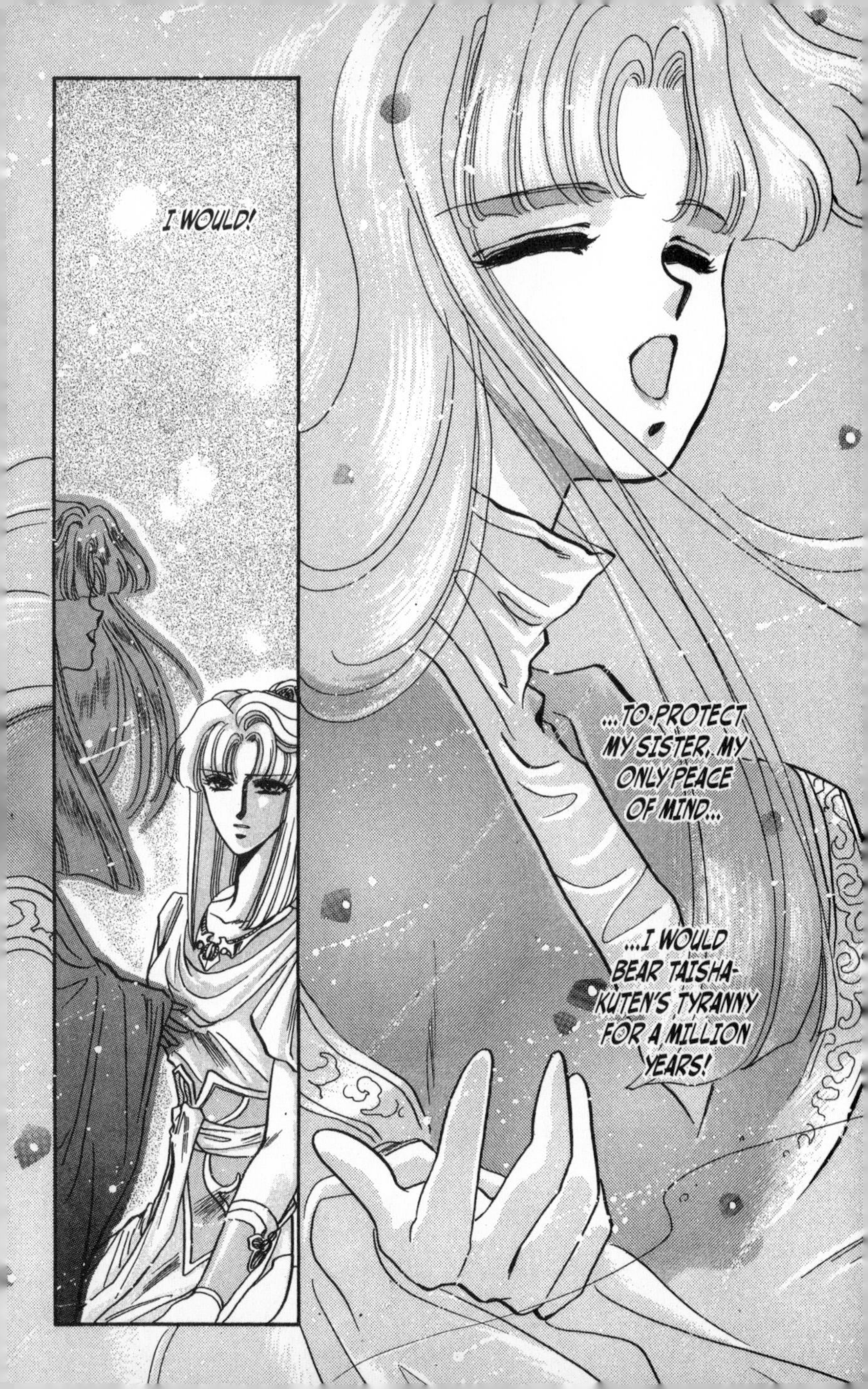
...TO PROTECT MY SISTER, MY ONLY PEACE OF MIND...
...I WOULD BEAR TAISHA-KUTEN'S TYRANNY FOR A MILLION YEARS!
I WOULD!

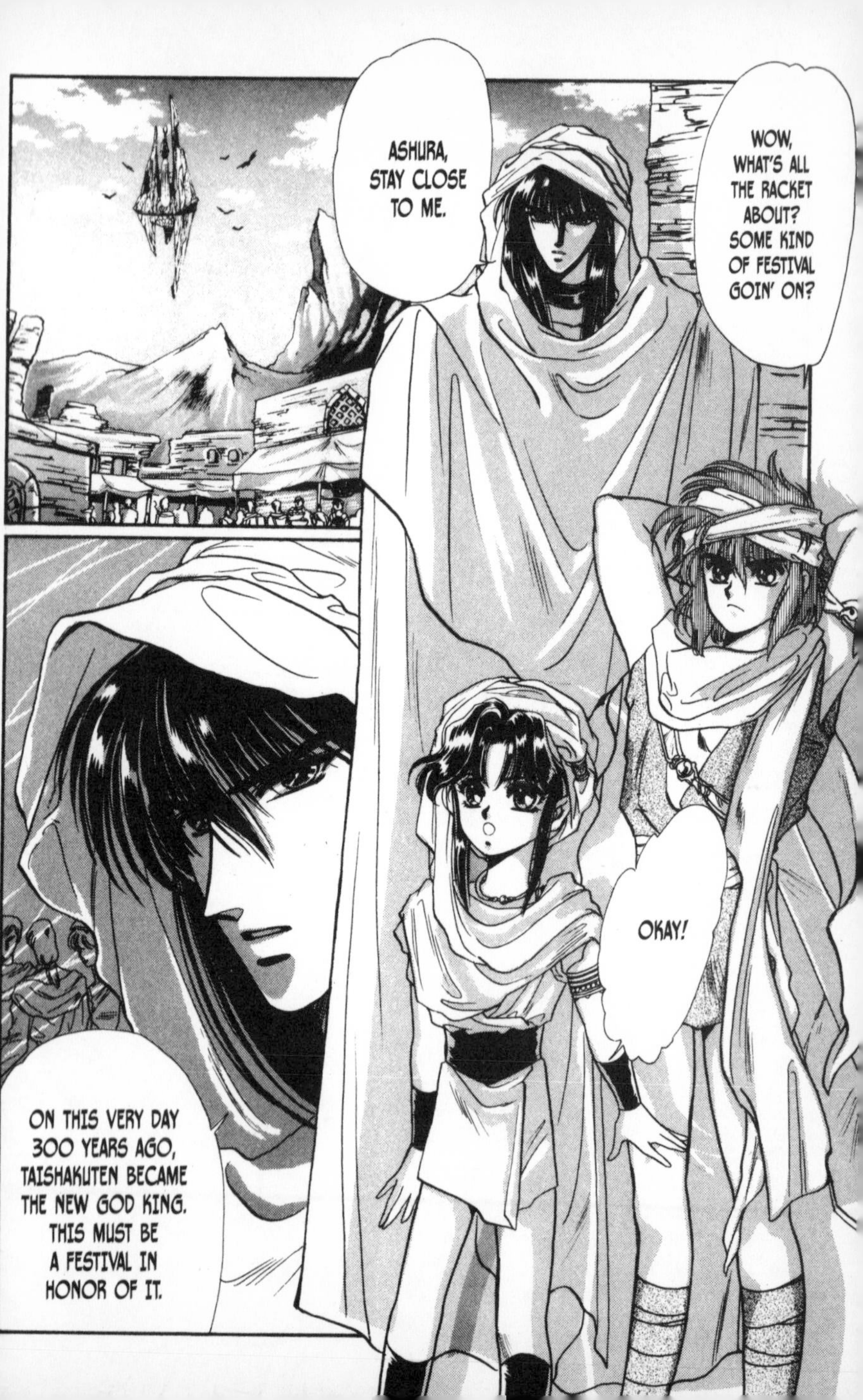
WOW, WHAT'S ALL THE RACKET ABOUT? SOME KIND OF FESTIVAL GOIN' ON?
ASHURA, STAY CLOSE TO ME.
OKAY!
ON THIS VERY DAY 300 YEARS AGO, TAISHAKUTEN BECAME THE NEW GOD KING. THIS MUST BE A FESTIVAL IN HONOR OF IT.

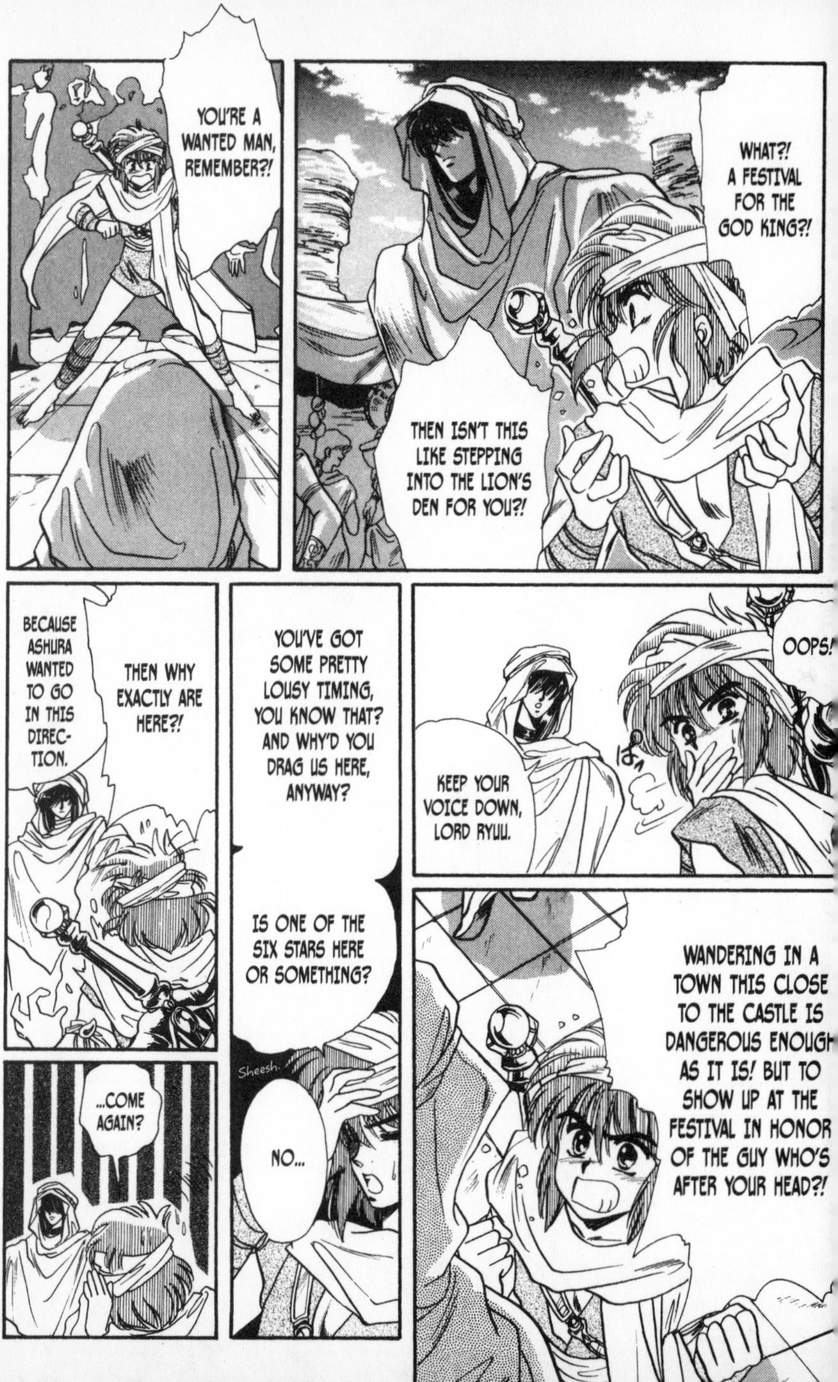
WHAT?! A FESTIVAL FOR THE GOD KING?!
THEN ISN'T THIS LIKE STEPPING INTO THE LION'S DEN FOR YOU?!
YOU'RE A WANTED MAN, REMEMBER?!
WANDERING IN A TOWN THIS CLOSE TO THE CASTLE IS DANGEROUS ENOUGH AS IT IS! BUT TO SHOW UP AT THE FESTIVAL IN HONOR OF THE GUY WHO'S AFTER YOUR HEAD?!
OOPS!
KEEP YOUR VOICE DOWN, LORD RYUU.
YOU'VE GOT SOME PRETTY LOUSY TIMING, YOU KNOW THAT? AND WHY'D YOU DRAG US HERE, ANYWAY?
IS ONE OF THE SIX STARS HERE OR SOMETHING?
Sheesh.
NO...
THEN WHY EXACTLY ARE HERE?!
BECAUSE ASHURA WANTED TO GO IN THIS DIREC-TION.
...COME AGAIN?

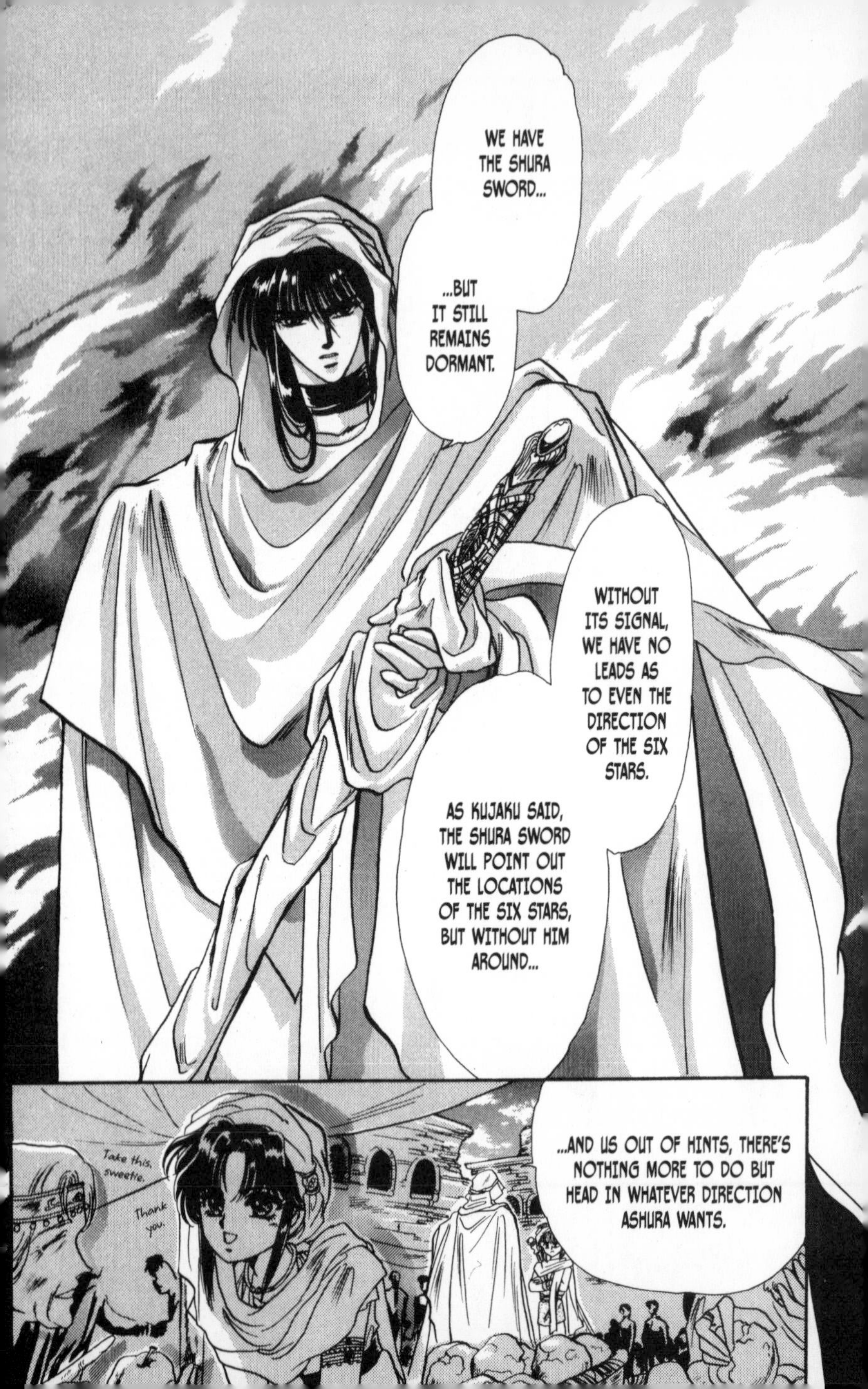
WE HAVE THE SHURA SWORD...
...BUT IT STILL REMAINS DORMANT.
WITHOUT ITS SIGNAL, WE HAVE NO LEADS AS TO EVEN THE DIRECTION OF THE SIX STARS.
AS KUJAKU SAID, THE SHURA SWORD WILL POINT OUT THE LOCATIONS OF THE SIX STARS, BUT WITHOUT HIM AROUND...
...AND US OUT OF HINTS, THERE'S NOTHING MORE TO DO BUT HEAD IN WHATEVER DIRECTION ASHURA WANTS.
Take this, sweetie.
Thank you.

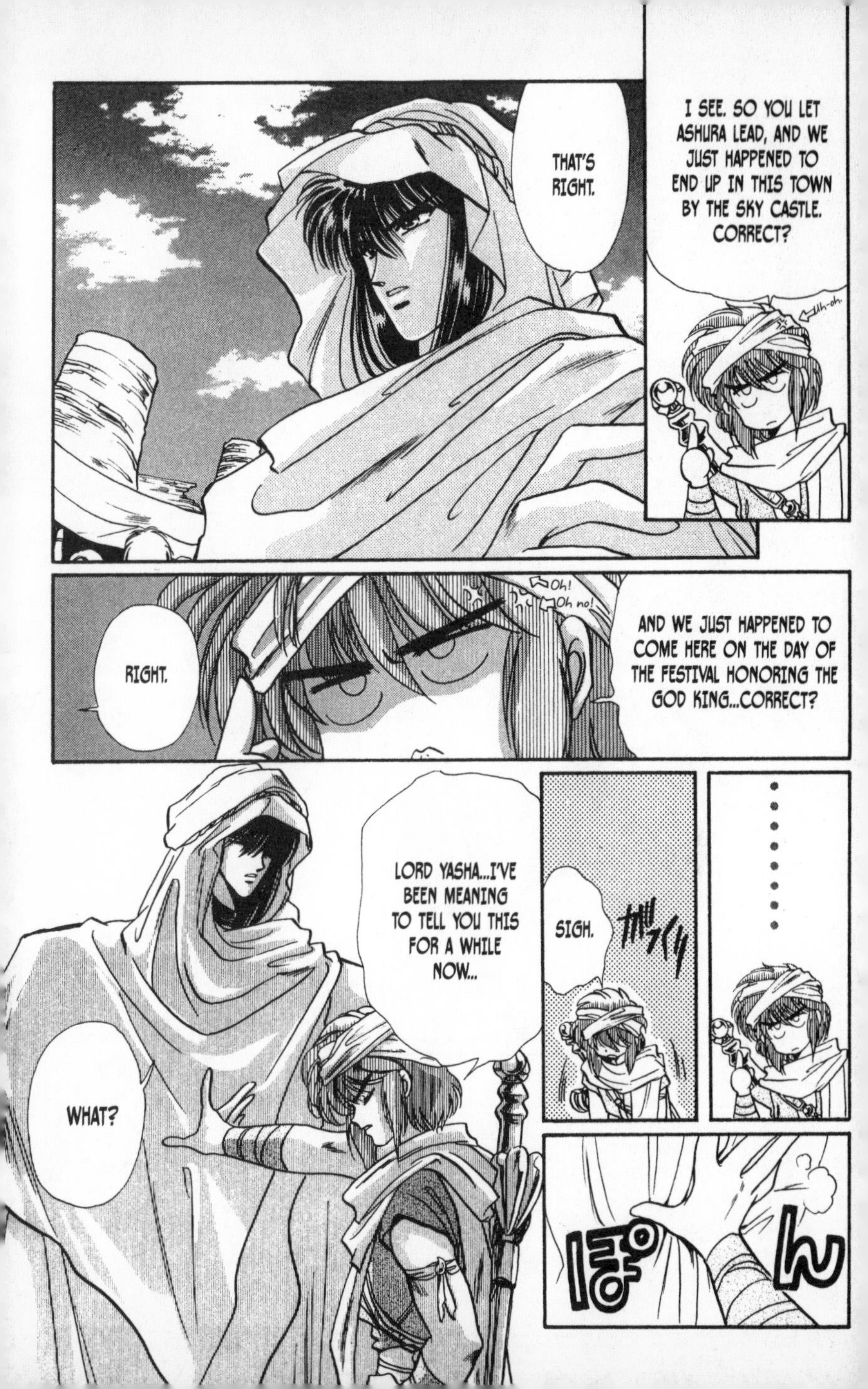
I SEE. SO YOU LET ASHURA LEAD, AND WE JUST HAPPENED TO END UP IN THIS TOWN BY THE SKY CASTLE. CORRECT?
Uh-oh.
THAT'S RIGHT.
AND WE JUST HAPPENED TO COME HERE ON THE DAY OF THE FESTIVAL HONORING THE GOD KING...CORRECT?
Oh!
Oh no!
RIGHT.
....
SIGH.
LORD YASHA...I'VE BEEN MEANING TO TELL YOU THIS FOR A WHILE NOW...
WHAT?

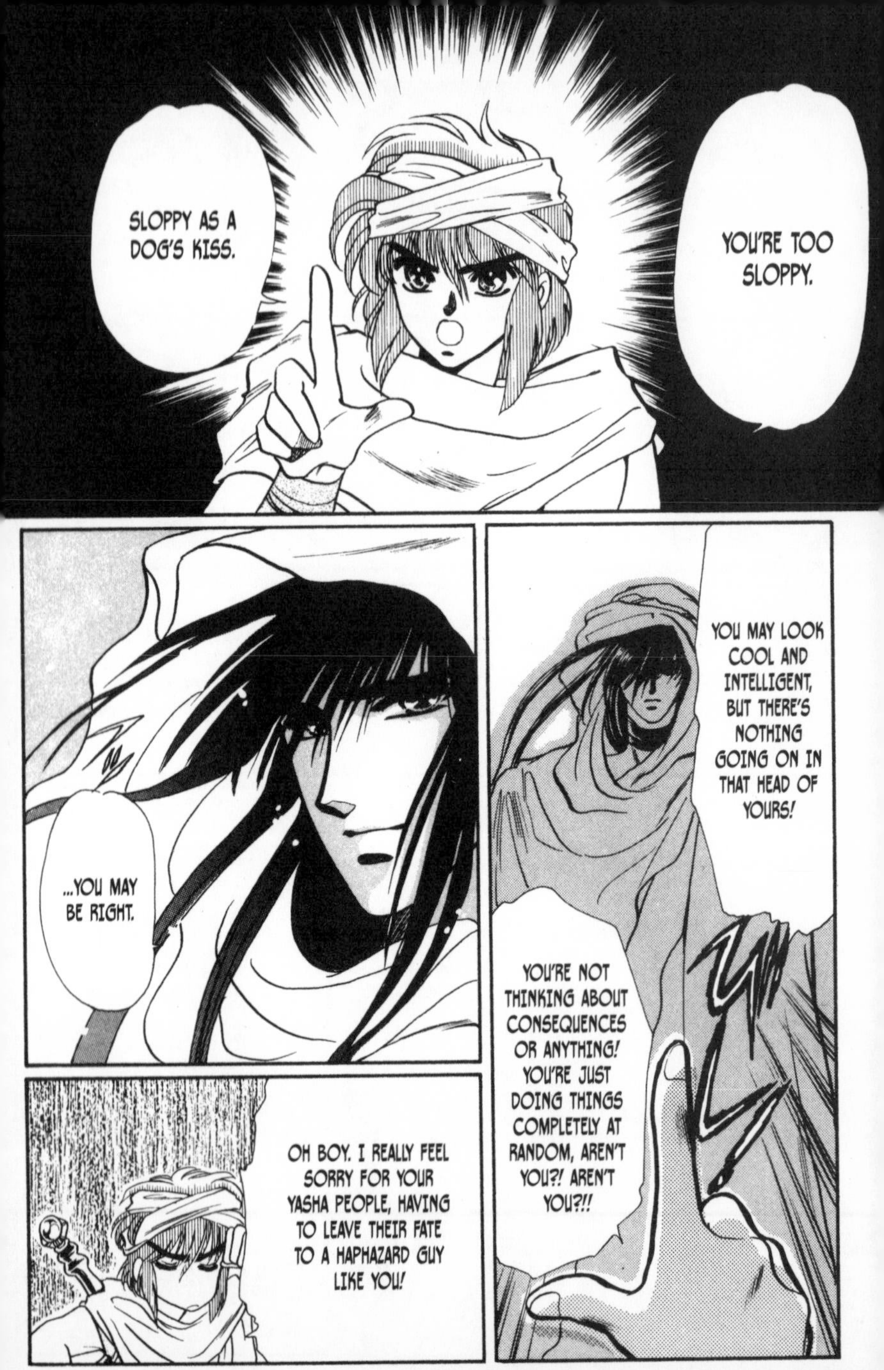
YOU'RE TOO SLOPPY.
SLOPPY AS A DOG'S KISS.
YOU MAY LOOK COOL AND INTELLIGENT, BUT THERE'S NOTHING GOING ON IN THAT HEAD OF YOURS!
YOU'RE NOT THINKING ABOUT CONSEQUENCES OR ANYTHING! YOU'RE JUST DOING THINGS COMPLETELY AT RANDOM, AREN'T YOU?! AREN'T YOU?!!
...YOU MAY BE RIGHT.
OH BOY. I REALLY FEEL SORRY FOR YOUR YASHA PEOPLE, HAVING TO LEAVE THEIR FATE TO A HAPHAZARD GUY LIKE YOU!

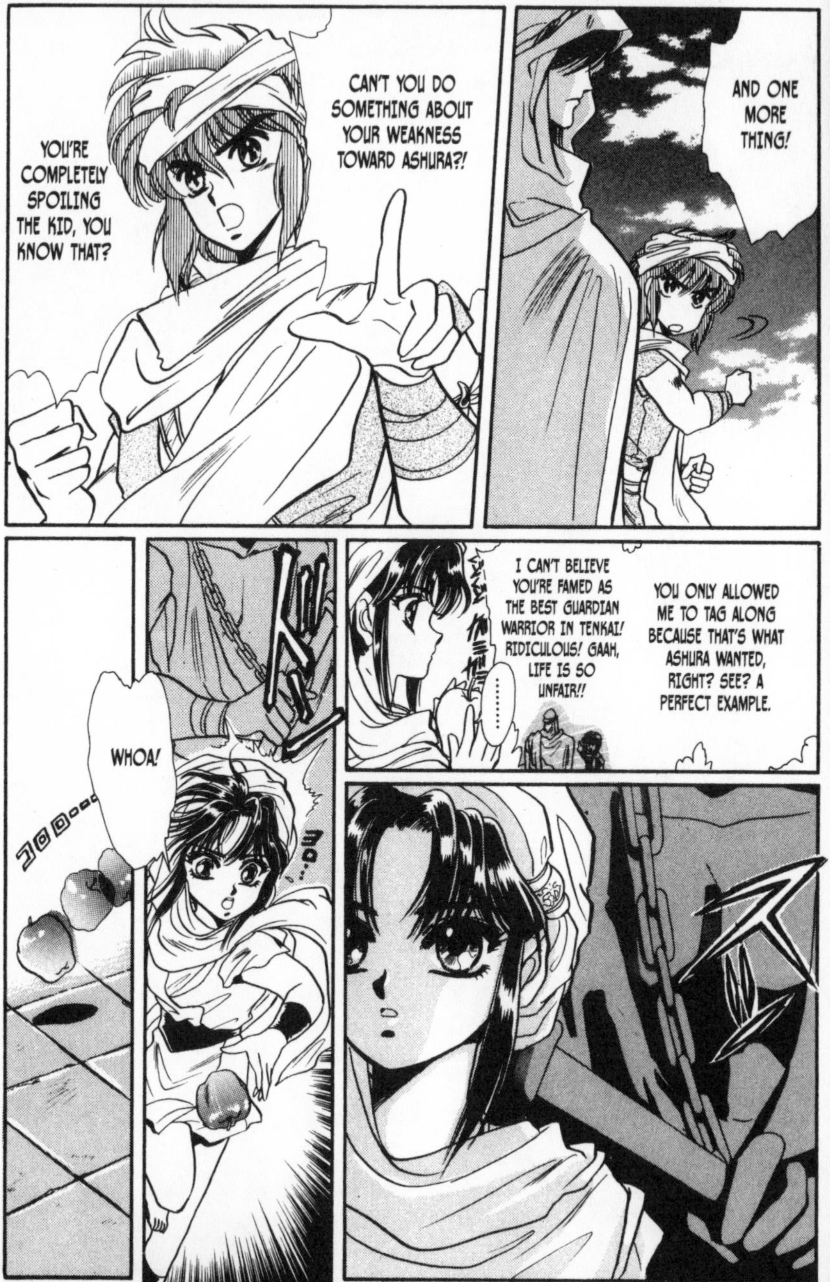
AND ONE MORE THING!
CAN'T YOU DO SOMETHING ABOUT YOUR WEAKNESS TOWARD ASHURA?!
YOU'RE COMPLETELY SPOILING THE KID, YOU KNOW THAT?
YOU ONLY ALLOWED ME TO TAG ALONG BECAUSE THAT'S WHAT ASHURA WANTED, RIGHT? SEE? A PERFECT EXAMPLE.
I CAN'T BELIEVE YOU'RE FAMED AS THE BEST GUARDIAN WARRIOR IN TENKAI! RIDICULOUS! GAAH, LIFE IS SO UNFAIR!!
....
WHOA!

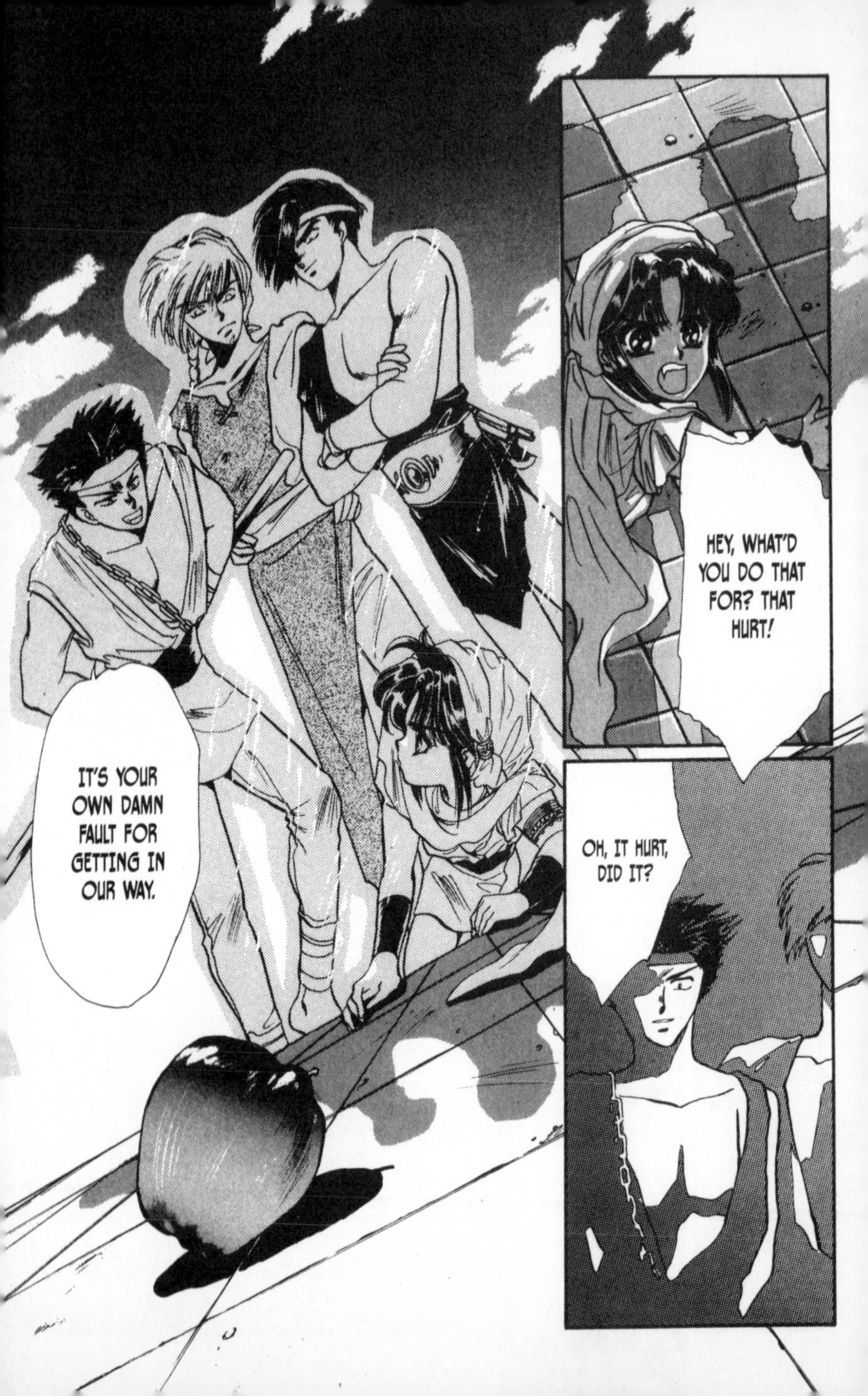
HEY, WHAT'D YOU DO THAT FOR? THAT HURT!
OH, IT HURT, DID IT?
IT'S YOUR OWN DAMN FAULT FOR GETTING IN OUR WAY.

A fight!

ASHURA!

I'M SAYING IF YOU APOLOGIZE AND GIVE US SOME COMPENSATION MONEY, WE'LL FORGET THE WHOLE THING EVER HAPPENED.

HE'S HOPELESS.

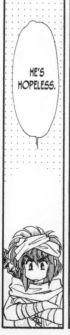

H-HEY! YASHA--!

113

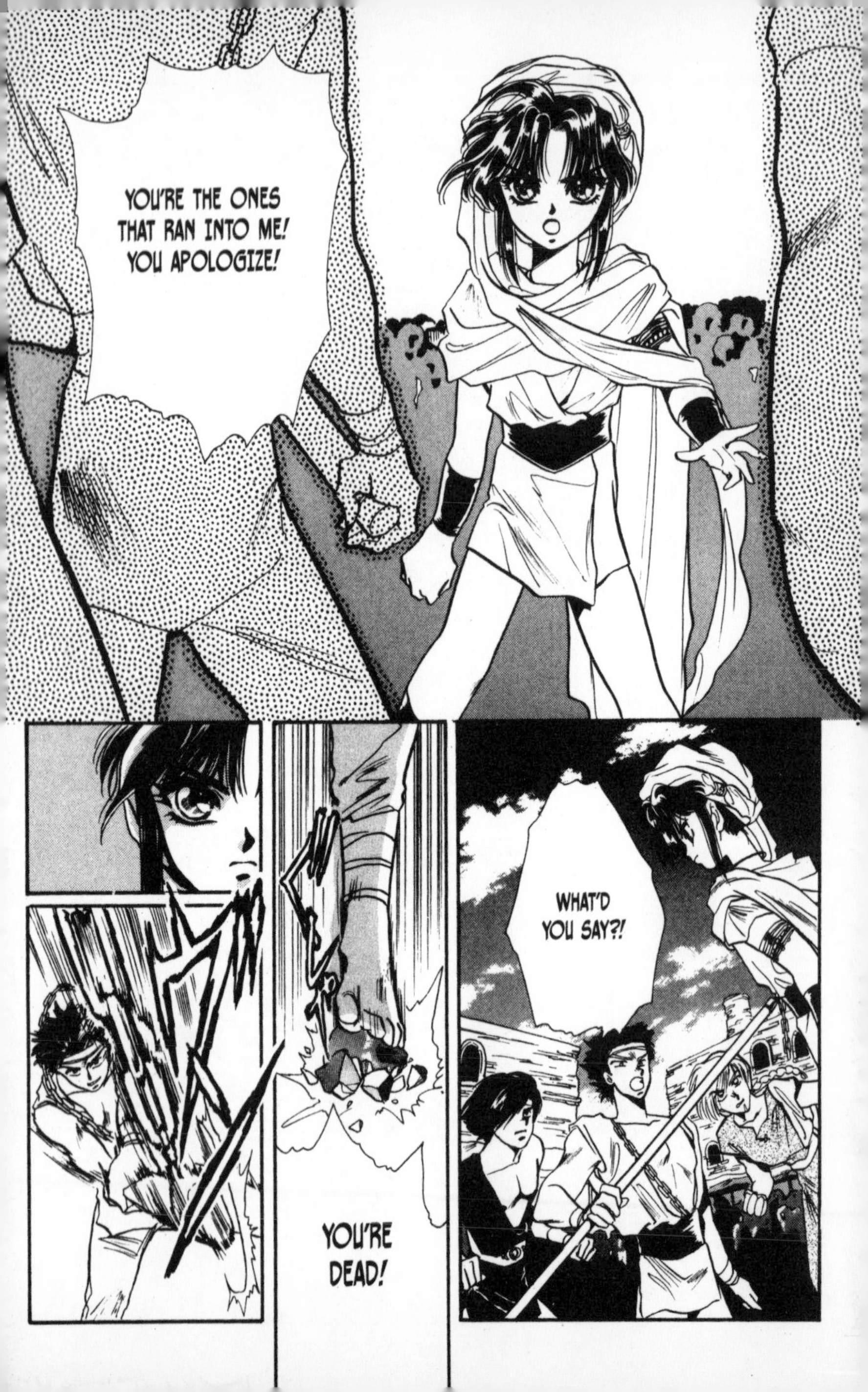
YOU'RE THE ONES THAT RAN INTO ME! YOU APOLOGIZE!
WHAT'D YOU SAY?!
YOU'RE DEAD!

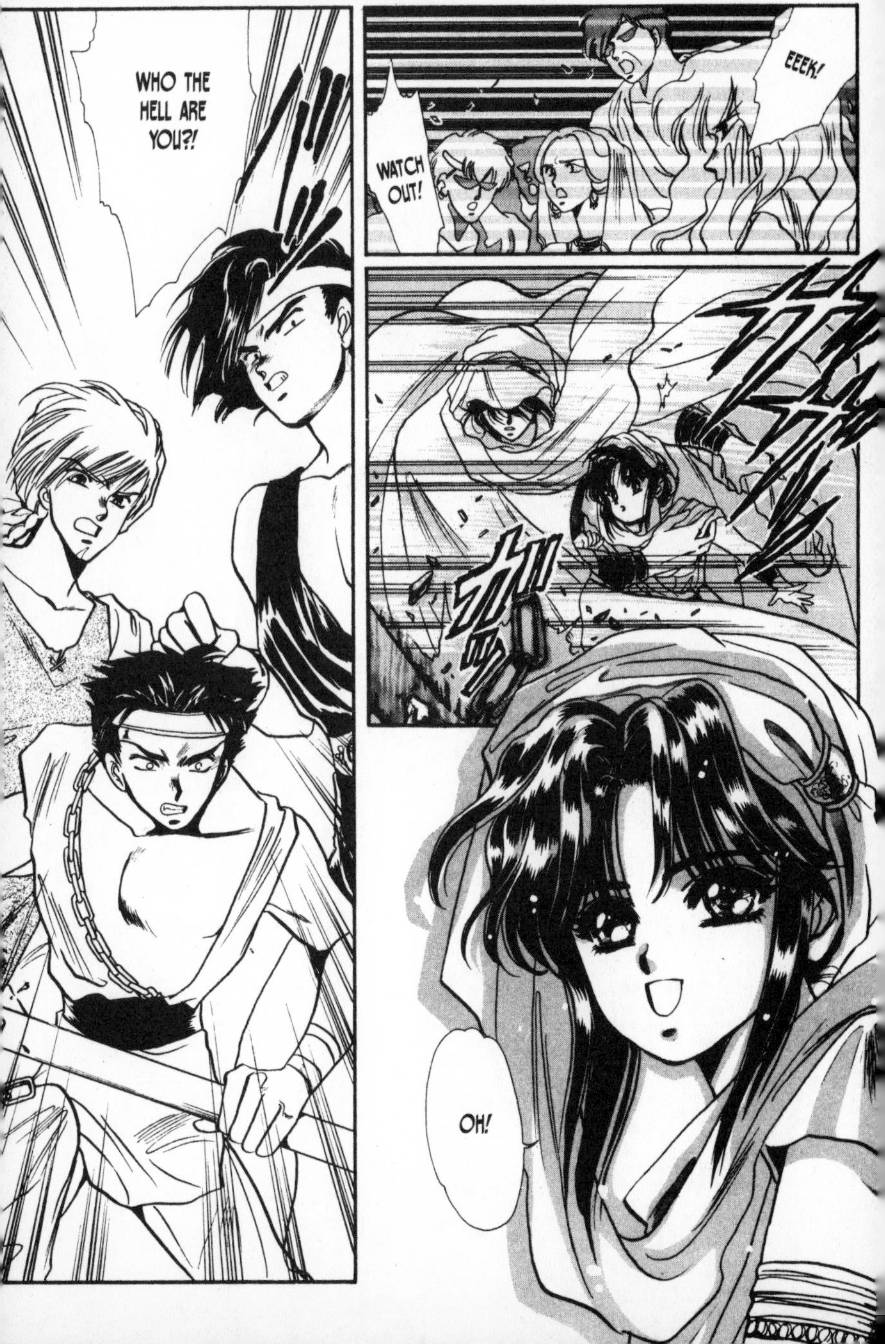
EEEK!
WATCH OUT!
OH!
WHO THE HELL ARE YOU?!

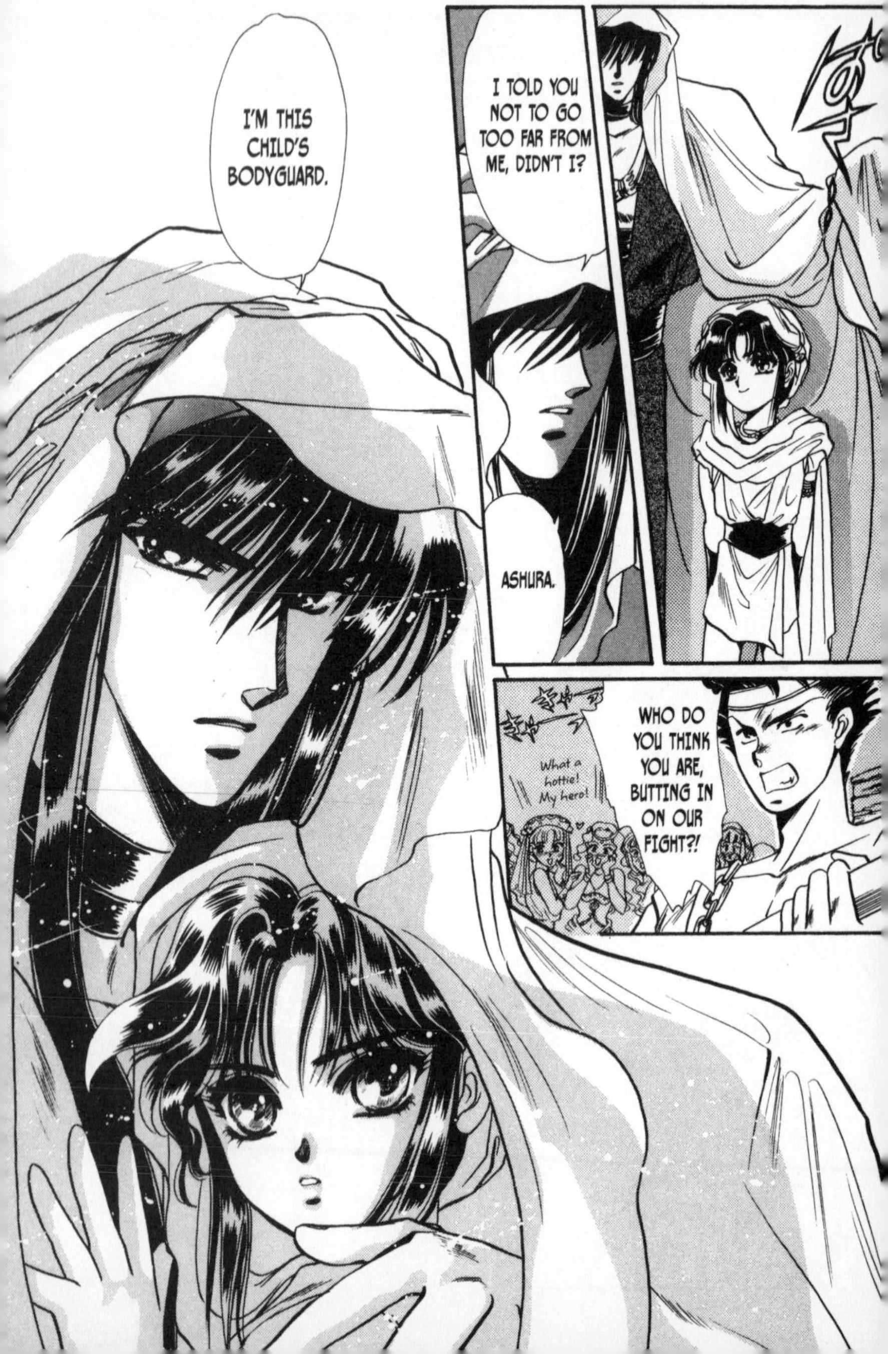
I TOLD YOU NOT TO GO TOO FAR FROM ME, DIDN'T I?
ASHURA.
WHO DO YOU THINK YOU ARE, BUTTING IN ON OUR FIGHT?!
What a hottie! My hero!
I'M THIS CHILD'S BODYGUARD.

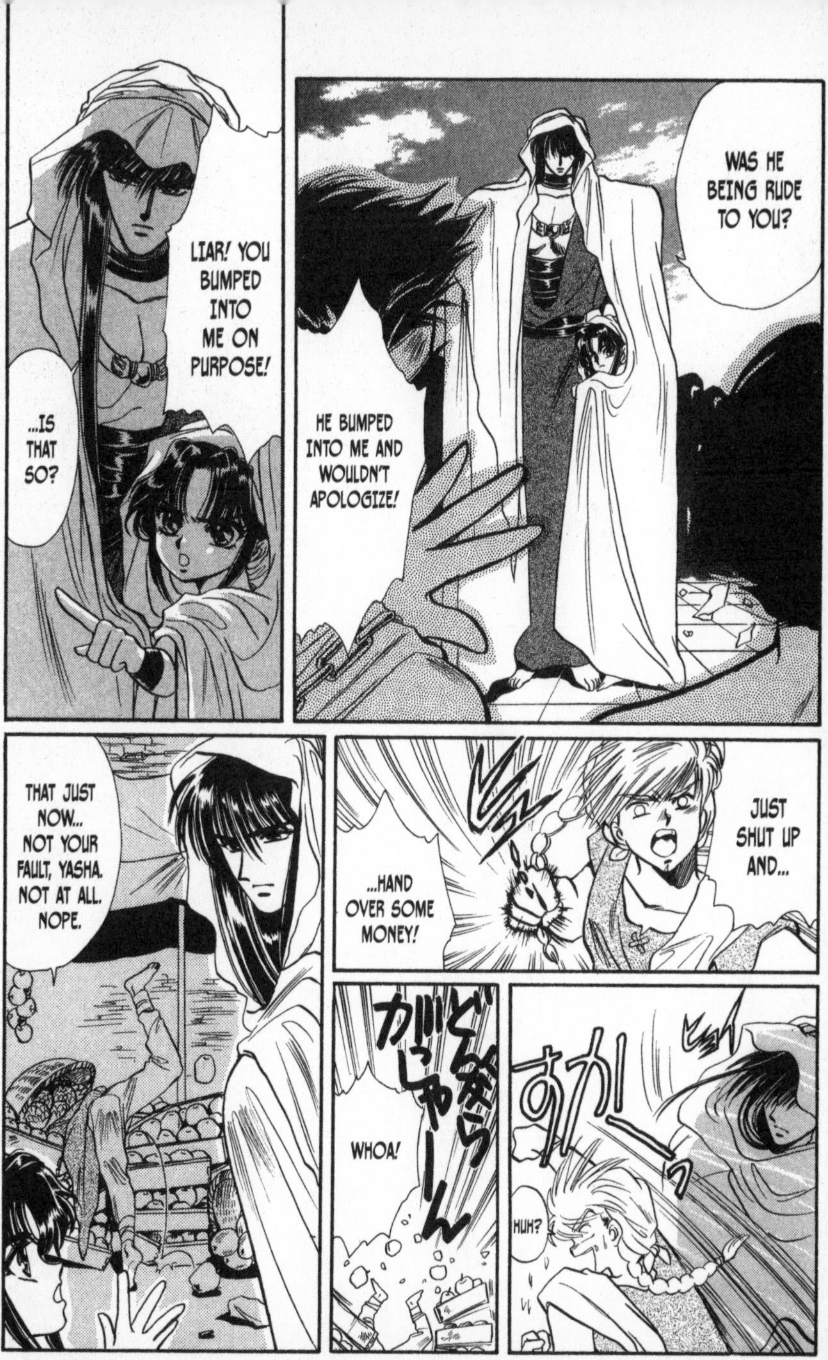
WAS HE BEING RUDE TO YOU?
HE BUMPED INTO ME AND WOULDN'T APOLOGIZE!
LIAR! YOU BUMPED INTO ME ON PURPOSE!
...IS THAT SO?
JUST SHUT UP AND...
...HAND OVER SOME MONEY!
すかーっ
HUH?
どんがら
がっしゃーん
WHOA!
THAT JUST NOW... NOT YOUR FAULT, YASHA. NOT AT ALL. NOPE.

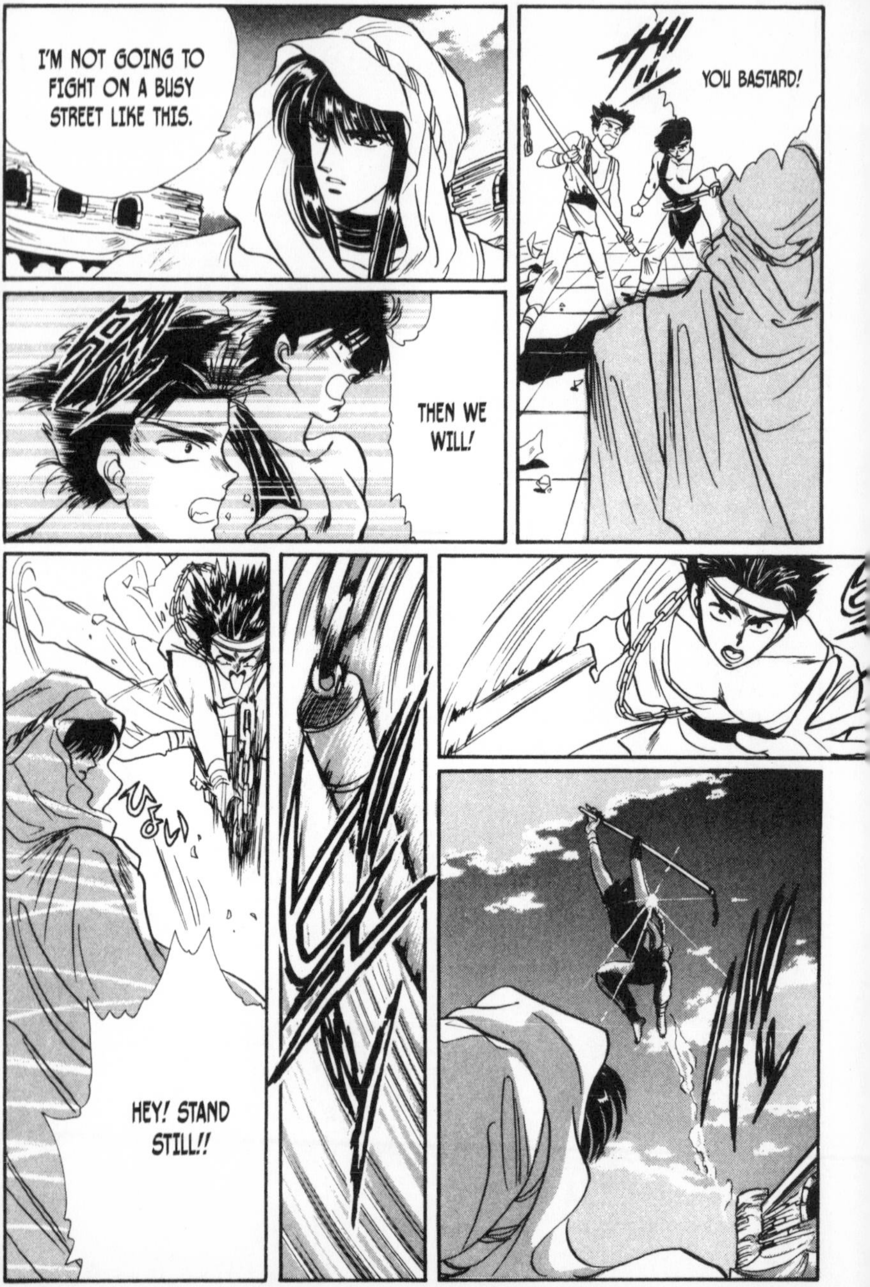
I'M NOT GOING TO FIGHT ON A BUSY STREET LIKE THIS.
THEN WE WILL!
YOU BASTARD!
HEY! STAND STILL!!

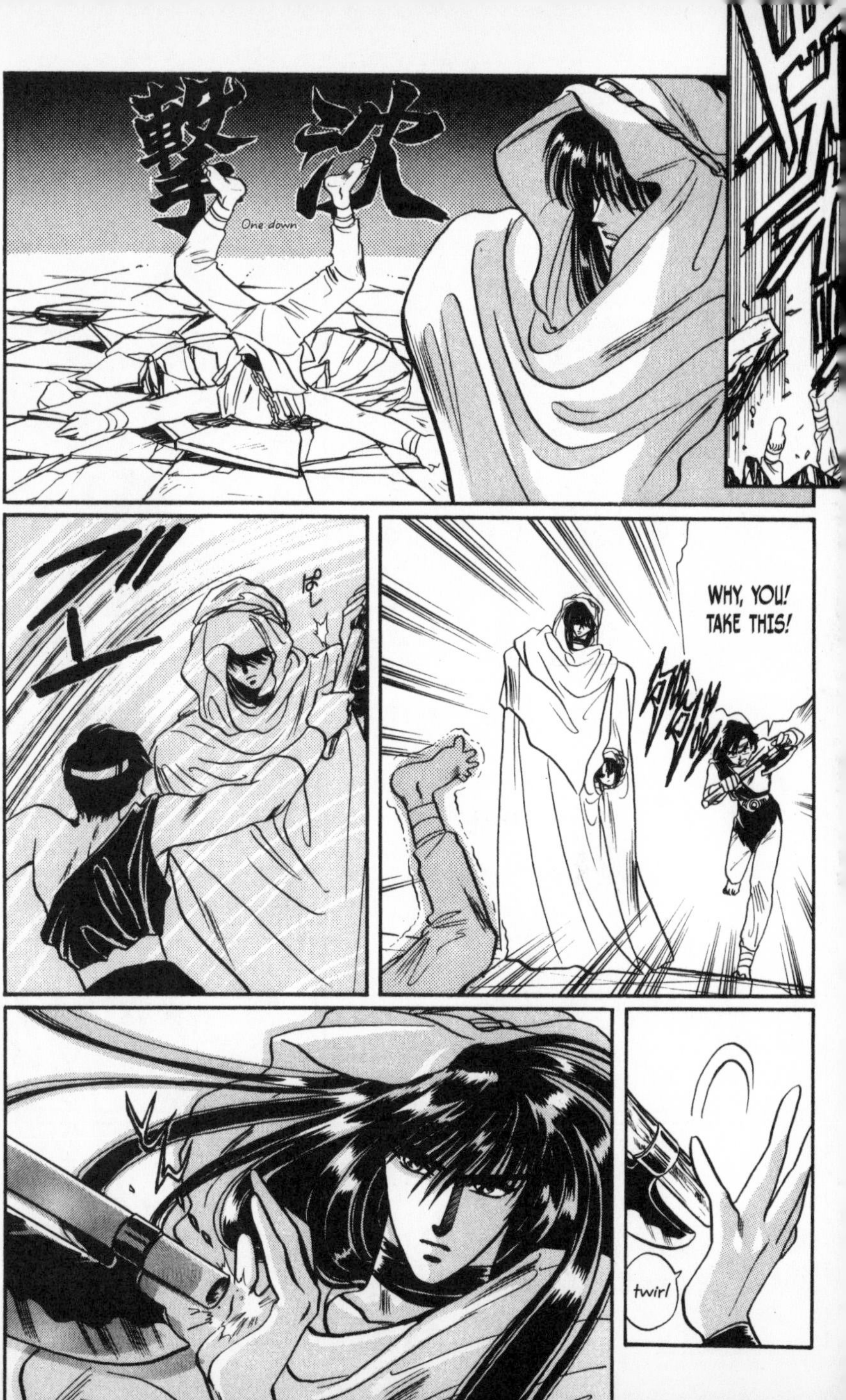

One down
WHY, YOU!
TAKE THIS!
twirl

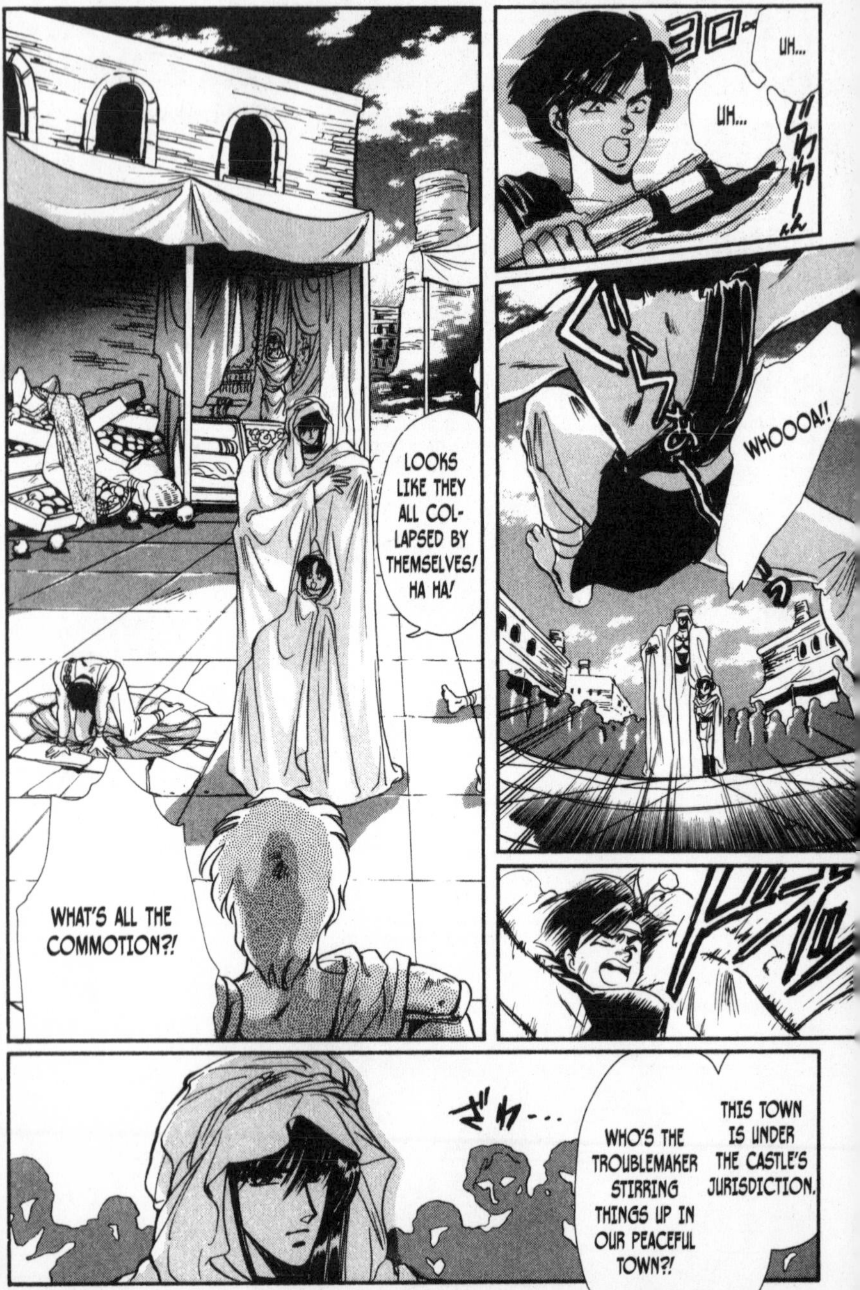

UH...
UH...
WHOOOA!!
LOOKS LIKE THEY ALL COL-LAPSED BY THEMSELVES! HA HA!
WHAT'S ALL THE COMMOTION?!
THIS TOWN IS UNDER THE CASTLE'S JURISDICTION.
WHO'S THE TROUBLEMAKER STIRRING THINGS UP IN OUR PEACEFUL TOWN?!

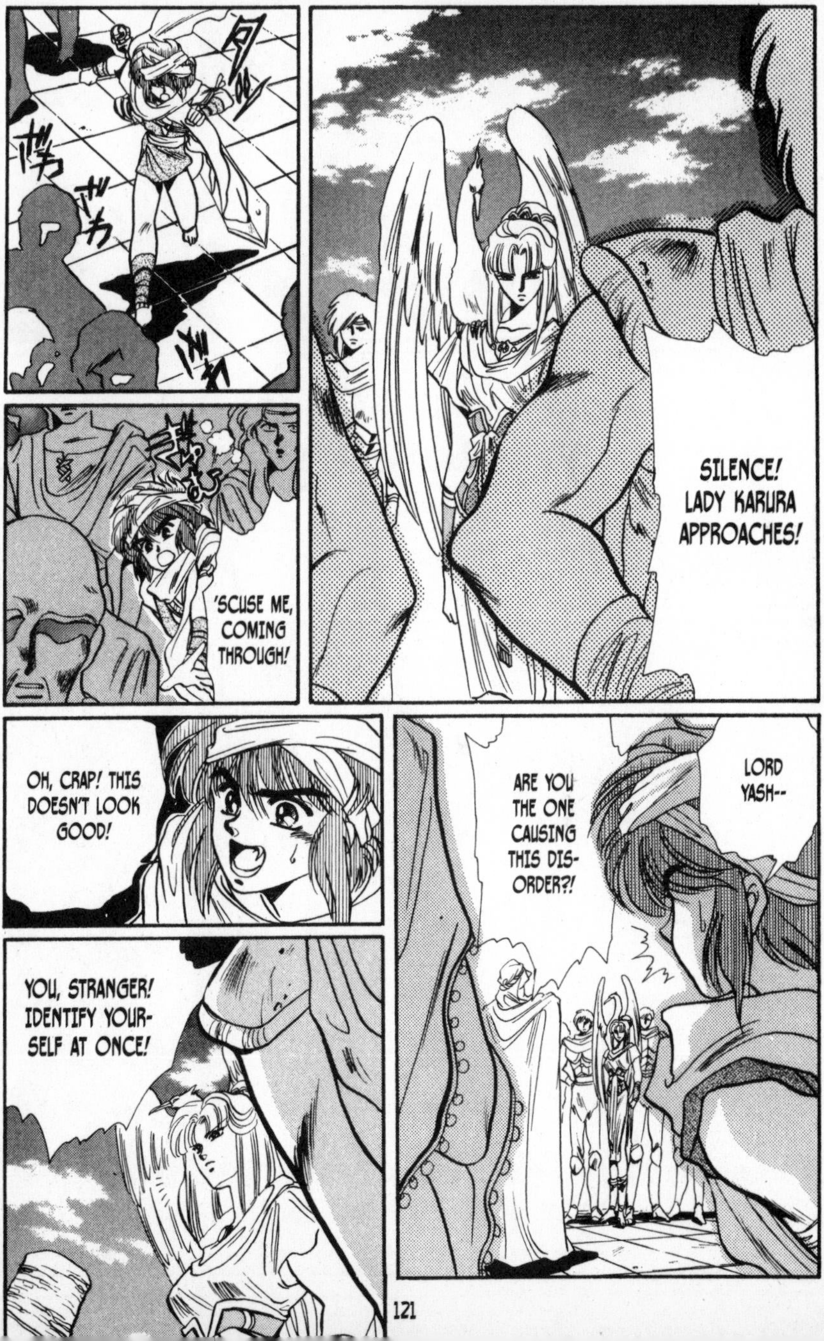
SILENCE! LADY KARURA APPROACHES!
'SCUSE ME, COMING THROUGH!
OH, CRAP! THIS DOESN'T LOOK GOOD!
YOU, STRANGER! IDENTIFY YOURSELF AT ONCE!
ARE YOU THE ONE CAUSING THIS DISORDER?!
LORD YASH--

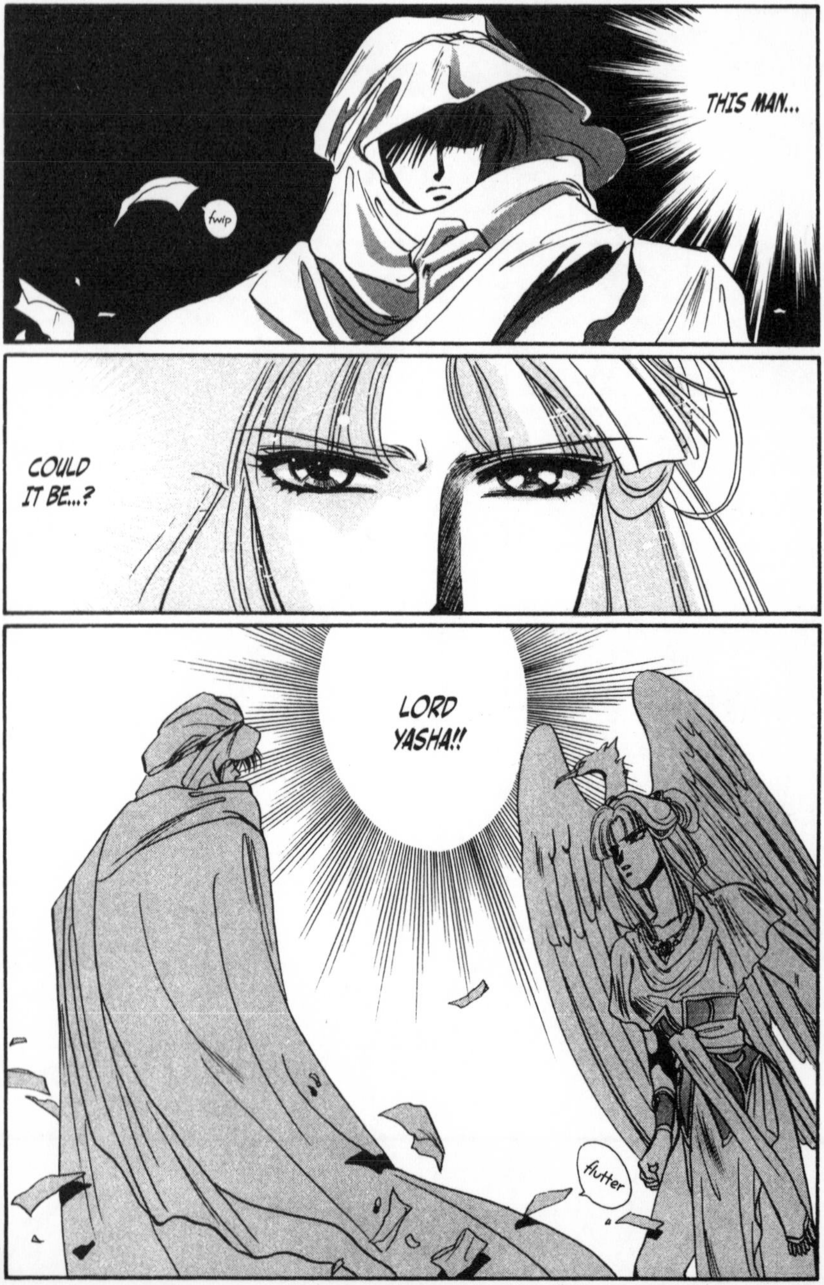
THIS MAN...
fwip
COULD IT BE...?
LORD YASHA!!
flutter

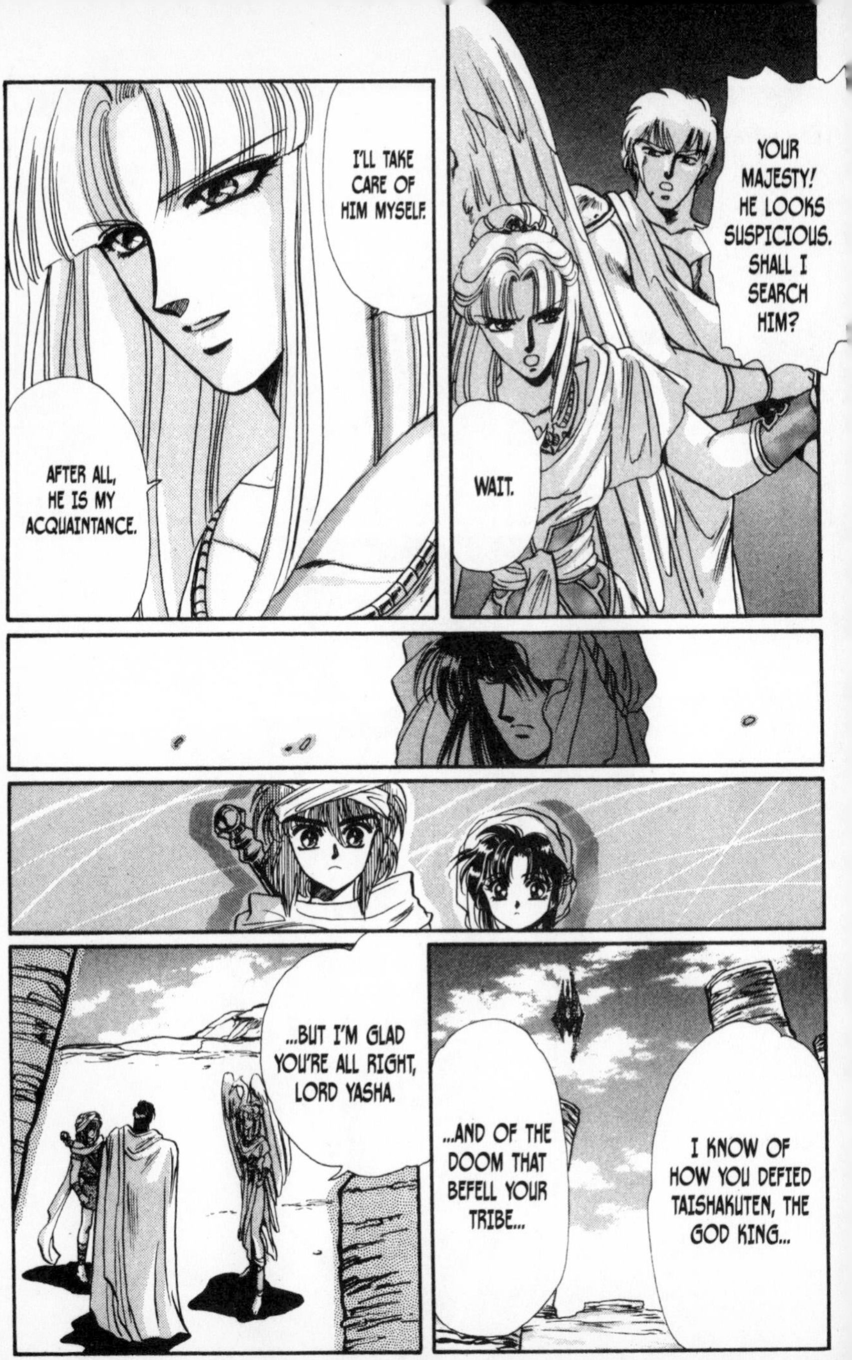
YOUR MAJESTY! HE LOOKS SUSPICIOUS. SHALL I SEARCH HIM?
WAIT.
I'LL TAKE CARE OF HIM MYSELF.
AFTER ALL, HE IS MY ACQUAINTANCE.
I KNOW OF HOW YOU DEFIED TAISHAKUTEN, THE GOD KING...
...AND OF THE DOOM THAT BEFELL YOUR TRIBE...
...BUT I'M GLAD YOU'RE ALL RIGHT, LORD YASHA.

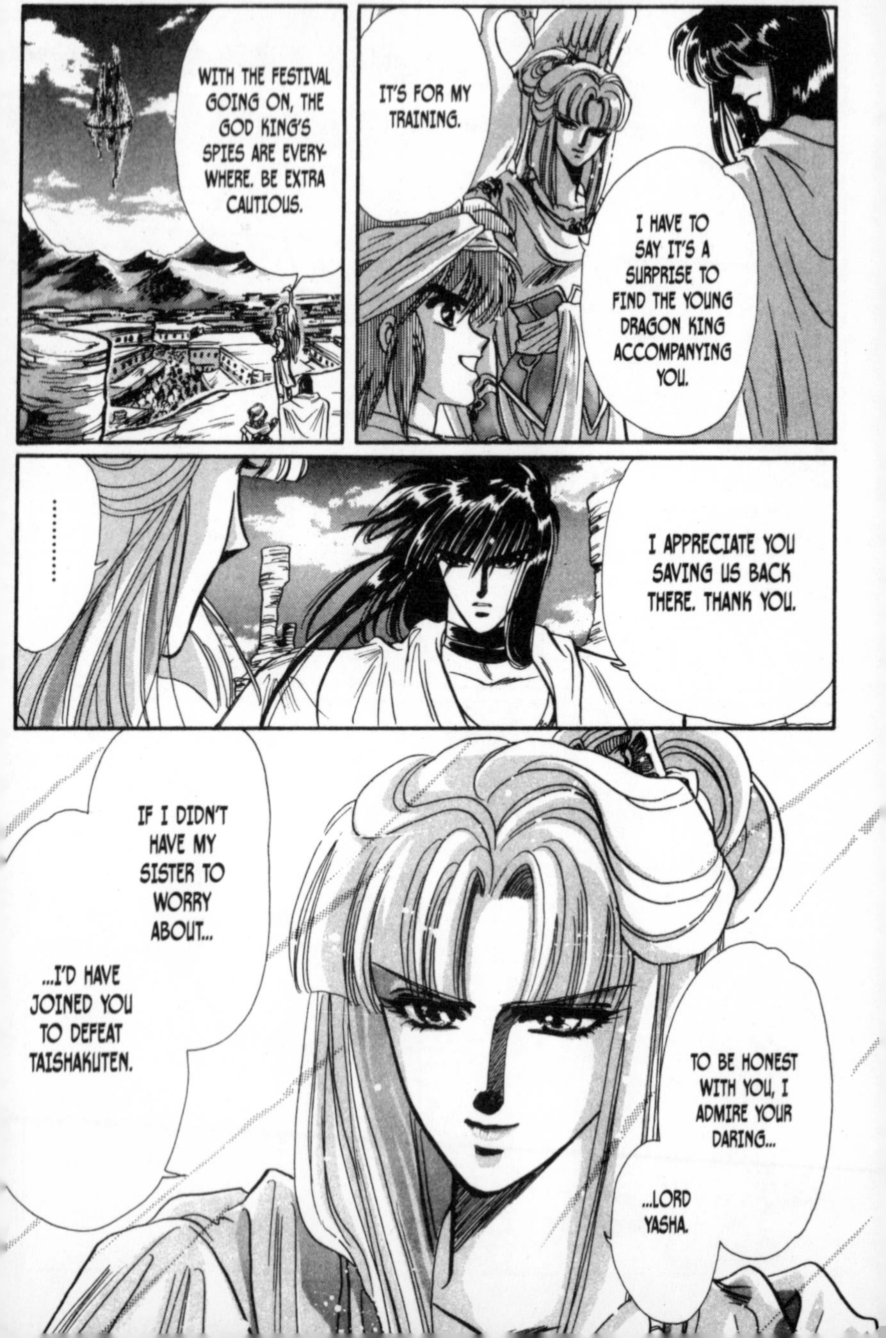
I HAVE TO SAY IT'S A SURPRISE TO FIND THE YOUNG DRAGON KING ACCOMPANYING YOU.
IT'S FOR MY TRAINING.
WITH THE FESTIVAL GOING ON, THE GOD KING'S SPIES ARE EVERY-WHERE. BE EXTRA CAUTIOUS.
I APPRECIATE YOU SAVING US BACK THERE. THANK YOU.
....
TO BE HONEST WITH YOU, I ADMIRE YOUR DARING...
...LORD YASHA.
IF I DIDN'T HAVE MY SISTER TO WORRY ABOUT...
...I'D HAVE JOINED YOU TO DEFEAT TAISHAKUTEN.

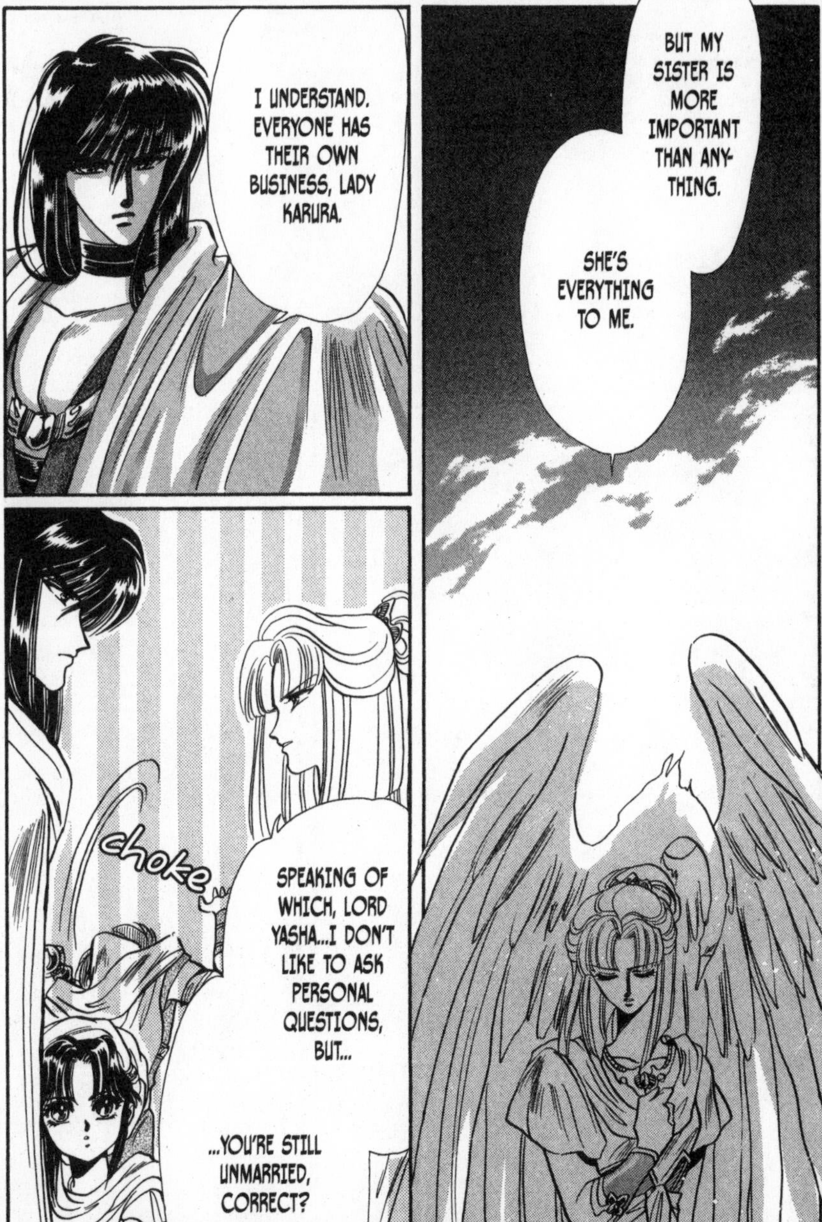
BUT MY SISTER IS MORE IMPORTANT THAN ANY-THING.
SHE'S EVERYTHING TO ME.
I UNDERSTAND. EVERYONE HAS THEIR OWN BUSINESS, LADY KARURA.
choke
SPEAKING OF WHICH, LORD YASHA...I DON'T LIKE TO ASK PERSONAL QUESTIONS, BUT...
...YOU'RE STILL UNMARRIED, CORRECT?

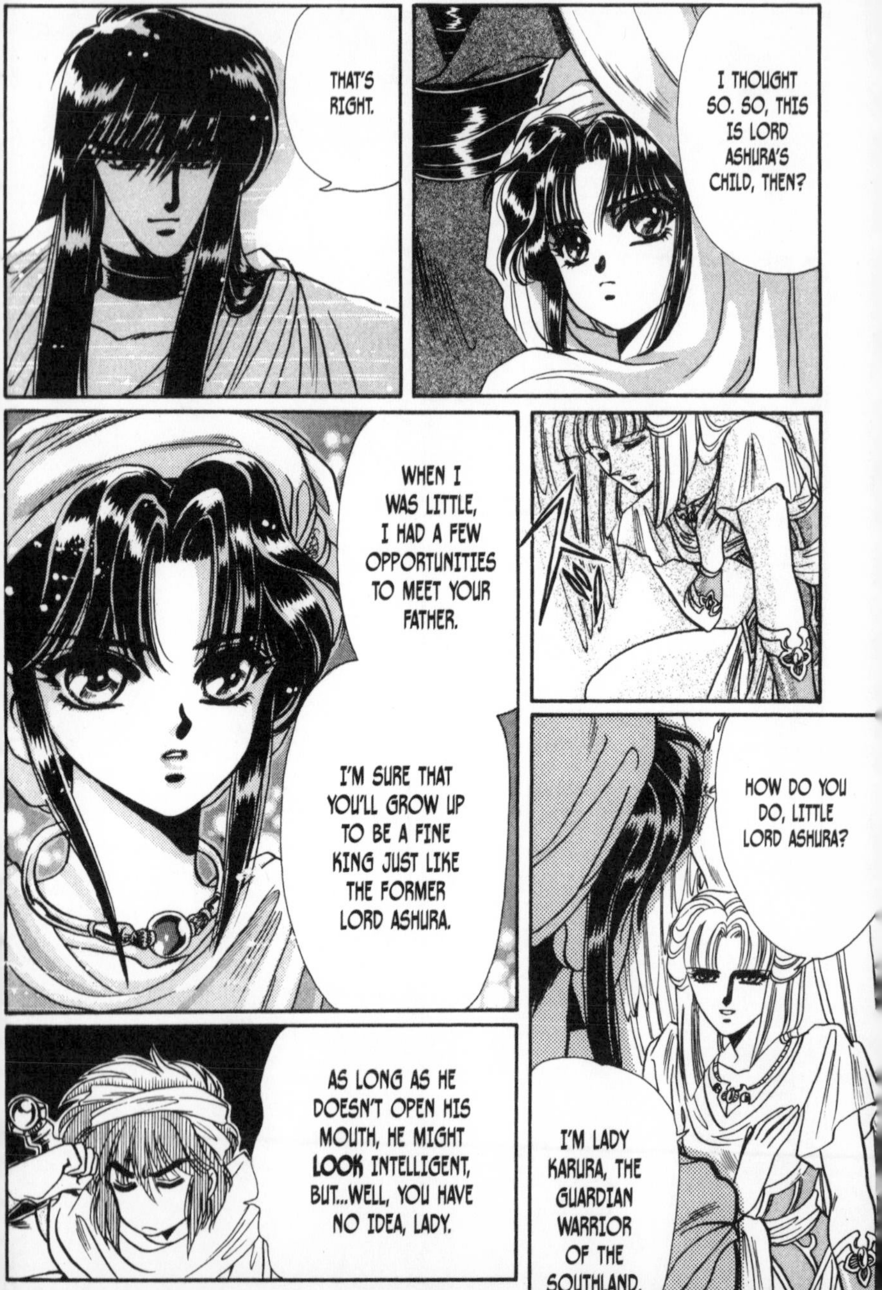
I THOUGHT SO. SO, THIS IS LORD ASHURA'S CHILD, THEN?
THAT'S RIGHT.
HOW DO YOU DO, LITTLE LORD ASHURA?
I'M LADY KARURA, THE GUARDIAN WARRIOR OF THE SOUTHLAND.
WHEN I WAS LITTLE, I HAD A FEW OPPORTUNITIES TO MEET YOUR FATHER.
I'M SURE THAT YOU'LL GROW UP TO BE A FINE KING JUST LIKE THE FORMER LORD ASHURA.
AS LONG AS HE DOESN'T OPEN HIS MOUTH, HE MIGHT LOOK INTELLIGENT, BUT...WELL, YOU HAVE NO IDEA, LADY.

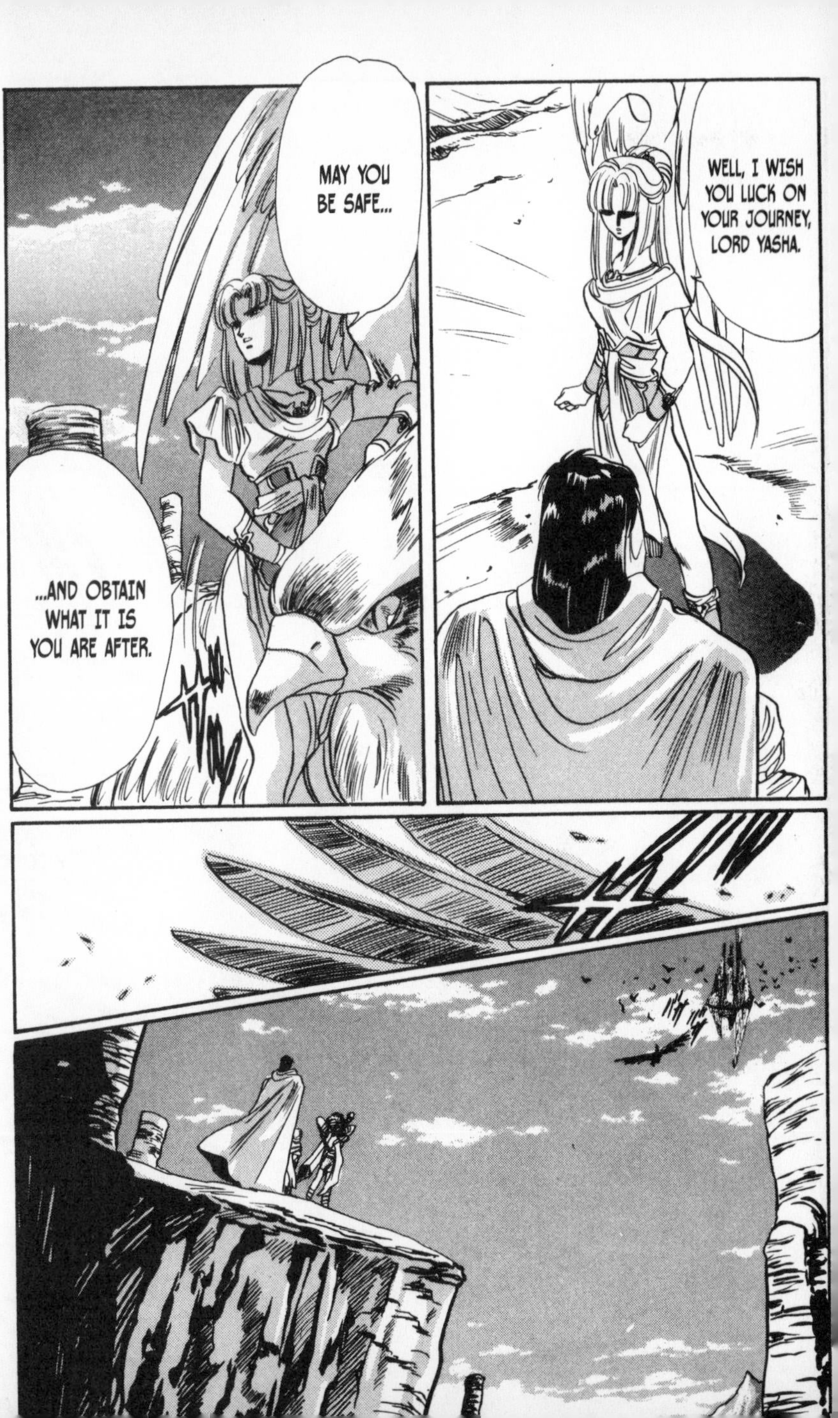
WELL, I WISH YOU LUCK ON YOUR JOURNEY, LORD YASHA.
MAY YOU BE SAFE...
...AND OBTAIN WHAT IT IS YOU ARE AFTER.

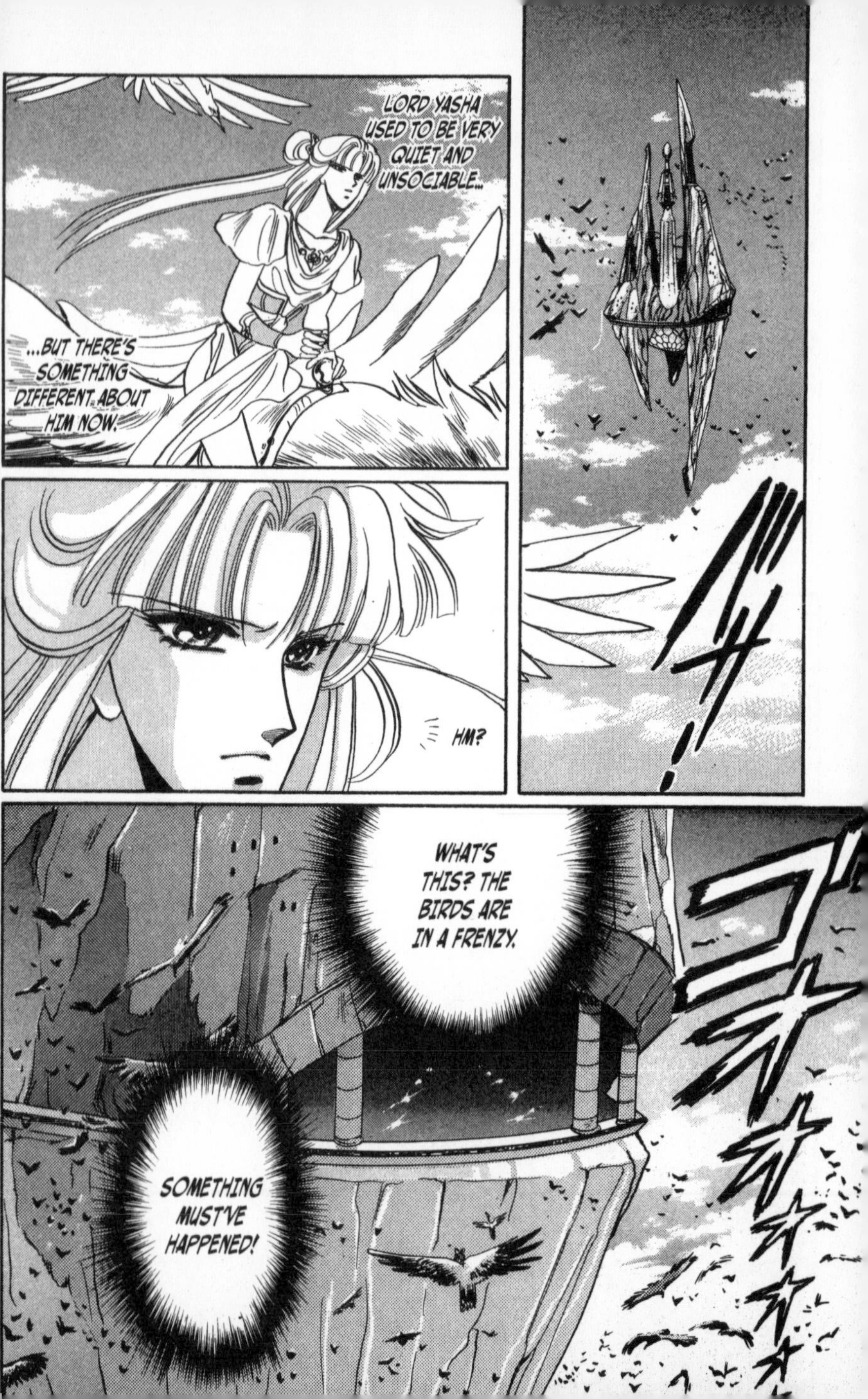
LORD YASHA USED TO BE VERY QUIET AND UNSOCIABLE...
...BUT THERE'S SOMETHING DIFFERENT ABOUT HIM NOW.
HM?
WHAT'S THIS? THE BIRDS ARE IN A FRENZY.
SOMETHING MUST'VE HAPPENED!

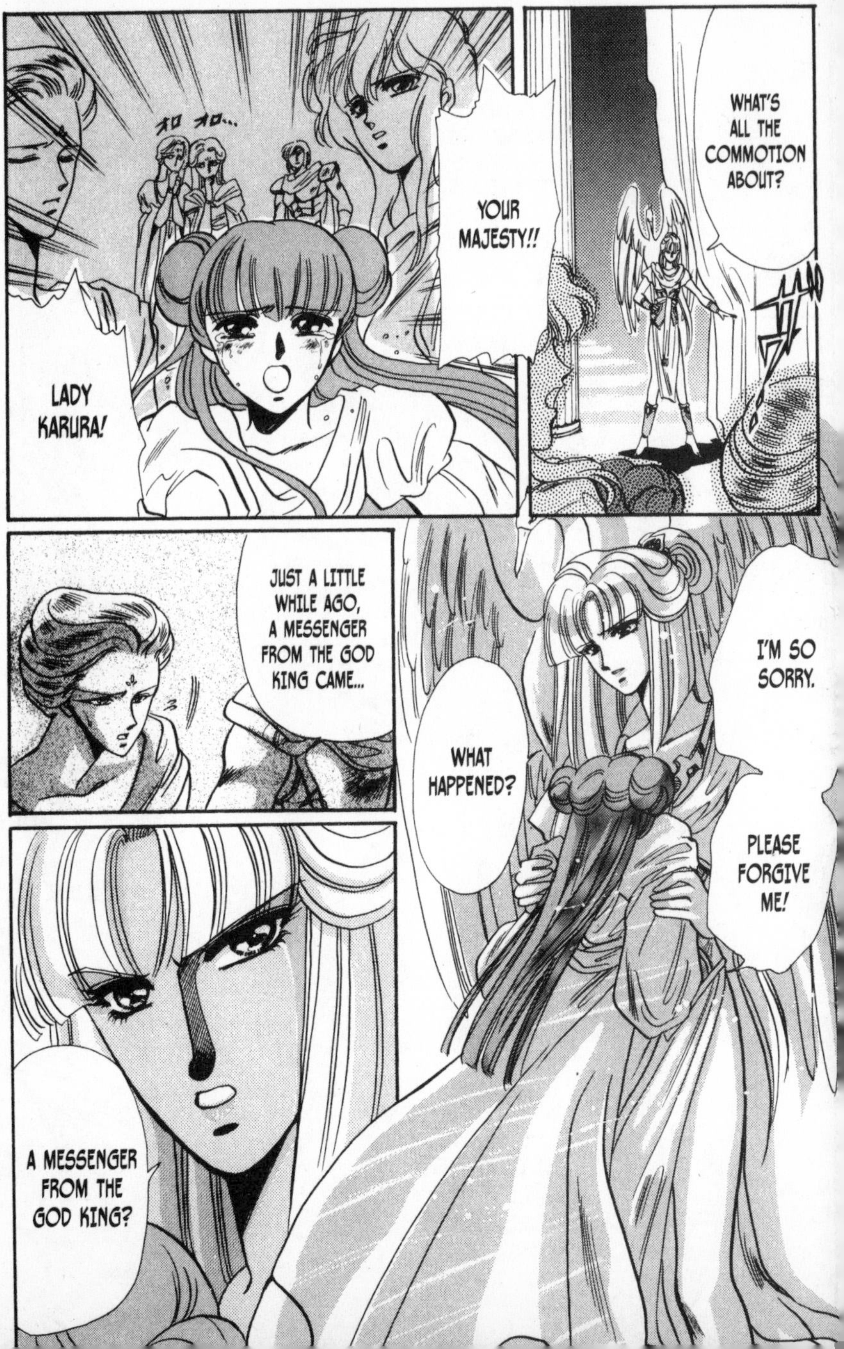
WHAT'S ALL THE COMMOTION ABOUT?
ザッ
YOUR MAJESTY!!
オロ オロ...
LADY KARURA!
I'M SO SORRY.
PLEASE FORGIVE ME!
WHAT HAPPENED?
JUST A LITTLE WHILE AGO, A MESSENGER FROM THE GOD KING CAME...
A MESSENGER FROM THE GOD KING?

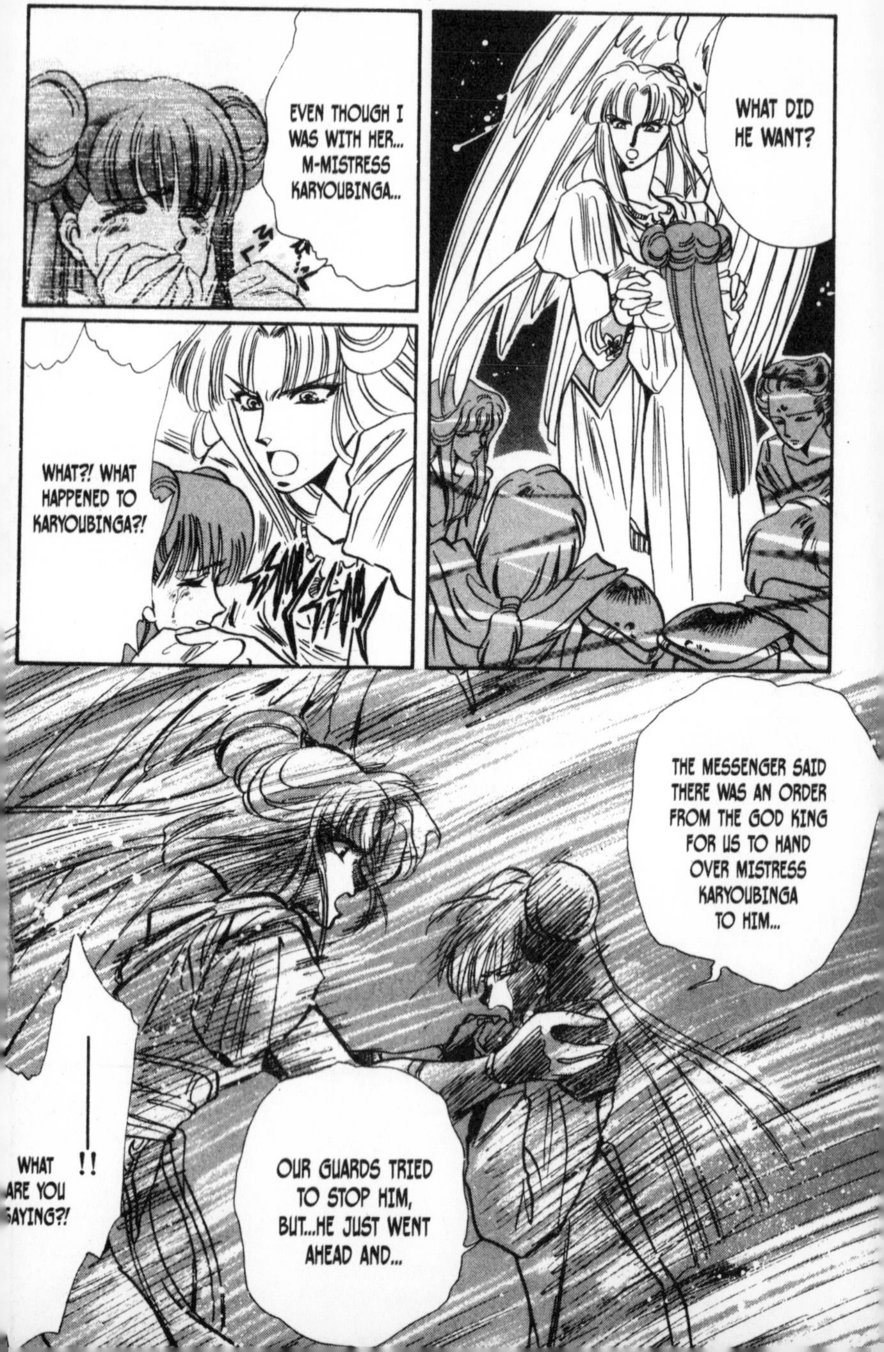
WHAT DID HE WANT?
EVEN THOUGH I WAS WITH HER... M-MISTRESS KARYOUBINGA...
WHAT?! WHAT HAPPENED TO KARYOUBINGA?!
THE MESSENGER SAID THERE WAS AN ORDER FROM THE GOD KING FOR US TO HAND OVER MISTRESS KARYOUBINGA TO HIM...
OUR GUARDS TRIED TO STOP HIM, BUT...HE JUST WENT AHEAD AND...
!!
WHAT ARE YOU SAYING?!

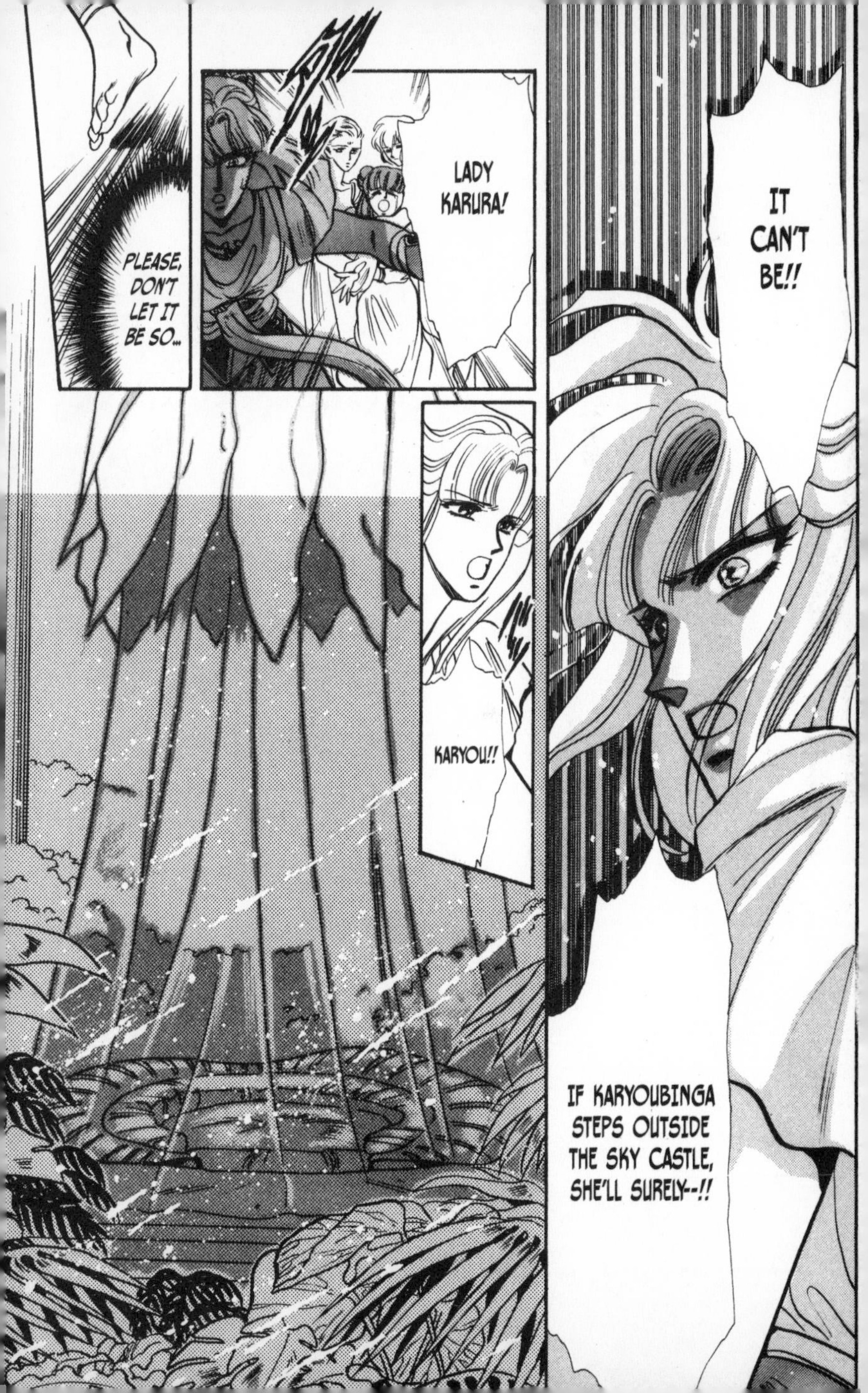
IT CAN'T BE!!
IF KARYOUBINGA STEPS OUTSIDE THE SKY CASTLE, SHE'LL SURELY--!!
LADY KARURA!
PLEASE, DON'T LET IT BE SO...
KARYOU!!

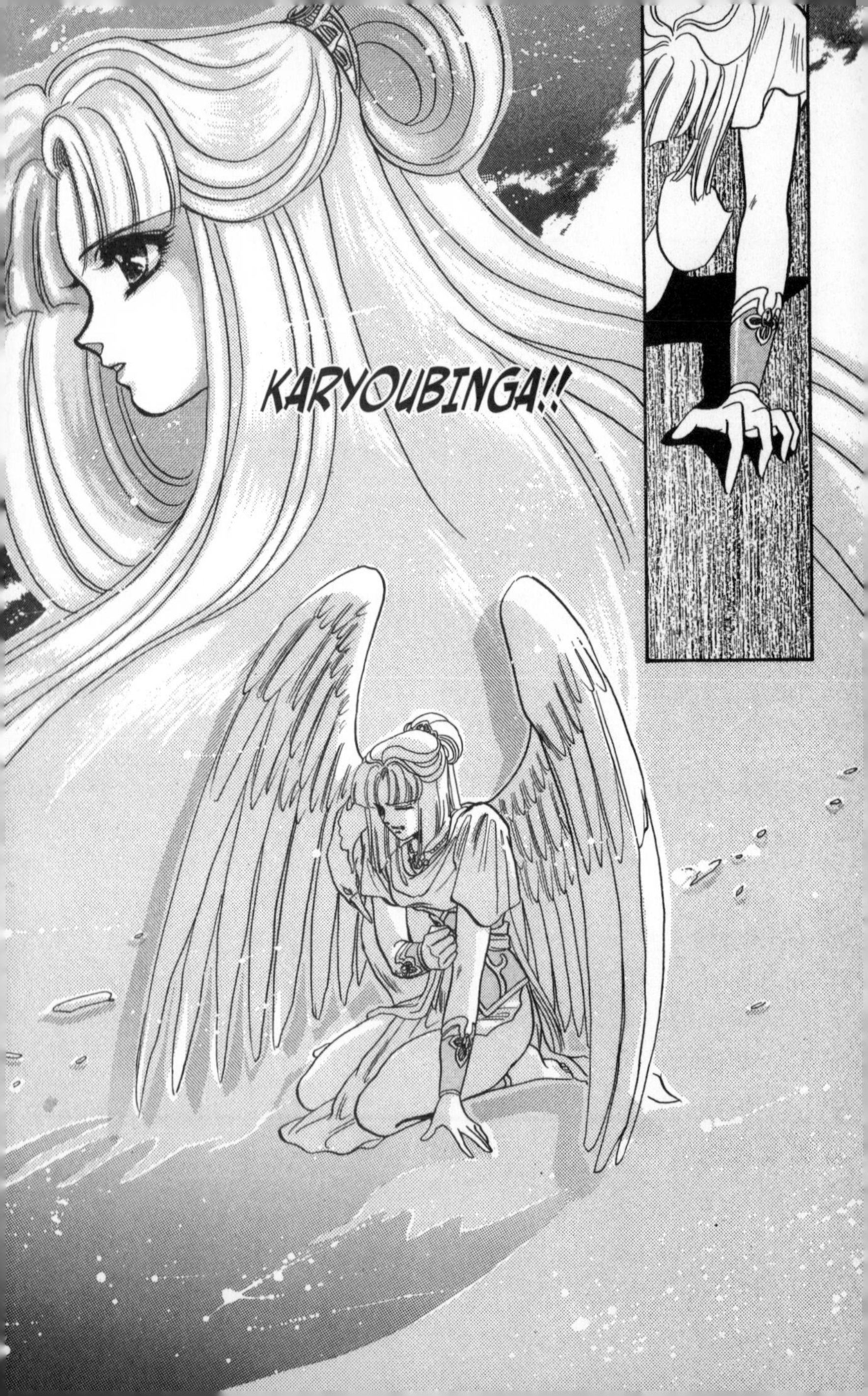
KARYOUBINGA!!

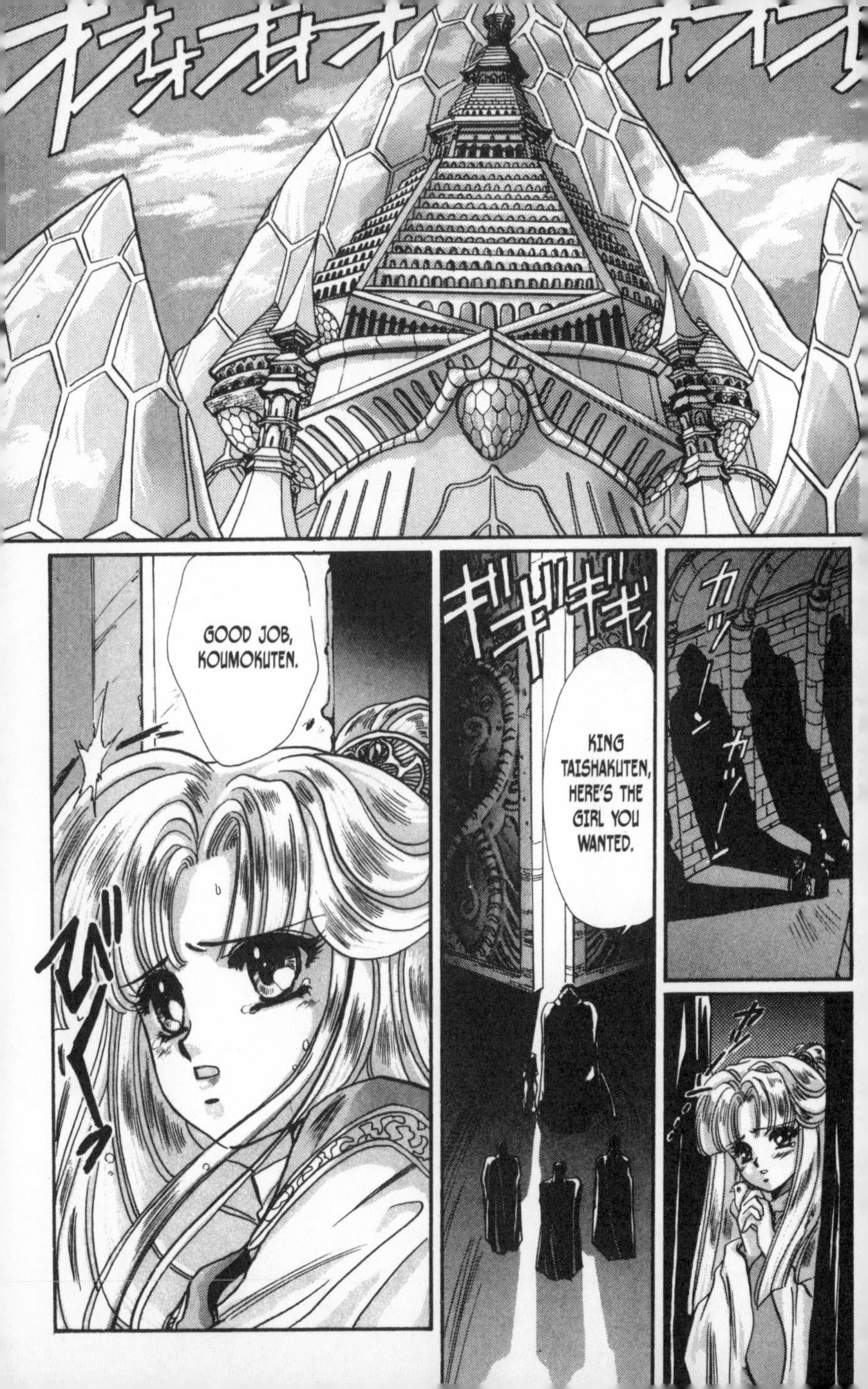
KING TAISHAKUTEN, HERE'S THE GIRL YOU WANTED.
GOOD JOB, KOUMOKUTEN.

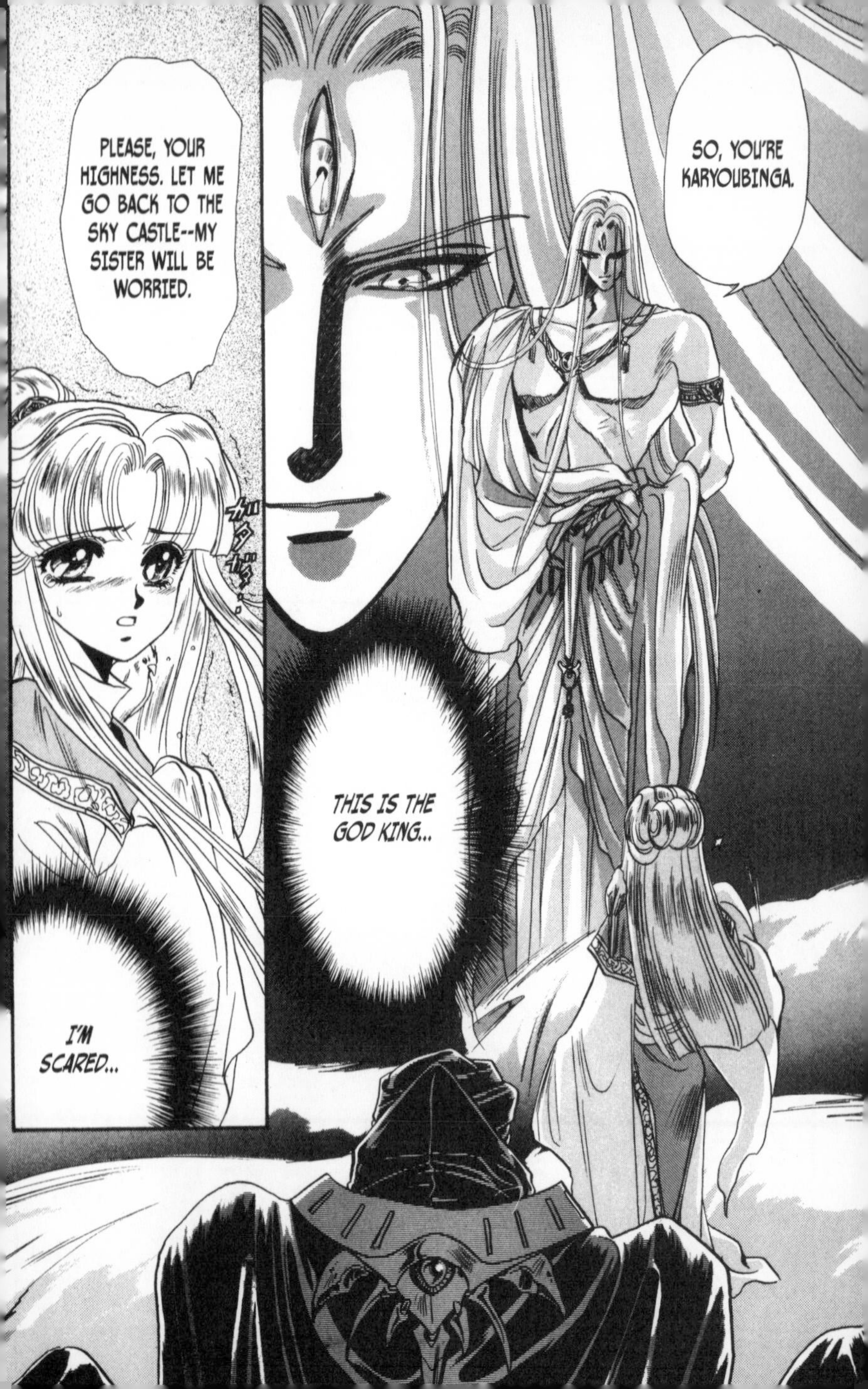
SO, YOU'RE KARYOUBINGA.
PLEASE, YOUR HIGHNESS. LET ME GO BACK TO THE SKY CASTLE--MY SISTER WILL BE WORRIED.
THIS IS THE GOD KING...
I'M SCARED...

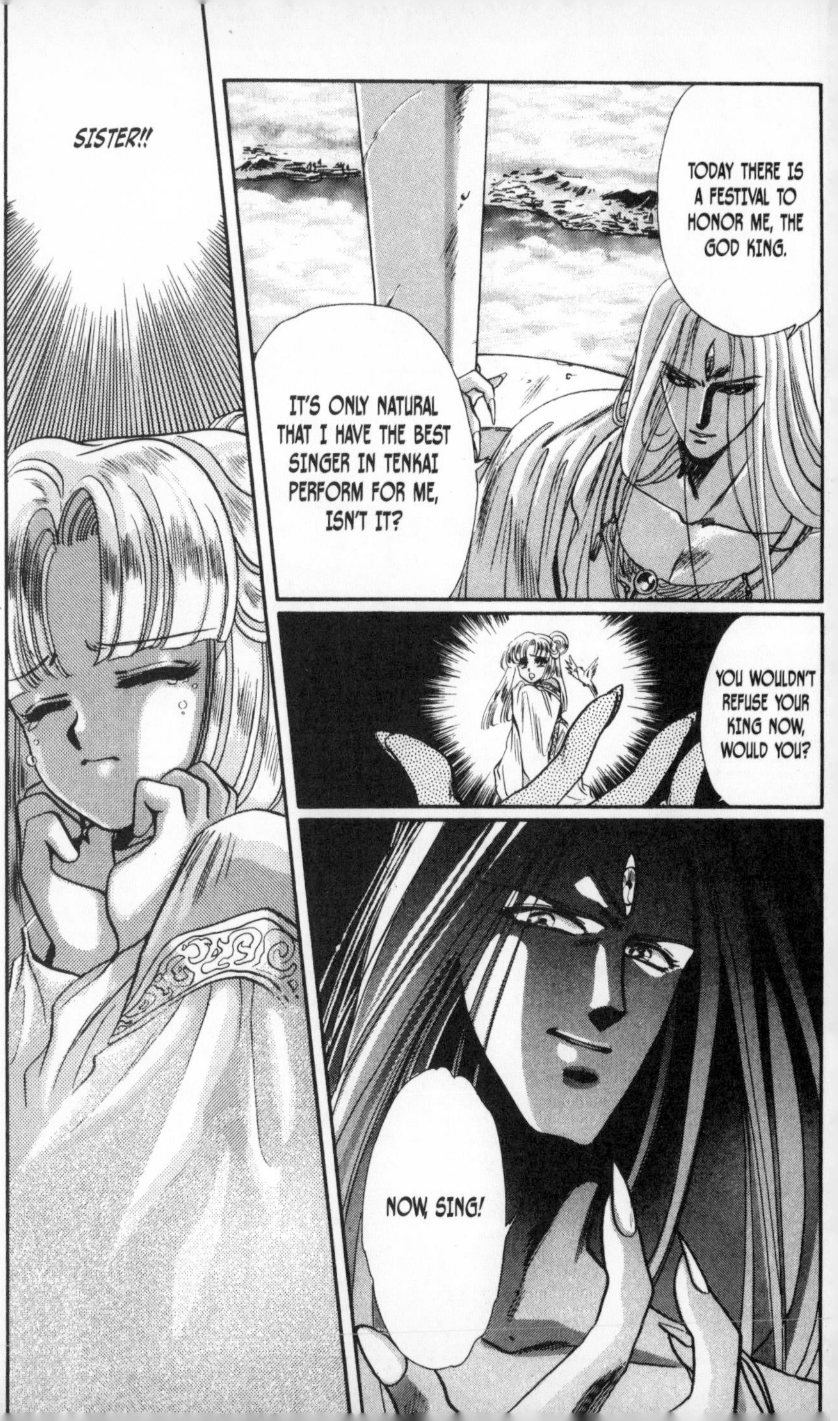
SISTER!!
TODAY THERE IS A FESTIVAL TO HONOR ME, THE GOD KING.
IT'S ONLY NATURAL THAT I HAVE THE BEST SINGER IN TENKAI PERFORM FOR ME, ISN'T IT?
YOU WOULDN'T REFUSE YOUR KING NOW, WOULD YOU?
NOW, SING!

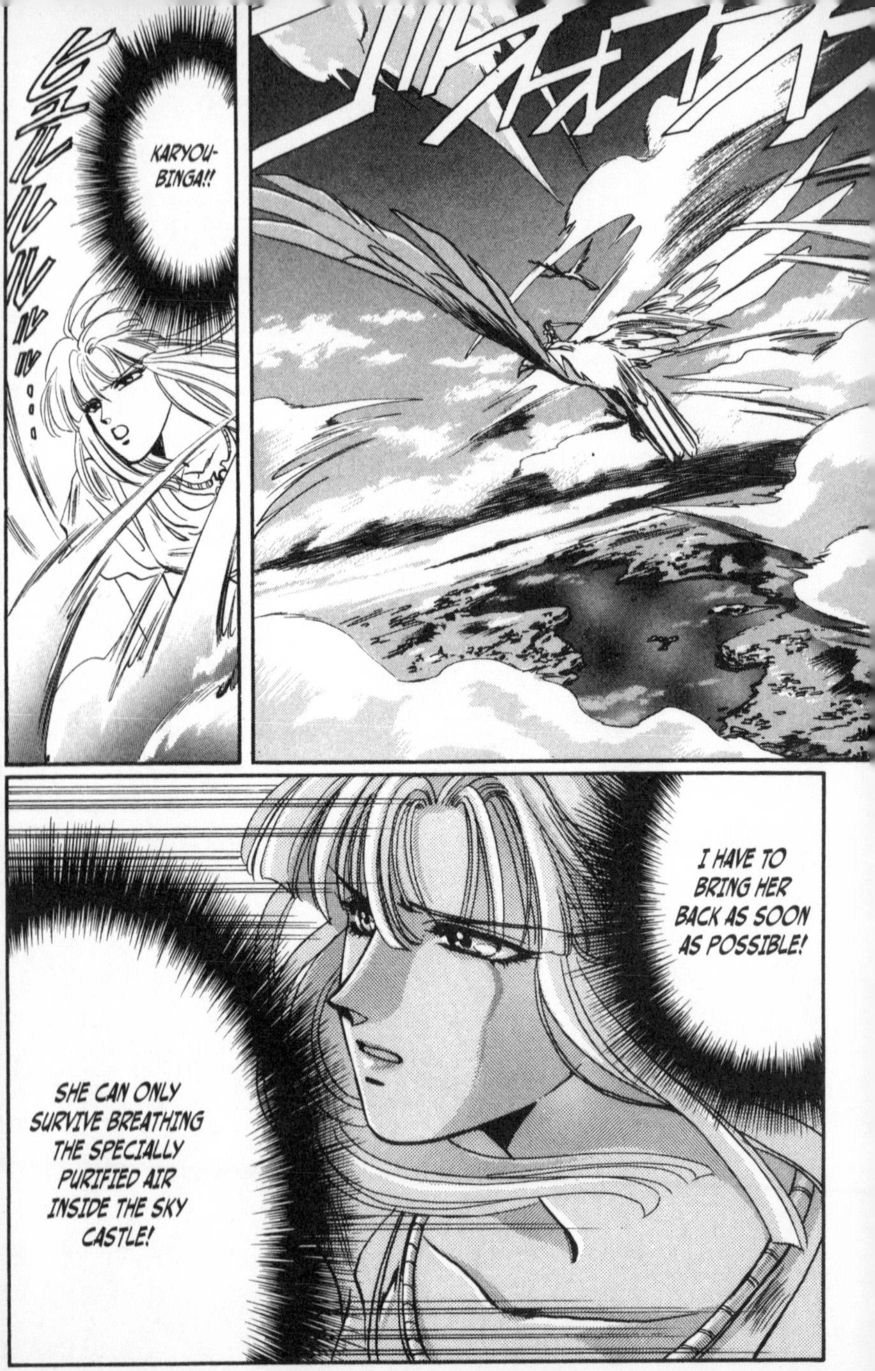
KARYOU-BINGA!!
I HAVE TO BRING HER BACK AS SOON AS POSSIBLE!
SHE CAN ONLY SURVIVE BREATHING THE SPECIALLY PURIFIED AIR INSIDE THE SKY CASTLE!

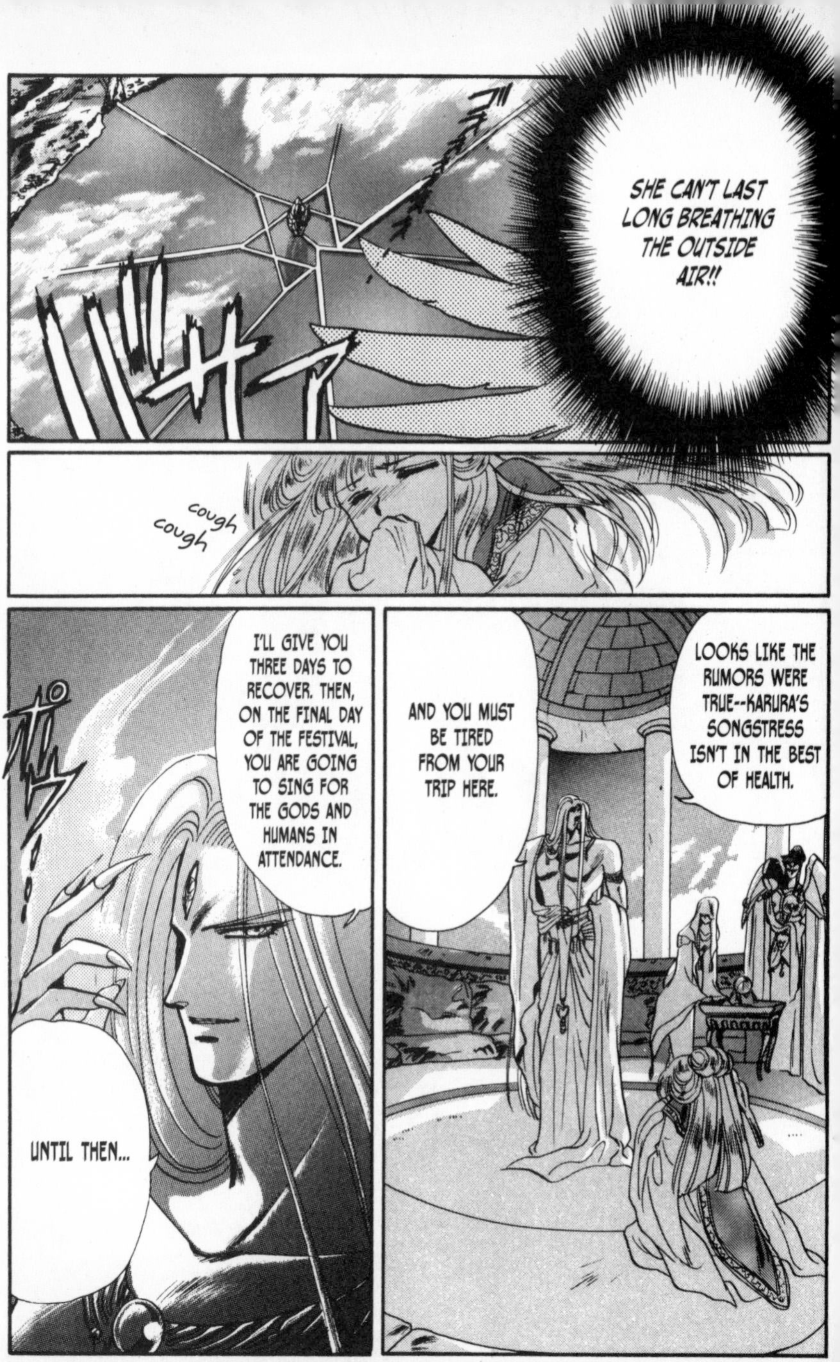
SHE CAN'T LAST LONG BREATHING THE OUTSIDE AIR!!
cough cough
LOOKS LIKE THE RUMORS WERE TRUE--KARURA'S SONGSTRESS ISN'T IN THE BEST OF HEALTH.
AND YOU MUST BE TIRED FROM YOUR TRIP HERE.
...
I'LL GIVE YOU THREE DAYS TO RECOVER. THEN, ON THE FINAL DAY OF THE FESTIVAL, YOU ARE GOING TO SING FOR THE GODS AND HUMANS IN ATTENDANCE.
UNTIL THEN...

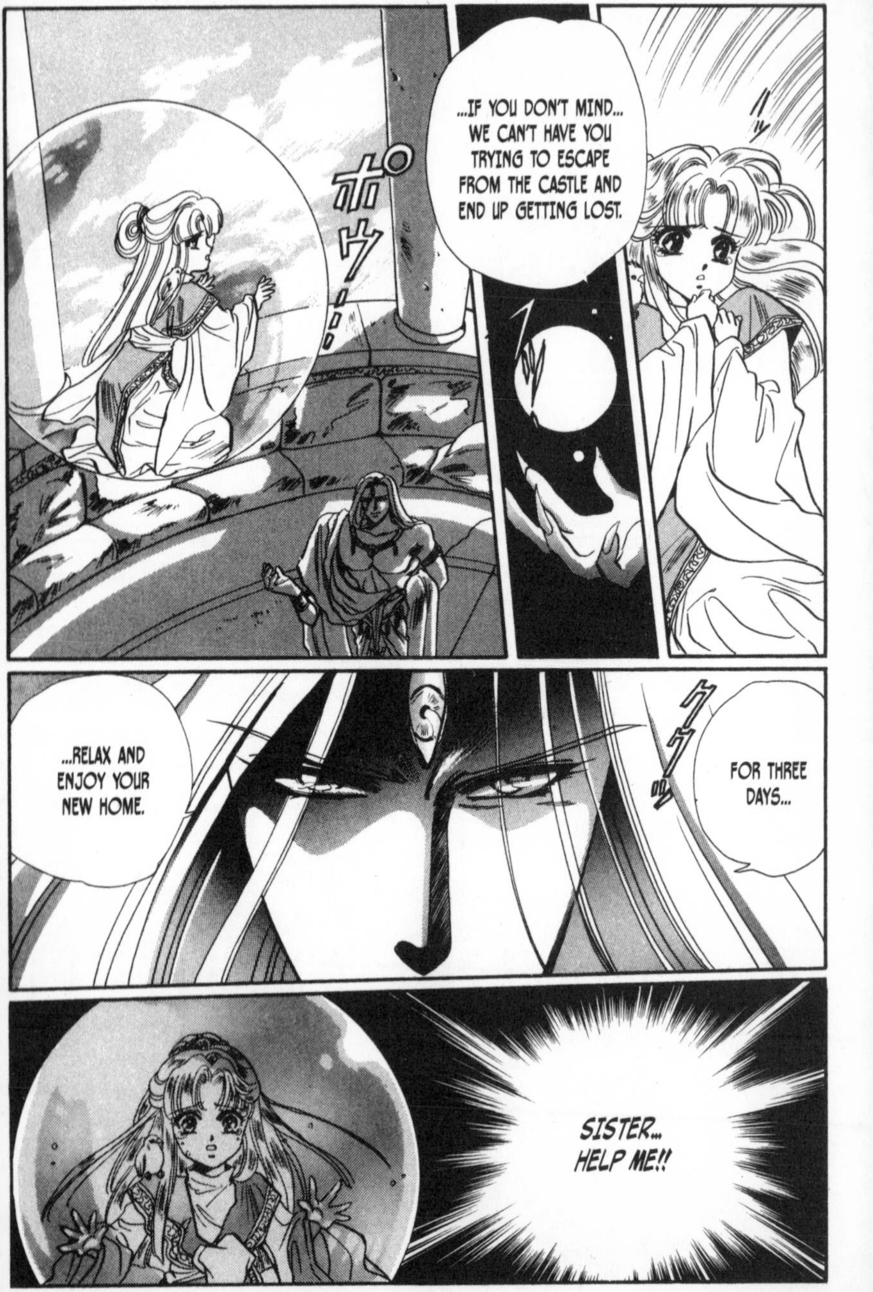
...IF YOU DON'T MIND... WE CAN'T HAVE YOU TRYING TO ESCAPE FROM THE CASTLE AND END UP GETTING LOST.
FOR THREE DAYS...
...RELAX AND ENJOY YOUR NEW HOME.
SISTER... HELP ME!!

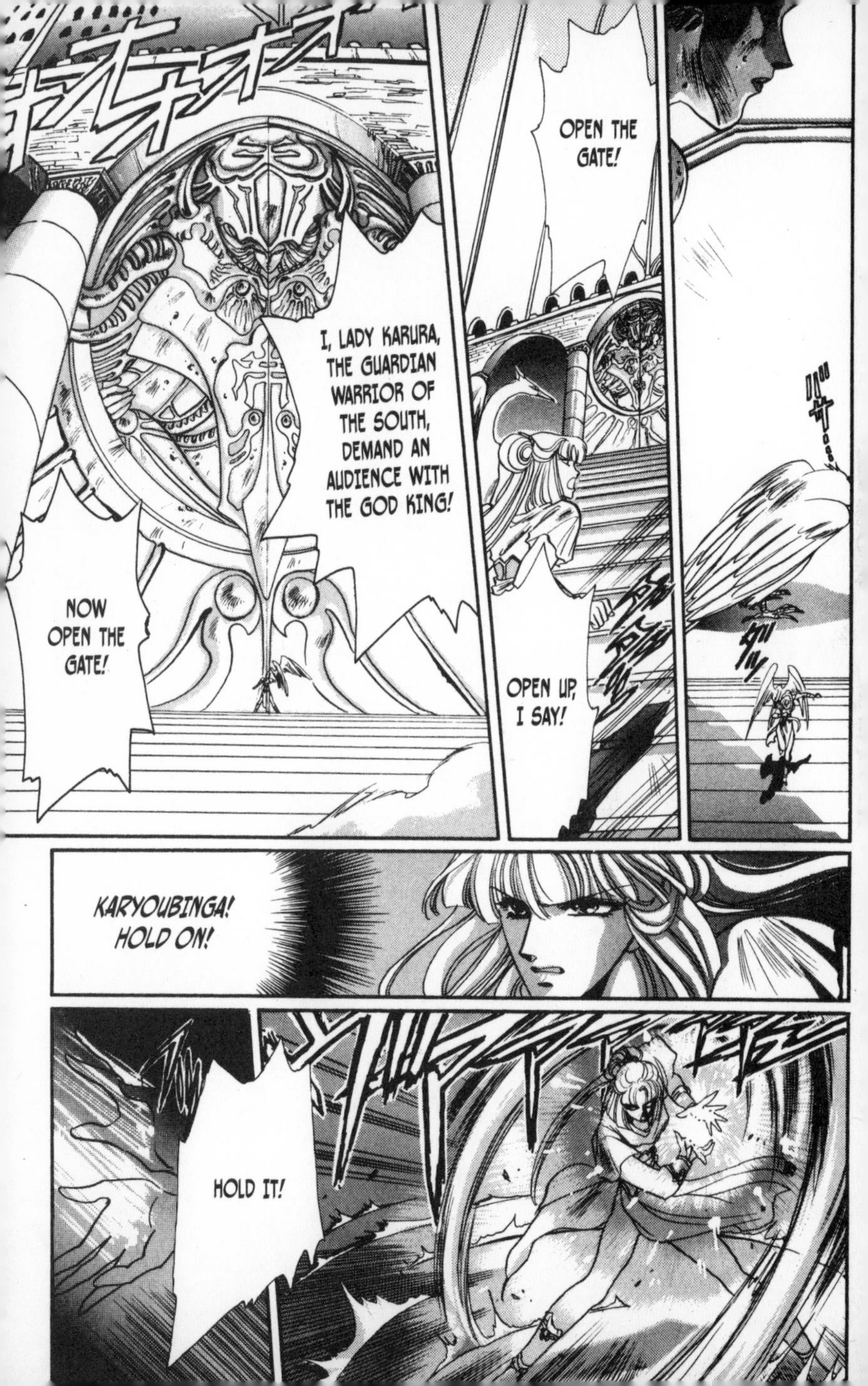
OPEN THE GATE!
OPEN UP, I SAY!
I, LADY KARURA, THE GUARDIAN WARRIOR OF THE SOUTH, DEMAND AN AUDIENCE WITH THE GOD KING!
NOW OPEN THE GATE!
KARYOUBINGA! HOLD ON!
HOLD IT!

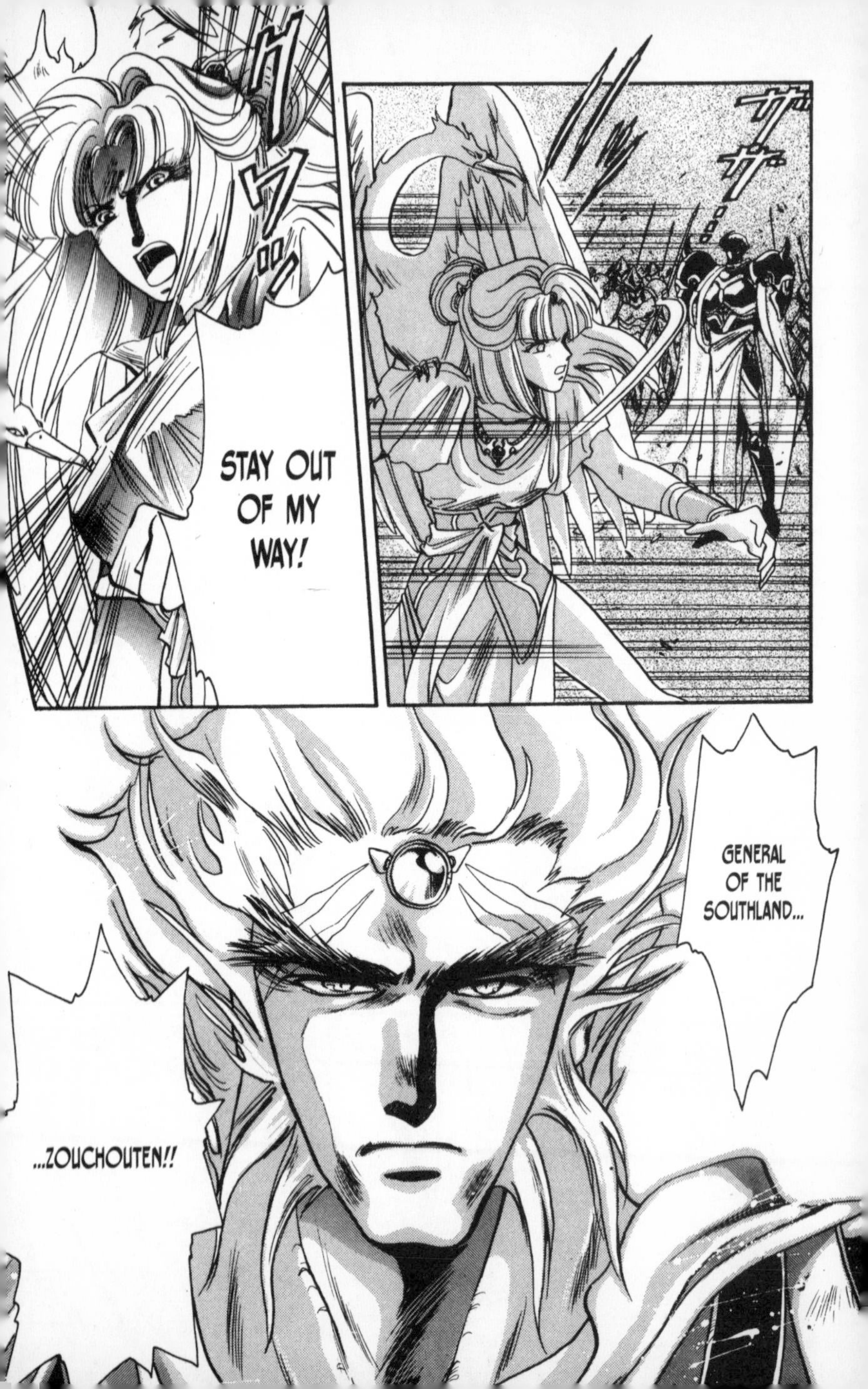
STAY OUT OF MY WAY!
GENERAL OF THE SOUTHLAND...
...ZOUCHOUTEN!!

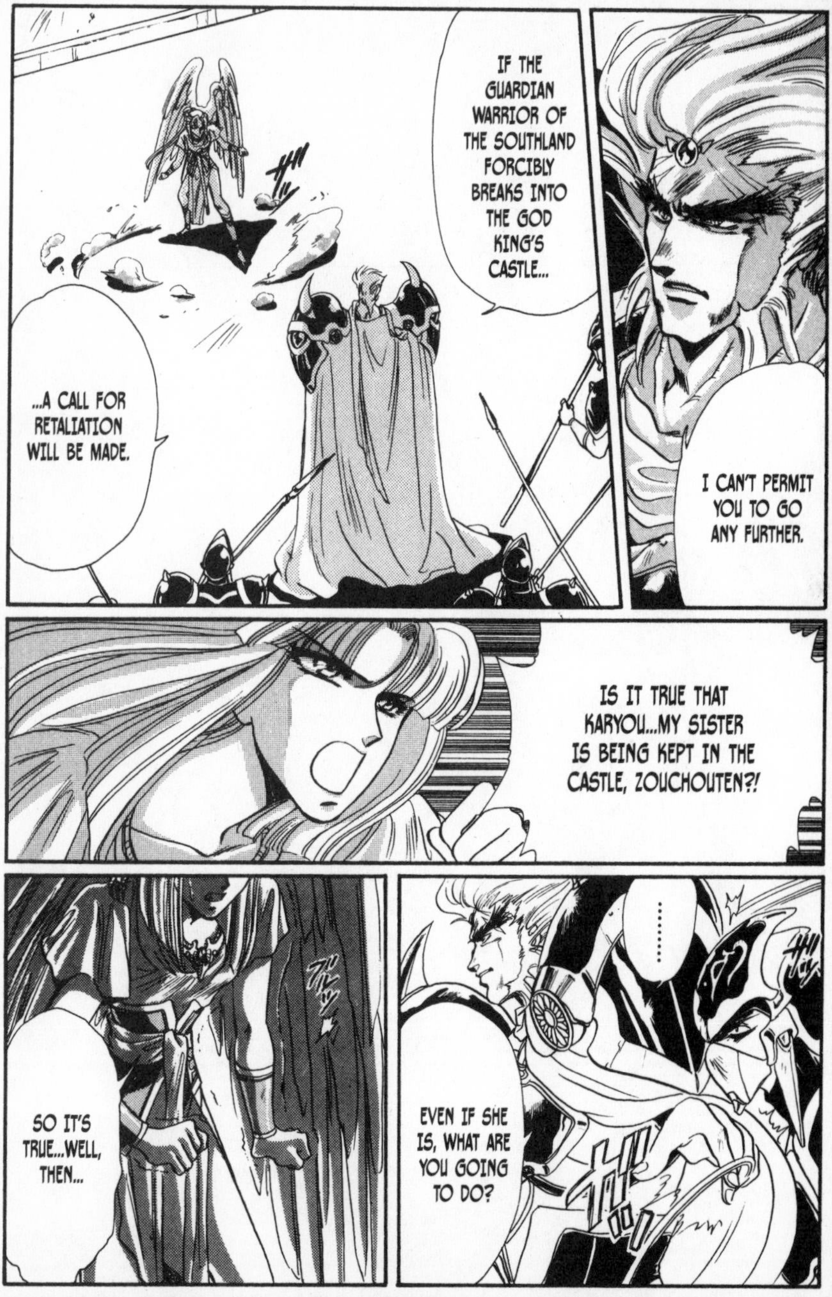

I CAN'T PERMIT YOU TO GO ANY FURTHER.
IF THE GUARDIAN WARRIOR OF THE SOUTHLAND FORCIBLY BREAKS INTO THE GOD KING'S CASTLE...
...A CALL FOR RETALIATION WILL BE MADE.
IS IT TRUE THAT KARYOU...MY SISTER IS BEING KEPT IN THE CASTLE, ZOUCHOUTEN?!
......
EVEN IF SHE IS, WHAT ARE YOU GOING TO DO?
SO IT'S TRUE...WELL, THEN...

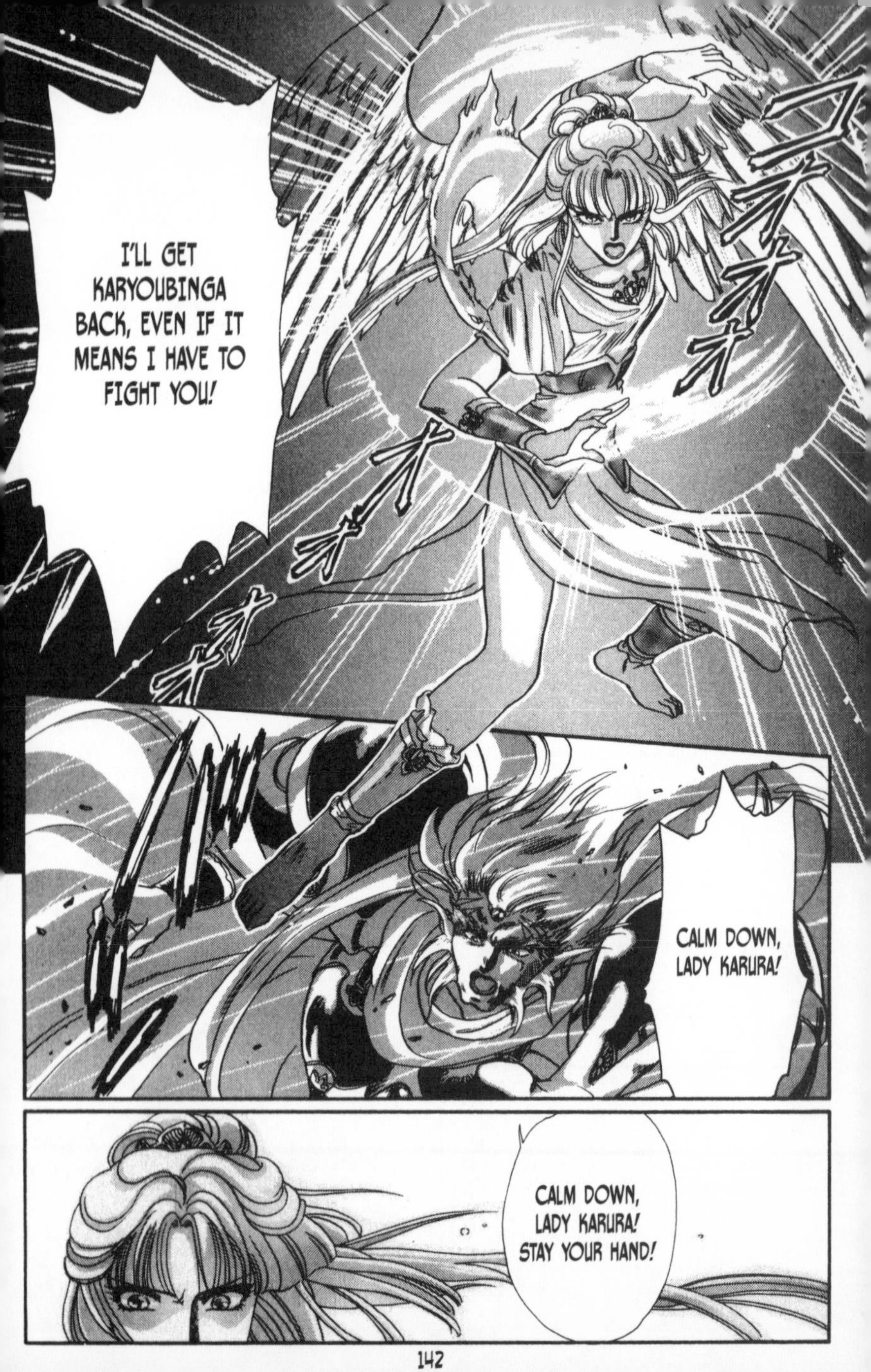
I'LL GET KARYOUBINGA BACK, EVEN IF IT MEANS I HAVE TO FIGHT YOU!
CALM DOWN, LADY KARURA!
CALM DOWN, LADY KARURA! STAY YOUR HAND!

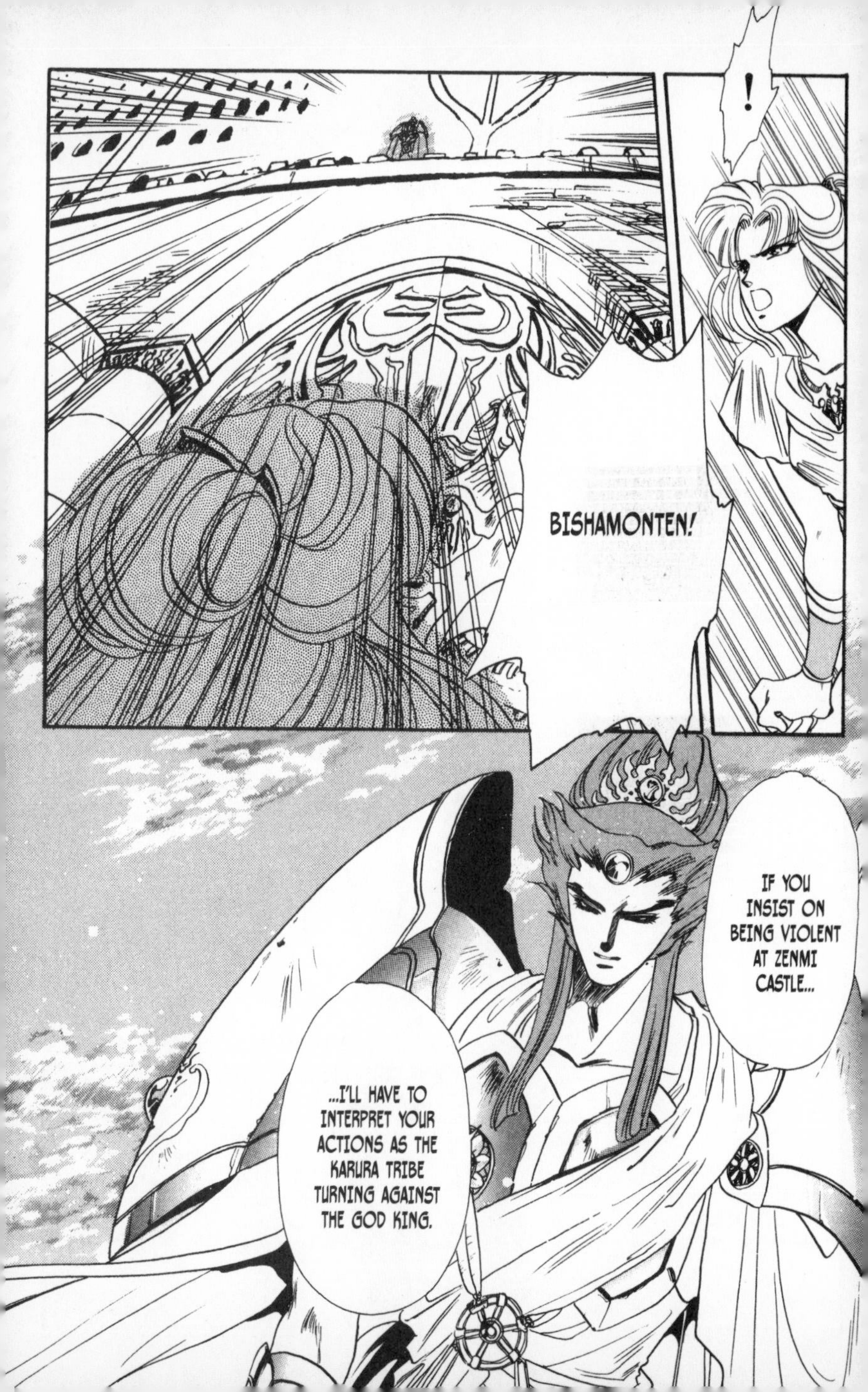
!
BISHAMONTEN!
IF YOU INSIST ON BEING VIOLENT AT ZENMI CASTLE...
...I'LL HAVE TO INTERPRET YOUR ACTIONS AS THE KARURA TRIBE TURNING AGAINST THE GOD KING.

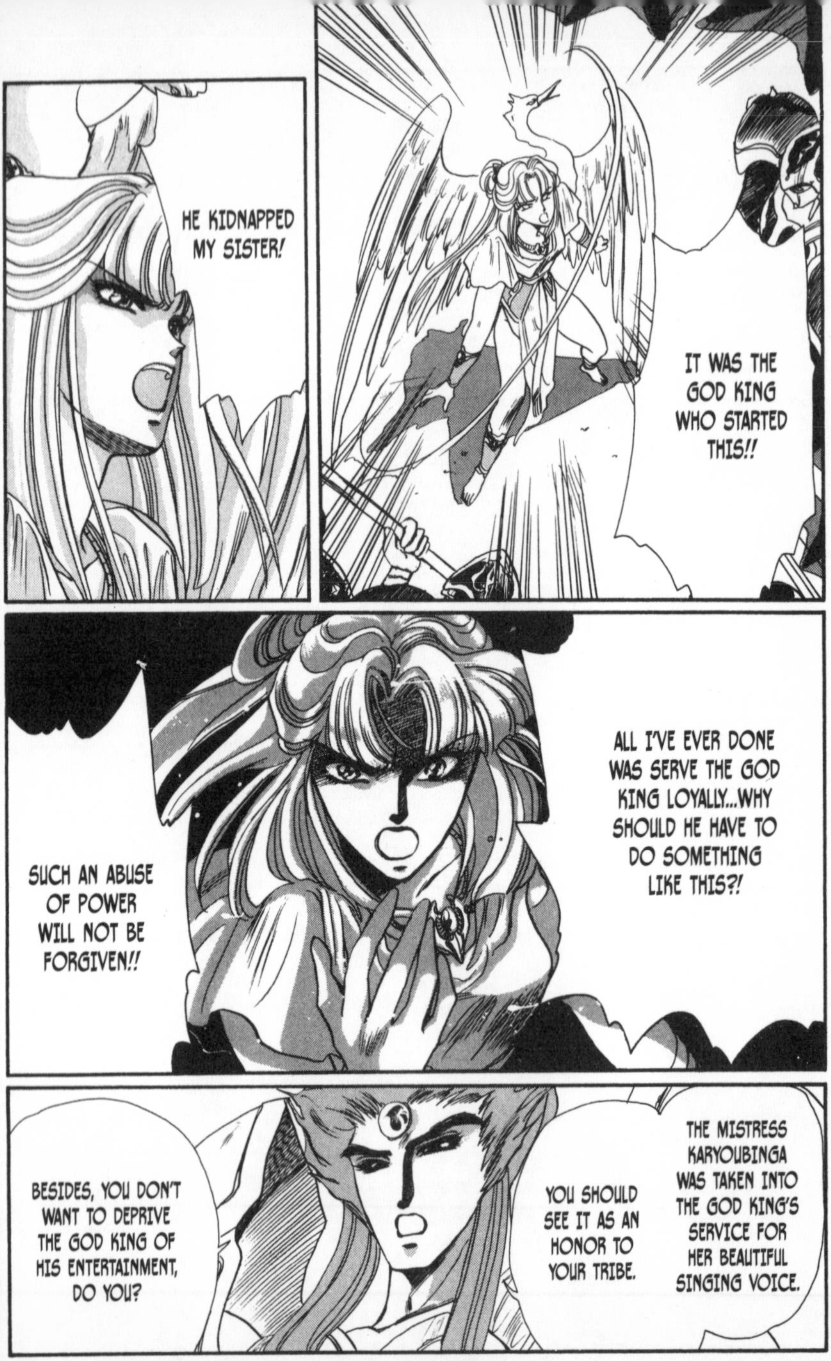
IT WAS THE GOD KING WHO STARTED THIS!!
HE KIDNAPPED MY SISTER!
ALL I'VE EVER DONE WAS SERVE THE GOD KING LOYALLY...WHY SHOULD HE HAVE TO DO SOMETHING LIKE THIS?!
SUCH AN ABUSE OF POWER WILL NOT BE FORGIVEN!!
THE MISTRESS KARYOUBINGA WAS TAKEN INTO THE GOD KING'S SERVICE FOR HER BEAUTIFUL SINGING VOICE.
YOU SHOULD SEE IT AS AN HONOR TO YOUR TRIBE.
BESIDES, YOU DON'T WANT TO DEPRIVE THE GOD KING OF HIS ENTERTAINMENT, DO YOU?

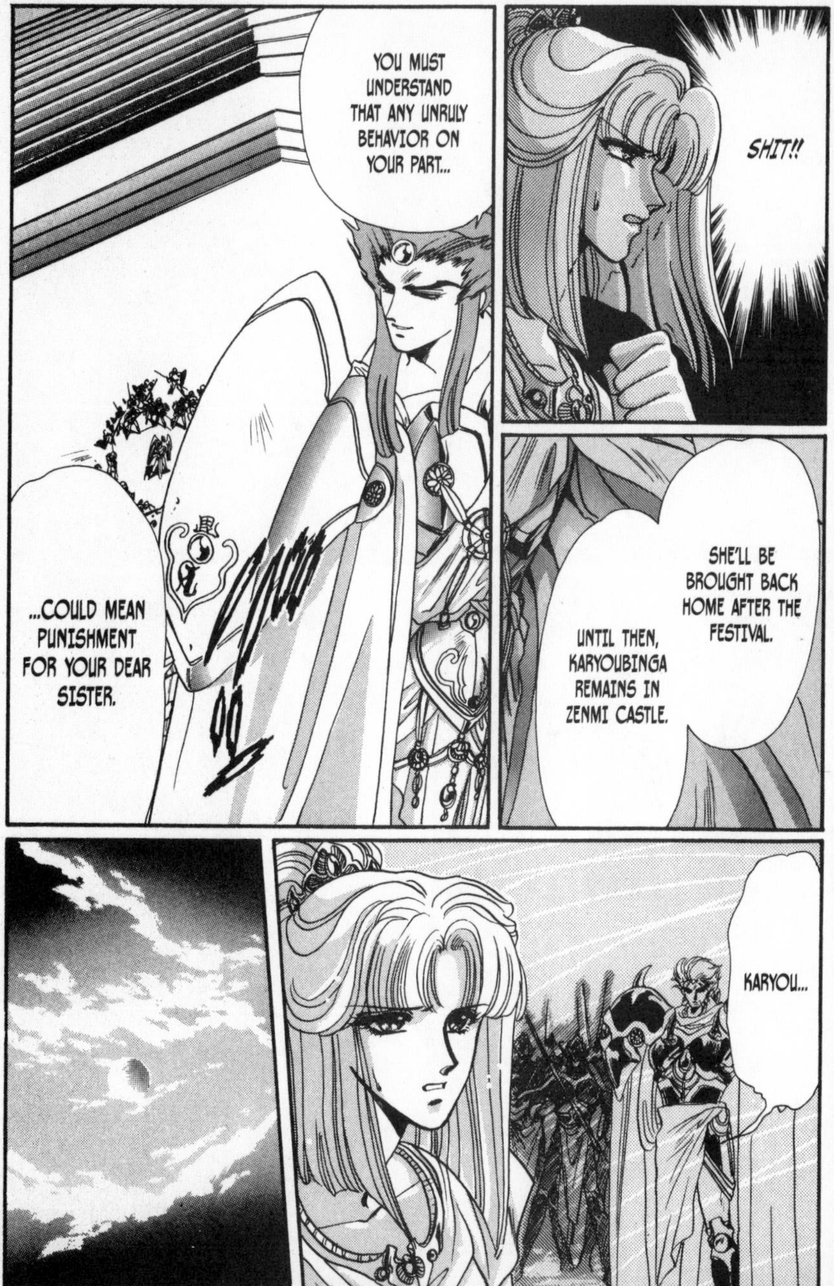
YOU MUST UNDERSTAND THAT ANY UNRULY BEHAVIOR ON YOUR PART...
SHIT!!
...COULD MEAN PUNISHMENT FOR YOUR DEAR SISTER.
SHE'LL BE BROUGHT BACK HOME AFTER THE FESTIVAL.
UNTIL THEN, KARYOUBINGA REMAINS IN ZENMI CASTLE.
KARYOU...

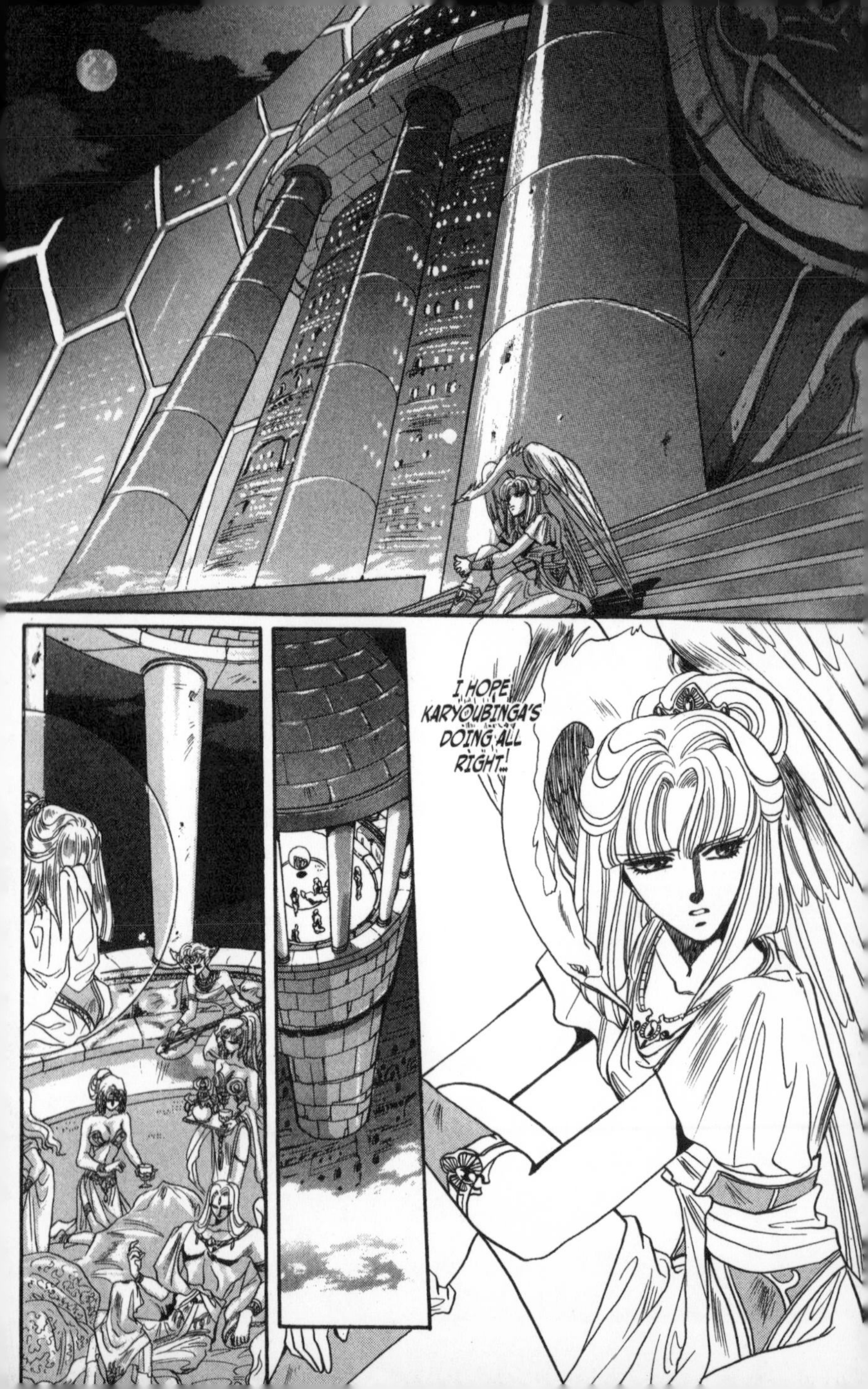
I HOPE KARYOUBINGA'S DOING ALL RIGHT...

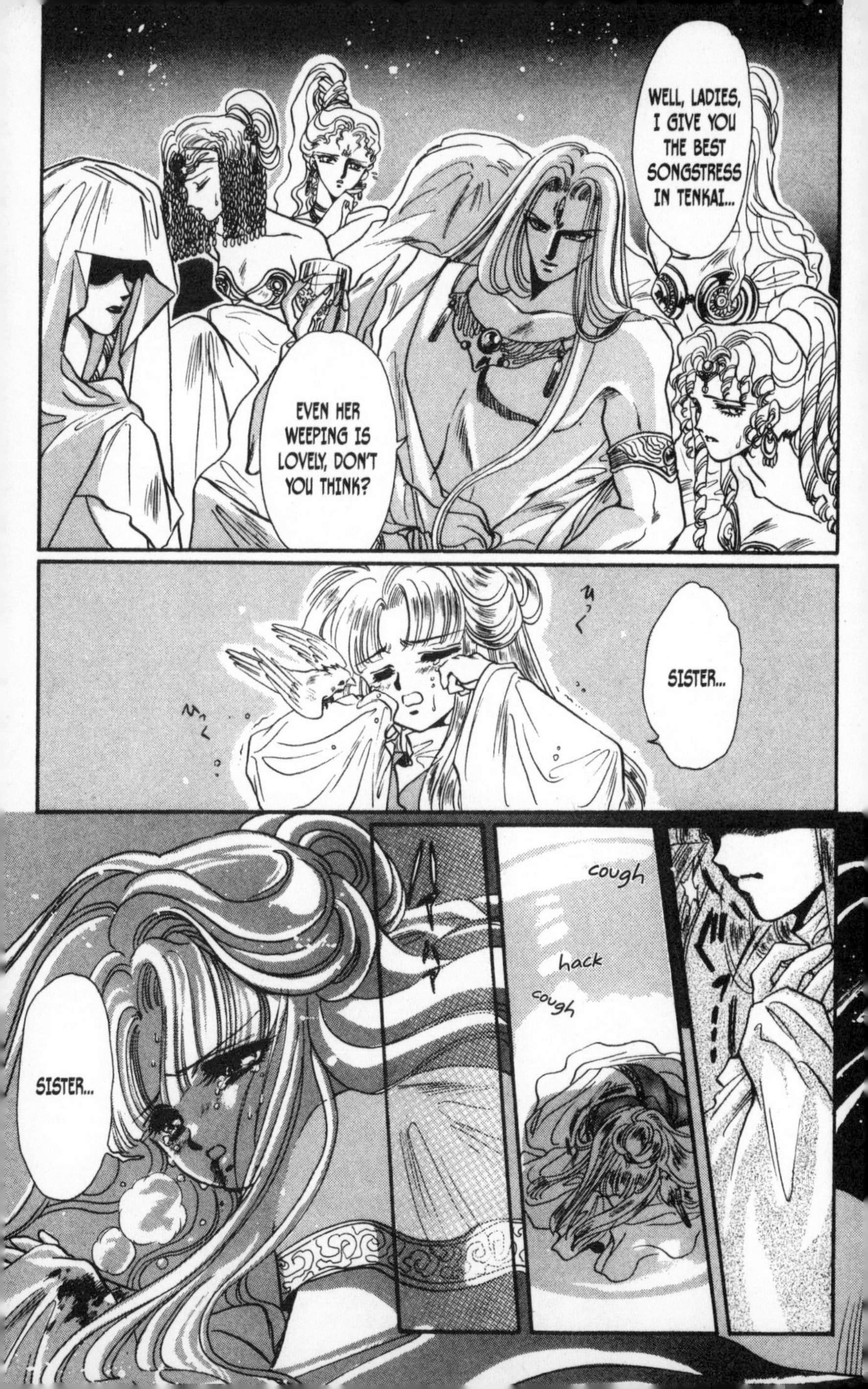

WELL, LADIES, I GIVE YOU THE BEST SONGSTRESS IN TENKAI...
EVEN HER WEEPING IS LOVELY, DON'T YOU THINK?
SISTER...
cough
hack
cough
SISTER...

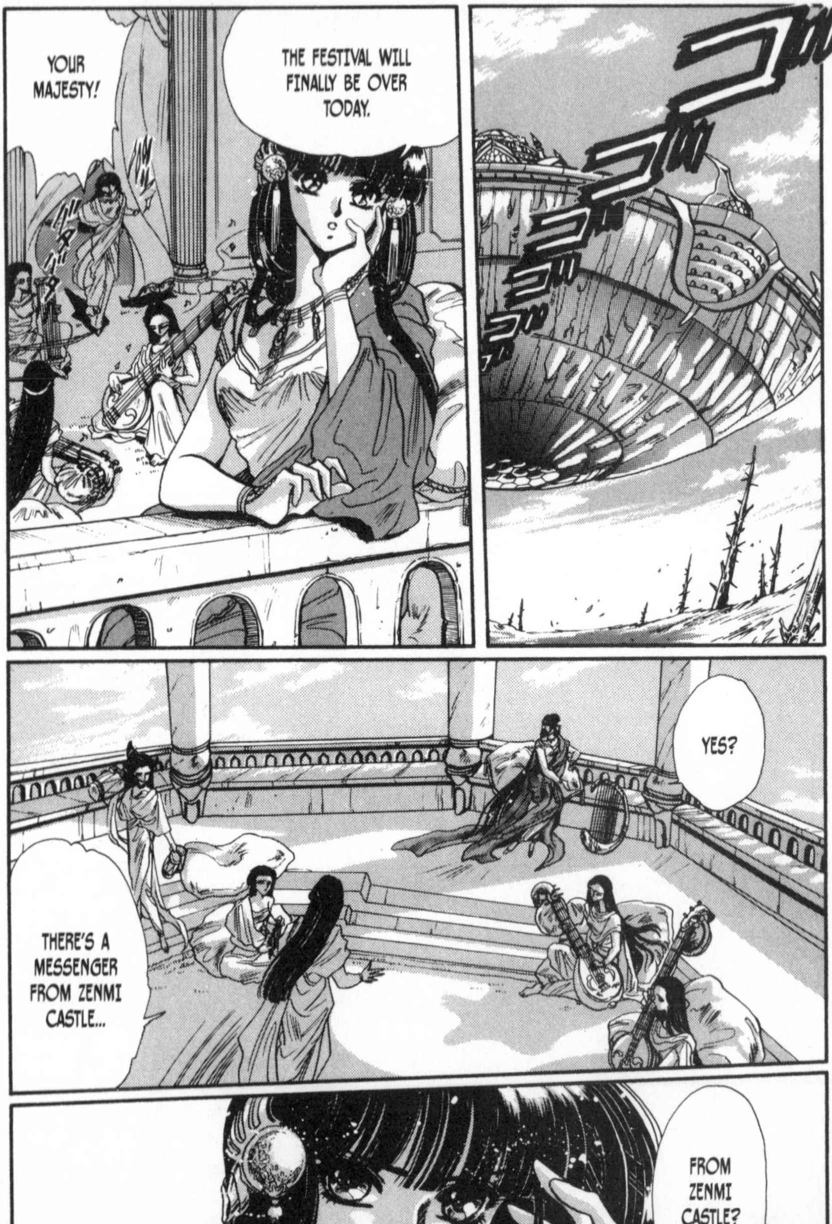
THE FESTIVAL WILL FINALLY BE OVER TODAY.
YOUR MAJESTY!
YES?
THERE'S A MESSENGER FROM ZENMI CASTLE...
FROM ZENMI CASTLE?

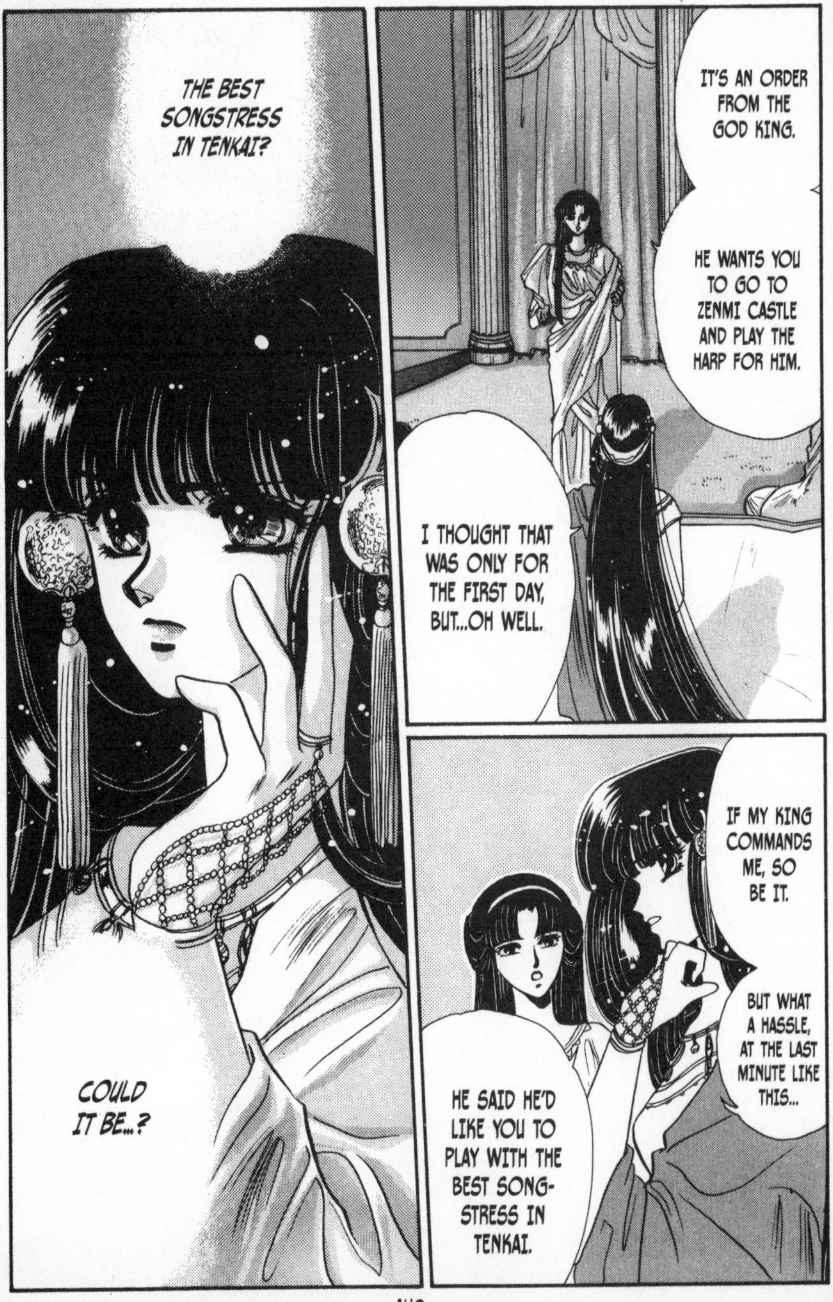
IT'S AN ORDER FROM THE GOD KING.
HE WANTS YOU TO GO TO ZENMI CASTLE AND PLAY THE HARP FOR HIM.
I THOUGHT THAT WAS ONLY FOR THE FIRST DAY, BUT...OH WELL.
IF MY KING COMMANDS ME, SO BE IT.
BUT WHAT A HASSLE, AT THE LAST MINUTE LIKE THIS...
HE SAID HE'D LIKE YOU TO PLAY WITH THE BEST SONG-STRESS IN TENKAI.
THE BEST SONGSTRESS IN TENKAI?
COULD IT BE...?

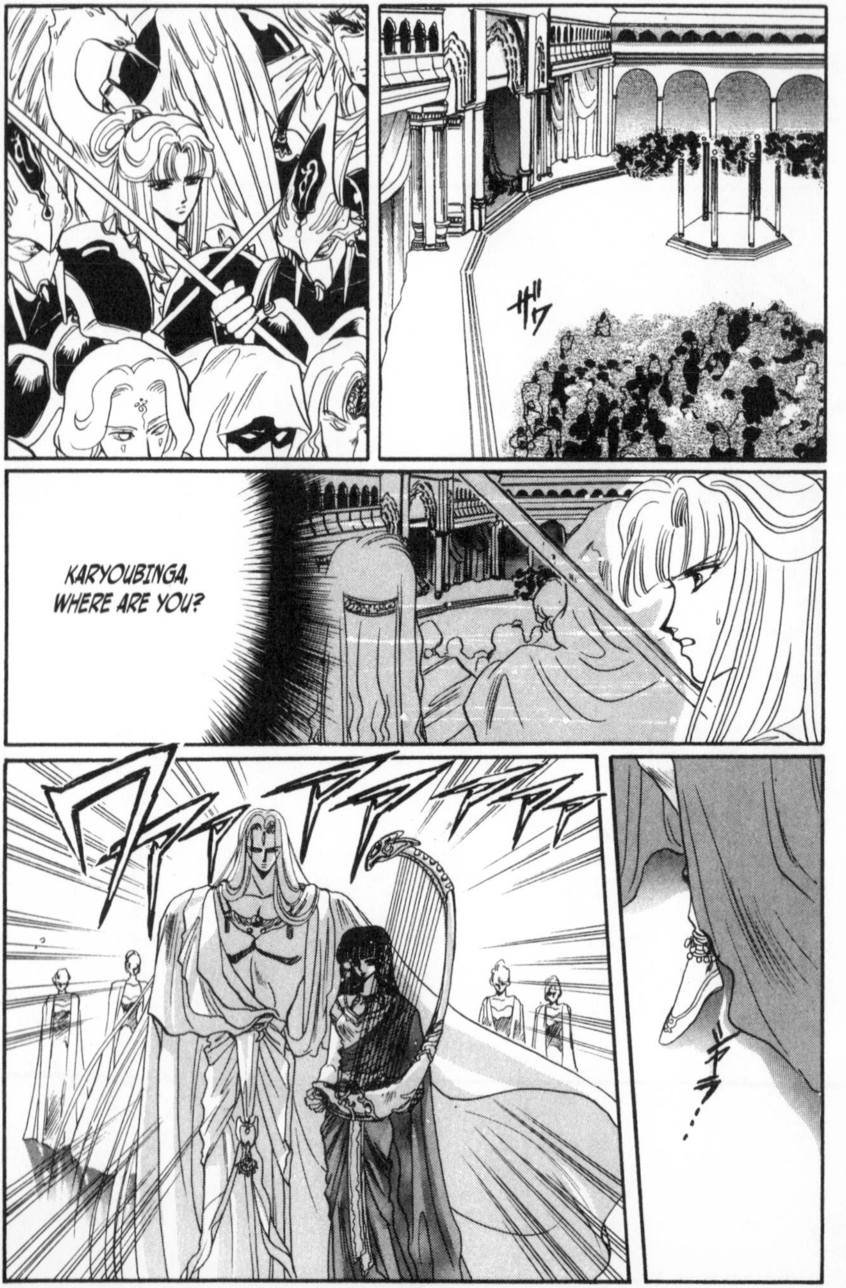
ザワ
KARYOUBINGA,
WHERE ARE YOU?

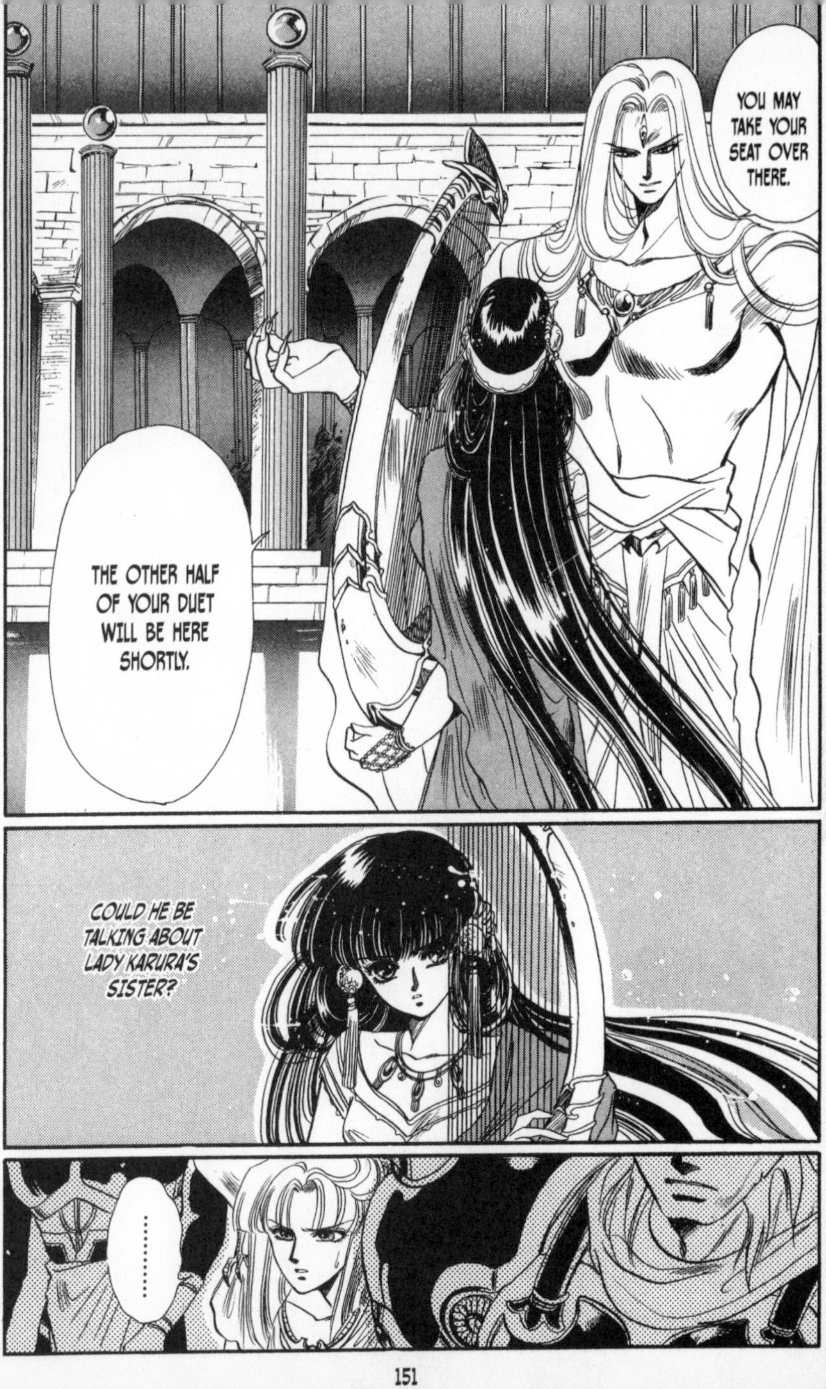
YOU MAY TAKE YOUR SEAT OVER THERE.
THE OTHER HALF OF YOUR DUET WILL BE HERE SHORTLY.
COULD HE BE TALKING ABOUT LADY KARURA'S SISTER?
......

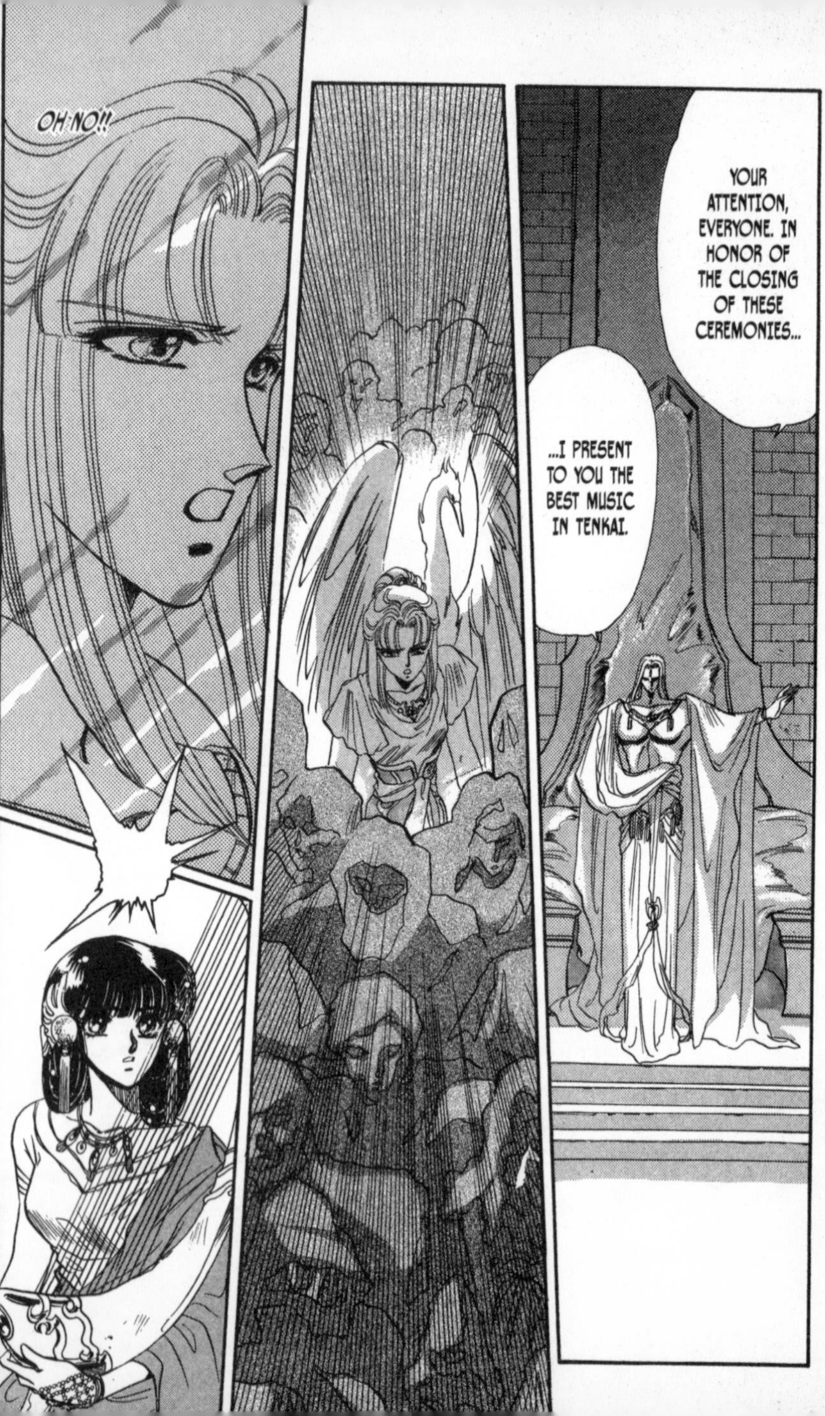
YOUR ATTENTION, EVERYONE. IN HONOR OF THE CLOSING OF THESE CEREMONIES...
...I PRESENT TO YOU THE BEST MUSIC IN TENKAI.
OH NO!!

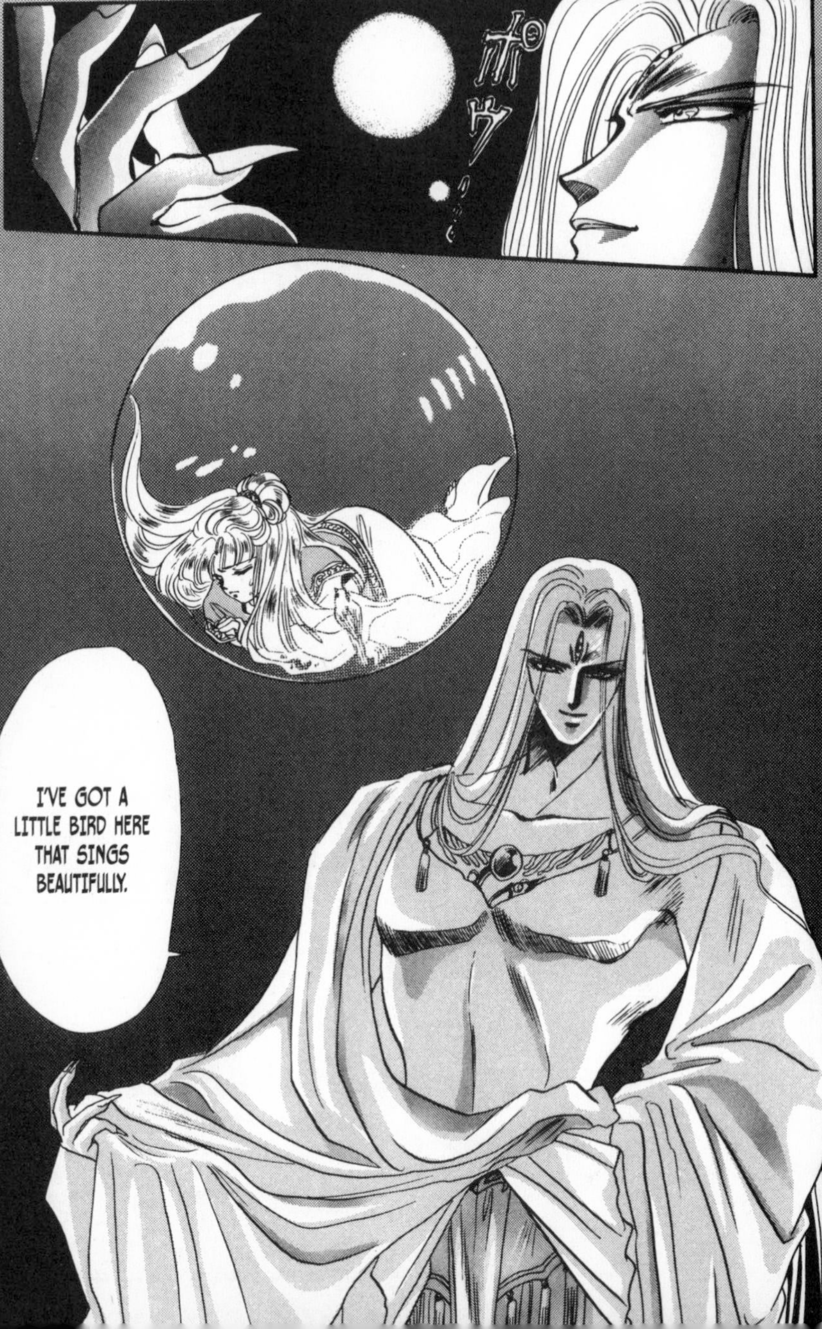
ポウ
I'VE GOT A LITTLE BIRD HERE THAT SINGS BEAUTIFULLY.

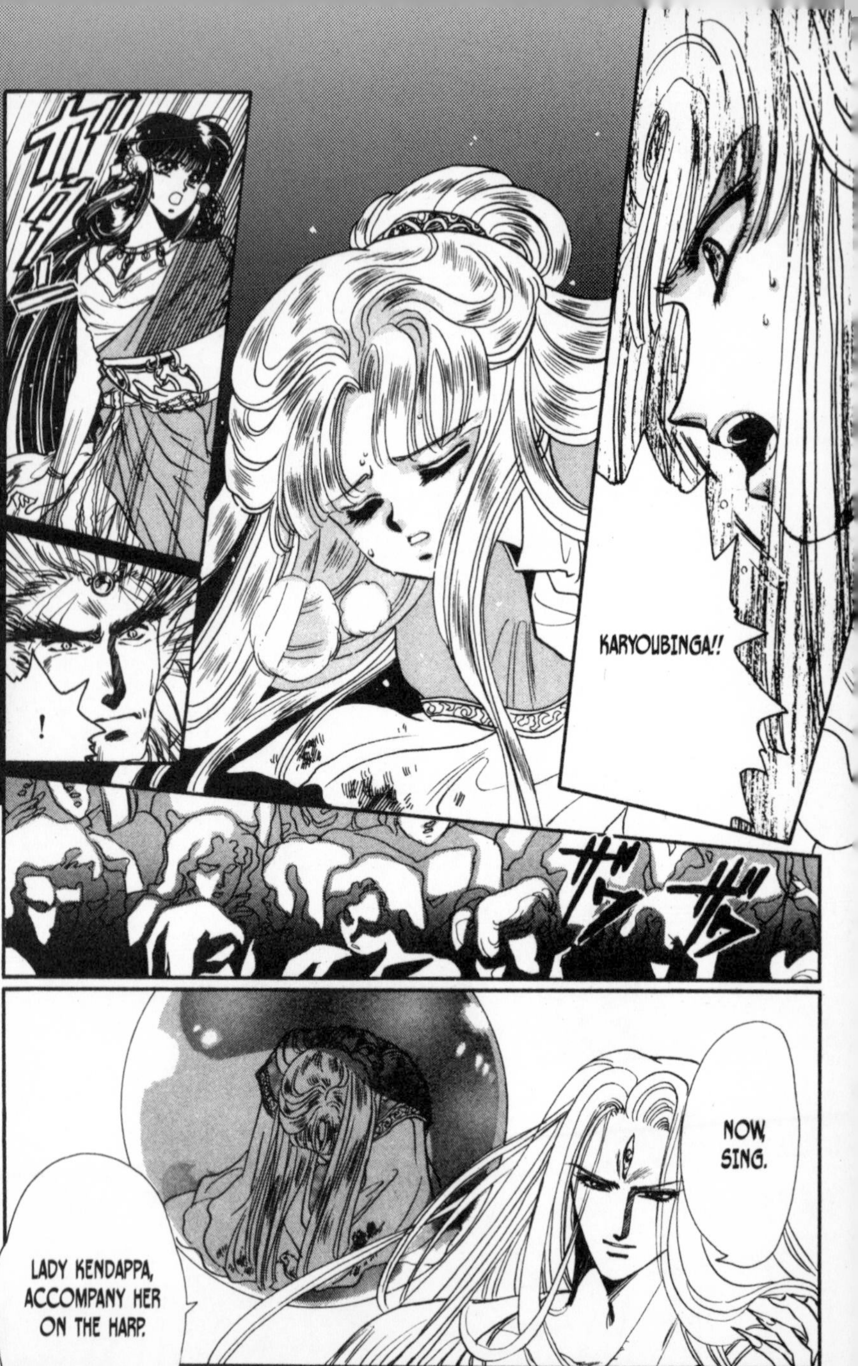
KARYOUBINGA!!
!
NOW, SING.
LADY KENDAPPA, ACCOMPANY HER ON THE HARP.

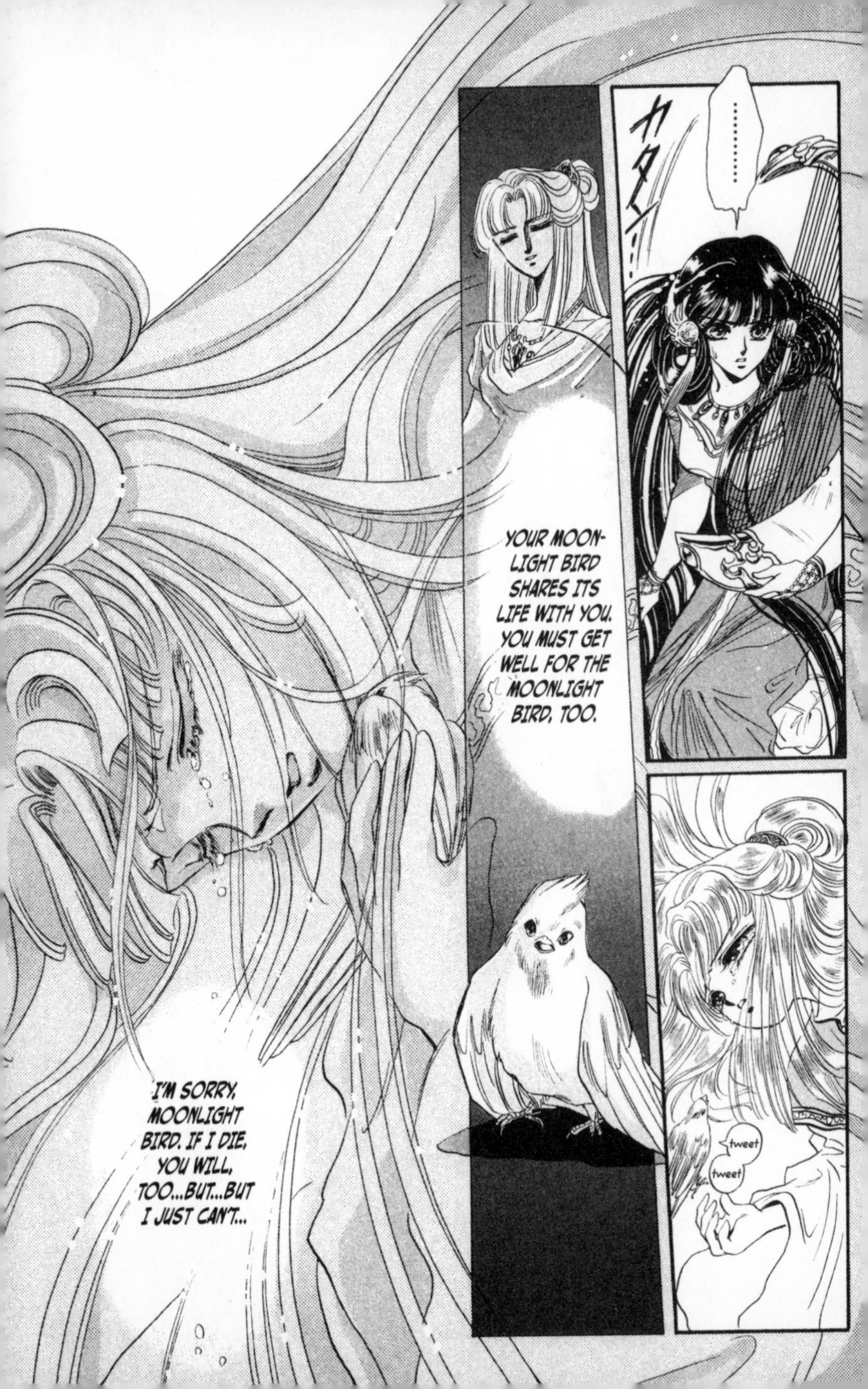
カタン
……
YOUR MOON-LIGHT BIRD SHARES ITS LIFE WITH YOU. YOU MUST GET WELL FOR THE MOONLIGHT BIRD, TOO.
tweet
tweet
I'M SORRY, MOONLIGHT BIRD. IF I DIE, YOU WILL, TOO...BUT...BUT I JUST CAN'T...

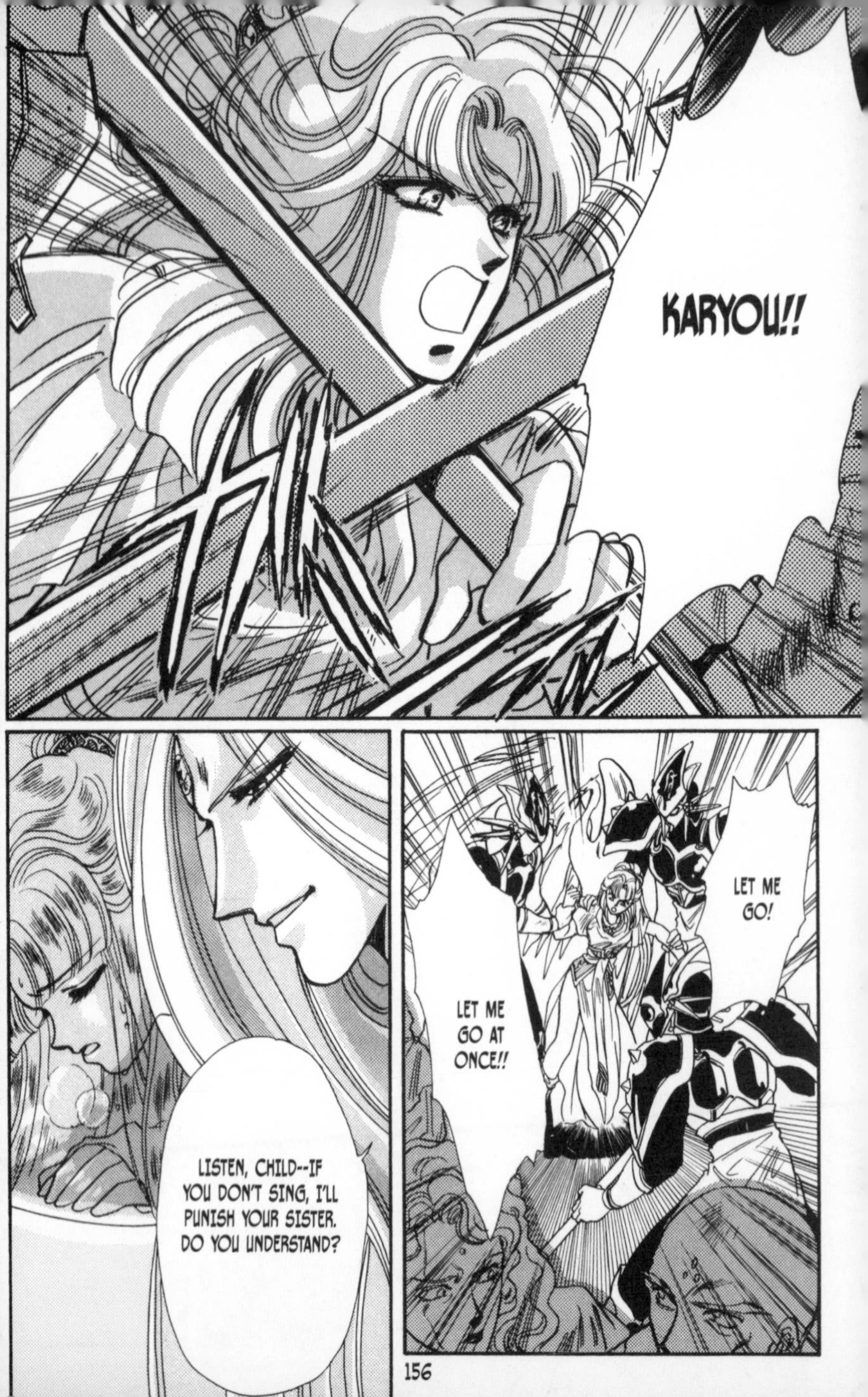
KARYOU!!
LET ME GO!
LET ME GO AT ONCE!!
LISTEN, CHILD--IF YOU DON'T SING, I'LL PUNISH YOUR SISTER. DO YOU UNDERSTAND?

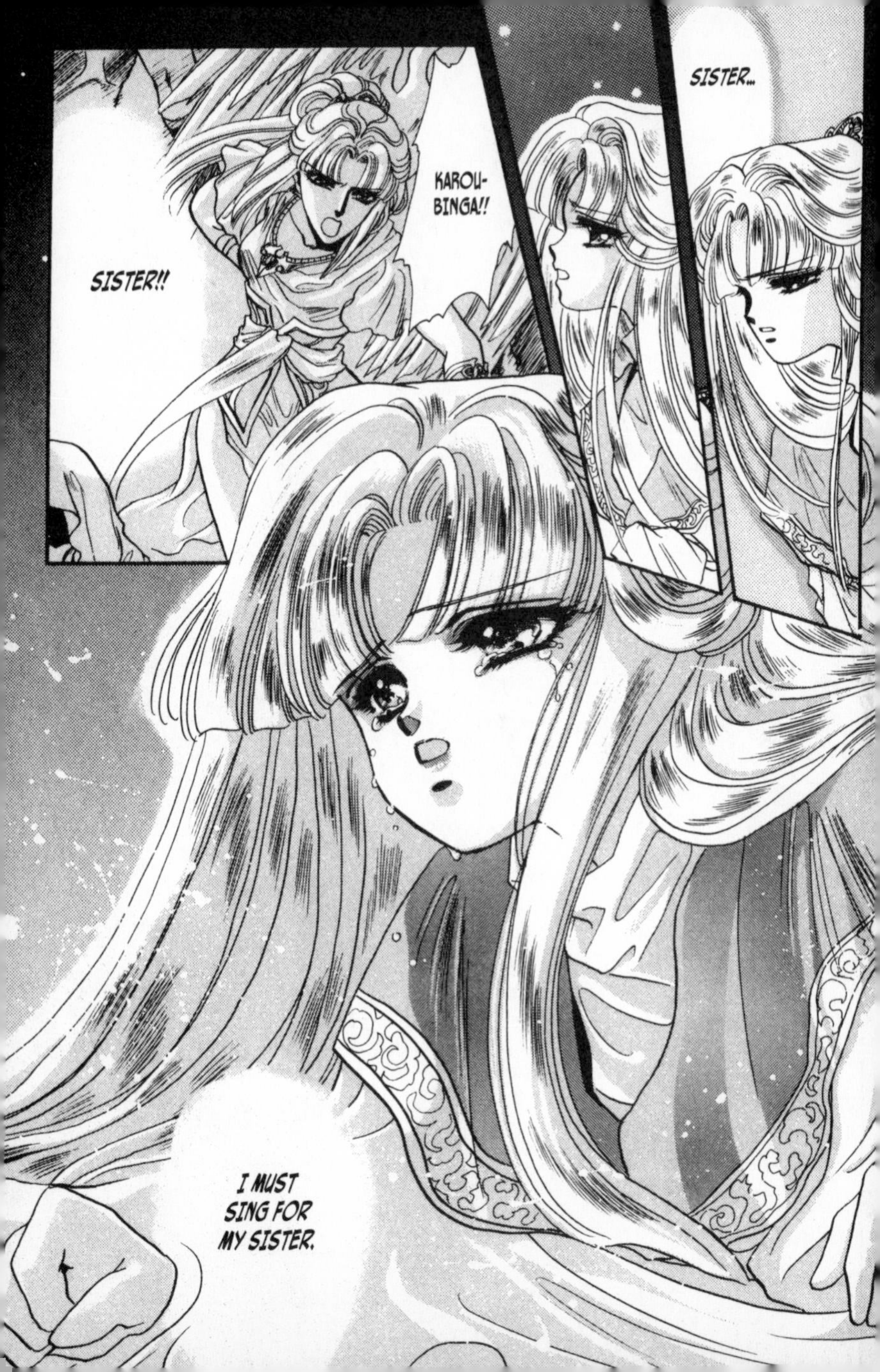
SISTER...
KAROU-
BINGA!!
SISTER!!
I MUST
SING FOR
MY SISTER.

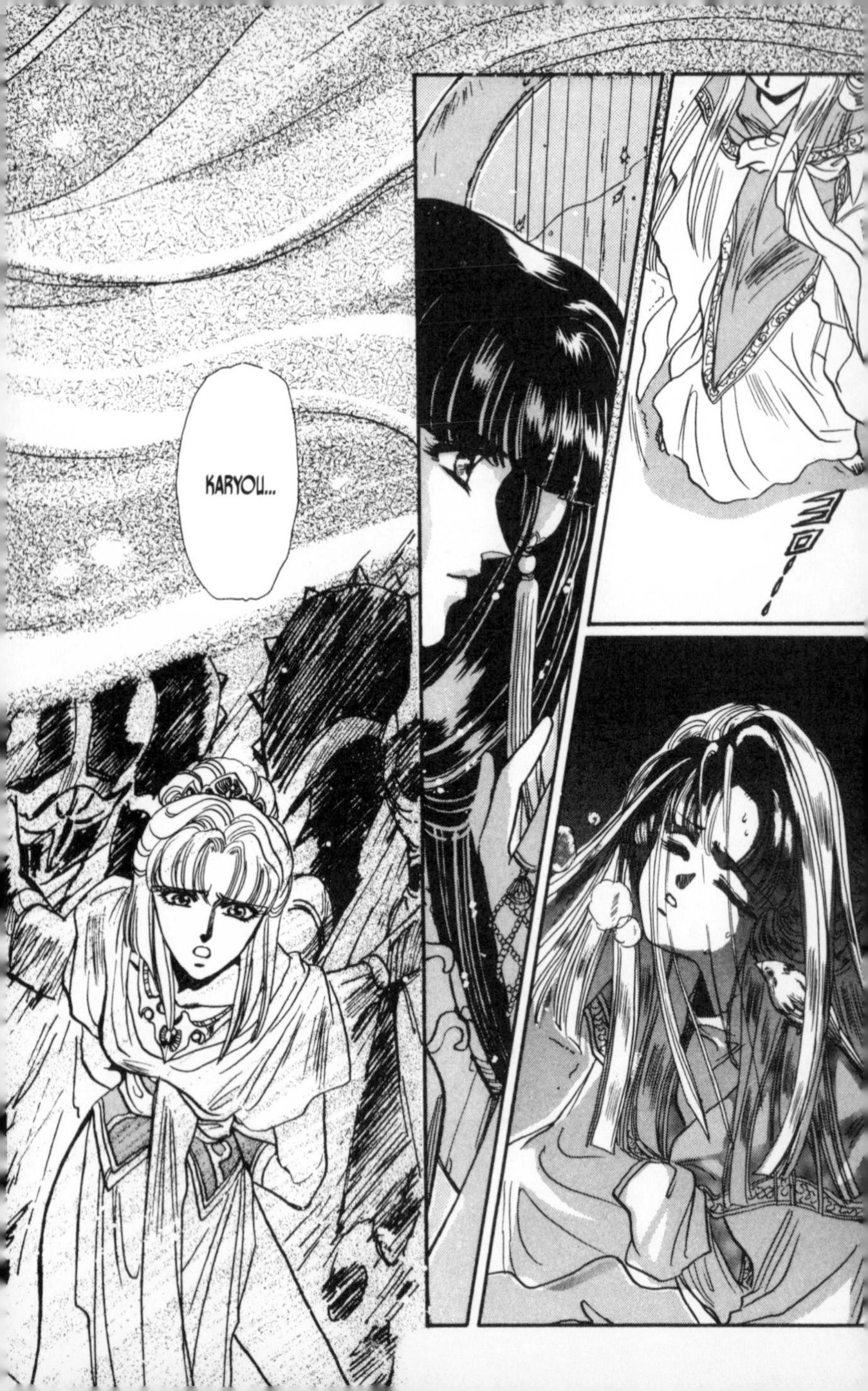
KARYOU...

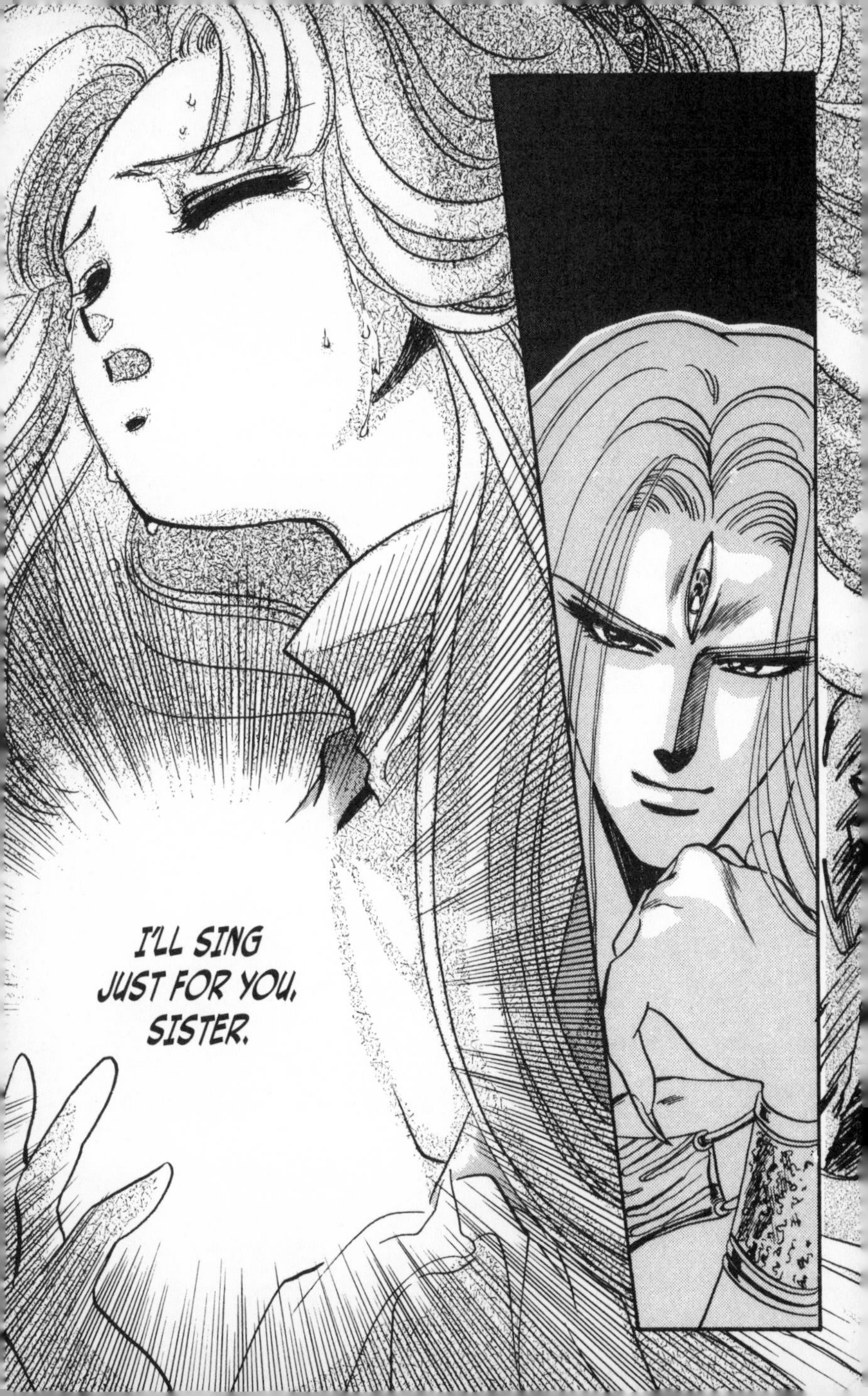
I'LL SING JUST FOR YOU, SISTER.

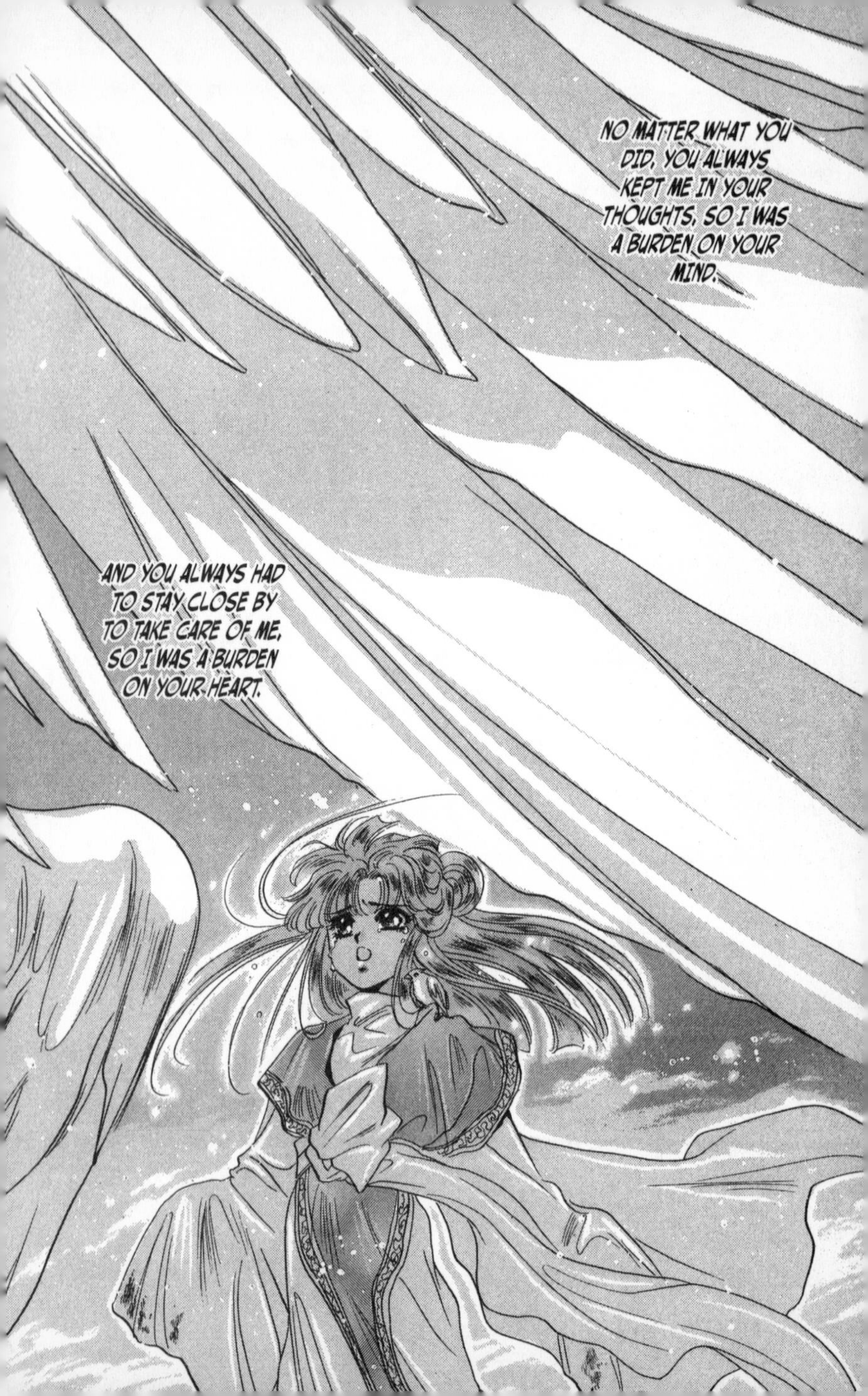
NO MATTER WHAT YOU DID, YOU ALWAYS KEPT ME IN YOUR THOUGHTS, SO I WAS A BURDEN ON YOUR MIND.
AND YOU ALWAYS HAD TO STAY CLOSE BY TO TAKE CARE OF ME, SO I WAS A BURDEN ON YOUR HEART.

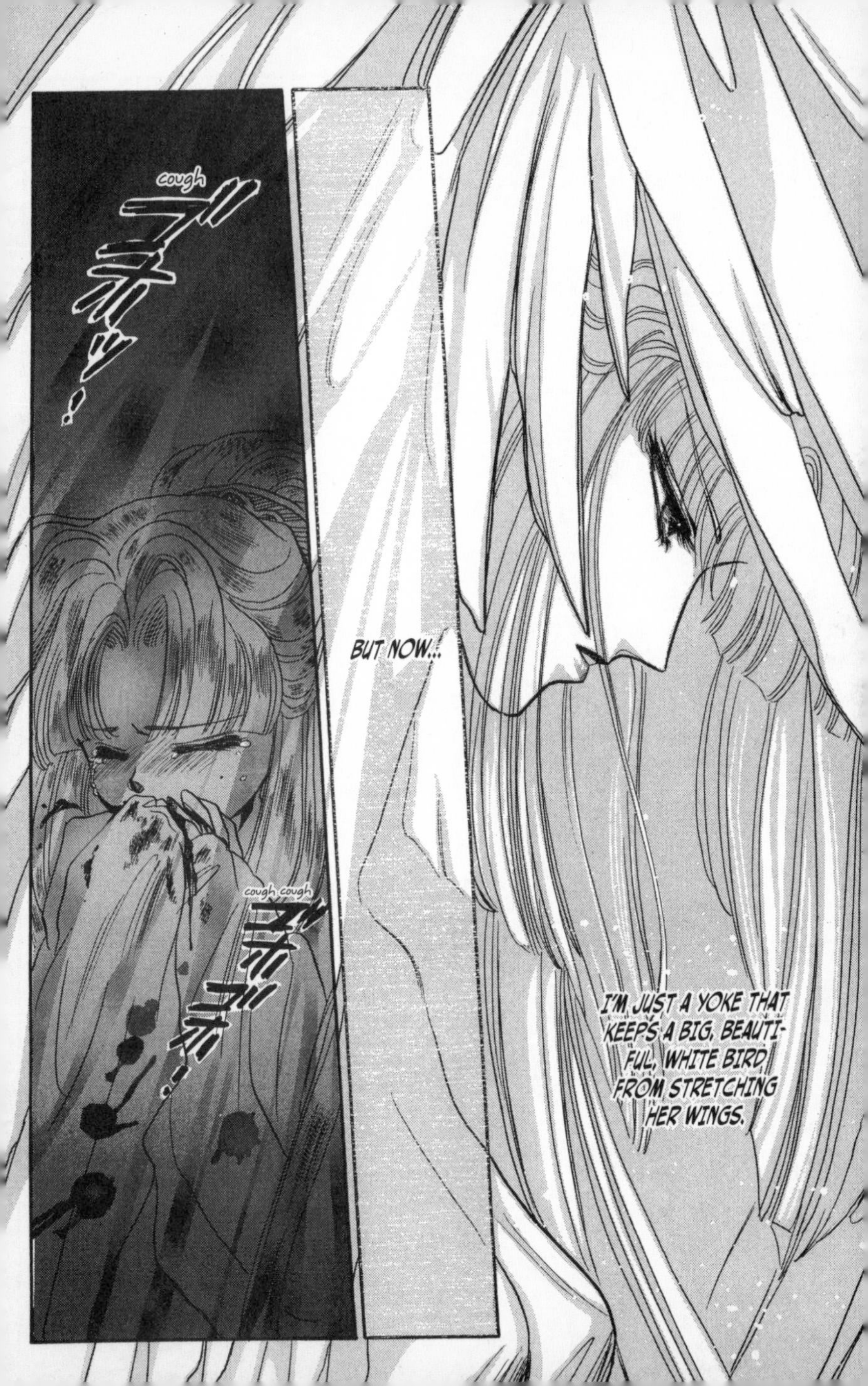
cough
cough cough
BUT NOW...
I'M JUST A YOKE THAT KEEPS A BIG, BEAUTI-FUL, WHITE BIRD FROM STRETCHING HER WINGS.

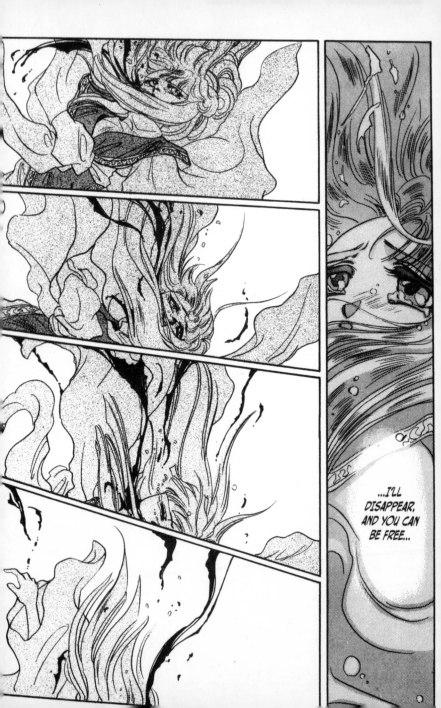

...I'LL DISAPPEAR, AND YOU CAN BE FREE...

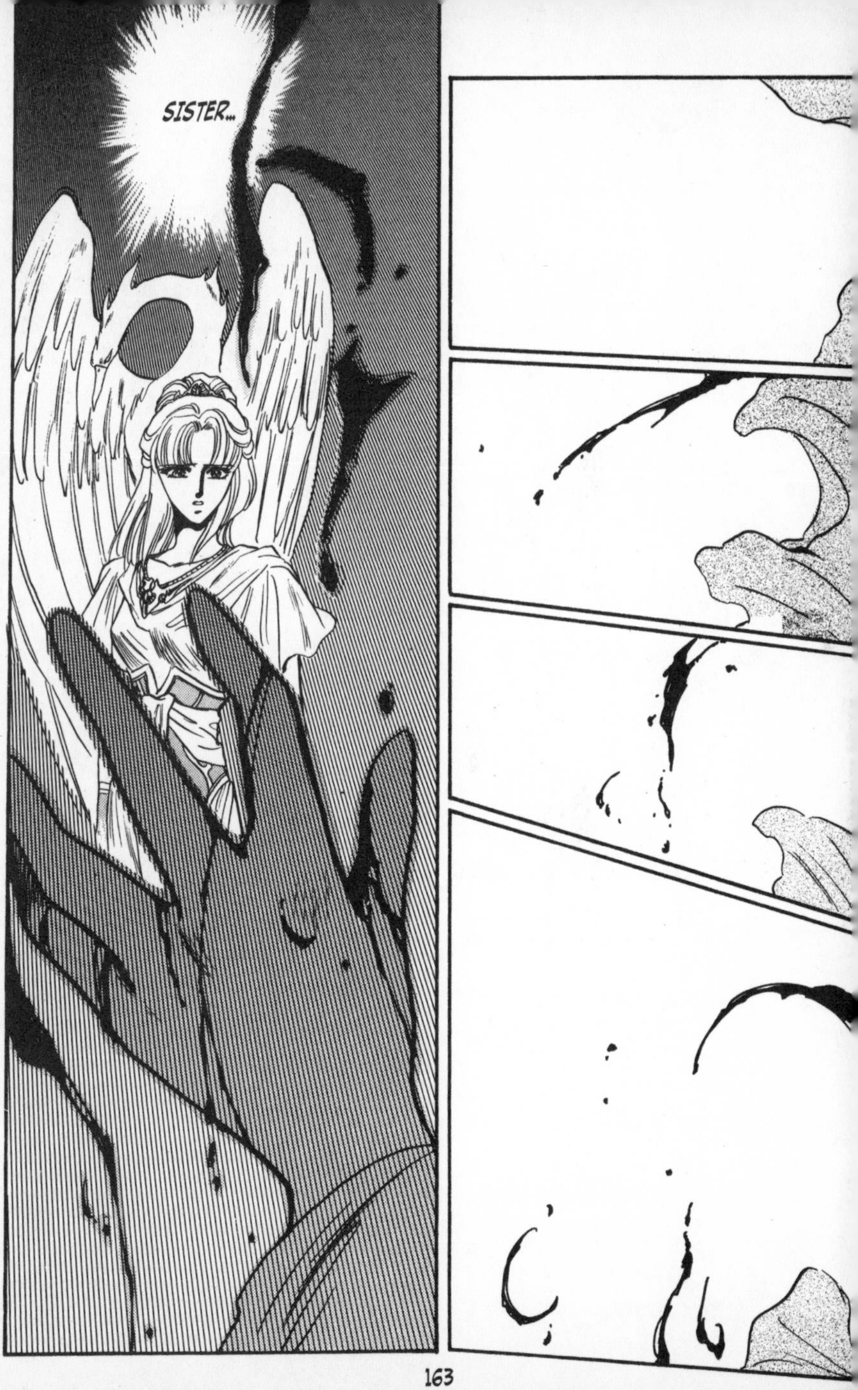
SISTER...

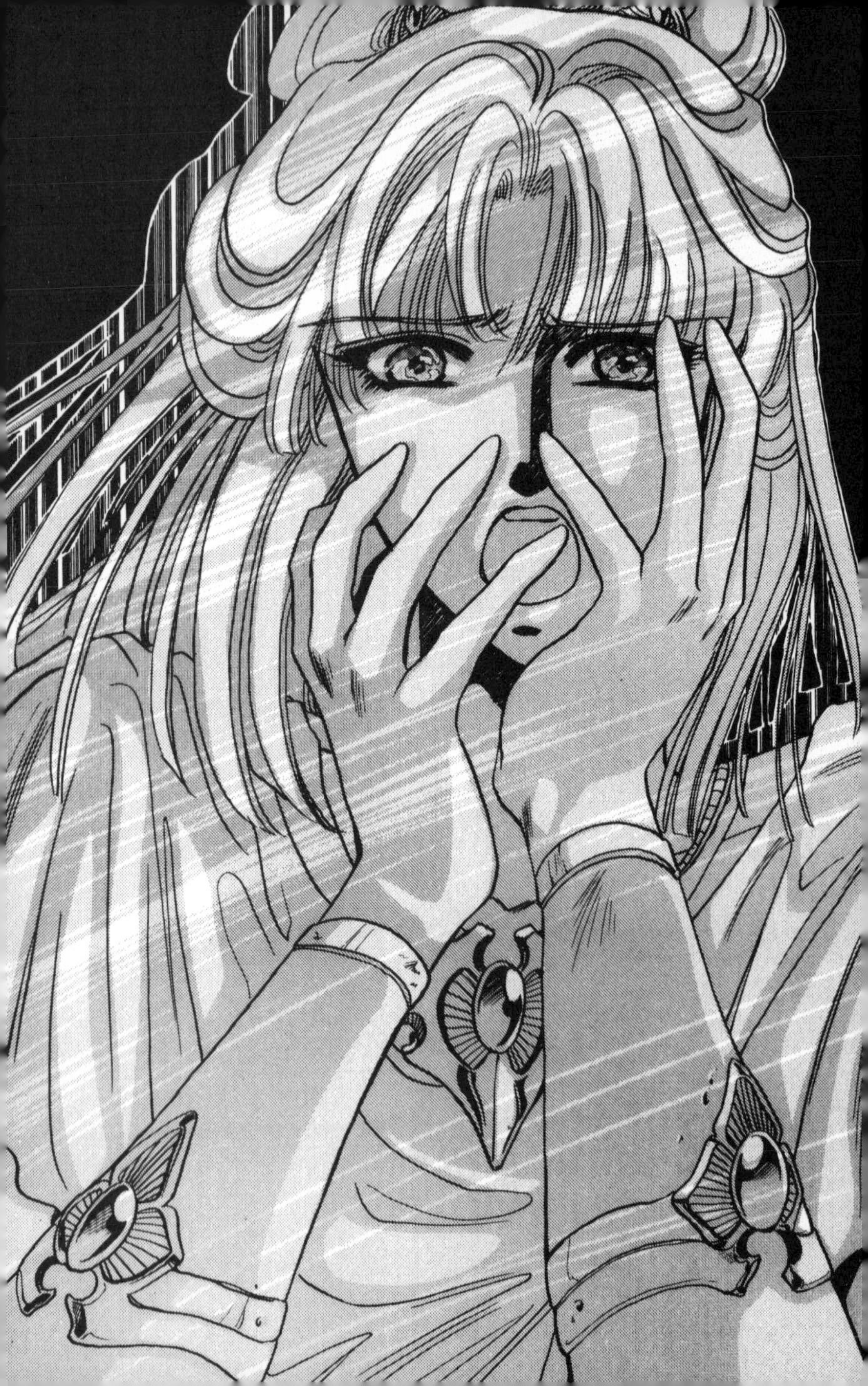

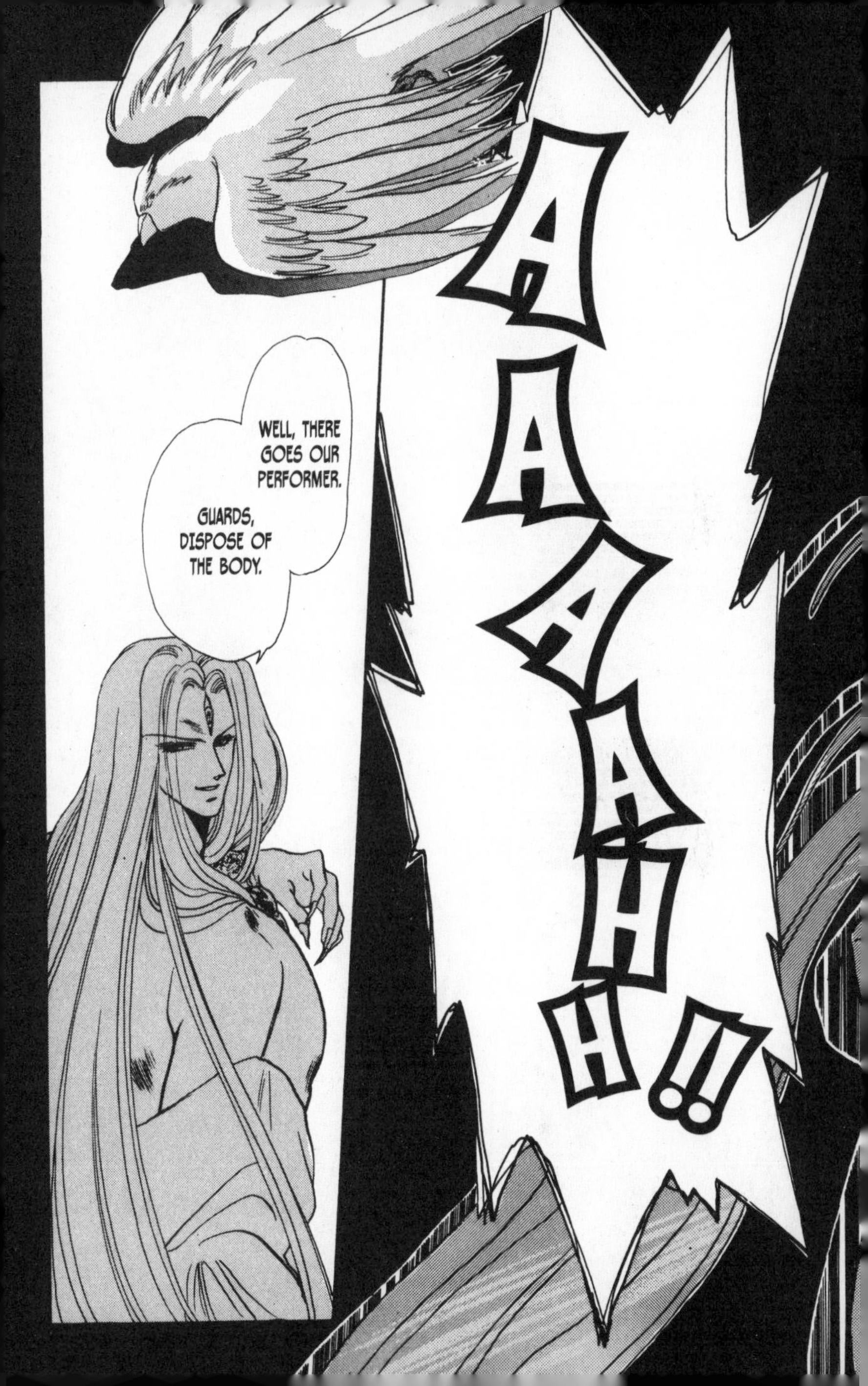
AAAAAAHH!!
WELL, THERE GOES OUR PERFORMER.
GUARDS, DISPOSE OF THE BODY.

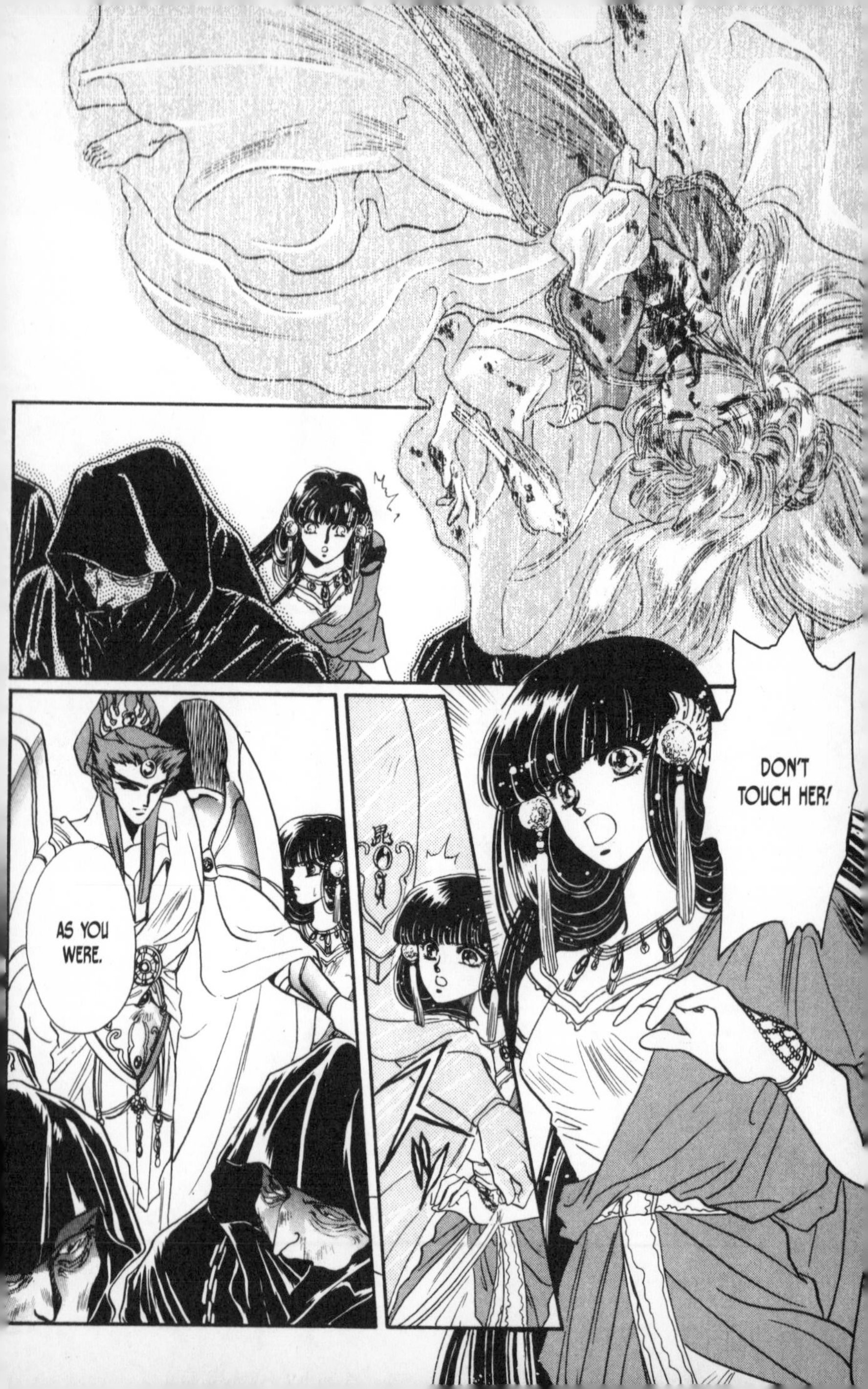
DON'T TOUCH HER!
AS YOU WERE.

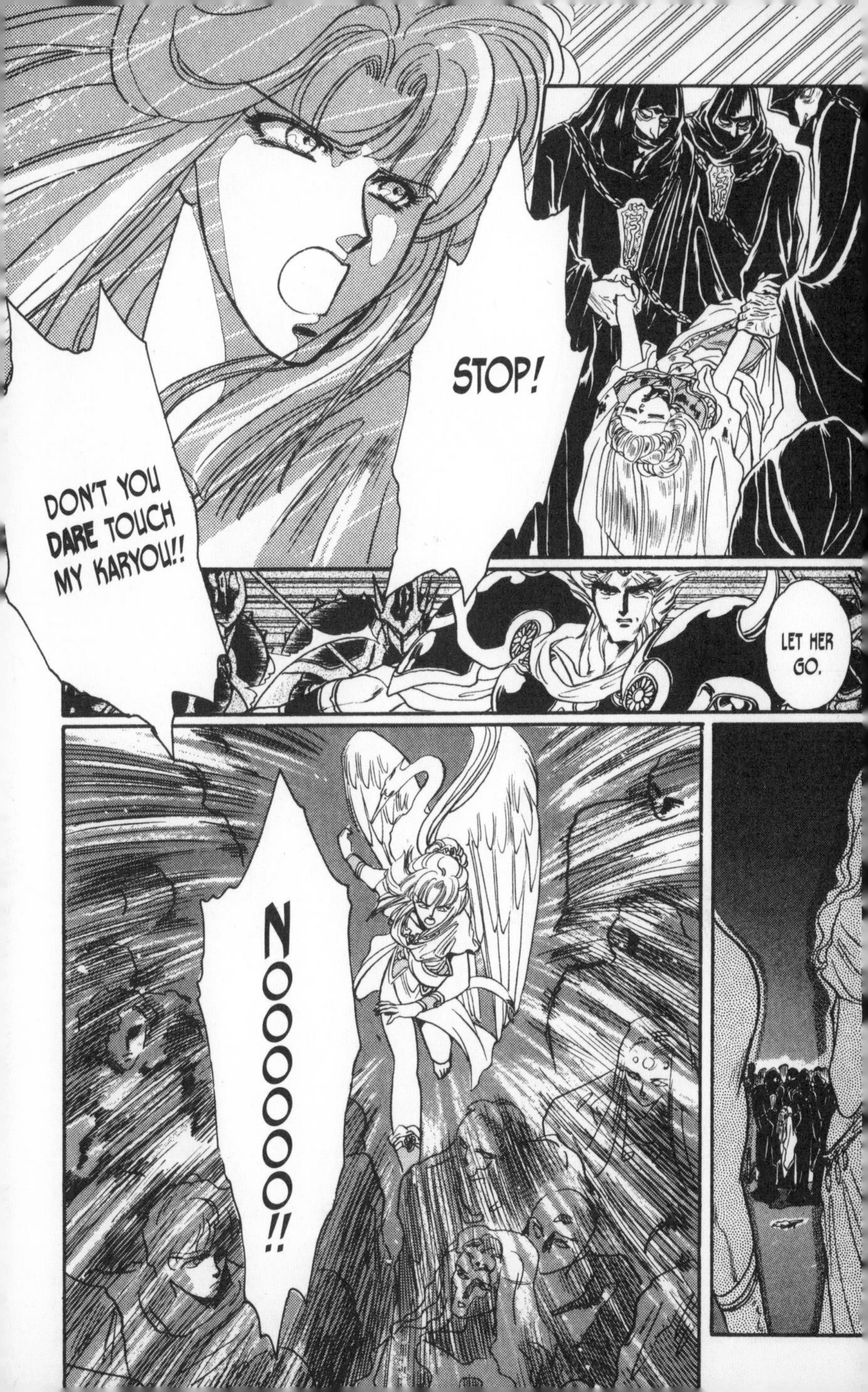
STOP!
DON'T YOU DARE TOUCH MY KARYOU!!
LET HER GO.
NOOOOOOO!!

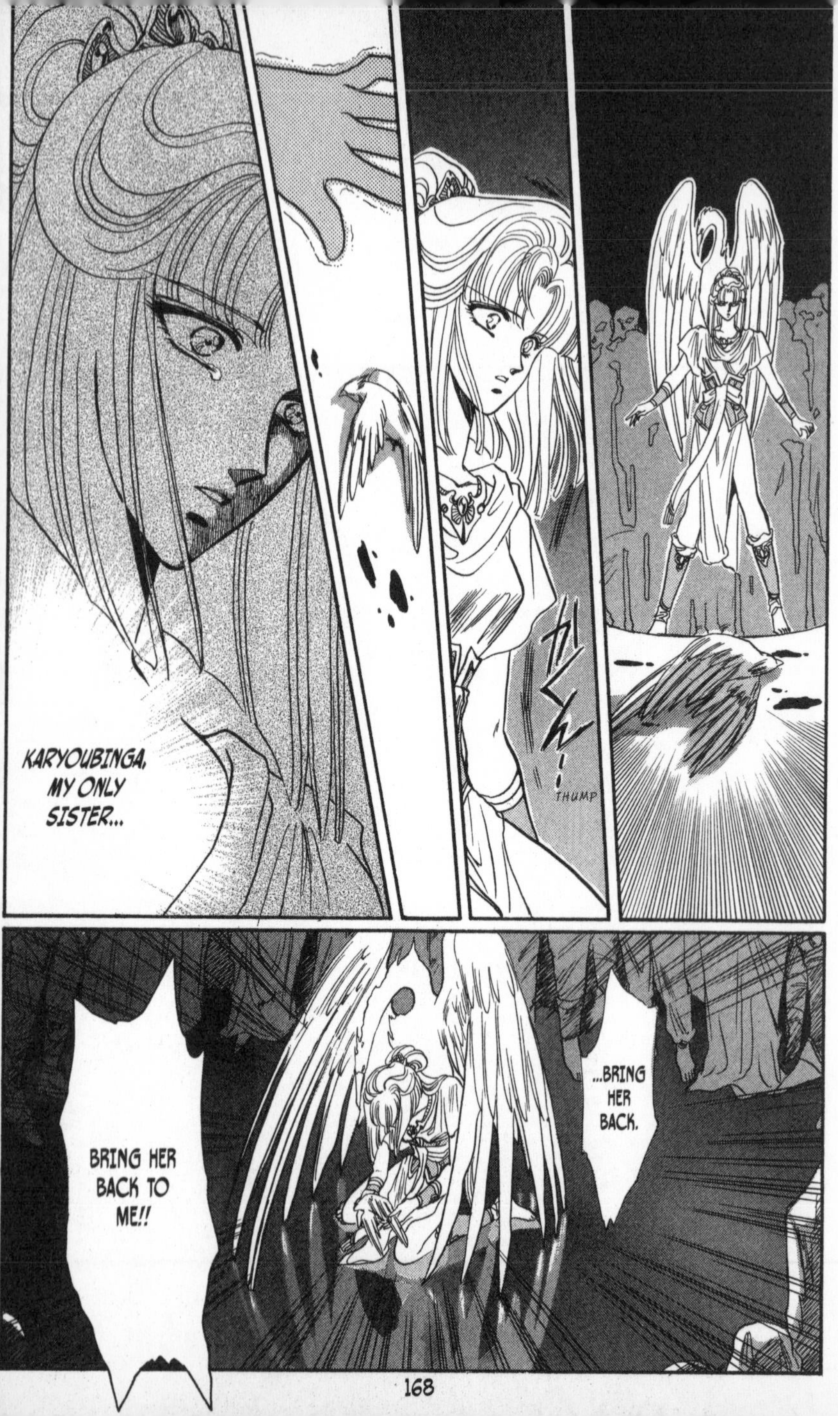
KARYOUBINGA, MY ONLY SISTER...
THUMP
...BRING HER BACK.
BRING HER BACK TO ME!!

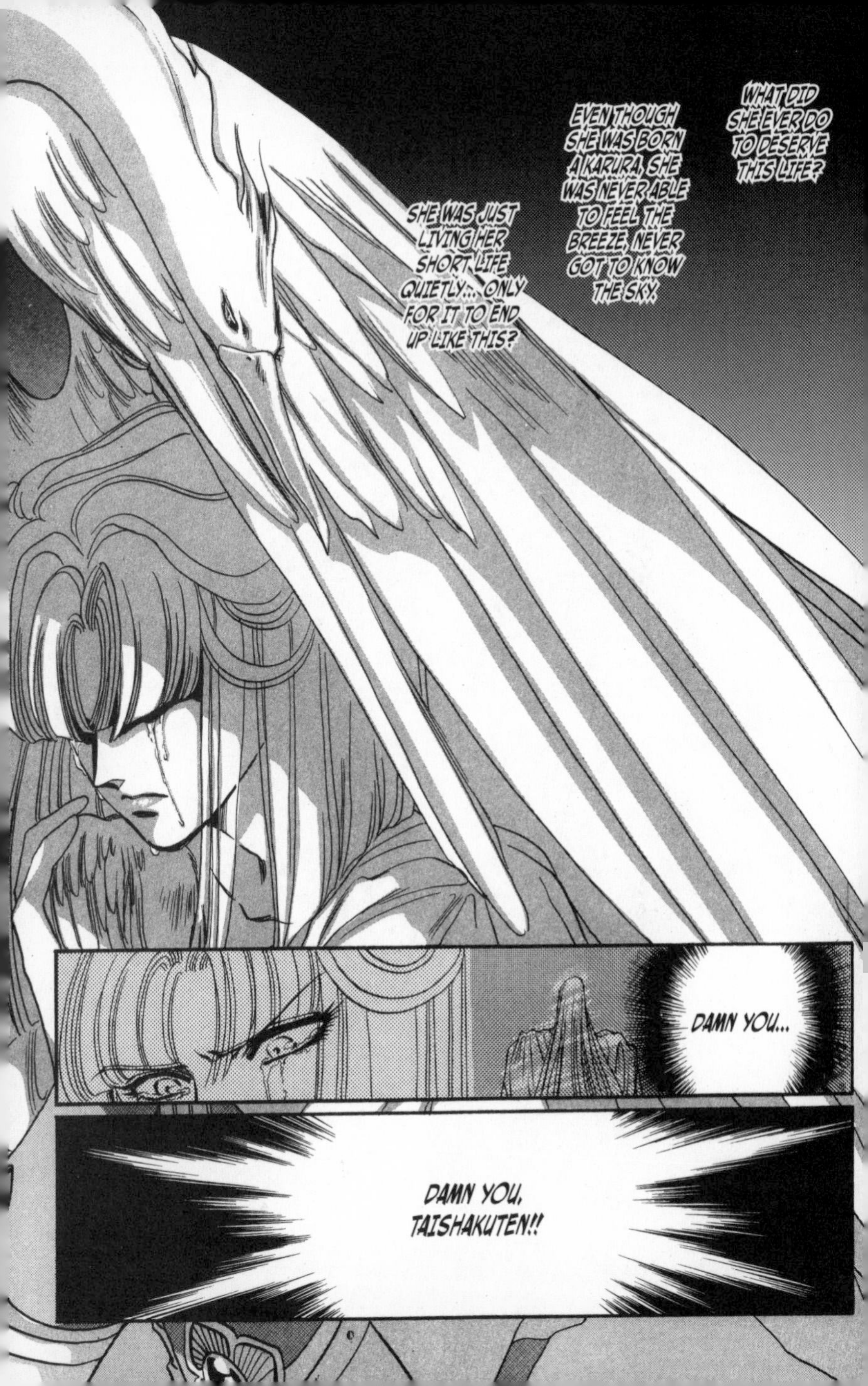
WHAT DID SHE EVER DO TO DESERVE THIS LIFE?
EVEN THOUGH SHE WAS BORN A KARURA, SHE WAS NEVER ABLE TO FEEL THE BREEZE, NEVER GOT TO KNOW THE SKY.
SHE WAS JUST LIVING HER SHORT LIFE QUIETLY... ONLY FOR IT TO END UP LIKE THIS?
DAMN YOU...
DAMN YOU, TAISHAKUTEN!!

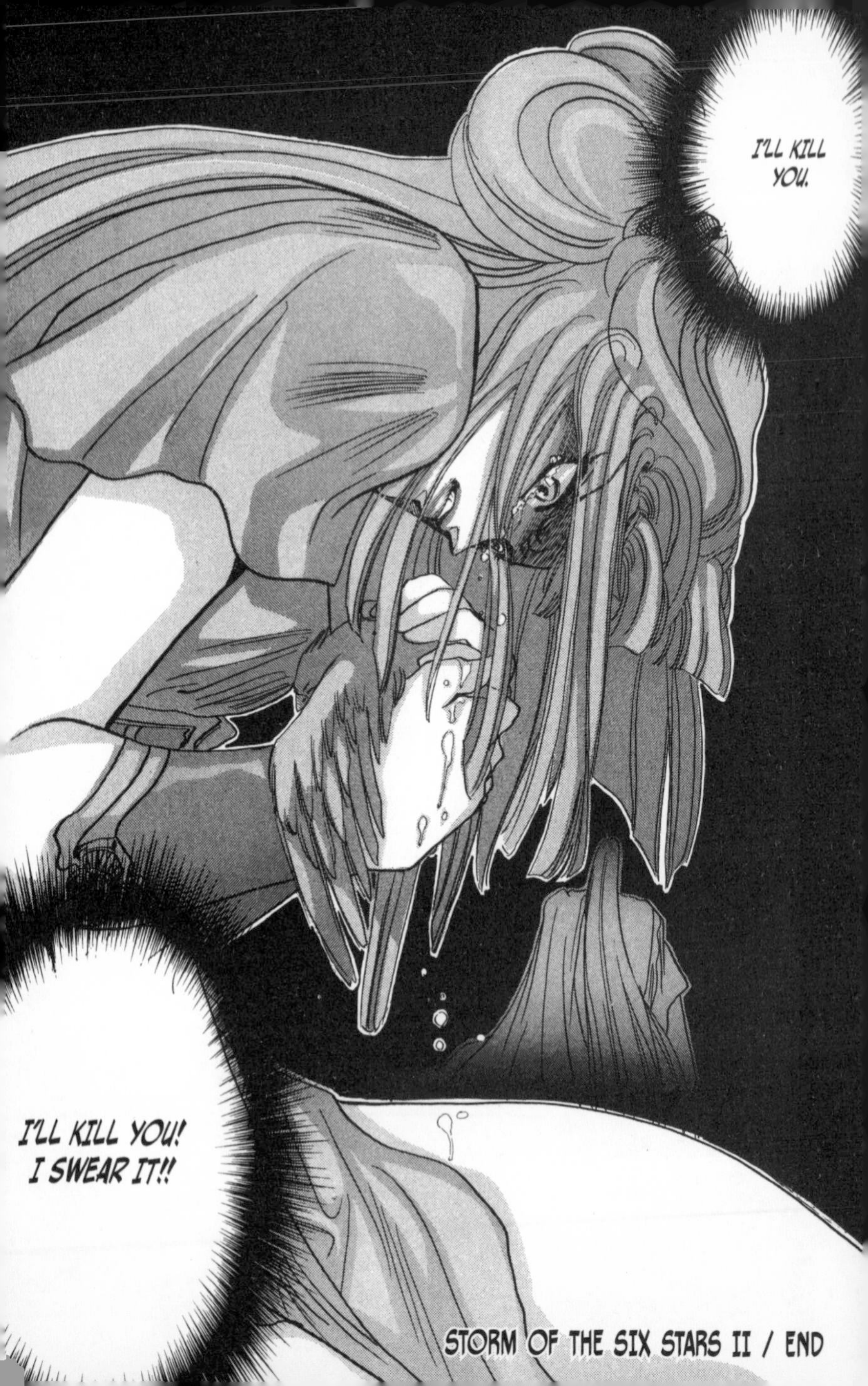
I'LL KILL YOU.
I'LL KILL YOU! I SWEAR IT!!
STORM OF THE SIX STARS II / END

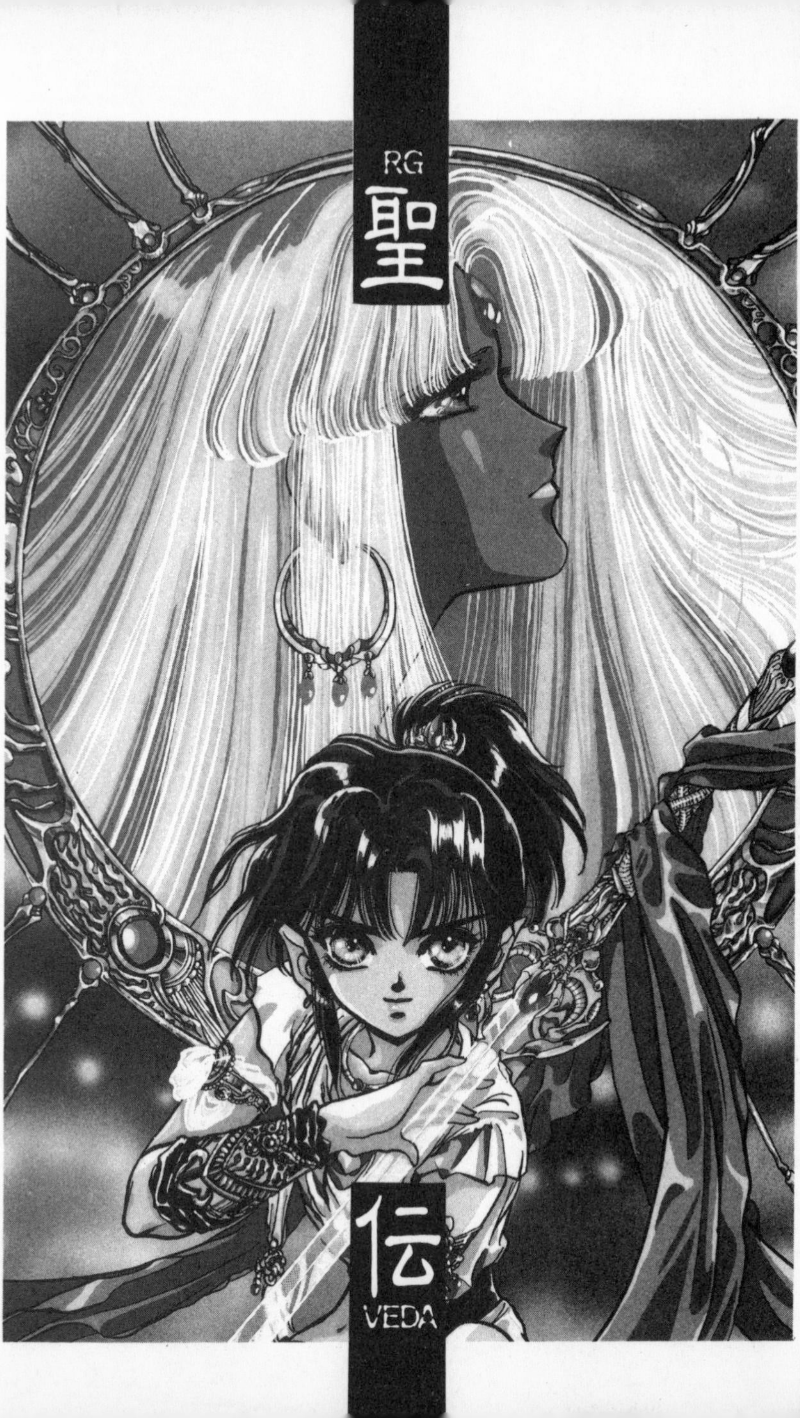
RG
聖
伝
VEDA

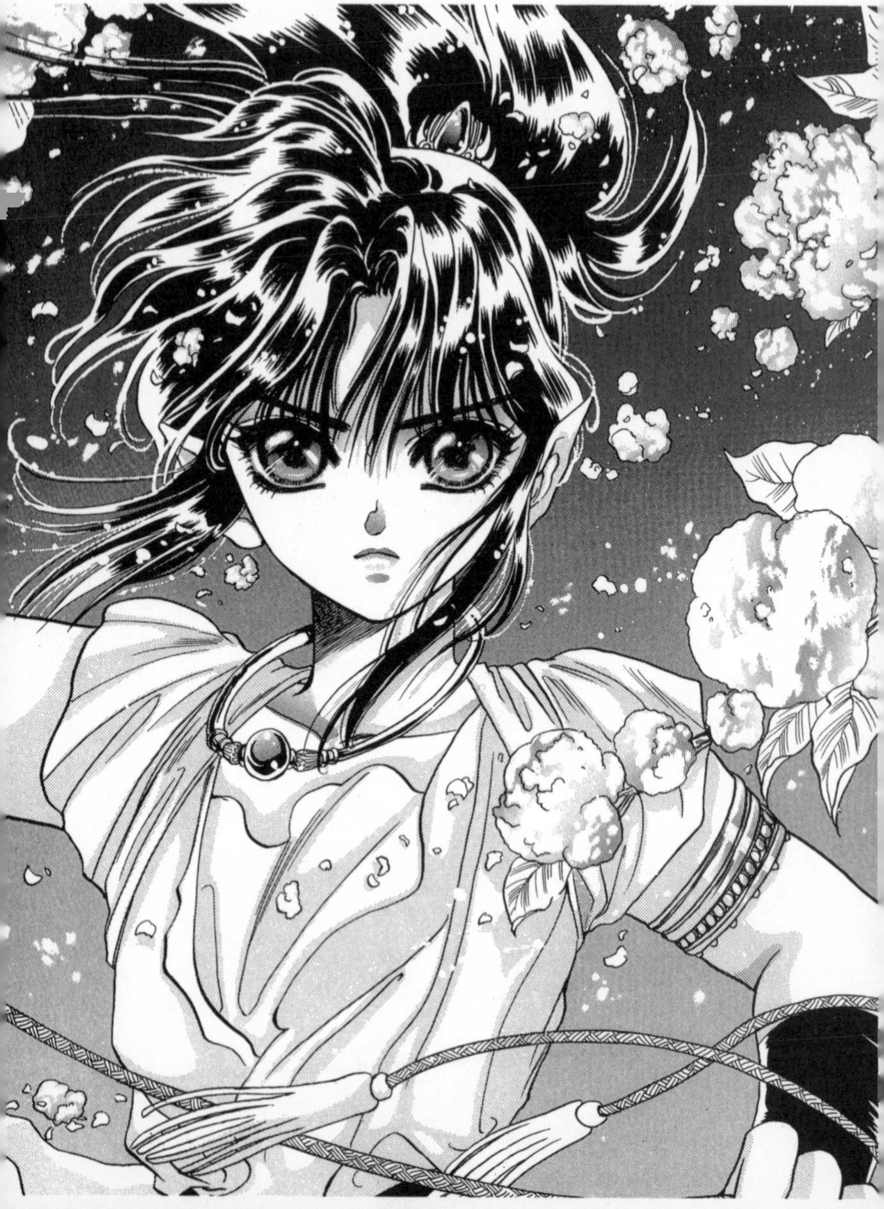

R G VEDA
聖伝

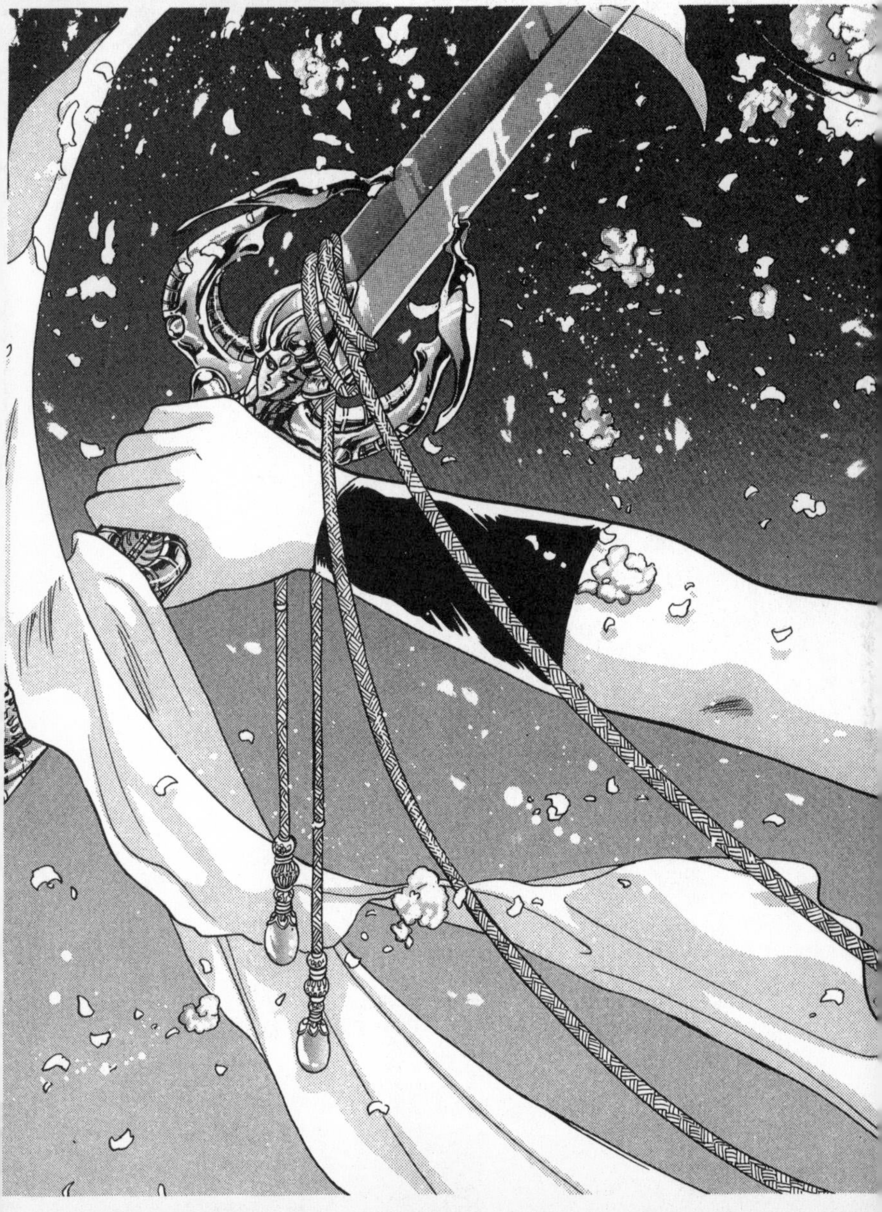

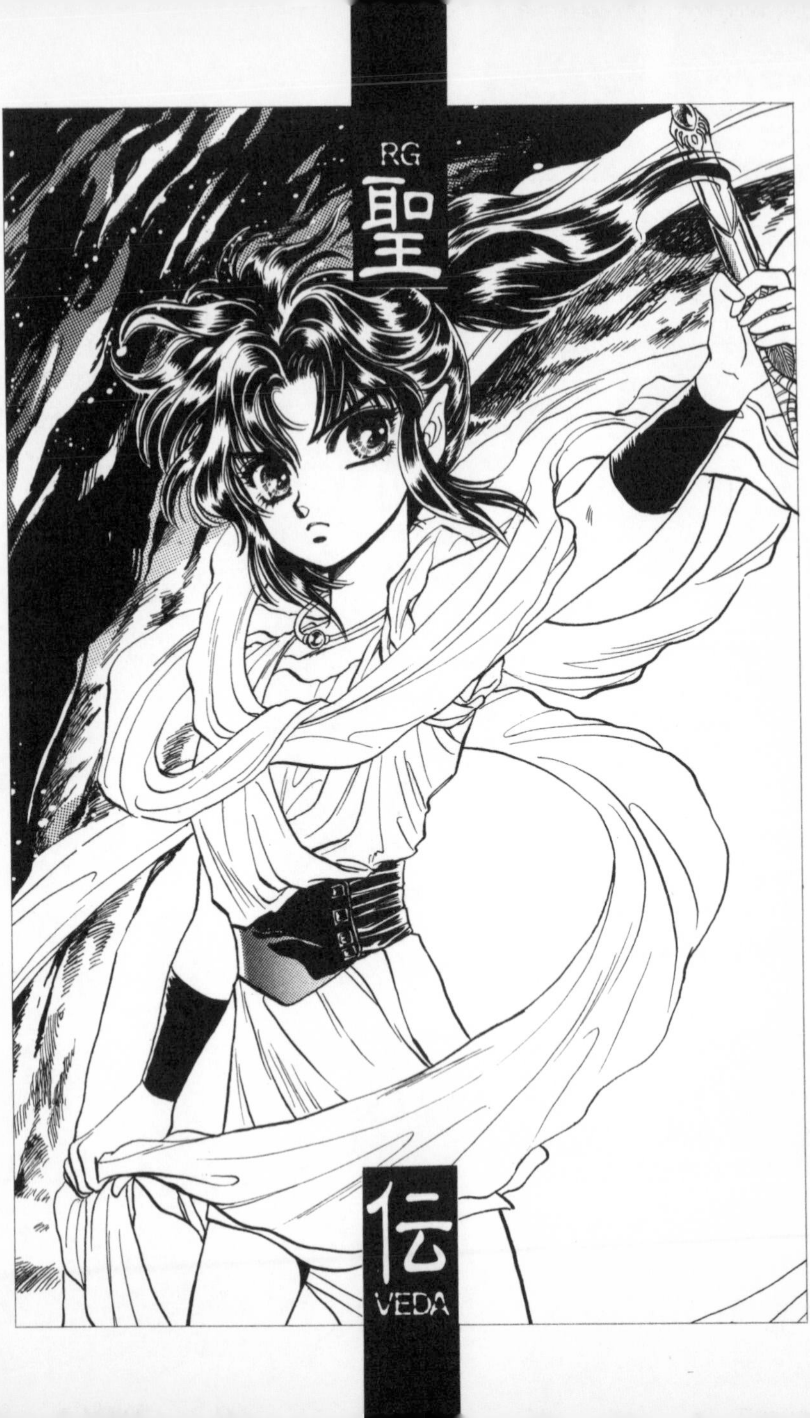
RG
聖
伝
VEDA

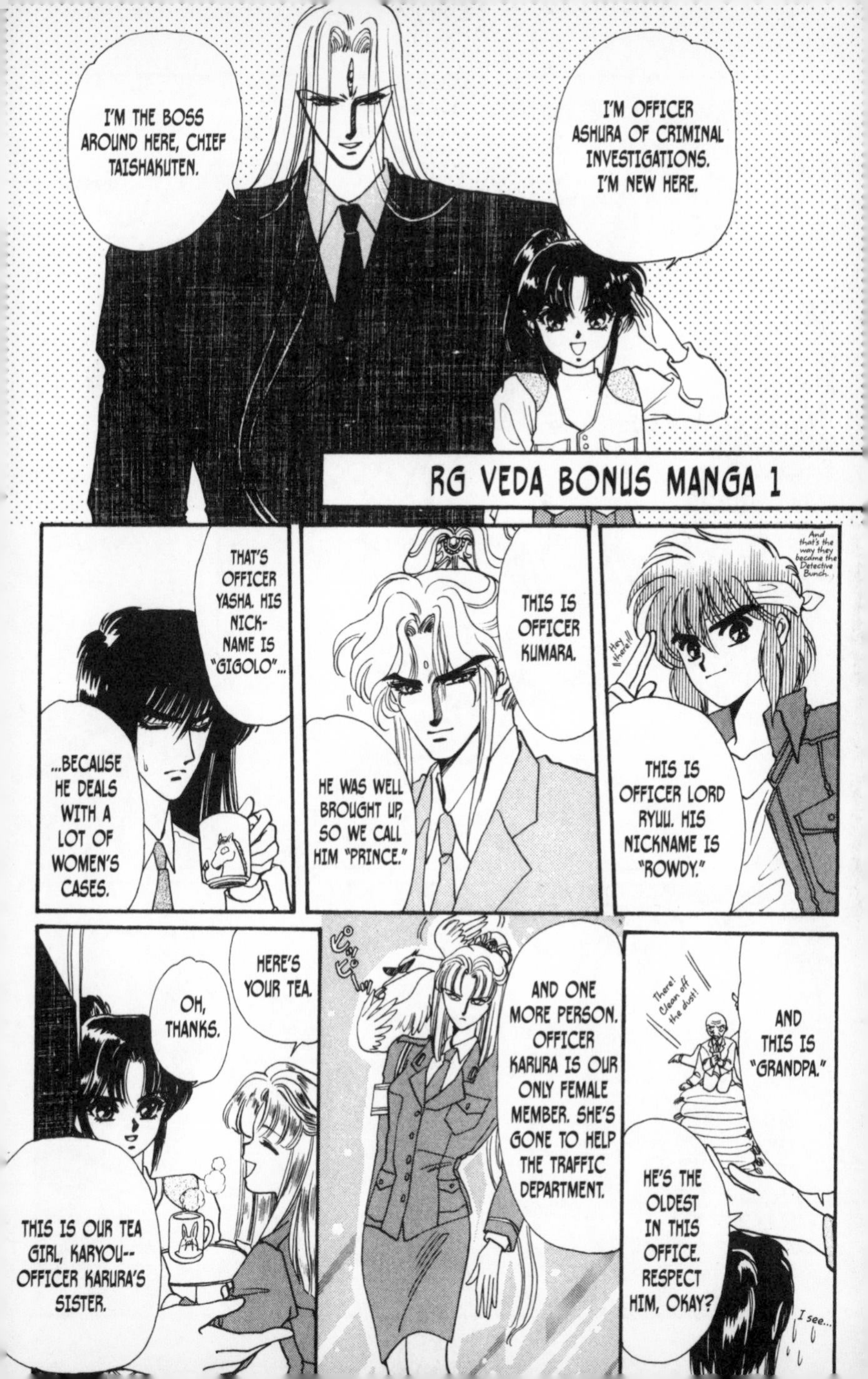
I'M OFFICER ASHURA OF CRIMINAL INVESTIGATIONS. I'M NEW HERE.
I'M THE BOSS AROUND HERE, CHIEF TAISHAKUTEN.
RG VEDA BONUS MANGA 1
And that's the way they became the Detective Bunch.
Hey there!!
THIS IS OFFICER LORD RYUU. HIS NICKNAME IS "ROWDY."
THIS IS OFFICER KUMARA.
HE WAS WELL BROUGHT UP, SO WE CALL HIM "PRINCE."
THAT'S OFFICER YASHA. HIS NICK-NAME IS "GIGOLO"...
...BECAUSE HE DEALS WITH A LOT OF WOMEN'S CASES.
There! Clean off the dust!
AND THIS IS "GRANDPA."
HE'S THE OLDEST IN THIS OFFICE. RESPECT HIM, OKAY?
I see...
AND ONE MORE PERSON. OFFICER KARURA IS OUR ONLY FEMALE MEMBER. SHE'S GONE TO HELP THE TRAFFIC DEPARTMENT.
HERE'S YOUR TEA.
OH, THANKS.
THIS IS OUR TEA GIRL, KARYOU--OFFICER KARURA'S SISTER.

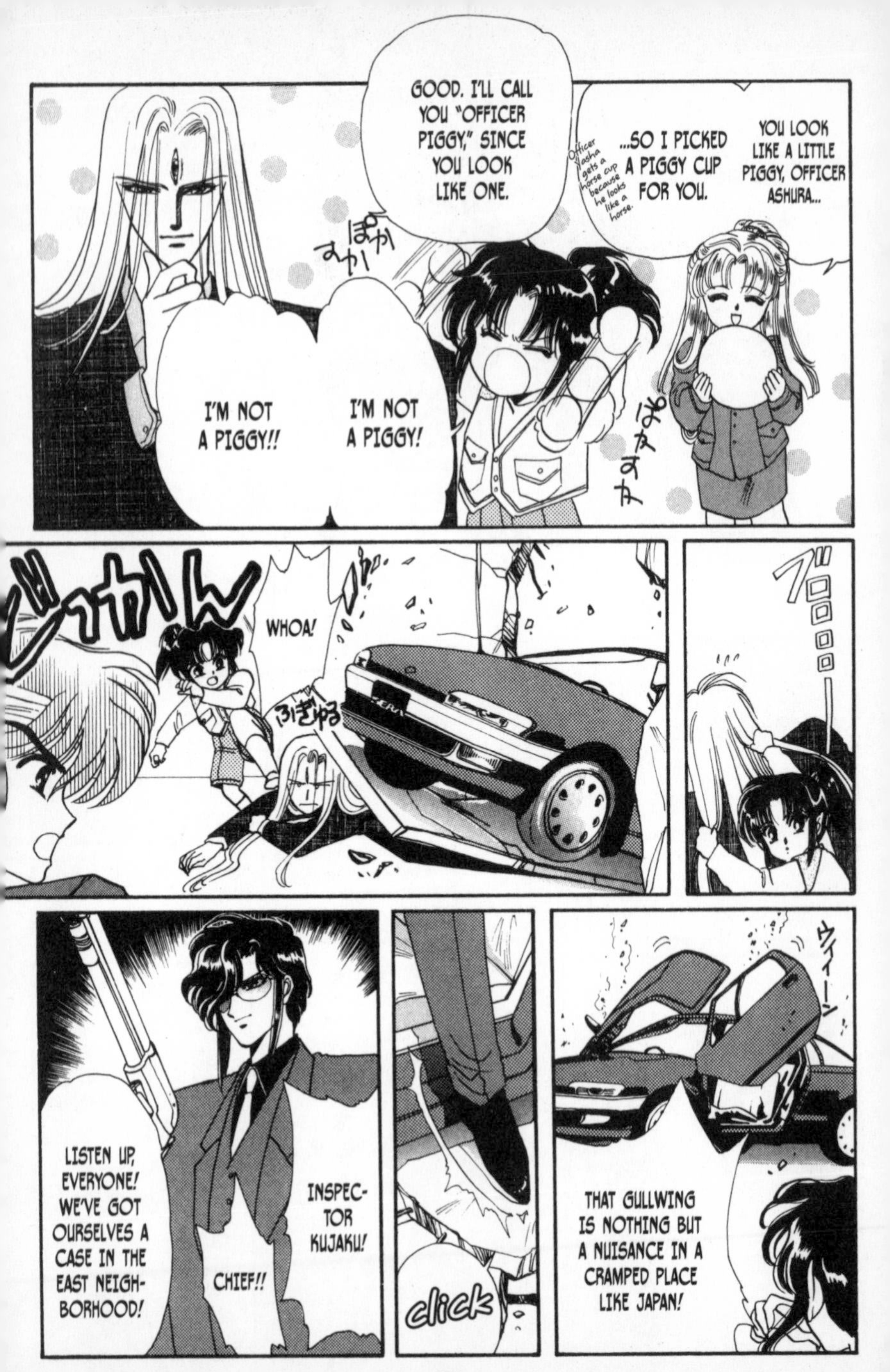
YOU LOOK LIKE A LITTLE PIGGY, OFFICER ASHURA...
...SO I PICKED A PIGGY CUP FOR YOU.
Officer Yasha gets a horse cup because he looks like a horse.
GOOD. I'LL CALL YOU "OFFICER PIGGY," SINCE YOU LOOK LIKE ONE.
I'M NOT A PIGGY!
I'M NOT A PIGGY!!
ブロロロロー
WHOA!
ふぎゅる
THAT GULLWING IS NOTHING BUT A NUISANCE IN A CRAMPED PLACE LIKE JAPAN!
ウイーン
click
INSPECTOR KUJAKU!
CHIEF!!
LISTEN UP, EVERYONE! WE'VE GOT OURSELVES A CASE IN THE EAST NEIGHBORHOOD!

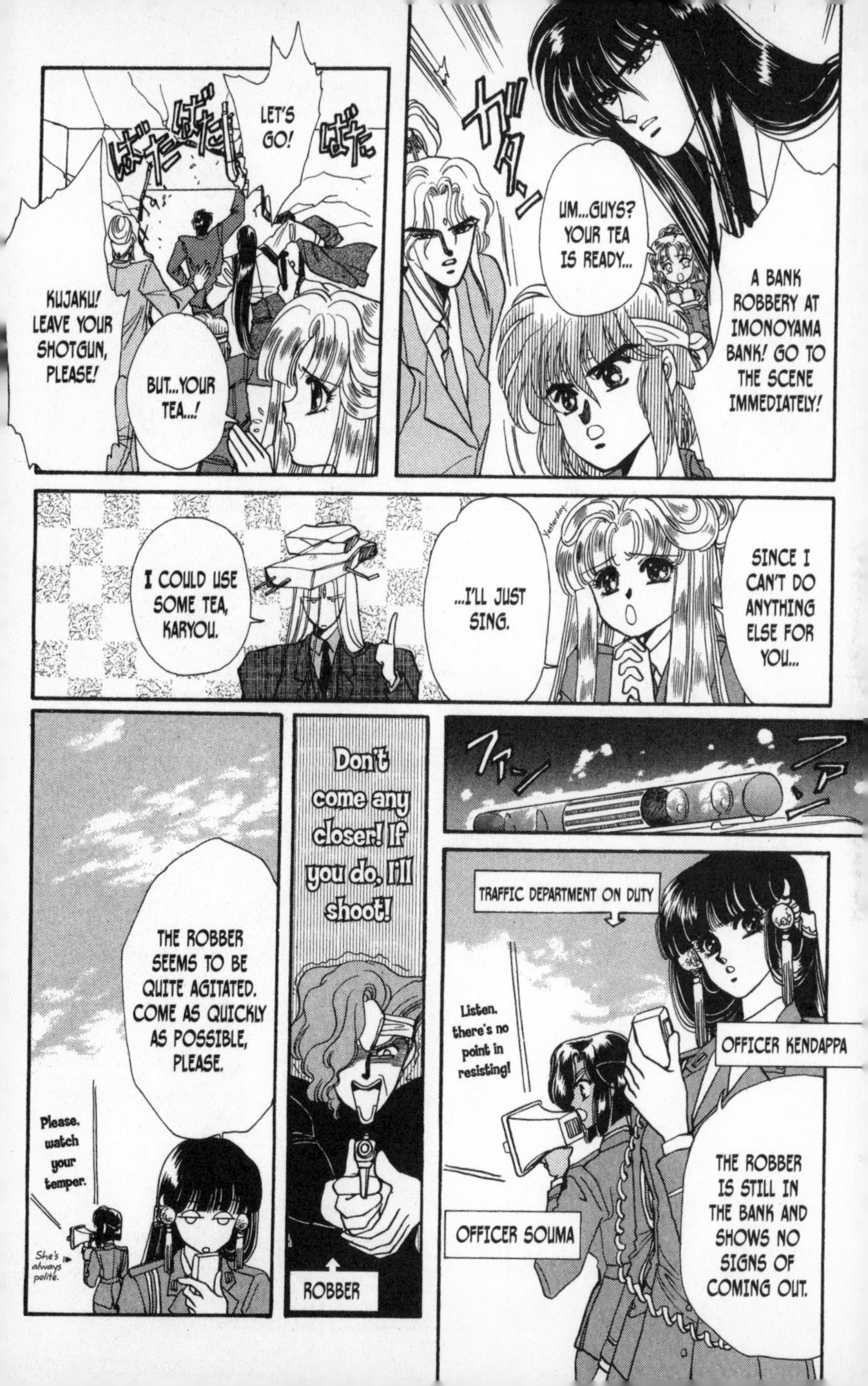
ガターン
A BANK ROBBERY AT IMONOYAMA BANK! GO TO THE SCENE IMMEDIATELY!
UM...GUYS? YOUR TEA IS READY...
ばた
LET'S GO!
ばたばた
KUJAKU! LEAVE YOUR SHOTGUN, PLEASE!
BUT...YOUR TEA...!
SINCE I CAN'T DO ANYTHING ELSE FOR YOU...
Yesterday...
...I'LL JUST SING.
I COULD USE SOME TEA, KARYOU.
TRAFFIC DEPARTMENT ON DUTY
OFFICER KENDAPPA
THE ROBBER IS STILL IN THE BANK AND SHOWS NO SIGNS OF COMING OUT.
Listen, there's no point in resisting!
OFFICER SOUMA
Don't come any closer! If you do, I'll shoot!
ROBBER
THE ROBBER SEEMS TO BE QUITE AGITATED. COME AS QUICKLY AS POSSIBLE, PLEASE.
Please, watch your temper.
She's always polite.

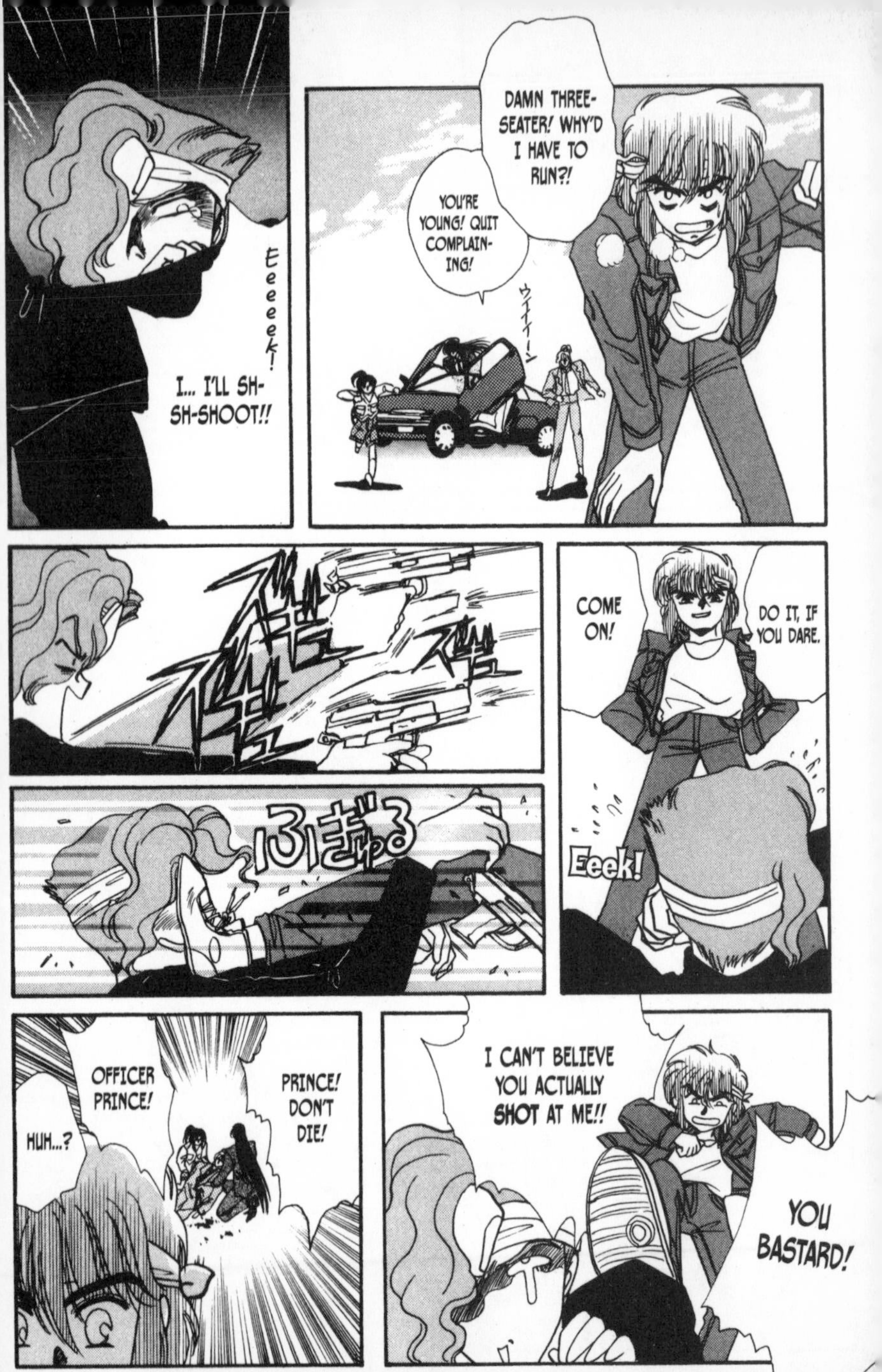

DAMN THREE-SEATER! WHY'D I HAVE TO RUN?!
YOU'RE YOUNG! QUIT COMPLAINING!
Eeeeeek!
I... I'LL SH-SH-SHOOT!!
COME ON!
DO IT, IF YOU DARE.
Eeek!
ふぎゅる
I CAN'T BELIEVE YOU ACTUALLY SHOT AT ME!!
YOU BASTARD!
OFFICER PRINCE!
PRINCE! DON'T DIE!
HUH...?

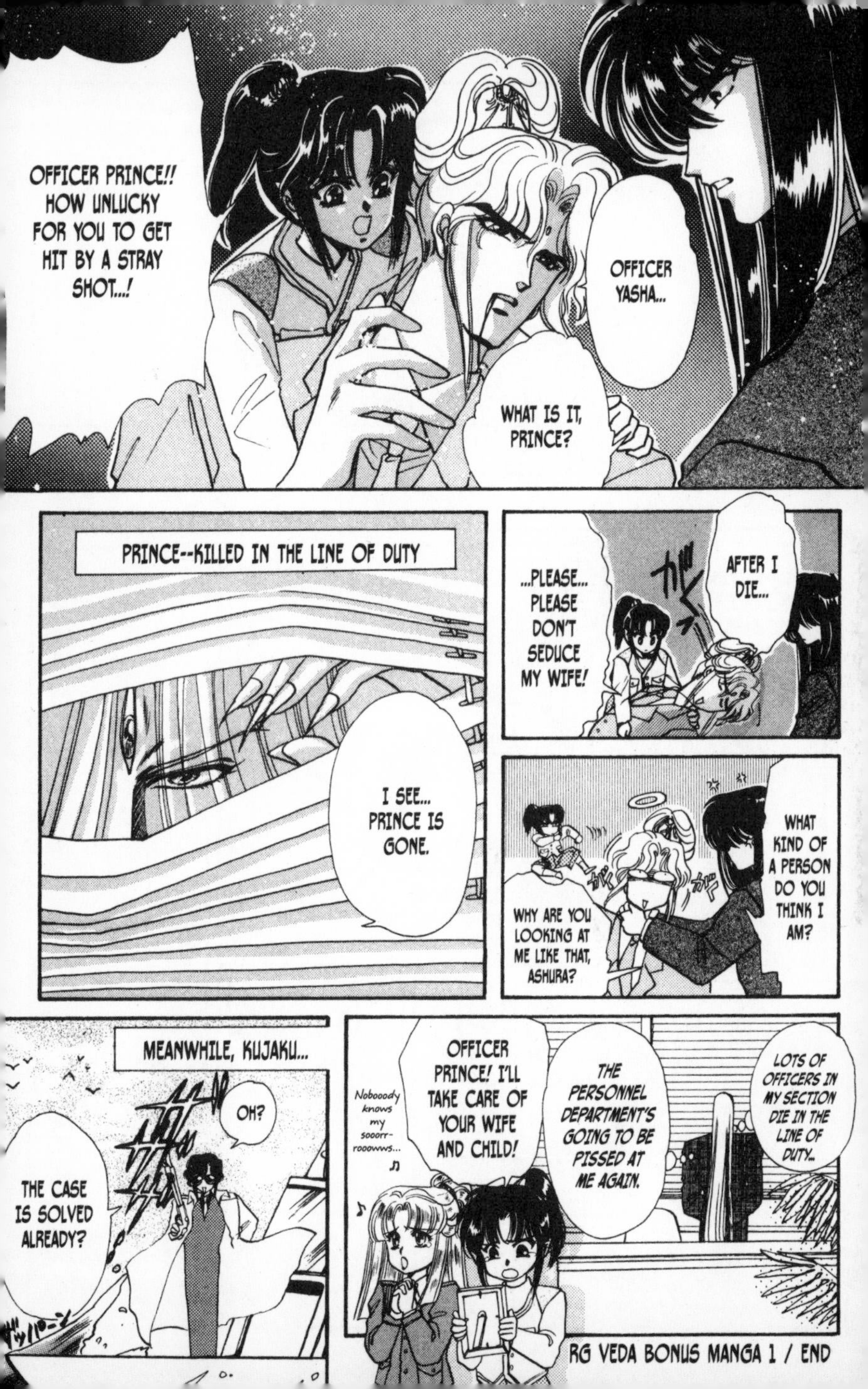
OFFICER YASHA...
WHAT IS IT, PRINCE?
OFFICER PRINCE!! HOW UNLUCKY FOR YOU TO GET HIT BY A STRAY SHOT...!
AFTER I DIE...
...PLEASE... PLEASE DON'T SEDUCE MY WIFE!
WHAT KIND OF A PERSON DO YOU THINK I AM?
WHY ARE YOU LOOKING AT ME LIKE THAT, ASHURA?
PRINCE--KILLED IN THE LINE OF DUTY
I SEE... PRINCE IS GONE.
LOTS OF OFFICERS IN MY SECTION DIE IN THE LINE OF DUTY..
THE PERSONNEL DEPARTMENT'S GOING TO BE PISSED AT ME AGAIN.
OFFICER PRINCE! I'LL TAKE CARE OF YOUR WIFE AND CHILD!
Noboooody knows my sooorrr-rooowws...
MEANWHILE, KUJAKU...
OH?
THE CASE IS SOLVED ALREADY?
RG VEDA BONUS MANGA 1 / END

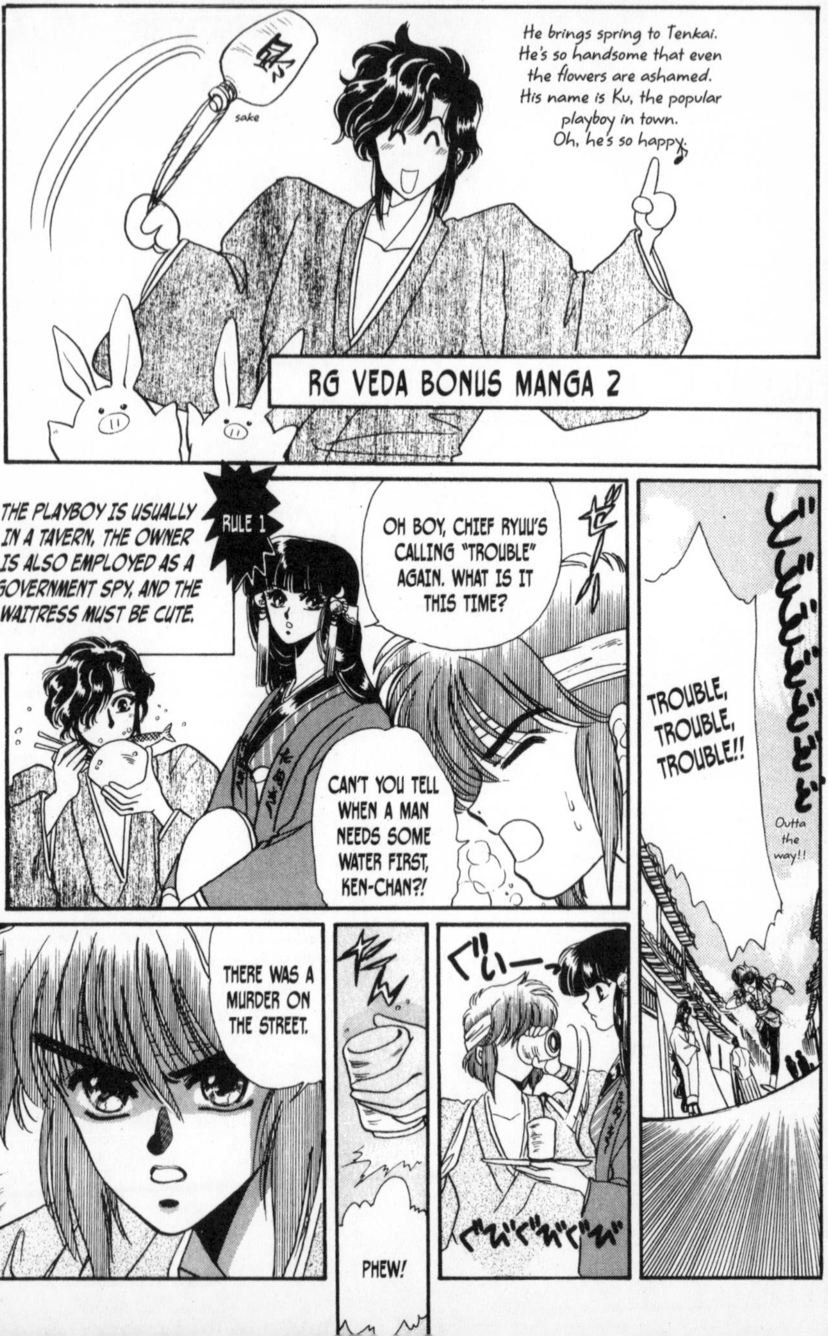
He brings spring to Tenkai. He's so handsome that even the flowers are ashamed. His name is Ku, the popular playboy in town. Oh, he's so happy.
sake
RG VEDA BONUS MANGA 2
TROUBLE, TROUBLE, TROUBLE!!
Outta the way!!
OH BOY, CHIEF RYUU'S CALLING "TROUBLE" AGAIN. WHAT IS IT THIS TIME?
RULE 1
THE PLAYBOY IS USUALLY IN A TAVERN, THE OWNER IS ALSO EMPLOYED AS A GOVERNMENT SPY, AND THE WAITRESS MUST BE CUTE.
CAN'T YOU TELL WHEN A MAN NEEDS SOME WATER FIRST, KEN-CHAN?!
PHEW!
THERE WAS A MURDER ON THE STREET.

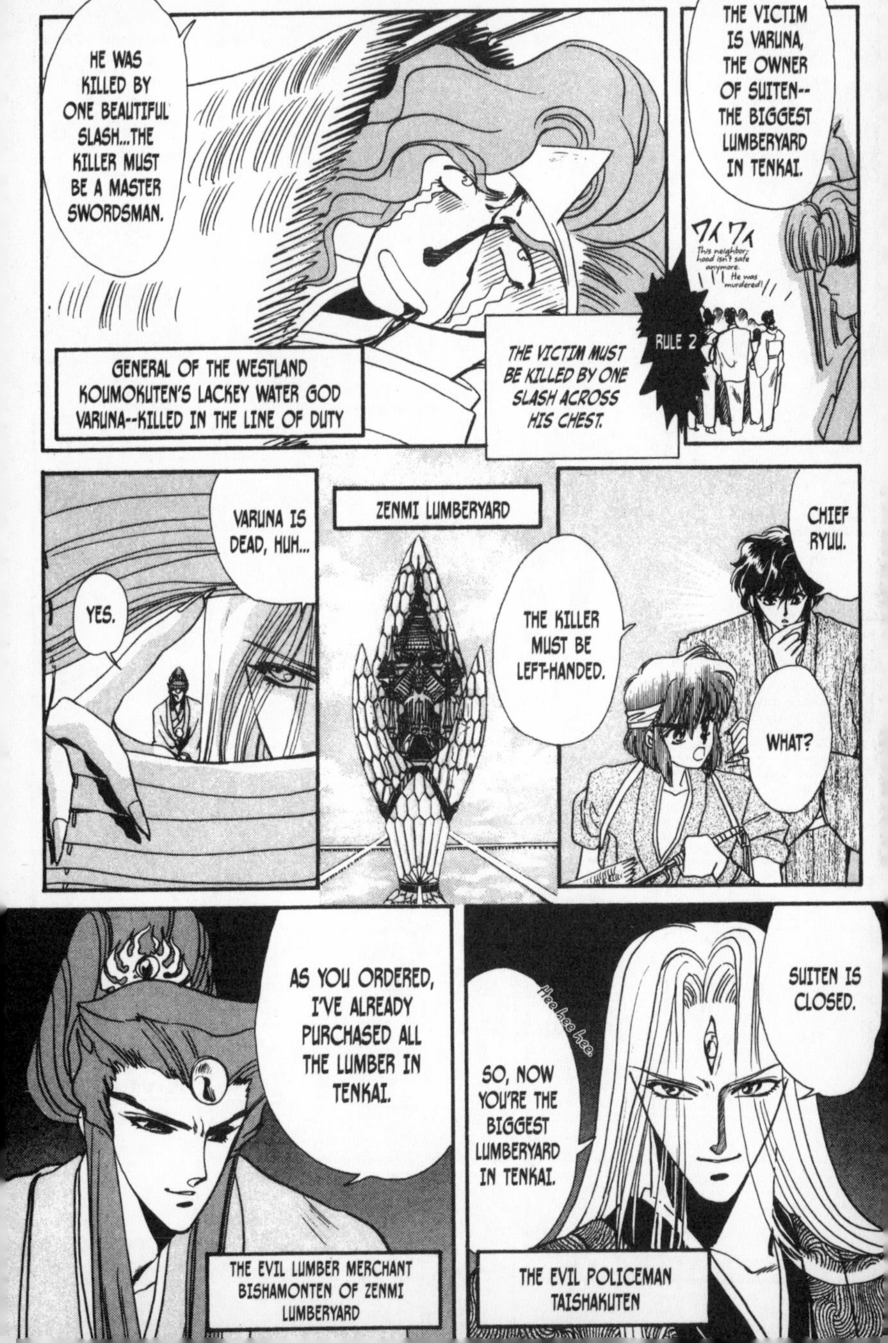
THE VICTIM IS VARUNA, THE OWNER OF SUITEN-- THE BIGGEST LUMBERYARD IN TENKAI.
ワイワイ
This neighborhood isn't safe anymore.
He was murdered!
RULE 2
THE VICTIM MUST BE KILLED BY ONE SLASH ACROSS HIS CHEST.
HE WAS KILLED BY ONE BEAUTIFUL SLASH...THE KILLER MUST BE A MASTER SWORDSMAN.
GENERAL OF THE WESTLAND KOUMOKUTEN'S LACKEY WATER GOD VARUNA--KILLED IN THE LINE OF DUTY
CHIEF RYUU.
THE KILLER MUST BE LEFT-HANDED.
WHAT?
ZENMI LUMBERYARD
VARUNA IS DEAD, HUH...
YES.
SUITEN IS CLOSED.
Hee hee hee.
SO, NOW YOU'RE THE BIGGEST LUMBERYARD IN TENKAI.
THE EVIL POLICEMAN TAISHAKUTEN
AS YOU ORDERED, I'VE ALREADY PURCHASED ALL THE LUMBER IN TENKAI.
THE EVIL LUMBER MERCHANT BISHAMONTEN OF ZENMI LUMBERYARD

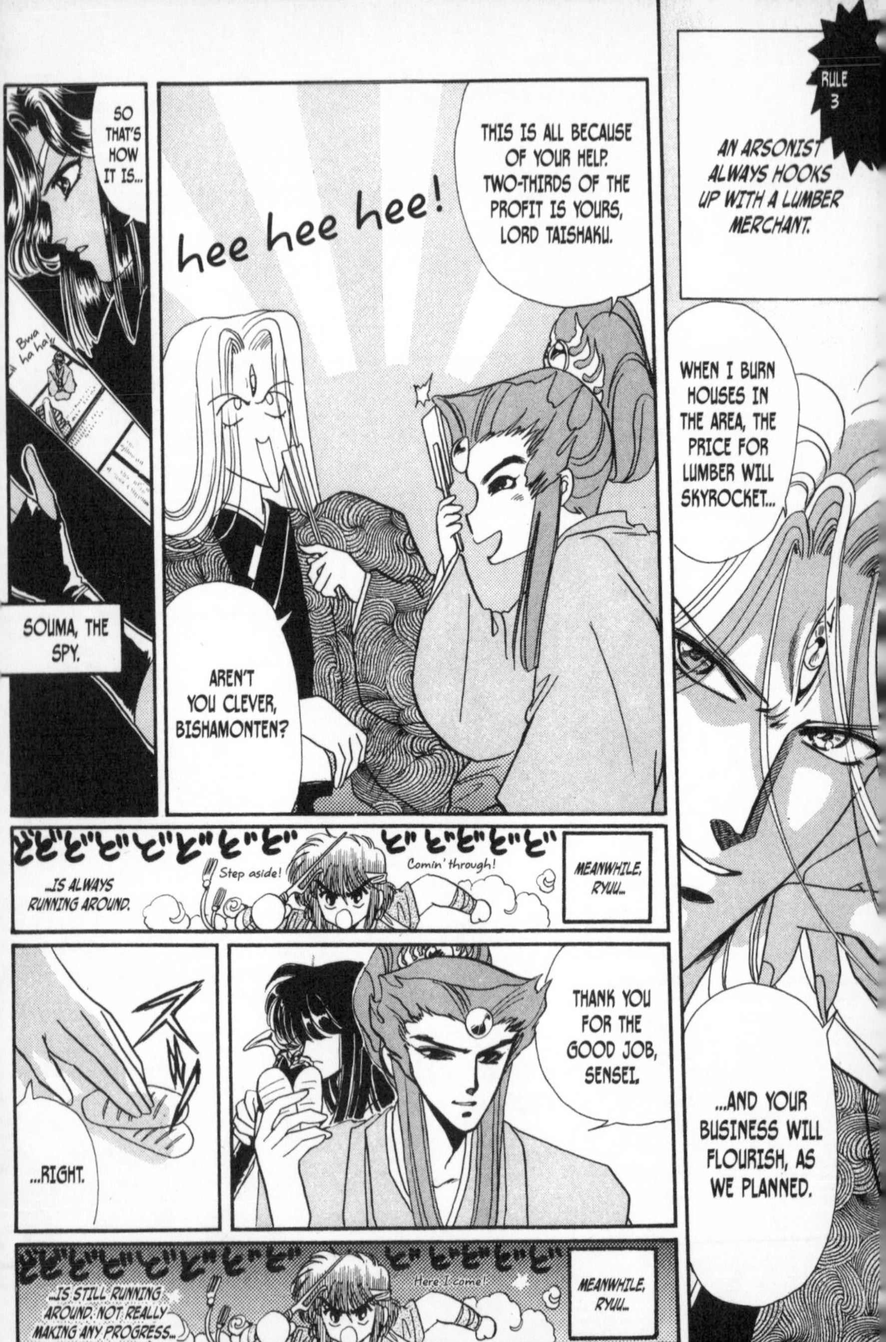
RULE 3
AN ARSONIST ALWAYS HOOKS UP WITH A LUMBER MERCHANT.
WHEN I BURN HOUSES IN THE AREA, THE PRICE FOR LUMBER WILL SKYROCKET...
...AND YOUR BUSINESS WILL FLOURISH, AS WE PLANNED.
THIS IS ALL BECAUSE OF YOUR HELP. TWO-THIRDS OF THE PROFIT IS YOURS, LORD TAISHAKU.
hee hee hee!
AREN'T YOU CLEVER, BISHAMONTEN?
SO THAT'S HOW IT IS...
Bwa ha ha!
SOUMA, THE SPY.
MEANWHILE, RYUU...
Comin' through!
Step aside!
...IS ALWAYS RUNNING AROUND.
THANK YOU FOR THE GOOD JOB, SENSEI.
...RIGHT.
MEANWHILE, RYUU...
Here I come!
...IS STILL RUNNING AROUND, NOT REALLY MAKING ANY PROGRESS...

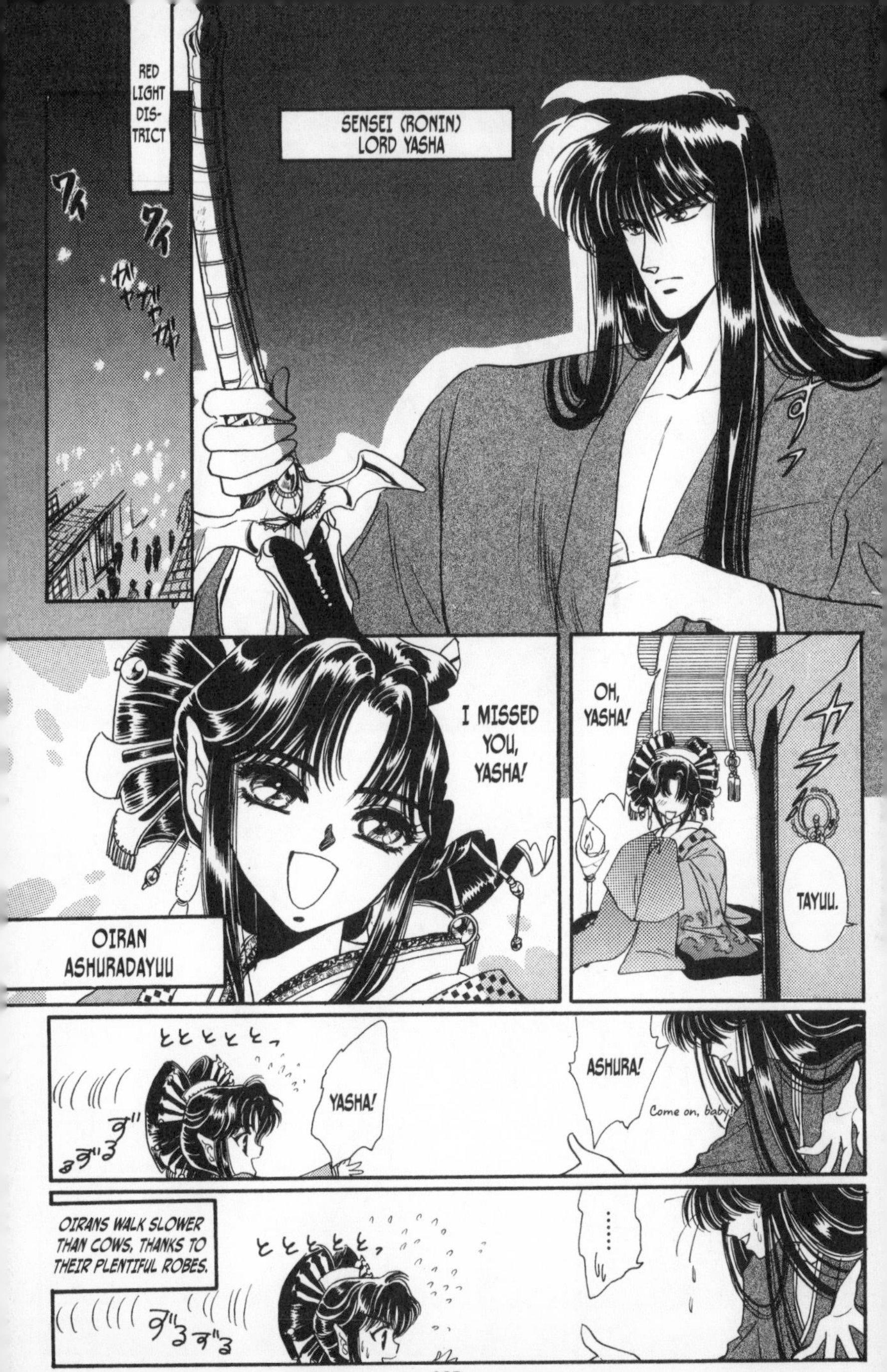
RED LIGHT DIS- TRICT
SENSEI (RONIN) LORD YASHA
TAYUU.
OH, YASHA!
I MISSED YOU, YASHA!
OIRAN ASHURADAYUU
ASHURA!
Come on, baby!
YASHA!
とととととっ
ずるずる
......
OIRANS WALK SLOWER THAN COWS, THANKS TO THEIR PLENTIFUL ROBES.
とととととっ
ずるずる

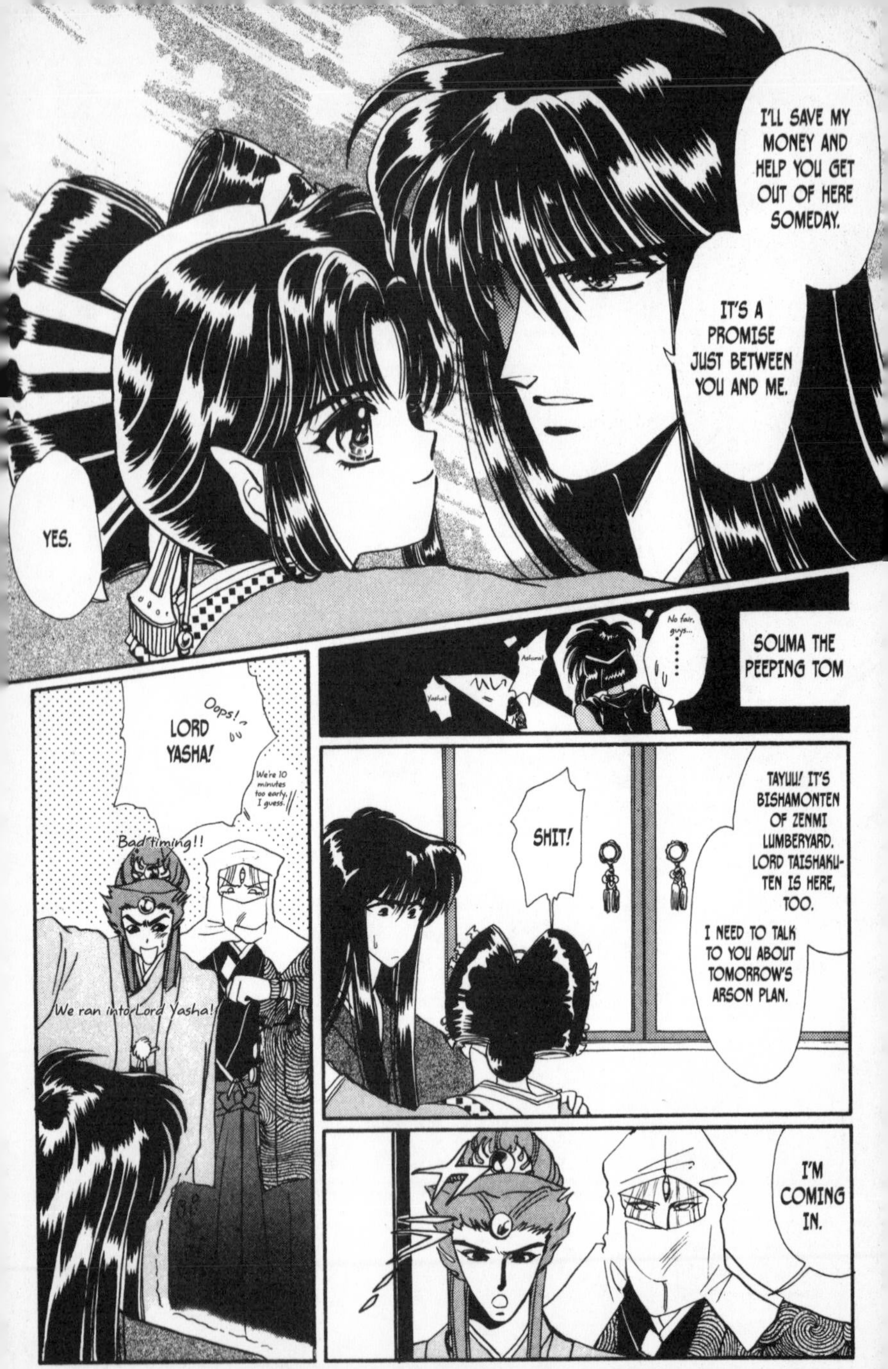
I'LL SAVE MY MONEY AND HELP YOU GET OUT OF HERE SOMEDAY.
IT'S A PROMISE JUST BETWEEN YOU AND ME.
YES.
SOUMA THE PEEPING TOM
No fair, guys... ......
Ashura!
Yasha!
TAYUU! IT'S BISHAMONTEN OF ZENMI LUMBERYARD. LORD TAISHAKU-TEN IS HERE, TOO.
I NEED TO TALK TO YOU ABOUT TOMORROW'S ARSON PLAN.
SHIT!
LORD YASHA!
Oops!
We're 10 minutes too early, I guess.
Bad timing!!
We ran into Lord Yasha!
I'M COMING IN.

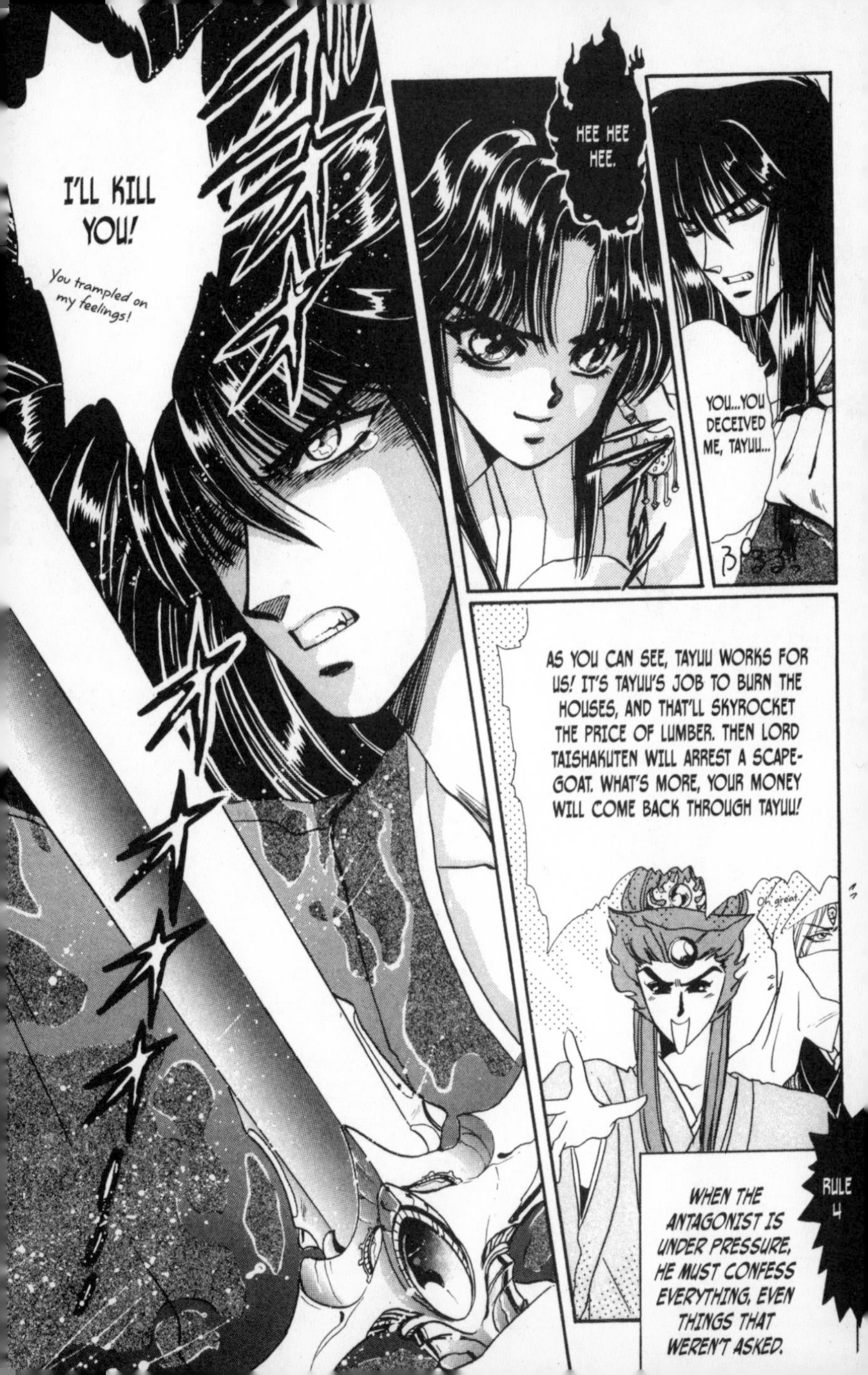
HEE HEE HEE.
YOU...YOU DECEIVED ME, TAYUU...
I'LL KILL YOU!
You trampled on my feelings!
AS YOU CAN SEE, TAYUU WORKS FOR US! IT'S TAYUU'S JOB TO BURN THE HOUSES, AND THAT'LL SKYROCKET THE PRICE OF LUMBER. THEN LORD TAISHAKUTEN WILL ARREST A SCAPE-GOAT. WHAT'S MORE, YOUR MONEY WILL COME BACK THROUGH TAYUU!
Oh great.
RULE 4
WHEN THE ANTAGONIST IS UNDER PRESSURE, HE MUST CONFESS EVERYTHING, EVEN THINGS THAT WEREN'T ASKED.

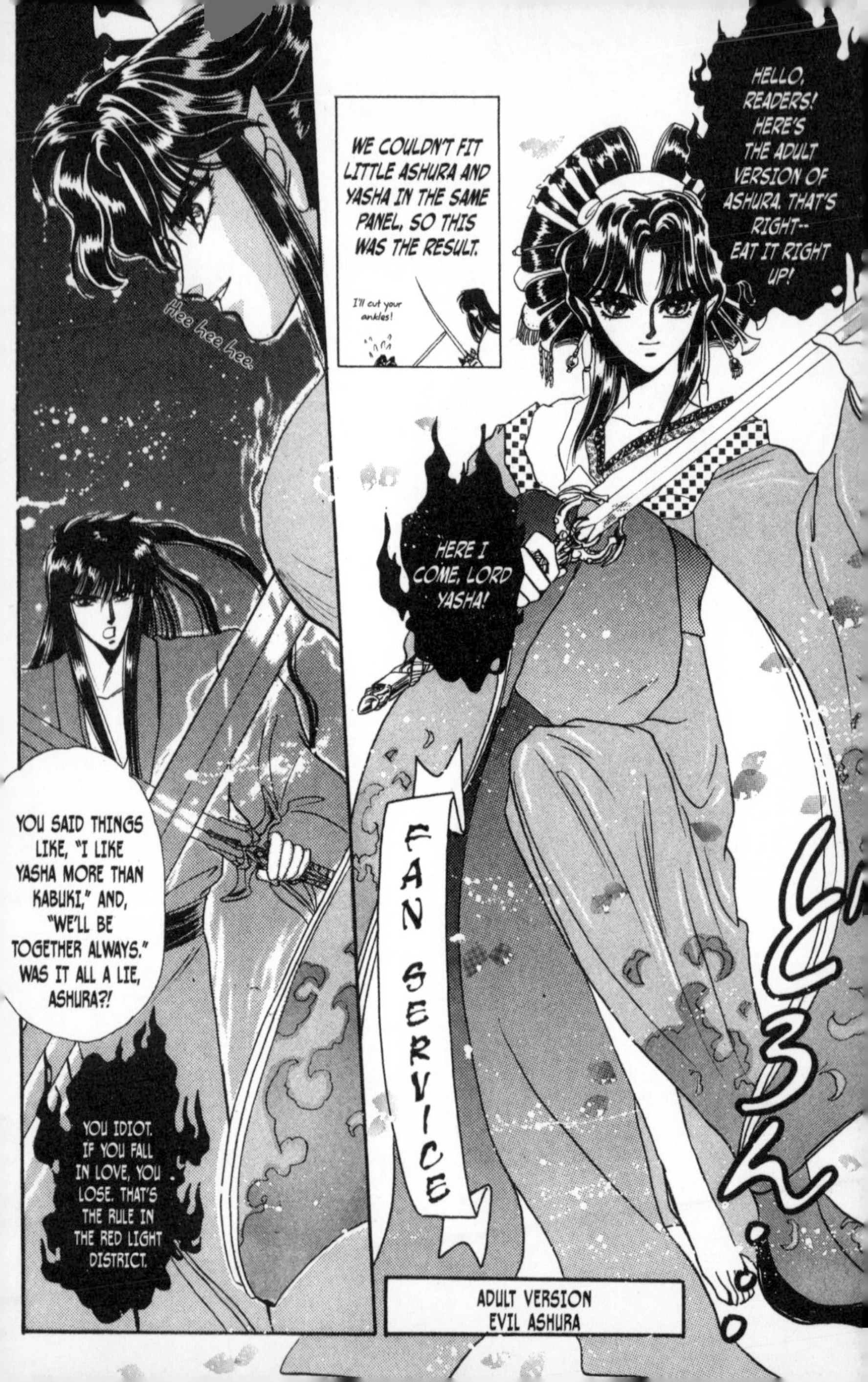
HELLO, READERS! HERE'S THE ADULT VERSION OF ASHURA. THAT'S RIGHT-- EAT IT RIGHT UP!
WE COULDN'T FIT LITTLE ASHURA AND YASHA IN THE SAME PANEL, SO THIS WAS THE RESULT.
I'll cut your ankles!
HERE I COME, LORD YASHA!
FAN SERVICE
ADULT VERSION
EVIL ASHURA
Hee hee hee.
YOU SAID THINGS LIKE, "I LIKE YASHA MORE THAN KABUKI," AND, "WE'LL BE TOGETHER ALWAYS." WAS IT ALL A LIE, ASHURA?!
YOU IDIOT. IF YOU FALL IN LOVE, YOU LOSE. THAT'S THE RULE IN THE RED LIGHT DISTRICT.

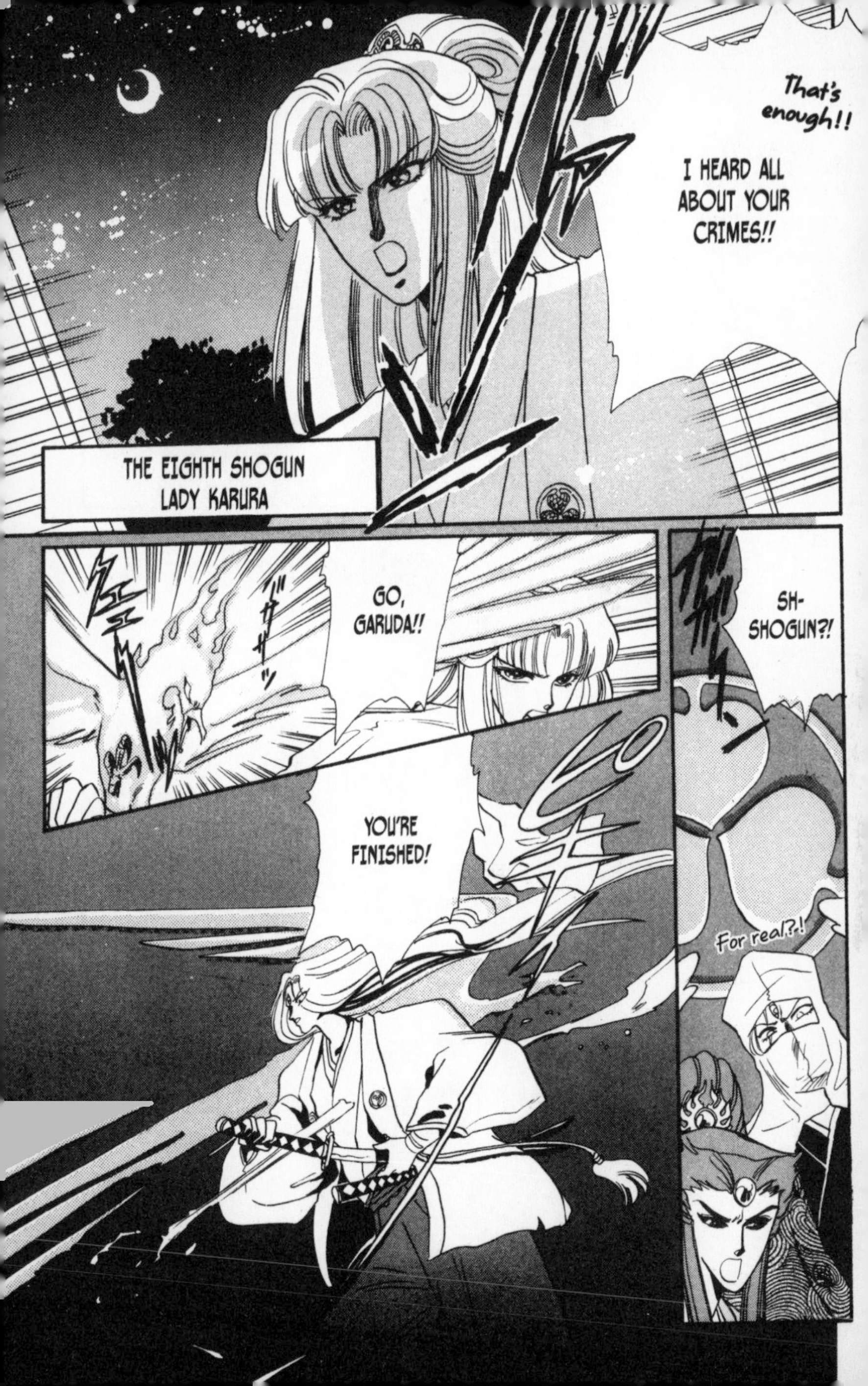
That's enough!!
I HEARD ALL ABOUT YOUR CRIMES!!
THE EIGHTH SHOGUN LADY KARURA
SH- SHOGUN?!
GO, GARUDA!!
YOU'RE FINISHED!
For real?!

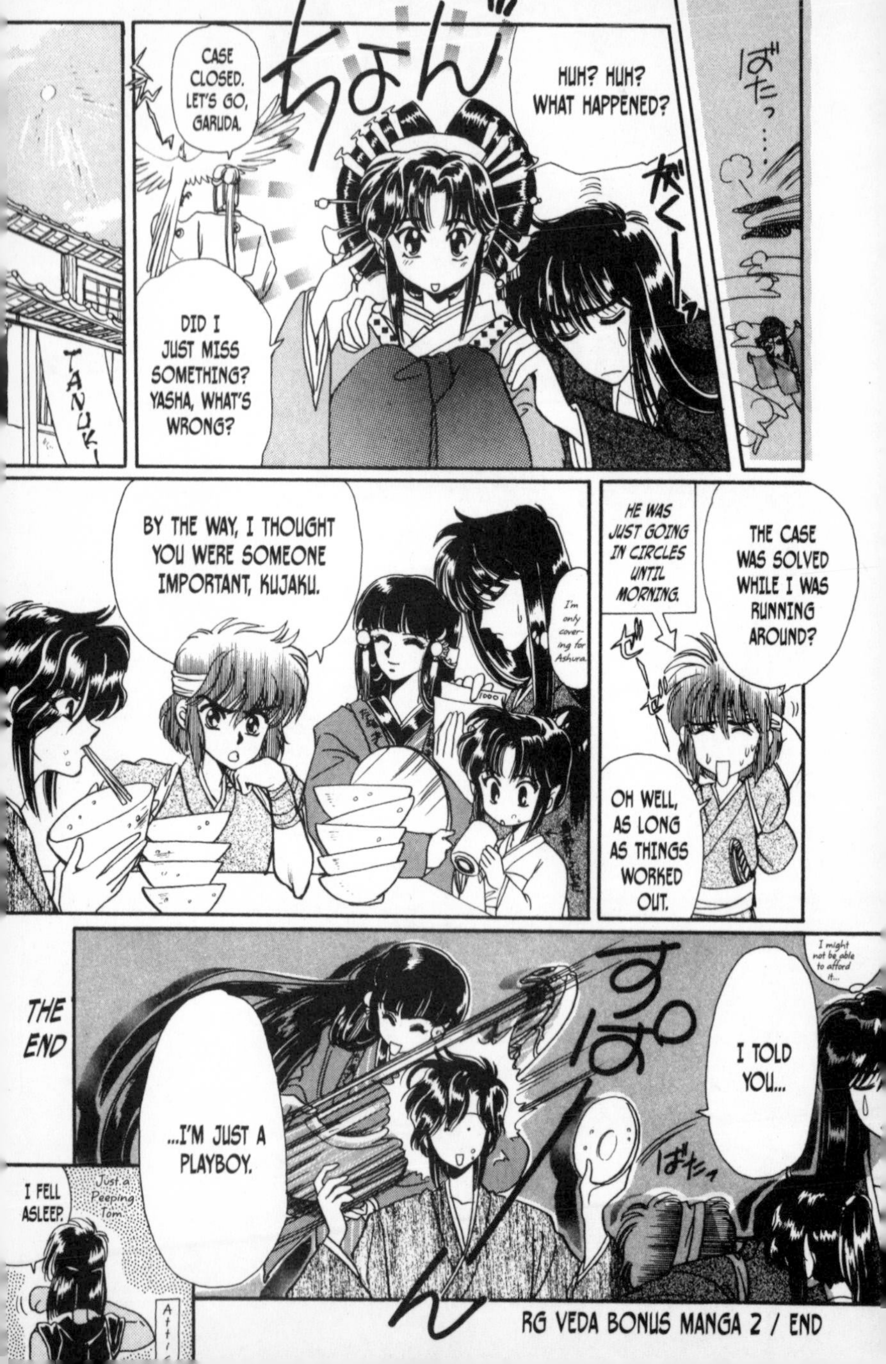
ばたっ……
HUH? HUH? WHAT HAPPENED?
ちょん
CASE CLOSED. LET'S GO, GARUDA.
DID I JUST MISS SOMETHING? YASHA, WHAT'S WRONG?
TANUKI
THE CASE WAS SOLVED WHILE I WAS RUNNING AROUND?
HE WAS JUST GOING IN CIRCLES UNTIL MORNING.
OH WELL, AS LONG AS THINGS WORKED OUT.
I'm only covering for Ashura.
BY THE WAY, I THOUGHT YOU WERE SOMEONE IMPORTANT, KUJAKU.
I might not be able to afford it...
I TOLD YOU...
...I'M JUST A PLAYBOY.
THE END
I FELL ASLEEP.
Just a Peeping Tom
RG VEDA BONUS MANGA 2 / END

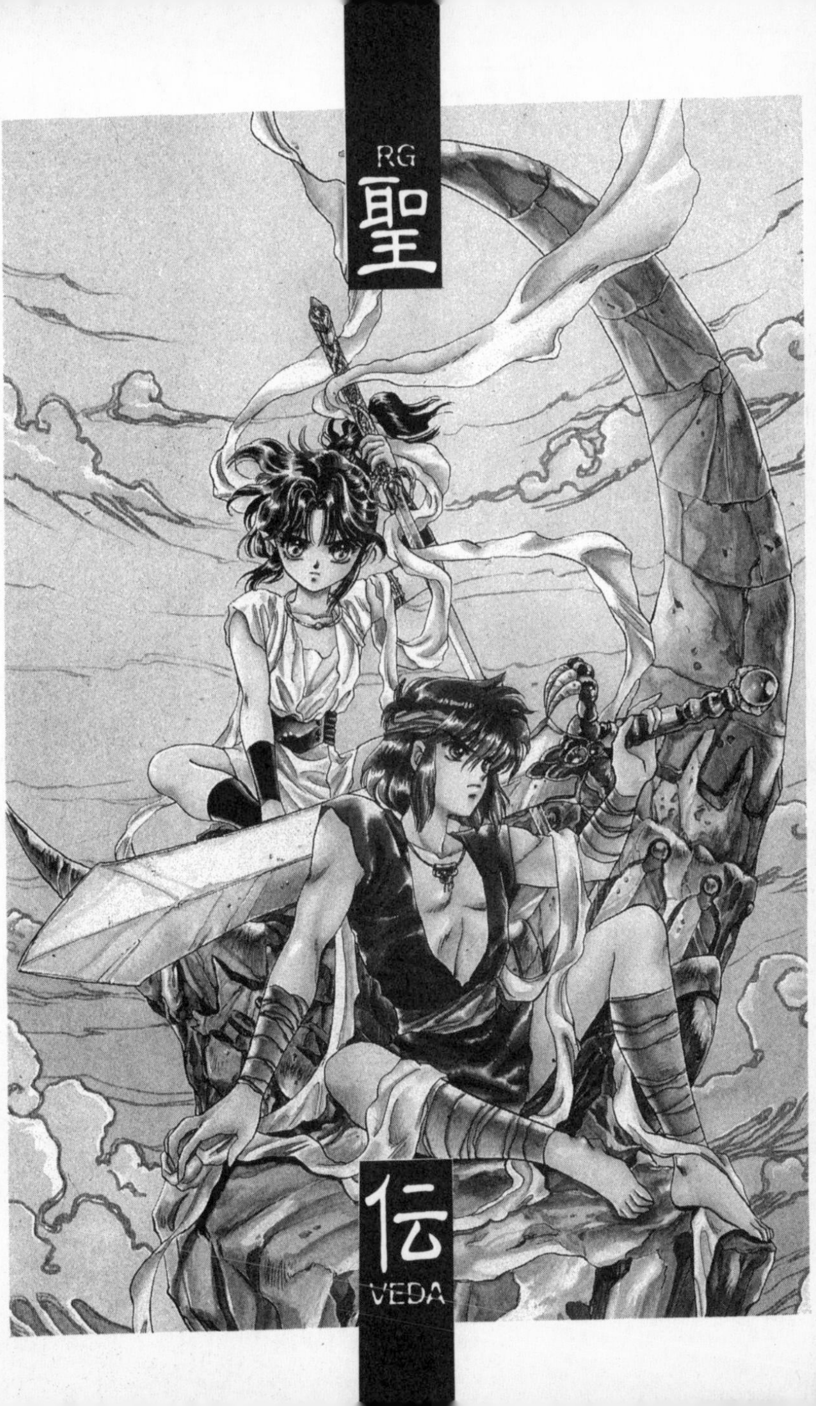
RG
聖
伝
VEDA

TOKYOPOP SHOP

TOKYOPOP MANGA SUPPLEMENT

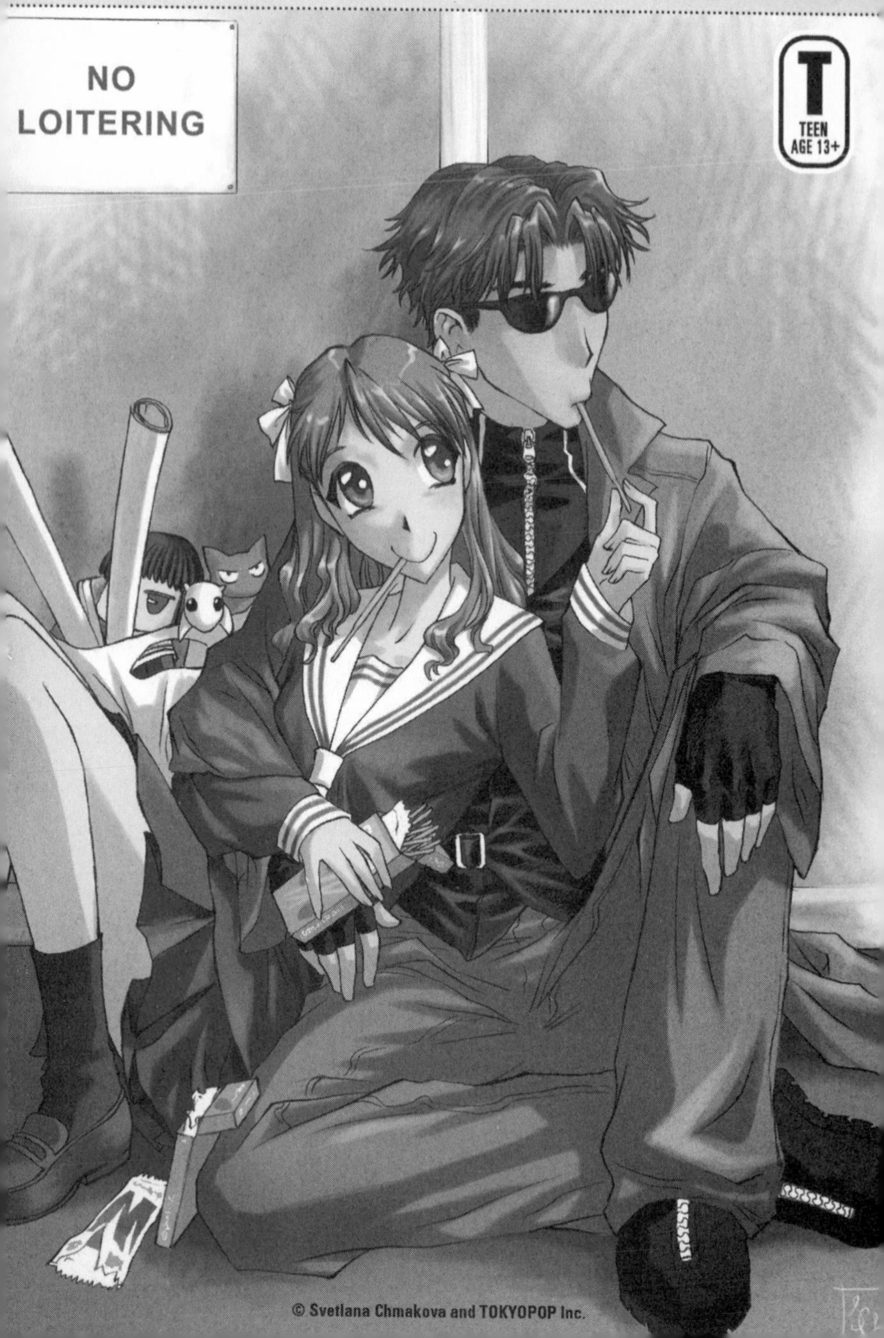
NO LOITERING
T
TEEN
AGE 13+